Founded in 1972, the Institute for Research on Public Policy is an independent, national, nonprofit organization.

IRPP seeks to improve public policy in Canada by generating research, providing insight and sparking debate that will contribute to the public policy decision-making process and strengthen the quality of the public policy decisions made by Canadian governments, citizens, institutions and organizations.

IRPP's independence is assured by an endowment fund established in the early 1970s.

Institute for Research on Public Policy

Institut de recherche en politiques publiques

Strengthening
Canadian
Democracy

Edited by Paul Howe, Richard Johnston and André Blais

Printed in Canada
Dépôt légal 2005

Bibliothèque nationale du Québec

National Library of Canada
Cataloguing in Publication Data

Howe, Paul, 1966-
Strengthening Canadian democracy /
Paul Howe, Richard Johnston, André Blais

Includes bibliographical references.
ISBN 0-88645-187-6

1. Democracy–Canada. 2. Canada–Politics and government.
I. Blais, André, 1947- II. Johnston, Richard, 1948-
III. Institute for Research on Public Policy. IV. Title.

JL193.H69 2004   320.471   C2004-904709-4

Proofreading
Timothy Niedermann

Interior Production
Chantal Létourneau

Cover Concept and Design
Schumacher Design

Cover Photo
Carrie MacPherson

Interior Grid Design
Studio Duotone inc.

Published by
The Institute for Research on Public Policy (IRPP)
L'Institut de recherche en politiques publiques
1470 Peel Sreet, Suite 200
Montreal, Quebec H3A 1T1
Tel: 514 985 2461   Fax: 514 985-2559
email: irpp@irpp.org   www.irpp.org

contents

Part C: The Broader Debate

Preface and Acknowledgements

Democracy, Winston Churchill famously quipped, is the worst system of government aside from all the others. Mr. Churchill presumably would have approved of refurbishment efforts designed to widen the gap between his preferred form of government and the other contenders.

Such is the sentiment behind this book. If a flawless system of government is an unattainable ideal, if intermittent conflict and distemper in the trenches of political life are unavoidable, there is nonetheless ample room to improve upon current democratic structures and procedures in many places, Canada among them. It is a sentiment shared by a growing number of Canadians who have come to feel that their democratic system, in manifold ways, falls short of their expectations and aspirations.

To advance public debate in this critical area, the Institute for Research on Public Policy launched the Strengthening Canadian Democracy project in 1999. Its purpose was twofold: to encourage discussion about the merits of current democratic practices and procedures along with possible alternatives; and to inform those deliberations with research of the highest calibre. Initiated soon after Hugh Segal assumed the Presidency of the IRPP, and bolstered by his enthusiastic backing and constructive advice, the project, we believe, has amply achieved these goals over the past four years.

The main charge for the editorial team — one of us then research director of the Governance Program at the Institute, the other two long-time collaborators on the Canadian Election Study and other projects — was to identify key areas of the democratic system potentially of concern and to commission research and commentary on these matters from recognized experts. This resulted in a series of papers, short and long, some academic in nature, others more policy-oriented, that has been published over the past several years in various IRPP formats. In light of the quality of the work produced and the centrality of the issue to current political debates, the decision was made to pull together much of this material in a single place. The result is the series of papers assembled in this edited collection.

The papers cover a wide range of topics relevant to current debates that are taking place at both the provincial and federal levels about the merits of various democratic reform alternatives. Richard Johnston sets the stage with his analysis of where we are and how we got here, specifically in reference to the Canadian party system. Highlighting the interplay between party politics and the electoral system, Johnston questions whether the latter might be in need of reform at this stage. The question is taken up in Louis Massicotte's subsequent paper, which offers a comprehensive analysis of the potential impact of switching from our current electoral system to one based on the principle of proportional representation. There follows, on the same theme of electoral reform, a series of shorter papers first presented at an IRPP conference held in May 2001, which canvas the full range of reform alternatives, as well as considering methods of effecting change in this area. Contributors to this section of the book are co-authors Matthew Mendelsohn and Andrew Parkin, Tom Flanagan, Jean-Pierre Derriennic, Paul Harris, David Beatty and John Courtney.

Longer papers that follow take up other issues relevant to current debates about the state of Canadian democracy. Jerome Black looks at the operation of the new voter registration regime — the so-called permanent voters list — in place since 1997, paying particular attention to its potential impact on electoral participation. Richard Nadeau and Thierry Giasson assess whether the media are, as is sometimes charged, partly responsible for the growing public distaste for politics and politicians, and suggest ways that media practices might be modified to offset any negative effects. Donald Blake undertakes a comprehensive enumeration of the rules and regulations surrounding electoral democracy in each of the provinces, as well as at the federal level, highlighting salient similarities and differences. And to round out the volume, Matthew Mendelsohn and Andrew Parkin contribute a second piece, this an in-depth examination of the advantages and drawbacks of using referendums as a decision-making tool for important policy issues.

Regrettably one volume could not contain all the worthy material generated by the project. The most significant omission is a series of working papers in

IRPP's *Policy Matters* series. The first of these pieces, by Jennifer Smith and Herman Bakvis, focussed on the regulations governing political finance, drawing contrasts between the Canadian and American approaches. Like other papers in the series, it hit on an issue that was soon to become a focus of concrete policy initiative, as the province of Manitoba (in 2001) and the federal government (in 2004) moved ahead with important new regulations in this area. Also in the *Policy Matters* series, Paul Howe and David Northrup reported the results of a national survey on the attitudes of Canadians towards current democratic procedures and possible reforms, an investigation that confirmed public disenchantment with the status quo and a widespread appetite for change. The same survey supported the research of Brenda O'Neill into the values and attitudes of young Canadians, a paper that has served as a valuable reference point for the growing debate on the pronounced disengagement of younger generations from the political system. Peter Dobell, meanwhile, contributed several pieces to the *Policy Matters* series on the mechanisms and machinery of parliament. This work too foreshadowed important initiatives in the area of parliamentary reform that are now in the works at the behest of Prime Minister Martin. And finally, Henry Milner provided a synopsis of his recent book on civic literacy, where he made the compelling case that citizens in many places, but Canada especially, are lacking the rudimentary understanding and knowledge required to participate in politics effectively; many, consequently, elect not to participate at all. These thoughtful papers can all be found at the website of the IRPP (www.irpp.org).

We would also be remiss were we not to acknowledge the invaluable service provided by the numerous reviewers who read the longer manuscripts in the series and provided incisive feedback. Of special note are two reviewers whose insightful remarks appeared in published form, as commentaries attached to Richard Johnston's analysis of the Canadian party system. Lisa Young offered her views on Johnston's prognosis and prescriptions, as did another commentator with good reason to ponder the future of the party system, Stephen Harper, now leader of the Conservative Party. These commentaries can be found at the IRPP website (as part of the *Choices* publication in which Johnston's paper first appeared).

While this wide-ranging research program was unfolding, efforts were also made to expand the circle of contact with the project by organizing events that would allow for a broader exchange of ideas and perspectives. Much of the credit for the success of these events must go to the hardworking staff at IRPP, who took the organizational lead in these matters. Soon after the project was underway, a series of public forums was held in several Canadian cities, starting in Halifax and wrapping up in Calgary, with stops in Ottawa and Vancouver along the way. These events brought together hundreds of interested citizens to hear the viewpoints of panelists from various walks of public life, as well as to offer their own opinions on the merits and demerits of Canadian democracy. The panelists who lent their time and erudition to these forums are to be thanked, as are the organizations that worked in partnership with IRPP in various cities: the Canada West Foundation in Calgary, and in Ottawa the Public Policy Forum and the Centre for Representation and Elections at Carleton University. Also not to be overlooked are the financial contributions provided by the Kahanoff Foundation that helped facilitate these and other events under the Strengthening Canadian Democracy umbrella.

Another important event for the project was the "Votes and Seats" conference held in Ottawa in May 2001. The focus at this gathering was electoral reform: should the Canadian electoral system be changed and if so, what would be the preferred model and how might change come about? Various commentators provided their responses to these questions, some of which are reproduced in this volume.

At the time of the "Votes and Seats" conference, the issue of electoral reform still seemed mired in its perennial position on the margins of Canadian political debate. That, however, soon changed. Various provincial governments across the country began investigating the possibility of switching electoral systems, principally with an eye to adopting some form of proportional representation. Keen to contribute to this evolving process, and with Geneviève Bouchard, the Institute's new Governance Research Director leading the way, the Institute organized two one-day forums, one in Toronto, the other in Montreal. These events provided a platform for the principal players steering the reform process in British Columbia, Quebec and Prince Edward Island to share their insights and experiences with enthusiastic audiences in both cities.

In a similar vein, the Institute organized a one-day roundtable in February 2002 designed to provide feedback and commentary on an important report issued by the Chief Electoral Officer following the 2000 election. "Modernizing the Electoral Process" was the latest in Jean-Pierre Kingsley's ongoing efforts to highlight areas of the electoral process in need of reform and to provide recommendations to Parliament for its consideration. Among the matters discussed that day were the largely unregulated realm of party leadership campaigns, potential new rules in the areas of political broadcasting and electoral financing designed to level the political playing field, and the efficacy of new methods of voter registration. The transcript from this enlightening event was subsequently published and can be found on the website of the Institute.

As the months wore on and democratic reform initiatives sprang up in other places such as Ontario and New Brunswick, it became evident that the timing of the project had been auspicious. The work of the IRPP and other organizations across the country has become part of a vibrant public debate aimed at rethinking some of the basic precepts and assumptions of Canadian democracy. As in many areas of public policy, the tree long-nurtured is at last bearing fruit.

Thanks are due to staff at the IRPP for their work on the project as a whole as well as their assistance in producing the current volume. Geneviève Bouchard has been steering the SCD initiative since her arrival at the Institute in 2001, taking it in important new directions. Suzanne Ostiguy McIntyre, vice-president of operations at the Institute, ably oversaw all administrative aspects of both the research and outreach dimensions of the project from the start. Murray Mincoff and Brian Fitzgerald provided both research and logistical support in the project's early days. Chantal Létourneau worked diligently and patiently on technical production for both the original papers as well as this book. Others at IRPP who lent their energy and enthusiasm to the project include Events Coordinator Suzanne Lambert and former communications director Graham Fox.

We must also, of course, express our gratitude to the contributors to this collection. Their reflections and analysis form the heart of this project. When approached by the editors to revise their previous work for the current project to reflect the shifting political landscape, they enthusiastically set to the task in the compressed time frame presented them.

Of course, the revision process could have continued indefinitely, for the arena of democratic reform is one of great activity, flux and fluidity. Inevitably, some of the particulars contained herein will prove superfluous or even erroneous in the months and years to come; indeed, the 2004 federal election, which came after the revision process for the book was largely completed, has already altered the political landscape in a number of relevant ways. This may, however, be a virtue in this instance. If our book is overtaken by events — if the analysis, in places, is left behind by a vibrant and fruitful process of political change and democratic reform — we will count it as a mark of success. We trust, too, that there are enough enduring verities and insights contained herein to sustain reader interest even as Canadian democracy is retooled for the twenty-first century.

Paul Howe
Richard Johnston
André Blais

Part A
Setting the Stage

Introduction

The New Landscape of Canadian Democracy

Paul Howe, Richard Johnston, André Blais

Much has changed in the real world of Canadian politics since the Strengthening Canadian Democracy project was initiated in 1999. Events of the final weeks of 2003 capped notable developments in the making for some time. Paul Martin became the country's twenty-first prime minister, his ascension to that position marked by the unprecedented step of a political party ousting a sitting PM. Meanwhile, the Canadian Alliance — itself having experienced internal turmoil, a caucus revolt and a change of leadership — persuaded the Progressive Conservative Party, after a lengthy courtship, to join forces in a new united party of the Right. Several months later, that new party mounted a surprisingly strong challenge in the June 2004 federal election, wresting enough seats from the reigning Liberals to produce the country's first minority government in over twenty years.

These developments are indicative of the restive quality of contemporary Canadian politics, of a widespread thirst for renewal — in ideas, in leadership — and an appetite for bold corrective measures. Alongside this agitation and turbulence, however, is another manifestation of the changing temper of the times, a significant disengagement from politics among the electorate at large. Much consternation was expressed when voter turnout fell to 61.2 percent in the 2000 federal election, the lowest level ever at the time. If the dominance of the Liberal Party and uncompetitive elections seemed partly to blame, the consistent and often sizeable decline in turnout in recent provincial elections, whether in Nova Scotia, New Brunswick, Ontario, Quebec or Manitoba (where only 54 percent of eligible voters turned out to cast a ballot in the most recent provincial election), suggested the disaffection ran deeper than this. The 2004 federal election confirmed these suspicions. Despite a lively campaign and a contest too close to call, only 60.5 percent of Canadian voters showed up to cast a ballot on June 28, a new nadir and a clear signal that vibrant elections alone will not suffice to rekindle political spirit among disengaged Canadians.

New Openings

As turnout numbers have declined amidst tumult in the party system, another change has slowly been taking form: governments and policy-makers are beginning to think seriously about ways to reinvigorate Canadian democracy. Following the 2000 election, Canada's chief electoral officer Jean-Pierre Kingsley indicated that reversing the decline in voter participation was an important priority for his office. His initial musing was that Canada might want to consider making voting mandatory, as a handful of countries around the world already does. More recently, the CEO's office has been probing the sources of the problem, expanding its research efforts to investigate key demographic groups who vote in low numbers, such as young adults and Aboriginal Canadians,[1] as well as considering technical improvements and innovations to facilitate voting, such as on-line voter registration.[2]

Various provinces have also been taking steps to rejuvenate democracy in their jurisdictions. British Columbia is furthest along in amending traditional democratic practices and procedures. Provisions for recall of members of the Legislative Assembly and for citizen-initiated referendums have been in place since 1995. The election of Gordon Campbell's Liberal government in 2001 has seen the introduction of other innovative measures. The first is fixed election dates. Henceforth BC will hold elections every four years on the nose rather than allowing the premier to pick the date. The second is the recent convening of the Citizens' Assembly on Electoral Reform, which is deliberating on the merits of alternative electoral systems and will put its recommendation for reform to the voters of British Columbia in a referendum that will accompany the next provincial election. The exercise is attracting national and international attention as the first where a government has coupled innovative techniques in deliberative democracy to direct democracy for binding decision on an important public policy issue.

Quebec has recently been building on a rich tradition of debate on the merits of different democratic procedures by undertaking a wide-ranging exploration of reform options in the past couple of years. This culminated in the convening of the Estates General on the Reform of Democratic Institutions in February 2003, which attracted over 1000 delegates, who gathered to discuss a broad gamut of issues raised in earlier public meetings held around the province. Unlike many initiatives that lose steam with a change in government, the momentum for democratic reform has not faltered since the election of Jean Charest's Liberal administration in April 2003. Of the various ideas on the table, the new government is pressing ahead most forcefully with electoral reform, promising legislation in 2004 that will introduce an element of proportional representation to Quebec's electoral system.

Other provinces are also considering whether a change to proportional representation might be for the better. After a number of lopsided election results, the government of PEI appointed a one-person Commission on Electoral Reform in January 2003 to consider the matter. Retired Chief Justice Norman Carruthers submitted his report in early 2004. While cautioning that more work needed to be done to engage and inform the citizens of PEI about the subject, and that a referendum would be the appropriate means of sanctioning any change, Carruthers did underline the merits of a mixed-member proportional system that would combine single member districts with top-up seats awarded to candidates from party lists.[3] Developments elsewhere also caught the commissioner's attention, prompting the recommendation that "a Prince Edward Island version of British Columbia's Citizen Assembly be used in this province to formulate a question for a referendum."[4]

Meanwhile in New Brunswick work has begun on Premier Lord's pledge during the 2003 provincial election campaign to reconsider any number of elements of the democratic system in that province. The Commission on Legislative Democracy has been established, its mission "to identify options for an enhanced citizen-centred democracy in New Brunswick."[5] Areas up for consideration include the electoral system, referenda, fixed election dates and an enhanced role for MLAs. Broad-based public consultation will help shape the recommendations that are to be submitted to the premier by December 2004.

Ontario, under the new leadership of Dalton McGuinty's Liberal Party, is similarly promising intensive investigation and public consultation in the near future on ways to make democracy work better in Canada's largest province. McGuinty has named a minister responsible for democratic renewal and created a secretariat to support his efforts. Elements of the system that will be scrutinized for possible reform include rules governing political financing, the electoral system and the role of MLAs. Also to be considered is the potential use of citizen juries to deliberate on policy issues (a technique akin to the Citizens' Assembly in BC but on a smaller scale).

At the federal level there have also been new initiatives and proposals. Principal among these is Bill C-24, which has established new rules for party finance that strictly limit donations from corporations and trade unions and provide for enhanced funding from the public purse. Other changes have come, or have been promised, in the area of parliamentary reform. In 2002, Parliament voted in favour of a new method of selecting committee chairs — a vote by committee members rather than selection by the prime minister. An attempt was also made to establish an independent ethics commissioner, but the relevant bill failed to pass into law before the dissolution of Parliament in November 2003. This was, however, among the items in the package of parliamentary reform that Paul Martin unveiled early on his campaign for the Liberal leadership and so will presumably materialize again, along with other promised changes, such as more free votes in the House of Commons and parliamentary review of government appointments.[6] There will undoubtedly be considerable pressure on the prime minister to deliver on these reforms and to consider others that may have escaped his attention.

Few would have foreseen five years ago that the very infrastructure of democracy would today be the most active area of public policy deliberation and innovation in this country. The traditional thinking was that political leaders would be reluctant to alter the structures and processes that had delivered them to power and afforded them ample rein to govern by their own lights. Countering that wisdom, any number have been boldly striking out in new directions, indeed unleashing forces — commissions, citizen assemblies, public consultations — that may, for better or worse, usher them ahead in directions and at a pace not entirely of their own choosing. It is truly one of the more striking developments in recent Canadian politics.

If the perceived urgency of the issue is one reason why politicians have taken up the cause in earnest, another development may have helped pave the way. The receding significance of the dominant political issue in Canada for much of the last four decades, national unity, has created an important vacancy on the public agenda. While it would be folly to declare the sovereignty movement in Quebec moribund — reports of its demise have proven to be premature time after time in the past — there can be no doubt that we are in the midst of a significant lull that has gradually settled over the province. If the atmosphere of relations was tense following the dramatic near miss of the 1995 referendum and the bitter debates engendered by the 1998 reference case on Quebec secession, the Supreme Court's capacious decision provided a measure of closure to at least one dimension of the debate, while the decline in PQ popularity allowed for the election of a new government more strongly committed to the Canadian federation than any other of the past several decades. The current context provides an opportunity not seen for many years to engage in reflection on fundamental issues other than our continued existence as a country.

This is not to say that earlier periods were entirely devoid of debate about the merits of Canadian democracy. Pressure for change often emanated from the West, where distance from the centres of economic and political power in Central Canada and a populist political culture produced periodic disaffection that partly manifested itself in calls for democratic reform. The federal election of 1921 saw the arrival in Ottawa of 65 MPs representing the fledgling Progressive Party, pressing for electoral and parliamentary reform. The party's success proved to be short-lived — its refusal to take up the mantle of Official Opposition or observe the conventions of party discipline contributed to its undoing — but it did represent an early expression of disquiet with some the settled assumptions of Canadian democracy. Western Canada was also, in the years between the wars, the site of considerable experimentation with different electoral systems — the alternative vote, the single transferable vote — at both the municipal and provincial levels (Manitoba, Alberta and Saskatchewan).[7] By the early 1950s, however, enthusiasm for these alternatives had abated and virtually all jurisdictions had reverted to single-member-plurality voting.

In the postwar period other sorts of changes materialized throughout the country, as some of the mechanisms of electoral democracy came under scrutiny and were updated to ensure fairer political competition and representation. Beginning in the 1950s, attention was focussed on inequities in the size of electoral constituencies, which led to the gradual introduction across the country of statutory requirements for redistribution by independent bodies that would reduce disparities between ridings while remaining sensitive to the effective representation of particular communities.[8] In recognition of the importance of money in the political process and its potentially nefarious effects, the *Canada Elections Act* (1974) introduced rules governing political contributions and spending aimed at both parties and other groups that might seek to influence the political process, as well as providing public funding for parties and candidates. Political patronage, that traditional lubricant of Canadian politics, also came under increased scrutiny and was, if not entirely exorcised from the political system, certainly trimmed back. All of this amounted to important democratic housekeeping, designed to clean up the system to ensure a more level playing field and greater integrity in government operations; it was not, however, so obviously designed to address the popular desire for a greater voice in government — a citizen-centred democracy, to borrow a phrase — that seems to underwrite much of the current angst and that might require more far-reaching changes.

When broader issues of structural reform arose in the postwar period, they were usually, in keeping with the priorities of the time, couched in the context of the national unity debate. Enhancing the democratic quality of political institutions could, it was argued, open up channels of voice and influence in

Ottawa for aggrieved regions of the country, thereby soothing regional tensions. So it was that the Pépin-Robarts Task Force on Canadian Unity, reporting in 1979, identified as one of the main benefits of proportional representation the assurance it would provide that all regions of the country would be adequately represented in the federal caucuses of the parties in Ottawa.[9] Similarly, Senate reform — often part of the mix whenever leaders gathered to discuss constitutional matters and an integral element of the Charlottetown Accord — was typically conceived as a means of tackling at once the democratic dysfunctionality of an appointed upper house and the inadequacy of regional representation at the federal level.

On one occasion, however, a significant audit of Canadian democracy was undertaken in its own right. The Royal Commission on Electoral Reform and Party Financing, chaired by Pierre Lortie, was appointed in 1989 and delivered its final report in February 1992. The "National Question" still hung over the proceedings. This was, after all, a time of intense constitutional debate and negotiation, marked by the unravelling of the Meech Lake Accord and the prolonged reconstitution efforts that eventually produced the Charlottetown agreement. But if the commission's work was overshadowed at the time by events of greater immediate consequence, it has stood the test of time as a thoughtful body of research and analysis that produced a wealth of recommendations dealing with matters of technical detail around the conduct of elections as well as larger issues, such as the representation of disadvantaged groups in elected bodies. Continued momentum for some of these ideas has come from Canada's chief electoral officer, who has had occasion over the past dozen years to draw upon the unfinished business of the Lortie Commission — recommendations never acted upon — in fashioning his postelection counsel to Parliament on ways to improve Canadian electoral democracy. The work of the Lortie Commission is, then, one important point of departure and a useful touchstone for current debates about ways to strengthen the democratic fabric in Canada.

For many, however, the ideas originating in officialdom have tended to focus on the finer points of democratic procedure, failing to probe larger questions around the basic design of our political institutions. The Lortie Commission for example, despite its formal title — the Royal Commission on Electoral Reform and Party Financing — did not consider whether the voting system itself might be changed, focussing instead on other elements of electoral democracy. Voices from outside the traditional corridors of power and from various points on the political spectrum began agitating for more, gradually coalescing over the course of the 1990s into a broad coalition of disparate groups united in their concern for the state of Canadian democracy. The Reform Party can be credited with lending the cause important early momentum in the latter part of the

1980s, with its populist-inspired program of democratic reform. Besides putting Senate reform back on the agenda, Preston Manning's Western-based organization championed the causes of direct democracy and an enhanced role for individual members of Parliament. Civil society was active in the cause as well, in the form of advocacy groups, academics, think tanks and the media, which, each in their own way, endeavoured to widen the range of options under consideration and provide forums for public deliberation and debate. Democracy Watch, an Ottawa-based watchdog founded in 1993, focused public attention on the inadequacy of mechanisms to ensure transparency and accountability in government. Fair Vote Canada more recently joined the fray as a national grassroots organization that has complemented the efforts of provincially based groups pressing for change to the single-member-plurality electoral system. As the cause in its various guises gained credibility and adherents, political parties aside from Reform started to take note and develop their own positions on the question of democratic reform. At the federal level, all the opposition parties — the NDP, Bloc Québécois and even eventually the Progressive Conservatives — added commitments to their programs to examine or implement such changes as proportional representation, citizen-initiated referenda or relaxed party discipline. They were joined by parties at the provincial level, including some in opposition who fashioned a democratic reform agenda that helped carry them into office (the Liberals in BC and Ontario) and others in power who recognized it as an issue worthy of serious consideration (the Conservatives in New Brunswick and the Parti Québécois).

So it is that pressure from below and pliability up above have come together at this juncture to put items of genuine significance squarely on the agenda. The venerable single-member-plurality electoral system is being seriously scrutinized in various quarters. The wisdom of stringent party discipline is coming into question. Allowing citizens to decide important policy questions on a more regular basis through the mechanisms of direct democracy is being contemplated. The innovative methods sometimes being used to explore these areas of reform exemplify the new willingness of governments to embrace public participation and deliberation. The BC Citizens' Assembly is the most notable example, but Quebec's Estates General also succeeded in bringing a broad coalition of citizens into the policy-making mix. Other provinces look likely to follow suit in the methods they will use to arrive at their recommendations for reform. It is difficult to imagine with the expectations that have been generated that the better part of the reform agenda will not come to fruition; or that the contagion of democratic renewal, once discussion and debate give way to actual reform, will not come to infect those parts of the country that have thus far proven resistant.

Broader Debates

But it is still early days with much discussion of alternatives yet to take place. For commentators, the fluidity of the current context presents both a risk and an opportunity: the risk of putting into print analysis and reflection that will quickly be outpaced by events, which is, however outweighed by the opportunity to intervene at an auspicious juncture and help influence debates as they unfold. From its inception the Strengthening Canadian Democracy project has endeavoured to provide a forum where various commentators, academic and otherwise, could draw upon their expertise to highlight critical issues and outline options for constructive democratic reform. If it has served this purpose to date, our hope is that it can contribute further by bringing together some of the earlier published work in this collected volume.

The project took two postulates as its starting point: judging by voter turnout levels and the disaffection with government captured by public opinion surveys, all is not well with Canadian democracy; and in seeking to reconnect Canadians with their political system, institutional remedies are likely to be the simplest and most effective. This institutionalist assumption is not shared by all who ponder the question of democratic disengagement. Some of these alternative viewpoints originate outside Canada, in countries that have also experienced a rising tide of democratic disaffection in recent times. The best-known is Robert Putnam's account of the American case in his book *Bowling Alone*. Surveying the broad sweep of American history, with special emphasis and a welter of statistical evidence on the period since the early 1960s, Putnam contends that negative attitudes toward government and declining political participation are but two elements of a broader pattern that has seen Americans retreating from community life in all its varied forms. America's stock of social capital — the web of voluntary connections, both informal and formal, and attendant norms of trust and reciprocity that together are the wellsprings of much collective action — has been depleted over the past forty years and must be replenished. The task will require a broad-based national effort in which citizens themselves have a vital role to play, reconnecting with one another as much as with government. The importance of reforming the institutions of American democracy, a recurring theme among critics, receives less emphasis in Putnam's account. While professing sensitivity to this perspective and allowing that both individual initiative and institutional change are needed to restore the fabric of American democratic life, he nonetheless closes his book with the admonition that "institutional reform will not work — indeed, it will not happen — unless you and I, along with our fellow citizens, resolve to become reconnected with our friends and neighbours."[10] The order of things seems clear enough.

Others who focus attention on societal evolution in their accounts of the challenges of contemporary democracy cast that evolution in a more positive light. Rising education levels coupled with access to rich and diverse information sources have, the thinking runs, produced critical citizens with high expectations of government and the skills and resources to think for themselves.[11] The issues that matter to citizens have changed too. Many — younger generations in particular, whose value priorities have been affected by the conditions of relative affluence in which they have come of age — are drawn to causes that do not slot easily into the traditional Left-Right classifications that have structured political competition in many places throughout the twentieth century. Postmaterialist issues, such as the environment and identity politics, are the new concerns of the day.[12] These varied changes have created a governing context in which citizens are less likely to subscribe to conventional practice, less inclined to participate in the prescribed manner. This perspective on societal evolution is persuasive and resonates with the Canadian experience, where events in the constitutional arena saw the gradual assertion of citizen power over the course of the 1980s and early 1990s, culminating in the public rejection of the elite-brokered Charlottetown Accord. It is, furthermore, complementary to our institutional focus. It is not that Canada's political institutions are intrinsically flawed and have never been adept at capturing public sentiment and translating it into effective public policy. But society has evolved to the point that there is now a significant mismatch between the political institutions and the citizenry they are meant to serve. Rejigging the citizen side of the equation — transporting us back to a time when people were less able or inclined to participate on their own terms and were consequently largely satisfied with the traditional mechanisms of representative democracy — is, on this interpretation, neither desirable nor feasible. The only sensible solution is to look at the institutions and see how they might be updated to create a citizen-centred democracy that will allow for the enhanced representation of diverse viewpoints and greater opportunity for more frequent and meaningful political participation.

These debates in the wider field are not our primary focus, but they provide some broader context for the book. That democratic disengagement is a widespread phenomenon affecting many countries and potentially resulting from multiple causes is worth bearing in mind in reflecting on the institutional arrangements of Canadian democracy. This broader context hovers in the background, and occasionally comes to the foreground, of many of the chapters in this book.

This Volume

The reflections and analyses that made up the Strengthening Canadian Democracy project took various forms: refereed papers published in IRPP's *Choices* series, working papers in its *Policy Matters* series, and events big and small that allowed for the exchange of ideas among academics, policy-makers and interested members of the general public. The current volume brings together a significant portion of this work (though interested readers will, as noted in the Preface, find more at the Institute's Web site). The items chosen for inclusion include the *Choices* papers, each of which takes up a single important theme, and a selection of shorter papers from an IRPP-sponsored conference on electoral reform, which first appeared in the Institute's monthly magazine, *Policy Options*. Where necessary, they have been updated to reflect developments since their initial publication. While these updates were undertaken prior to the 2004 federal election, which clearly altered the political landscape in significant ways, the new configuration of political power in Ottawa has not affected the deeper patterns and trends of Canadian democracy that are the principal focus of the papers.

The research series began with Richard Johnston's retrospective analysis of the abiding conundrum of Canadian party politics and so does the book. Canadian political parties have constantly struggled to straddle the regional divisions that represent this country's deepest faultlines. The Liberals have traditionally played the game well and been rewarded with office more often than any other party. The Conservatives have experienced more sporadic success, cobbling together coalitions that have suffered from internal tensions, the latest of which dissolved when the Mulroney coalition that had brought the West and Quebec into the Tory fold, splintered into Reform, the Bloc and a much diminished PC remnant. The lesson from history is that Canada's electoral system, despite its obvious incentives for opposition parties to rally under a single banner, has never really managed to forge two parties with enduring pan-national appeal. Real electoral competition has been lacking. While the parties of the Right have now come together in the new Conservative Party of Canada, the question remains whether the underlying centrifugal forces remain in effect and will produce a return to the patterns of the past. Inasmuch as the frailties of the Canadian party system are rooted in abiding structural divisions, the question arises whether a different electoral system might be better suited to the Canadian electoral environment.

Louis Massicotte's paper leads off the second section of the book, "Part B: Electoral Reform," and picks up where Johnston's ends: what would be the effect of introducing proportional representation at the federal level in Canada? While the issue is under consideration in several provinces at the current time, there is not the same consideration being given the matter in Ottawa. The discussions that are unfolding in British Columbia, Quebec, New Brunswick and PEI will help inform any debate that might transpire at the federal level, but there are distinct dimensions to be considered in the pan-Canadian context, in particular the issue Johnston highlights, the regional and cultural diversity of Canada. Massicotte takes this into account, along with other factors relevant to an assessment of PR, including perennial anxieties over the durability of governments and the quality of governance under a proportional system. In the end he is persuaded that a change to PR would fulfill many of the hopes of its advocates without any serious deleterious side effects.

The electoral system deserved, in our view, special attention and consequently an IRPP conference was organized in May 2001 that generated other valuable insights and analyses on the subject. Attendees from all parts of the country joined invited guests from New Zealand, a former prime minister, the Rt. Hon. James Bolger, and Paul Harris, former chief executive of the New Zealand Electoral Commission. A full range of perspectives was on offer, including firsthand accounts of the change to a PR system in New Zealand that took place in 1996. We reproduce here a selection of those shorter papers, which originally appeared in IRPP's magazine *Policy Options*.

The first offers a counterpoint to Massicotte's advocacy of proportional representation. Tom Flanagan suggests that if Canadians are intent on electoral reform — and he himself is of the view that the electoral system is probably not of primary importance — we should look seriously at another system used elsewhere, the alternative vote. Leaving our current electoral system intact but for the substitution of ballots that would allow voters to rank candidates in order of preference would, in Flanagan's view, represent the preferred reform alternative. Flanagan's reasoning echoes Johnston's when he argues that the most pressing concern is to give voters real electoral choice by facilitating the creation of a viable alternative to the governing Liberals. While the merger of the Tories and Alliance would appear to promise just that without electoral reform, Flanagan cautions that the divisive tendencies that pulled parties apart in the past may yet surface again. He remains convinced that the alternative vote is a change worth considering.

The next contribution comes from Jean-Pierre Derriennic. It provides a thoughtful reflection on the values that should underpin the choice of electoral system. In Derriennic's view, a just system should encourage governments to treat all citizens as equals, allow for the expression of a diversity of political viewpoints, and empower citizens to remove governments they find objectionable. Drawing on these basic principles, Derriennic contends that both SMP and PR suffer from significant shortcomings that could be rectified through the use of the alternative vote. He also underlines that the alternative vote mechanism of ranking candidates in order of preference is compatible not only with our current single-member-constituency system but also with proportional systems, as is the case for the Irish single transferable vote. Whatever precise model is selected, it is clear, in Derriennic's view, that improvements could be made upon the current system.

Paul Harris offers insights from the New Zealand experience with electoral reform — the forces that produced reform in the first place and its subsequent reception by New Zealanders. The switch from SMP to PR was a long process that began in the mid-1980s and was finally in effect for the 1996 election. Harris — who served as research director for the Royal Commission that started the ball rolling with its 1986 endorsement of German-style PR — reports that the experience with the new system has been mixed, corroborating the sentiment expressed by other contributors that no electoral system is perfect. The piece here updates that experience, however, to include the 2002 election and reports that New Zealanders appear, after a lengthy transition period, to be settling into their new system. If there is still some lingering debate about the wisdom of the reform, it does not appear likely to be undone at this stage.

Three further papers speak to potential mechanisms of change. How might electoral reform come about? How *should* it come about? David Beatty is an enthusiastic advocate of judicial intervention to impose a change in electoral system. He describes the constitutional challenge that is being mounted by the Constitutional Test Case Centre at the University of Toronto Law School on behalf of the Green Party of Canada in the Ontario Superior Court of Justice. Surveying past court decisions in the area of electoral law, Beatty believes the case can be made that our current electoral system violates section 3 of the Charter, the right to vote, as well as section 15, equality rights. At this stage, it will take considerable time for the case to make its way through the court system; Beatty urges the federal government to use its power of referral to put the case directly before the Supreme Court of Canada.

Another route to electoral reform is outlined by Matthew Mendelsohn and Andrew Parkin. They first consider the circumstances that are likely to precipitate reform, drawing lessons from the experiences of other countries that have changed their electoral systems in recent years. The obstacles, they adduce, are considerable but not insurmountable. They next offer prescriptions for the decision-making mechanisms that should guide a reform process. Given that Mendelsohn and Parkin appear later in the book making a cogent case in favour of direct democracy, it is not surprising they argue in this shorter piece for a process that involves citizens deeply at all stages. The authors must be given full marks for prescience, as their advocacy of a citizens' forum to deliberate on the alternatives and formulate a proposal for ratification in a public referendum has taken concrete form in the Citizens' Assembly process in British Columbia. The current updated piece reflects on that exercise in light of their analysis.

We end the electoral reform section with a cautionary piece. John Courtney counsels prudence on two counts. First, he questions the wisdom of changing electoral systems, arguing that our method of electing representatives to

Parliament is but one element in a complex and interconnected institutional structure. Changes to the electoral system may have unanticipated — and negative — effects on other important components, such as our political parties. His second observation is that electoral reform requires a particular confluence of circumstances and conditions that seems to be lacking in Canada. In light of developments since the piece was first written, we invited Courtney to revisit the latter part of his analysis to determine its continued applicability. Had the conditions for electoral reform he identified fallen into place or were some of them less critical than initially supposed? Or were we, the editors, jumping the gun in suggesting the analysis might need revisiting? No province, after all, has actually changed its electoral system just yet. Courtney offers his assessment of the implications of current developments for the proposition that change is not readily effected.

The final section of the book, "Part C: The Broader Debate," turns to other elements of the institutional architecture of Canadian democracy. The first contribution is Jerome Black's examination of an important administrative change that took place in 1997. In that year, the method used to compile voters lists for federal elections was changed from door-to-door enumeration to a permanent voters list, officially entitled the National Register of Electors. Black raises important questions about the forces and motivations that led to the change, as well as its effects on voter turnout, both in the aggregate and among those groups most likely to fall through the cracks of the new registration regime. Finding flaws, he outlines measures Elections Canada is taking and others it might consider to help shore up the new system. It is a trenchant critique that highlights the need to look closely at what might appear, at first blush, to be an administrative modification of no great consequence.

In the next paper, Richard Nadeau and Thierry Giasson examine an important intermediary institution, the news media, the lens through which most aspects of political life are filtered for public viewing. Increasingly, some would contend, those who report from the political theatre are engaging in a sniping and superficial journalism that highlights personality and conflict at the expense of serious and thoughtful coverage of politics. The worst culprit is television, where a shallow treatment of the day's events is the norm. The result has been a steady erosion of confidence in our political institutions and leaders. In investigating these claims, Nadeau and Giasson provide an extensive review of past research in the area and conclude that criticisms of the media may be overdone; further evidence would be needed to establish incontrovertibly the link between media coverage and democratic malaise. At the same time, there is sufficient concern about current media practices to warrant consideration of certain reforms that would encourage more edifying political journalism.

Much of the analysis in the book focuses on the federal level of Canadian politics. Donald Blake turns our attention to the provincial level, providing a detailed investigation of the rules and procedures that govern electoral democracy in different jurisdictions across the country. Fully updated to take account of the many changes since its initial publication, the paper highlights the strengths and weaknesses of different provinces across a variety of areas: redistricting procedures, regulations on political financing, the rules governing candidacy and voting and election outcomes. It also provides comparisons with the federal level on these same dimensions. The general conclusions are that significant progress has been made in a number of important areas and the provinces fare well when compared to the federal level.

Finally, Matthew Mendelsohn and Andrew Parkin consider the merits of direct democracy, in particular the use of referendums as a policy-making instrument. Their careful and considered analysis is aimed at countering the facile dismissal of this particular tool of democracy by those who see it as a conservative ploy designed to accomplish policy goals that cannot be achieved through the mechanisms of representative democracy. Drawing on a rich comparative analysis, the authors conclude that referendums are not of any intrinsic ideological hue and can have varied effects on policy depending on the context in which they are deployed and the rules governing their use. Through a systematic elaboration of important variants on referendum mechanisms, they outline the models they believe are most consistent with some of the better traditions of Canadian democracy. Mendelsohn and Parkin's paper is an important contribution toward the development of nuanced understandings and positions on a device which is probably the most simple and direct method of empowering citizens and which must be given due consideration.

The topics addressed in the book, and in the Strengthening Canadian Democracy project as a whole, naturally represent only a sampling of those that might have been included. Since the project's inception, a number of issues have gained greater public prominence and are likely to find their way onto the democratic reform agenda; indeed some have already been broached in components of the SCD project that could not be contained within this volume. Recent revelations about the generous gifts bestowed on federal cabinet ministers by corporate interests have raised new concerns about definitions of unethical behaviour and ways of policing it. Extremely low voter turnout among young Canadians in the federal election of 2000[13] raises questions about this particular subgroup: what are the principal sources of youth disengagement and what can be done to tackle the problem? In the wake of the federal election of 2004, it might be asked whether more invigorating and enlightening election campaigns are part of the solution. The leaders debates, for example, have failed to produce compelling discussion on policy issues in recent years, have failed by all accounts to inform and inspire voters. Can we not do better? Recent developments outside Canada — the recall campaign in California; the ongoing process of democratic renewal in Great Britain — also invite consideration and analysis by Canadians interested in thinking through the full gamut of possibilities for restructuring our democratic system.

Looking Ahead

All signs point to continued vitality on this front. The project of democratic renewal will remain a staple of Canadian political debate for the foreseeable future. It is heartening to see this issue animating citizens, engaging us in dialogue with one another and with our political representatives. In an earlier period, when the attention of Canadians was focussed on constitutional reform, one of Canada's leading political commentators, Peter Russell, saw fit to ask whether we were ready to become a sovereign people. Could we come together to embrace foundational principles that would henceforth govern our common life together?[14] Our constitutional endeavours were not entirely fruitless, but failed to produce that elusive final consensus, leaving us in a state of deep division and weariness. The debate on democratic reform has the potential to revivify our political community, producing not only a more vibrant and dynamic democracy, but also a deeper comity among the individuals and communities that make up this diverse country. If a sovereign people is one that has decided how best to govern itself after a full and honest reflection on the alternatives, we may be taking an important step toward that goal as we fashion a new democratic future together.

Notes

1. Recent issues of Election Canada's magazine *Electoral Insight* have explored voting patterns among these two groups (see Vol. 5, nos. 2 and 3 (July and November 2003)).

2. A 2003 study conducted by the CGI consulting group concluded that on-line voter registration is "technologically feasible" but should be implemented incrementally. See Elections Canada, "On-Line Voter Registration Feasibility Study — Executive Summary," Electoral Law and Policy, at www.elections.ca

3. *2003 Electoral Reform Commission Report*, pp. 82-97, at Elections Prince Edward Island Web site, www.gov.pe.ca/election

4. *2003 Electoral Reform Commission Report*, p. 103.

5. Web site of the New Brunswick Commission on Legislative Democracy, www.gnb.ca/0100/index-e.asp

6. Indeed, the first significant application of this principle came in late summer 2004, when two proposed Supreme Court appointments were reviewed by parliamentary committee.

7. Dennis Pilon, "The History of Voting System Reform in Canada," in Henry Milner (ed.), *Making Every Vote Count* (Peterborough, ON: Broadview Press, 1999), pp. 111-21.

8. John Courtney, *Commissioned Ridings* (Montreal: McGill-Queen's University Press, 2001).

9. Task Force on Canadian Unity, *A Future Together: Observations and Recommendations* (1979), pp. 104-06.

10. Robert Putnam, *Bowling Alone* (New York: Touchstone, 2001), p. 414.

11. Russell Dalton, *Citizen Politics*, 3rd ed. (New York: Chatham House Publishers, 2002).

12. The postmaterialist perspective, first developed by American political scientist Ronald Inglehart, is applied to the Canadian case in Neil Nevitte, *Decline of Deference* (Peterborough, ON: Broadview Press, 1996).

13. One recent analysis of the 2000 election, which corrects for the tendency of surveys to produce inflated estimates of voting, estimates a turnout rate of 22.4 percent for those aged 18 to 20 and 27.5 percent for those aged 21 to 24. See Jon H. Pammett and Lawrence LeDuc, "Explaining the Turnout Decline in Canadian Federal Elections: A New Survey of Non-Voters" (Elections Canada: 2003), p. 20.

14. Peter H. Russell, *Constitutional Odyssey: Can Canadians Become a Sovereign People?*, 2nd ed. (Toronto: University of Toronto Press, 1993).

1

Canadian Elections
at the Millennium

Richard Johnston

Electoral democracy in Canada is sick. Whatever its faults, the old system at least delivered true competition for office and intermittent circulation of parties in government. Now, only the Liberal Party seems poised to govern, but its base for governance is weak. Its traditional competitors, the Progressive Conservatives and, to an extent, the NDP, have behaved like fading great powers, unwilling to admit that their sun is setting. Its new competitors, Reform (later the Canadian Alliance) and the Bloc Québécois, has harboured only an illusion of major-party status. The Bloc cannot seek to grow, for that would defy its nature. Yet its very existence may compromise the expression of Quebec's interests. The Alliance did seek to grow, but has risked repeating the cycle that led to the old system's collapse. The merger of the Alliance and the PCs may correct some of these tendencies, but the early indications give reason for scepticism. Voters, meanwhile, seem more and more reluctant to play the game at all.

How did we get here? Where, if anywhere, can we go? The paper begins by outlining where "here" is: a Liberal government weak in the country but strong in the House; an opposition too fragmented to mount a serious challenge to the Liberals; complacency on the surface of politics, but reasons for apprehension. Then follows an account of how we got here. It acknowledges that certain features of Canada's predicament are local manifestations of global trends. It also acknowledges that the old system was, in a way, racing against time, as the underlying fundamentals of Quebec's relationship with the rest of Canada evolved.

But, in keeping with the theme of the Strengthening Canadian Democracy project, my emphasis is on structural factors, on the electoral system in particular. Special attention is given to strategic choices by the Conservative Party, choices that responded fully to the electoral system's logic and brought that party striking success, but that in 1993 brought it low. As the Conservative Party evolved, so did third parties. Some third-party change was not so much evolution as backwash from Tory initiatives. But some also reflected true third-party initiative, notably on the left. The implication in my account is that even the modest competitiveness of the old system was something of an illusion, that deep down only the Liberals could govern on a continuing basis. All along, the system may have been badly aligned with Canadian society. What the 1990s did was bring that fact out in sharp relief.

Finally, the paper looks downstream, to consider where the system might go from here. One possibility is that it already embodies natural, self-correcting tendencies, that true contestation for power will be restored. It seems more likely, though, that the system really is broken. This time the call for institutional redesign may not be a false alarm.

Where Are We Now?

In seats and votes, the political pattern after 1997 has been a mixture of opposites. The Liberals, the party of government, seem weak in the country but strong in the House of Commons. This disjunction represents the culmination of several trends, which together make the government's true position more problematic than it seems on the surface. On the Opposition side, the Alliance, the principal alternative to the Liberals, also has a weak vote base, weaker by far than any earlier pretender to government. In absolute number of seats, the Alliance is also weak. Yet it is not the smallest Official Opposition in history. Indeed Reform/Alliance after 1997 was stronger than the Liberals were after the 1984 election and 2000 reinforced this fact. These observations also held, roughly, for the other main party of opposition, the Bloc Québécois. For all three parties, the secret to this disjunction lies in Canada's first-past-the-post (FPTP) electoral formula.

Equally important is who was missing from the House, at least in force. The Conservatives, one of the traditional parties of government, were fatally weakened. So may have been the New Democratic Party, another pillar of the pre-1993 order. There is no mistaking how far these parties fell in popular esteem. But their standing in the House both exaggerated their plight and worsened it, by a self-fulfilling process. If the Liberals, Reform/Alliance and the Bloc were beneficiaries of FPTP, the Conservatives and NDP were its victims.

Figure 1
Popular Vote

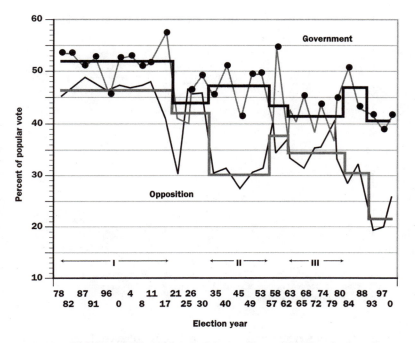

Source: Chief Electoral Officer of Canada, *Report*, various years. Analyses by the author.
Note: Thin lines track year to year variation. Circled years are majority governments.
Thick lines track electoral periods. Roman numerals denote party systems.

Popular weakness and parliamentary strength

The popular basis of the Chrétien government was the weakest of any majority government in Canadian history. Figure 1 indicates one facet of this weakness, by plotting government and opposition vote shares since 1878.[1] For visual clarity, the figure groups elections into structurally distinct periods. The "First Party System," 1878-1917, captures an era of close two-party competition. The next period, 1917-35, is a transition over which the first system died, but slowly and in a manner that only partly foreshadowed the next system. That system, the "Second Party System," 1935-57, was absolutely dominated by the Liberals. The years 1957-63 brought a second transition. As with the first system, the first election in the transition ended the old system but barely revealed the next one. The "Third Party System," 1963-84, saw the return of Liberal dominance, this time less overwhelming than in 1935-57. The last two periods mark the Mulroney-Campbell and Chrétien governments respectively. If the Conservatives' nine years in power hardly qualify as a system in their own right,

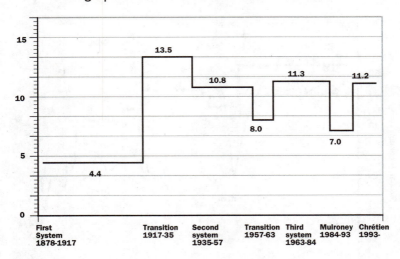

Figure 2

Geographic Concentration of Government Vote

Source: Chief Electoral Officer of Canada, *Report*, various years. Analyses by the author.
Note: Entry is standard deviation of government party vote share across provinces. Higher number means more concentrated.

a government so powerful and so long-lived does not seem like a mere transition. The pattern established in 1993 may last indefinitely and so qualify as a "Fourth" system, but it is too soon to say. In that pattern, the Liberals' average share was almost two points lower than in their last protracted stay in power, 1963-84. Only one other majority government, elected in 1945, had a vote share as weak as the Liberals' 1993 one, 41 percent. And at 38.5 percent in 1997, the Liberals reached a new majority-government low. Indeed, of all *minority* governments only two had smaller votes.[2] The 1997 share was even smaller than a handful of earlier opposition shares. The 2000 vote was only a small correction.

Yet the Liberal pattern could be said to extend a trend originating in the 1920s. Since 1921, vote majorities have been rare and the trend has been generally downward, although the Mulroney Conservatives broke the trend temporarily. The downtrend is especially clear for the Liberals, the usual party of government.

The Chrétien government's base was also narrow geographically, and this too continued a trend. Figure 2 plots one measure of geographic concentration, the standard deviation of the governing party's vote share across provinces. The higher the standard deviation the more concentrated in one or a few provinces the party is. In one sense, the 1990s are not unusual at all, as sectional narrowness characterizes almost all governments since 1917. But the 1990s extend a

Figure 3
Parliamentary Strength

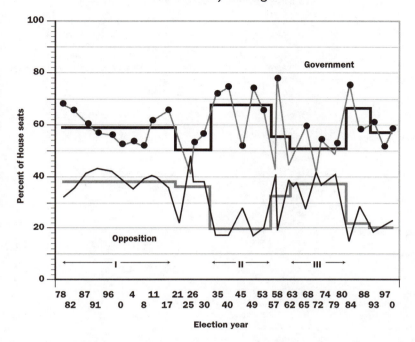

Source: Chief Electoral Officer of Canada, *Report*, various years. Analyses by the author.
Note: Thin lines track year to year variation. Circled years are majority governments.
Thick lines track electoral periods. Roman numerals denote party systems.

disturbing pattern. When Conservative forces rally to form a government, they produce geographically quite inclusive electoral coalitions. But the rally never lasts long. Thus, the typical pattern has been Liberal government with a base that is both narrow and eroding.

For all that, the Chrétien government was strong in the House, as figure 3 reveals. It returned consecutive majorities, the first Liberal government to do so since 1953, and the majorities have not been weak by this century's standards. The 1997 majority was thin, to be sure, but the 1993 margin was very comfortable, larger than any returned by Pierre Trudeau. The 2000 majority was also quite one-sided. Set against more than a century of elections, the parliamentary Liberals were neither peculiarly strong nor peculiarly weak. Three periods in figure 3 exhibit stronger governments and three exhibit weaker ones.

Although the Chrétien government's vote reproduced, even exaggerated, the regionally confined pattern of the Trudeau era, the party was more inclusive in seats. In 1993, the Liberals returned MPs from all 10 provinces. The retreat in 1997 still left

Table 1

Party Ratings by Vote, 1993, 1997, 2000 Elections

	Party being rated					
	Conservative	Liberal	NDP	Reform/ Alliance	Bloc Québécois	Average *N*
1993						
Conservative	58.0	55.2	33.9	40.9	28.3	372
Liberal	35.3	72.2	38.8	38.8	29.8	1,121
NDP	31.2	58.1	57.4	36.1	28.5	175
Reform/Alliance	38.0	57.2	31.4	69.5	27.7	522
Bloc Québécois	32.5	50.4	34.8	37.1	71.5	366
1997						
Conservative	66.1	51.9	36.4	31.0	18.8	403
Liberal	46.0	72.3	39.5	31.1	15.7	859
NDP	39.1	51.3	71.0	26.0	18.6	235
Reform/Alliance	36.5	42.7	27.8	70.7	7.6	492
Bloc Québécois	43.3	37.0	35.1	17.4	70.0	219
2000						
Conservative	68.3	51.1	36.2	32.9	39.2	209
Liberal	43.4	75.5	37.1	29.4	27.1	787
NDP	39.7	52.4	66.2	20.8	41.9	195
Reform/Alliance	41.6	38.8	26.0	74.1	36.5	539
Bloc Québécois	41.5	38.5	34.3	33.7	69.5	199

Sources: The 1992-93 Canadian Election and Referendum Study (principal investigator: Richard Johnston) and the 1997 and 2000 Canadian Election Studies (principal investigator: André Blais). Data furnished by the Institute for Social Research, York University. Analyses by the author.

them with beachheads in nine. It is even tempting to propose that representation of regions improved in 1997 relative to 1993, in that more than one province was vital to maintaining the thin Liberal majority. Where in 1993, only Ontario MPs were a large enough block to deny their co-partisans a majority by unilateral withdrawal, in 1997, this was true outright of four provinces and almost true of two others.[3] This stands in contrast to the effective exclusion of Trudeau's last government from all of Western Canada. And 2000 restored much of the 1993 pattern.

The Liberal Party was also the nearly universal second choice, according to the Canadian Election Study data in table 1. Party groups are identified by self-reported vote in each survey's post-election wave. Preference orders are inferred from party ratings on a 100-point scale. The Liberal tug was especially strong in 1993, when supporters of the four other parties rated the Liberal Party far more highly than any other but their own. Where non-Liberal voters typically rated their own party about 65 on the scale, they rated the Liberals in the mid-to-high 50s. Party differences in Liberal rating were small. New Democrats rated the Liberals slightly higher than their own party, and even Bloc Québécois supporters rated the Liberals fairly highly. Tempers had clearly frayed by 1997, as the ratings gap between the Liberals and voters' own parties widened considerably. In 1997, non-Liberal supporters rated their own party a little higher than in 1993, about 69 points, and rated the Liberals much lower, in the mid-40s. Gaps among voting groups were also wider, as Conservatives and New Democrats still rated the Liberals (just) over 50 while Blocistes and Reformers rated them around 40. Even so, only Bloc supporters typically named a party other than the Liberals (the Conservatives, in this case) as their second preference. The pattern for 2000 is much like that for 1997.

Similarly, the Chrétien government enjoyed remarkable support between elections. Soon after each election, support in most polls — measured by respondents' willingness to vote for the Liberal Party if an election were held that day — soared. Support surges — "honeymoons" — have been the norm after majority victories, but since 1993 honeymoons have lasted entire Parliaments.[4] If the Liberal crashes in the 1997 and 2000 campaigns strongly suggest that these elevated support levels are illusory, they nonetheless seemed to colour media coverage of the government and, perhaps, to embolden the government itself. Certainly, the Chrétien governments did not seem as much on the defensive as their predecessors were.

Fragmented opposition

It is clear, then, that the disjuncture between the Chrétien government's popular weakness and parliamentary strength had little to do with the Liberal Party itself. The obvious place to look is across the aisle, to the Opposition. And after 1993 the outstanding fact about the Opposition was its fragmentation.

First, consider the simplest facts, as revealed by figures 1 and 3. The first lesson of figure 1 is that opposition forces have fragmented even more than government ones. Where over the twentieth-century governments lost about 10 percentage points in the popular vote, the Official Opposition lost over 25 points. Fifteen of these 25 points were lost *before* the emergence of Reform and the Bloc. Of course, other opposition parties picked up the slack, as voters alienated from the governing party still must go *somewhere*. But that is the very point: they became less and less likely to cluster around a single pole of opposition.

This accounts for the disjunction, already hinted at, between the top line in figure 1 and its equivalent in figure 3: where governments' vote shares have mainly shrunk, their seat shares have waxed and waned with no real trend. Governments in the transitional period of 1917-35 were weaker than in the old two-party framework that prevailed before 1917.[5] But the Liberal governments of the 1935-57 period were arguably the most powerful in Canadian history, even though their popular base was smaller than in the pre-1917 systems. In the 1957-84 period, governments were weakened again. John Diefenbaker's stunning 1958 victory was offset by the thinness of his 1957 and 1962 pluralities.

Renewal of the Liberals after 1963 left them barely able to control House majorities. The Liberal grip on the House did tighten after 1968, but their majorities remained slim. Then, in 1984, the tide turned back toward governing parties. The Conservatives' parliamentary strength under Brian Mulroney, in his first House at least, rivaled that for the 1935-57 Liberals, and the Chrétien Liberal government was also comfortably situated.

Clearly important to the ebb and flow of Government House strength in figure 3 is the ebb and flow of opposition fractionalization indicated by the bottom lines of figure 1. Although the opposition vote trend is downward, it is not unbroken. Relative to earlier periods, the Official Opposition strengthened in 1957 and remained strong until 1984. The initial strengthening, 1957-63, was a bit artifactual, as it represented the temporary exile of the highly resilient Liberal Party. More consequential is the fact that the Conservatives were so much stronger in opposition in the 1963-84 period than in the 1935-57 one. The Conservatives' long-term vote gain (figure 1) around 1960 was modest, about five points. But the seat gains (figure 3) this brought were spectacular: a near doubling of the typical Conservative seat share, from under 20 percent to over 35 percent. This surge is a major theme below, for in it lie the seeds of the Tory debacle of 1993.

With the Liberals' defeat in 1984, opposition fragmentation resumed. Some of this reflected the thinning of the Liberals' own base, whose continuance into the 1990s makes that party weak in the country if not in the House. Some of this 1984 fragmentation reflected further strengthening of the NDP, of which more below. Then came the 1990s and the emergence of Reform as the main pole of opposition.[6] But Reform was weak, far weaker in popular vote than even the pathetic Conservative and Liberal oppositions of 1935-57 and 1984-88.

In seats, however, those particular oppositions were no stronger than Reform. Indeed, for most years between 1935 and 1957, Conservative oppositions were slightly weaker than Reform and the 1984-88 Liberals, with only 14 percent of seats in the House, were the weakest in history. Reform clearly squeezed many more seats per vote out of the system than did earlier weak oppositions. The secret of Reform's success in seats was the party's very narrowness in votes. Reform dominated only two provinces but there it was very dominant. Indeed, "too many" of its votes, strategically speaking, were concentrated in Alberta. Reform's most "efficient" province, from this perspective, was British Columbia. Curiously, Reform became less efficient in its 2000 guise as the Alliance.

If Reform and, even more, the Bloc were somewhat more efficient than some earlier oppositions, they were stunningly more efficient than the Conservatives and the NDP. Each of these latter parties was only weakly differentiated by region, and neither dominated any single province. Only in Atlantic Canada did the Conservatives remain competitive. In Quebec and Ontario the Conservatives served mainly to split the vote, among federalists in Quebec and on the centre-right in Ontario. The NDP was most competitive in its ancient heartland, Saskatchewan, but in no sense did it dominate that province any more.

Both parties used to be major players, of course, but in 1993 each lost *two thirds* of its former vote. For both, 1993 was an all-time low, 1997 was only marginally better, and 2000 was a serious setback. The Tories' previous low came in a bitter election, 1945, in which the whole landscape trembled. Fortunately for the Tories, this was also a bad year for the Liberals.[7] And the 1945 low was still eleven points above the Tories' 1993 result and eight points above the 1997 one. For the NDP, the 1993 share was smaller even than the CCF share in this party's first outing, in 1935. Each party took a geographic profile that sustained a large party under the logic of FPTP and saw it forced downward across the board. Each party survived because of residual organization, but also because of strength at the provincial level.

The worst of both worlds?
Canadians may thus be paying a price for our FPTP electoral system without getting a commensurate benefit. The price is distortion of voters' party preferences. The benefit is supposed to be the simplification of alternatives, which promotes, in turn, decisiveness and the clarification of lines of accountability. table 2 conveys the total scope of distortion as well as the extent of simplification, election by election and with median values for selected periods.

Distortion is indicated by the leftmost column, labeled "disproportionality." Its values indicate, roughly, the total deviation of seat shares from vote shares.[8] Most values in table 2 are fairly typical of FPTP systems. On average, Canadian results are more distorted than those for US House elections, much less distorted than in India, and about the same as in the United Kingdom and New Zealand.[9]

"Simplification" is indicated by the two rightmost columns in table 2, labeled the "effective number of parties." The "effective" number attempts to make precise an intuition about the "real" number of parties in a system. Consider first a system with two parties. If each party is exactly the same size, then the number must be two. If one is a little larger than the other we may still feel comfortable calling the system a two-party one. What if one party is twice the size of the other? At the other extreme, what about a party too small to be a factor in the real competition? The "effective number" measure translates these concerns into a continuous index by taking a notion of fractionalization — a system is more fractionalized the larger the number of parties and the more equal their shares — and turning it upside down.[10] Table 2 applies the "effective number" measure to both vote and seat shares.

The 1993, 1997 and 2000 elections score high, that is, above the all-elections median, on both distortion and fragmentation. On distortion, none of these

Table 2

Disproportionality and Defractionalization

Year	Disproportionality	Effective number of parties		
		Electoral	Parliamentary	
Second system				
1935	21.4	3.3	1.9	
1940	19.7 — Median	2.8 — Median	1.7 — Median	
1945	7.9 19.7	3.7 2.9	2.9 1.9	
1949	21.0	2.9	1.7	
1953	14.2	2.9	2.1	
Transition				
1957	2.6	3.0	2.9	
1958	20.9	2.4	1.6	
1962	7.1	3.2	2.8	
Third system				
1963	7.6	3.2	2.6	
1965	10.5	3.3	2.6	
1968	12.9 — Median	3.0 — Median	2.3 — Median	
1972	6.7 9.6	3.3 3.1	2.8 2.5	
1974	9.6	3.0	2.4	
1979	10.8	3.1	2.5	
1980	9.0	2.9	2.4	
Mulroney-Chrétien				
1984	21.0	2.7	1.7	
1988	11.3	3.0	2.3	
1993	17.6	3.9	2.4	
1997	12.6	4.1	3.0	
2000	13.8	3.8	2.5	
Median of all elections	13.1	3.1	2.4	

Source: Chief Electoral Officer of Canada, *Report*, various years. Analyses by the author.

elections is an extreme case. But every other election with above-average disproportionality was a landslide, a radically "simplified" result. The 1993-2000 elections, in contrast, produced highly fractionalized Houses, with the 1997 result the most fragmented in history.

So here too the rules have changed. In the past, the more distorted the result, the smaller the effective number of parliamentary parties. The 1935-88 relationship was:

$$\text{Effective Number} = 3.2 - 0.07 * \text{Disproportionality.}[11]$$

By this relationship, a result as disproportionate as the 1993 one should produce a House of 2.0 parties, not the 2.4 that actually emerged. In 1997 the House "should" have the equivalent of 2.3 parties, not 3.0. In 2000, the number "should" have been 2.2.

So many parties appeared in the House because so many appeared in the electorate. The 1993-2000 elections featured a record number of electoral parties, with only 1945 coming close among earlier results. The number of electoral parties testifies to the long-run failure of the old system at simplifying the alternatives. The argument for FPTP in terms of consolidation and simplification has two parts, but only one part seems to hold in Canada. The first part, the one that works, is called the "mechanical" effect, the reduction in the effective number of parties as votes are translated into seats. Table 2 shows that, without fail, the number of parliamentary parties is smaller than the number of electoral parties, sometimes spectacularly so. A "psychological" effect is supposed to follow from this, but here the argument breaks down. Mechanical distortion on this scale should create powerful disincentives against fractionalization of the vote. Some voters sense that their votes will be wasted and move strategically to a party that is both acceptable and viable. Parties pull candidates back where they are not viable, and potential donors and volunteers restrain their largesse. Truly infeasible parties should thus fade and die, leaving two large parties, each competitive for power and each willing to accept underrepresentation when it loses as the price of controlling outright majorities when it wins. In the long run, this should mitigate, although of course not eliminate, the appearance of disproportionality.[12]

In the second system, 1935-57, the typical outcome was dramatically distorted. The typical disproportionality value, 19.7, was larger even than the actual value for 1993. The typical mechanical effect was to strip one whole party from the system (compare the electoral and the parliamentary medians for the system). The second-system pattern, then, was to take a somewhat fragmented vote and, through massive distortion, produce a one-sided House, a House with fewer than two effective parties. By rights, this "should" have produced a downtrend in the effective number of electoral parties, as insurgent voters and elites were discouraged. Instead, the number of electoral parties stayed close to three, and then, after 1960 and the transition to the third system, kicked up over three. In the third system, the typical pattern was to take a quite fragmented vote and turn it into a modestly less fragmented House. The 1984 and 1988 elections scaled the fragmentation back a bit, but did not depart from the basic disproportionality-fractionalization relationship of earlier elections.

Now we have returned to distortion on the scale of the second system, 1935-57, but with parliamentary fragmentation exceeding that of the third system, 1963-84. In the second system, oppositions were weak. Even if they occasionally embarrassed the government, they never came close to threatening its existence.[13] In the third system, it was governments that were weak. From 1993 to 2000, the pattern rather resembled the second system, in that governments were strong in the House out of proportion to their strength in the country. And in 2004, the

Liberal government lost its majority, yielding a situation in which both government and opposition are weak.

So we may have the worst of both worlds. It is a given that FPTP produces more disproportionality than does the main alternative, a proportional representation (PR) formula.[14] To the extent that disproportionality is mitigated, it is because parties that validly represent bodies of opinion are suffocated. FPTP has other pathologies too, which this paper also chronicles. These things are all bad in themselves. But their flip side should be the creation of simple choices, effective governments and credible oppositions. The Canadian system has done a reasonable job in empowering government, in that most of the time single-party seat majorities appear. On the opposition side, the Canadian system has done a poor job for years, as oppositions have often been weak. And now the system may be on the verge of failing to empower governments. A multiparty legislature where no single party holds a majority is not a bad thing in itself. But if such a legislature becomes the norm, we must then ask whether there is any more point in accepting distorted results.

Apprehensions

For the 1990s, the pattern may have been messy but tolerable. The Liberal government enjoyed the full measure of majority power. This may or may not be a good thing in itself but good or bad, the power of House majorities is not an issue peculiar to that decade. The government's majority was more "manufactured" than most, but manufacturing is, again, not a new issue. The government's program did not provoke widespread opposition. And its standing between elections was eerily high.

"Eerie" does seem the right word, for the suspicion lingered that the absence of sharp debate and popular unrest made for an inadequate test of the government's true standing.[15] In the 1997 election, for instance, the government's support dropped sharply over the campaign, and its seat majority seems to have been saved only at the end. In 2000, the issue was similarly in doubt.

The situation at present carries some echoes of the mid-1950s. Accounts of that period suggest popular distress at a government unresponsive to forces on either right or left, and arrogant toward the House of Commons. But none of the great parliamentary battles of the mid-1950s registered in downtrends, not even blips, in poll readings of government approval. What was missing, we must infer, was someone able to articulate the discontent as leader of a plausible alternative government. Only in 1957 could John Diefenbaker become the tribune for expressing the discontent.[16] Two things about Diefenbaker are relevant. One was his undoubted political skill. The other was that he inherited a party that, although weak, was still a consolidated, pan-Canadian alternative.

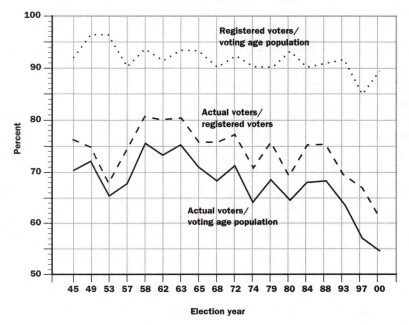

Figure 4

Postwar Turnout

Election year

Current discontent with the Liberal government does not seem on the scale of that in 1957. But in the absence of a credible alternative to the Liberals, how would Canadians express such discontent?

One answer might be, by exiting the arena entirely. And voters may already be sensing the impasse as, according to Figure 4, turnout in 1993 and since has been below the postwar average.[17] From 1945 to 1988, turnout as conventionally calculated, the number voting as a percentage of the number registered (the middle line in Figure 4), averaged 75.4 percent, with no trend. The corresponding figures for 1993 and 1997, respectively, are 69.6 and 67.0. The 1993 number is probably an underestimate as, outside Quebec, the voters list was carried over from the 1992 referendum and almost certainly had a surplus of the deceased and the recently moved. But most of the drop was real,[18] and there is no explaining away lower turnouts in 1997 and 2000.

Indeed, this indicator understates the problem. As a gauge of overall eligibility to vote, the number of registered voters has deteriorated, with a particularly dramatic drop in 1997. As a percentage of the voting age population, the registration rate used to fluctuate between 90 and 94 percent, and did so right down to and including 1993, according to the top line of figure 5.[19] But in 1997, the registration rate dropped to just over 85 percent. Why it dropped so dramatically is beyond the scope of this paper. It could be that the 1990s brought so large an immigration flow that the meaning of "age-eligibility" is different for the 1990s as compared with earlier decades. It could be that administrative changes account for the drop, as Elections Canada embarked on a transition to a permanent voters list in 1997.[20] A partial correction occurred in 2000, but the registration level was still below the earlier norm.

Whatever the reason for the drop in registration, turnout relative to age-eligibility now looks bad. From 1945 to 1988, there may have been a net downtrend in turnout calculated this way, but the trend was very modest. Turnout so measured averaged over 70 percent until 1965, then began a gradual drop. Only once since 1968 has the rate exceeded 70 percent. The 1993 rate, just below 64 percent, was a new postwar low. But 1993 pales in comparison to 1997, at 57 percent, and to 2000, at 55 percent.

This puts Canada near the bottom of the industrialized-world turnout league tables. Measured by this standard, Canada comes off only a little better than the US. In the 1996 US House election, for instance, turnout measured this way was 49 percent, a very disturbing figure but not that much below Canada's. No other G-7 country besides the US has turnout as low as Canada's, and only Japan and France have comparable rates. In round numbers, Canada is now 10 points below the United Kingdom, 15 points below Germany, and 30 points below Italy. Canada has never had peculiarly high turnout, but the gradual decline from the 1960s to the 1980s, followed by the precipitate drop in the 1990s, has taken us from the lower middle of the pack to very near the back.[21]

How Did We Get Here?

A global problem?

Does the shattering of old patterns reflect a global process of cultural and technological change? An argument along these lines has considerable currency and deserves to be taken seriously. This section outlines some arguments and reviews cross-national evidence. The review unveils commonalties of politics at the millennium, but it also suggests that differences among countries are as striking as convergences. Some, at least, of our problems are home-made. In particular, some originate in the strategic logic embedded in the electoral system.

That the Western world has undergone a culture shift in the last thirty years seems undeniable. The strongest statement along these lines lies in the work of Ronald Inglehart,[22] who claims that the ubiquitous prosperity of the postwar industrial world produced a generation with no experience of material want. This generation is thus largely unmoved by older controversies over shares of the material pie. The new sensibility resists old, consolidated forms of political action: big parties, big unions, the state generally. Moreover, newer, higher-order "postmaterial" drives are not easily shed, even if economic conditions worsen. The shift is thus permanent and is differentiated by period of birth. Canada, unsurprisingly, is not exempt from this culture shift.[23]

The claims are hotly contested, but the broad sweep of the thesis seems intuitively right. If the Inglehart thesis is hampered by weak measures and loose conceptualization,[24] it nonetheless captures the culture shift in gross outline. The political agenda has either shifted or expanded, as claims rooted in identity and in secular individualism (admittedly somewhat contradictory bases) have gained ground. That many groups and political actors resist these claims is part of the point. How parties respond to this broadening and reorientation of debate is the concern of the most influential interpretations of the evolution of both the right and the left in Europe. Herbert Kitschelt, for instance, shows how, for all of Western Europe, the old capitalist/socialist dimension has been supplemented, although not supplanted, by an authoritarian/libertarian one. As well, the balance of electoral power has shifted to the right. The axis of competition in most countries combines the old and the new dimensions.[25]

If the form of the challenge is ubiquitous, response to it by voters and parties is not. Some old parties, constrained by internal politics, failed to adapt to the modified agenda, and suffered accordingly. Others were able to absorb the new lines of conflict. The difference is political, and, notwithstanding evolutionary cultural universals, the centrality of politics makes each country rather unique. This pattern — the importance of each country's actual political history and the weakness of continent-wide trends — runs through most recent systematic investigations of European electoral patterns. For example, the psychological claim of parties has, on average, diminished, in the sense that fewer voters claim to identify with a party and, perhaps most critically, fewer claim a strong attachment. But in some countries partisanship so measured has actually intensified and in others, little change is visible. In general the differences among countries are more striking than the generality of the downtrend.[26] Similarly, there appears to be no continent-wide trend toward party-system fragmentation or toward systematically higher levels of volatility.[27] Trust in political institutions shows no Europe-wide trend, although individual countries exhibit movement. As with partisanship, trust is affected by political factors, and here a specific pattern sticks out: the more frequent is governmental turnover, the lower is the average level of trust.[28]

Also showing no Europe-wide trend, but rather a collection of country-specific stories, is electoral turnout.[29] It is true that the countries most immediately comparable to Canada, the big, rich countries of the G-7, exhibit declining turnout. Of these, only Italy shows no trend. Calculating turnout the same way as before in this paper, as a percentage of the age-eligible population, and plotting trends, other countries have seen turnout drop in the postwar period from five (UK) to twelve (France) points. With a fifty-year postwar downtrend of 9.5 points, Canada's drop is a bit greater than the G-7 average. Timing varies considerably across the G-7. In the US, the UK and France, turnout has been dropping in small steps for many years. In Germany, the downtrend seems to start in the 1980s. Only Japan is like Canada in seeing virtually the entire drop postponed to the 1990s. There may, then, be a story about secular change in turnout that is almost G-7-wide. But as with the European examples, differences across countries are at least as striking as the generalities.

One element in the "postmaterial" pattern does have real resonance in Canada, the rise of identity politics. The identities in question may be ancient, but their expression was inhibited by material want and global military insecurity. More recently, however, the very success of the West, economically and militarily, has loosened restraints on identity demands. In Europe, the consolidation of the Union has empowered national minorities in relation to their central governments, as, ironically, the cost of ethnic assertion has dropped.

This is a theme already familiar to Canadians. The emergence of the Bloc Québécois represents a certain electoral coming-of-age for Canada's largest national minority, as forces already strong in Quebec's provincial politics are now projected onto the federal scene. Here too, however, it does not suffice merely to allude to global patterns. The oddity of this universal trend is that it represents the re-emergence of the particular, as arguments are couched increasingly in terms of history, memory, and place. This too directs us back to the indigenous elements in the country's partisan history. The place to start is the electoral system.

The centrality of the electoral system

Clearly the electoral system is implicated in much of the earlier discussion. It was responsible for the vote-seat distortions that mark the 1990s. More generally, it affected the parliamentary power of winning parties, somewhat independently of their own vote-drawing power. A system with this much power constitutes a powerful set of strategic incentives in its own right. It does not just translate behaviour, it is an active force in shaping it.

To see how this is so, begin by reconsidering the seat-vote disjunctions discussed above. One indicator of disjunction is the ratio between the two quantities — seats and votes — for a given party. Winners under FPTP almost always have ratios greater than 1.0: they win a larger percentage of seats than of votes. Losers, including the Official Opposition, commonly have ratios under 1.0: they win a smaller share of seats than of votes. The Liberals' 1993 ratio, 1.47, is the fourth highest in history, after the 1935 and 1949 Liberal landslides and the 1984 Conservative one. It is slightly larger than the ratio for the 1958 Conservative landslide. Of course, the Liberal victory in 1993 was no landslide, just a comfortable majority. What makes the ratio so high is that this comfortable majority was generated by so weak a popular vote share. At 1.32, the 1997 ratio is lower than in 1993 but still well above the median for majority governments. In 2000, the ratio moved back up to 1.41.

Does this mean that the Chrétien government somehow changed the informal vote-to-seat translation rules? Far from it. Indeed, the Liberals won fewer seats in the 1990s than they "should" have, given the old rules. What *did* change, as already outlined, was the fragmentation of the opposition. Consider this simple representation of the how Liberal and Conservative votes traditionally combined to produce Liberal seats:

Liberal Seat % = 3.6 + 1.86 * Liberal Vote % - 0.90 * Conservative Vote %.[30]

What this means is that a Liberal vote gain of one percentage point would increase the party's seat share by 1.86 points or, depending on the size of the House, five or six seats. Stated this way, the relationship assumes that the Liberal shift is not accompanied by a Conservative shift. If the Liberal gain comes at the Tories' expense, that is, the Conservative vote share also drops a percentage point, then the Liberals would gain another two or three seats. Of course, these relationships also work in reverse, for Liberal losses and Tory gains. In the typical election, Liberal gains were in fact complemented by Tory losses, and vice versa. But not entirely. A striking long-run pattern in figure 1, where government and opposition are compared, is *asymmetry*. Notwithstanding consolidation of opposition in and after John Diefenbaker's period at the Tory helm, the underlying story has been a widening gap between government and opposition. The Tories' collapse in the 1990s may be the final chapter in that story. It was certainly a gift to the Liberals.

Were the Liberals able to cash the gift in completely? Not quite, it turns out. Just cranking the 1993, 1997 and 2000 Liberal and Conservative votes through the equation above would yield Liberal seat shares of 65.5, 58.3 and 68.6 percent, respectively. In fact, Liberal shares were rather lower each time, 60 percent in 1993, 50.8 percent in 1997, and 57.5 in 2000. So even though the seat/vote ratios seem high, they were not high at all given the weakness of the ancient foe. Why then did the Liberals not extract even more seats from the system? The answer has two parts.

First, the Liberals were too concentrated geographically for their own good. In certain provinces, they "worked" the map just right. British Columbia and Quebec may be examples: weak shares province-wide, but sufficiently concentrated (too concentrated in Quebec, perhaps) in the metropolitan centres to guarantee a decent representation. But in Ontario and, in 1993, Atlantic Canada, the Liberals wasted votes. The Liberal shares were so huge in those places that no amount of opposition consolidation would have turned more than a handful of seats, if any. No consolidation occurred, of course, and so the Liberals could have won about as many seats with a rather smaller vote, such that the "surplus" could have been put to better use in other regions.

Second, although the opposition was fragmented overall, it was not equally fragmented everywhere. Of the four serious opposition parties, two — the Conservatives and NDP — were geographically dispersed and two — Reform/Alliance and the Bloc — were concentrated. The concentration of the latter two limited the ability of the Liberals to capture seats. Put another way, Reform/Alliance and the Bloc captured so much of the old Tory vote in BC, Alberta, and Quebec that they did not so much fragment that vote as replace it.

In this narrative lies a generalization about the first-past-the-post system. Success under FPTP is not just a matter of accumulating votes. Also important is how those votes are distributed across the landscape, as parties are encouraged to think geographically. What it means for a party to think geographically is contingent, however, on how many votes it starts with: the fewer the votes, the more concentrated in one or a few places they should be. Conversely, the more votes a party controls, the more spread out they should be.[31] Opposition parties in the 1990s illustrate both sides of the first proposition: Reform/Alliance and the Bloc benefited from concentration; Conservatives and New Democrats suffered from dispersion.

FPTP in Canada is often criticized for sowing division, for encouraging parties to adopt regionally divisive strategies. The logic of the previous paragraph suggests that the criticism cannot be made unconditionally. Unquestionably, FPTP encourages small parties to make narrow appeals and, to the extent that small parties flourish, the House may become a cacophony of sectionalism. This did seem to be a story of the 1990s. But large parties are encouraged to broaden their appeal, to craft geographically inclusive coalitions and to look for issues that cut through region.[32] And most Canadian governments have, in fact, succeeded in pursuing an inclusive strategy.

First consider the place of Quebec, arguably the historic pivot for government. Figure 5 plots the place of Quebec and the other regions in the formation of governments. For each region, the smooth top line is its total number of seats in the House, a gauge of potential influence. The jagged line below is the number of seats from the region won by the Canada-wide winner, a gauge of the region's actual influence. In all but three elections from 1935 to 1988, the winner also won a majority of Quebec seats. In over half the cases, withdrawal of Quebec seats would have deprived the winner of a House majority. In four of those nine, withdrawal would also have denied the winner a plurality, also the case with the three minority governments in which Quebec was well represented. The three elections in which the winner secured fewer than 20 Quebec seats were all Conservative victories, all minority governments, and all short-lived. Over most of this period, Quebec adhered to the Liberals and made them the only feasible party of government. That government might be weak, indeed a minority for critical periods, but installation of an alternative, Conservative government required an extraordinary and unsustainable concatenation of forces. All that seemed to change with Quebeckers' willingness to support the Mulroney Conservatives. This apparently heralded the return of true two-party competitive politics, as the 1984 swing toward the Tories mirrored the earlier 1887-96 swing away from them. Quebec thus played the pivot in two equally vital ways: it arbitrated two great realignments; between these realignments, it made the Liberals virtually the sole feasible party of government.

Some of this power reflects mere size, for Quebec has always held a large body of seats, 65 at the beginning and 75 now. At present Quebec controls slightly under 25 percent of the House, and in earlier decades the share was larger. But Quebec's importance goes beyond mere numbers. The province's voters also used their voting power effectively, by consolidating support for a party that enjoyed significant support elsewhere and, when switching, doing so nearly wholesale. Comparisons with Ontario (panel B in figure 5) are instructive. Over this period, Quebec's total number of seats always lagged behind Ontario's, and the gap has widened. But each major party's range of outcomes was 10 seats greater in Quebec than in Ontario. In Quebec, the Liberal minimum was 12 seats and the maximum, 73, for a range of 61. The corresponding Conservative numbers were 1 and 63, for a range of 62.[33] In Ontario, the Liberal minimum and maximum were 14 and 64, for a range of 50. The Conservative numbers were 17 and 67, also a range of 50. The difference in seat pattern follows one in popular vote, as the range of vote shares was much greater in Quebec than in Ontario. This vote flux in Quebec is then translated into seat flux with remarkable efficiency, as spatial variance in vote shares within Quebec is low.[34] Thanks to this consolidation of seats, Quebec representation in government almost always bulked about as large as Ontario's. Indeed, in nine of the seventeen 1935-88 parliaments, Quebec members on the government side outnumbered Ontario ones.

On one hand, this is a story of sectionalism. Quebecers appear to act on a sense of provincial interest, and major parties respond. On the other hand, Quebec seats never suffice by themselves to constitute a government. To win a majority, a party must, at the very least, match the Quebec total with seats from other regions. Usually, the requirement for seats outside Quebec has been greater.[35]

The other big lump of seats is Ontario, of course, but before 1993 Ontario did not play its weight. Over the years since 1935, the province's total number of seats grew, but until 1993 its average number of *government* seats shrank. In one sense, then, the province became less, not more of a counter in the government game. It is true that when the whole country swung one way, so would Ontario.

Figure 5

Regional Strength: House versus Governing Party

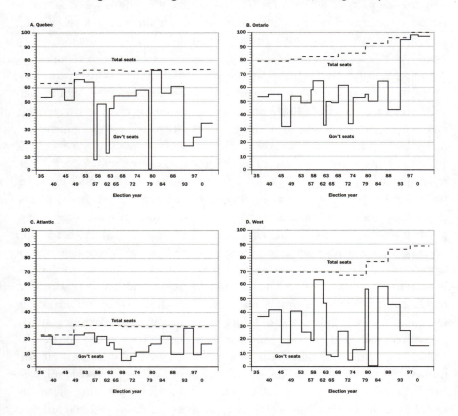

Thus in the 1958, 1968, and 1984 sweeps, the winner's Ontario share was 60 to 70 seats. But these shares were not sustainable and three times the winner captured fewer than 40 Ontario seats. In contrast to the Quebec case, two of these three cases involved Liberal winners, in 1945 and 1972. Each time, the Liberals' weakness in Ontario was a setback to the government, but only a temporary one. The essential fact about Ontario in comparison with Quebec, according to comparison of panels A and B, is the greater fragmentation in its seat shares.

But Ontario is still bound to be important simply for its sheer bulk: currently it holds roughly one-third of all House seats. In the typical pre-1993 House, about 50 government seats were from Ontario, smaller than the typical Quebec share but still more than one-third of the requirement for a majority.

Atlantic Canada also usually found a place at the table. It was next to impossible for this region to contribute more seats than Ontario to the winner. By the end of the period the whole region controlled fewer seats than British Columbia, not to mention Ontario or Quebec. Even so, from the 1930s to the early 1960s the region rivaled Ontario as a source of government seats. Over the whole period, Atlantic Canada contributed about half as many seats as Ontario to governing parties. Twice, 1945 and 1962, Ontario largely abandoned the governing party, so that the Atlantic region held as many government seats as the biggest province.

So far, then, the story is one of inclusion. The very biggest place is well represented but not absolutely dominant. The smallest region is almost always present in some kind of force and occasionally rivals the biggest region. Quebec plays a key role by consolidating internally and, if an acceptable alternative presents itself, by swinging en masse. This is worth underlining. Whether or not one considers Canada a binational state, few doubt that the biggest challenge is the continued integration into the pan-Canadian scheme of the one jurisdiction with a francophone majority. The FPTP electoral formula has historically facilitated — and may even have forced — a linguistically inclusive strategy on prospective governing parties.[36] Three of four regions routinely win serious representation at the centre. Presumably this reflects active solicitation by the major parties.

The problem, of course, is the West. For most of this century the region has dwarfed the Atlantic provinces, and in recent years has pulled away from Quebec as well.[37] British Columbia alone now has as many seats as Atlantic Canada. But this has not been cashed in on power at the centre. Over half the time from 1935 to 1988, the government party returned more seats from Atlantic Canada than from the West. Only five times did the region contribute seats in proportion to its intrinsic strength, and two of these (1962 and 1979) were short-lived minority governments.

It might have been tempting to see the Mulroney years as the region's political coming of age. Not only was the West the springboard for the Mulroney government's majority, the majority in question lasted two parliaments, the first consecutive majorities since 1953, the first for the Tories since 1891. The Conservatives' strength in the West, when joined to a breakthrough in Quebec, seemed to form the basis for the first real two-party politics since the 1890s. It was not to be, of course. The key element in the 1993 election was the evaporation of Tory strength, most dramatically in these very regions. To understand that evaporation we have to go back to how that strength was built in the first place.

The other party that evaporated in 1993 was the NDP. Its pre-1993 history, in many ways, complemented that of the Tories. The NDP exists, arguably, because the Diefenbaker Conservatives pre-empted some of the old CCF base. But by reconstituting itself in a particular way, the NDP also changed the character of third-party activity. The explosion of 1993 was, in part, a recrudescence of forces that, between them, the post-Diefenbaker Tories and the NDP redirected.

The 1993 cataclysm was not all old West wine in new Reform bottles. The official opposition in 1993, after all, was the Bloc Québécois. For the West, 1993 arguably just restored an old pattern. The real novelty was the shrinkage of Quebec's presence at the centre of power. Figure 5A indicates that 1993 and 1997 were the only ones in living memory in which Quebec had, for more than a few months, fewer than 30 seats on the government side of the House. This may signal a fundamental change to the informal rules of government formation. It certainly signals a fundamental change in Quebec's own orientation to the system.

First moves: Conservatives to the west, NDP to the east

Between the 1950s and the 1980s the Conservative Party made itself a progressively more formidable electoral force. Some of this it accomplished just by growing. Equally important, however, was the party's efficient response, whether intentional or accidental, to the electoral map. Figure 6A, "Tories move out of Centre," illustrates the first step, accomplished mainly under John Diefenbaker's leadership. The light line gives the 1935-53 pattern, not a pretty picture for a party pretending to alternative-government status. The party's places of relative strength were places of absolute weakness. The Conservatives averaged about 40 percent of the vote in Ontario and the Atlantic provinces, some ten points behind the typical Liberal share. In the rest of the country their typical share was simply pathetic: just over 20 percent in Quebec and around 20 percent in the four Western provinces. The Western reading is true for the whole period, but understates how much worse things were in that region than in Quebec. Two elections infused with wartime passion, 1940 and 1945, polarized French and English Canada and drove the Quebec Tory share under 20 percent. In the other three elections, the Tories' Quebec vote hovered around 30 percent. This fluctuation mattered hardly at all in seats, as the Tories won few in Quebec throughout the period. Countrywide, the Tories received an average vote share of 30 percent and a seat share of 19 percent.[38] In this period, the Conservatives were barely plausible as an opposition party much less as a governing one.

In the West, Conservative weakness was not matched by Liberal strength. Both old parties were weak in the region, so Western politics was third-party politics. The West was the primary site for Canada's first great electoral insurgency, the Progressive movement of 1921. Just as Alberta was the epicentre of the 1921 earthquake, so was it the main site for third-party activity in the 1935-57 system, where, according to figure 6b, parties out of the mainstream averaged over 50 percent of the vote. British Columbia and Saskatchewan were not far behind, however, as third parties routinely pulled in over 40 percent, and the gap between Manitoba and all provinces to its east was large. The Western parties numbered two: Social Credit, which dominated Alberta and gained importance in BC; and the Cooperative Commonwealth Federation (CCF), with special strength in BC, Saskatchewan and Manitoba.

In this period, then, Canada harboured two geographically segregated party systems. In the East, the two old parties prevailed, only weakly challenged by

Figure 6

Geographic "Rotation" — Second to Third Systems

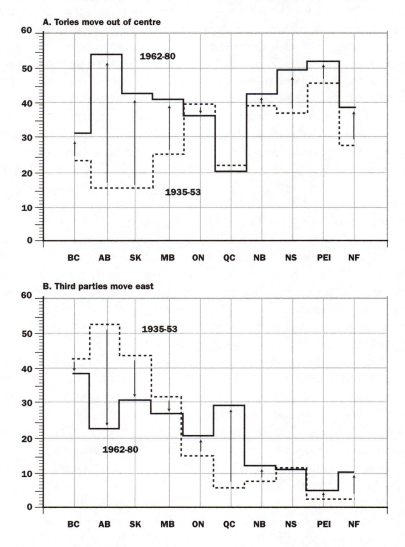

A. Tories move out of centre

1962-80

1935-53

BC   AB   SK   MB   ON   QC   NB   NS   PEI   NF

B. Third parties move east

1935-53

1962-80

BC   AB   SK   MB   ON   QC   NB   NS   PEI   NF

insurgents. In Quebec the Conservatives were terminally weak, but were complemented less by third-party activity than by hegemonic Liberal strength.[39] In the West, third parties were strong, in some places the prevailing force.

Between the 1950s and the 1960s, the Conservative Party gained considerable ground, less by augmenting its vote than by increasing its geographic efficiency. Where the party's average vote share moved up only 4 points, to 34 percent, its average seat share doubled, to 38 percent. The modesty of the net vote gain reflects the offsetting of massive gains in medium-sized provinces by modest losses in large provinces, as indicated by figure 6A. Where before the Conservatives thrice squandered 30 percent of the Quebec vote on virtually no seats, now they wasted fewer votes.[40] Their decline in Ontario left them weak in the province, but their seat position there was already weak. In the West, conversely, they moved up dramatically, such that they tended to win outright majorities in Alberta and solid pluralities in Saskatchewan and Manitoba. The figure understates how well the party did in BC. Where in the 1960s the party reverted to its abject shares of the earlier system, in the 1970s it marched toward a plurality position, comparable to those in Saskatchewan and Manitoba. The party initially moved up in the Atlantic provinces, then fell back. In the 1962-80 elections, then, the Conservatives were a party initially of all outlying regions and then quite distinctively a party of the West.

As the Tories became more a party of the West, the West became less distinctively the home of third parties, as indicated by Figure 6B. In every Western province the third-party total fell, while third-party voting became a fact of life elsewhere. In BC and Alberta, Social Credit just evaporated. In Saskatchewan and Manitoba, the party losing ground was the successor to the CCF, the NDP. Within the West, BC displaced Alberta as the province with the largest ongoing third-party presence. Ontario moved up to a level comparable to the Prairie West. Most notable, however, was the rise of third-party voting in Quebec. In 1962 an incarnation of Social Credit burst on that province's scene and lasted for nearly the entire period, weakening only at the end.

If all this still left Canada with a regionally differentiated system, the pattern of differentiation was sharply modified from before. The West remained distinctive from the East, but only in the strength of parties, no longer in their identity. The dominant party in the region, the Conservatives, had a significant presence everywhere else except Quebec. The West gave the Liberal Party a weak share, but Liberals still remained in the region's game. The West was distinctive in that its second-place (in some provinces, first-place) party, the NDP, was overall the system's third party, but the NDP was now more competitive for the biggest prize of all, Ontario. The most distinctive region was now Quebec, the only province clearly dominated by the Liberals yet also the new home of Social Credit.

As third-party voting spread, it became, as it were, domesticated. This is the point of figure 7. Between 1921 and 1988, the total third-party vote became progressively less episodic, less susceptible to short-term flux. In part, this reflects the emergence of the CCF, later the NDP. The original Western impulse, in 1921 toward a loose grouping called the Progressives, embodied at least two tendencies. One was protest, which produced surge and decline, according to the state of the wheat economy. The other was programmatic, and this impulse finds its clearest expression in the CCF-NDP, whose series is dominated not by

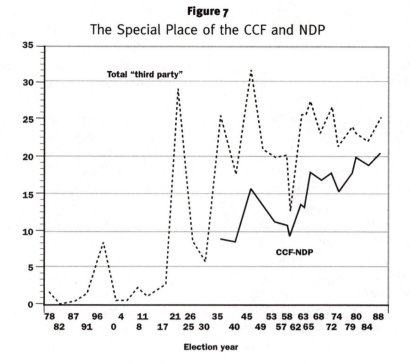

Figure 7

The Special Place of the CCF and NDP

Total "third party"

CCF-NDP

Election year

short-term flux but by gradual growth. Between the second and third party systems, short-term flux lost importance generally, although it did not disappear. Third-party activity increasingly came to mean NDP activity. Although the total third-party vote, and thus the non-NDP vote, surged in 1962, this did not signal a classic Western insurgency. Rather, it was the appearance of Social Credit in Quebec. Even this surge only temporarily delayed the NDP's rise to monopoly of the third force.

Second move: Conservatives to Quebec

The 1962-80 Conservative pattern — strong and growing in the West, consolidation elsewhere except Quebec — left the party powerful in opposition but still infeasible as a party of government. After 1962, they never won more than 36 percent of the total vote, and only twice more than 40 percent of the seats. Their high point is telling. In 1979, on 36 percent of the vote they received 48 percent of seats, a remarkable showing for so modest a vote. But they won hardly any seats in Quebec and were lucky to win as many as they did outside that province.

As argued above, seats in Quebec tend to be available *en bloc*. For the Conservatives to win an outright seat majority, then, the obvious move was to invade Quebec, and this they did in 1984. Their 1980-84 transition looked simple: under the leadership of Brian Mulroney, they just added Quebec to the pre-existing coalition. Figure 8A indicates that almost all their gain over the 1962-80 system came in Quebec.[41] This gave them a smashing victory in 1984 and helped ensure that their 1988 majority was still comfortable. About half the Quebec gain came at the expense of the Liberal Party.

The other half came from Social Credit. Figure 8B records that the third-party total in Quebec dropped by half, and this drop in turn is about half the total Conservative gain. After 1984, Quebec exhibited one of the weakest third-party shares, and most of this accrued to the NDP. The disappearance of Social Credit in Quebec completed the "domestication" of third parties. Figure 7 indicates that 1984 brought the smallest non-CCF/NDP component ever in total third-party voting. The 1988 pattern was essentially the same, although the slight widening of the NDP/"total" gap in that year was a warning sign: it reflects Reform's first candidacies in Alberta.

Of course, the Conservative move into Quebec was not as simple as all that. The Tories exploited Quebec's province-focused nationalism, which, for all its growth and prominence in provincial politics, was blocked in federal politics. The Liberals had been mobilized to fight that nationalism even as they asserted another, rights-based version of the francophone project. By their openness to Quebec nationalism, the Tories, perhaps inadvertently, expanded the agenda of federal politics.[42]

In one sense, the 1984 and 1988 elections indicate the resilience of Canada's old parties. The very oldest, the Liberals and the Conservatives, continued to dominate the system. Indeed, they appeared to have restored much of the system's pre-1921 competitive balance. Although they could not banish third-party voting, both of them were competitive for national office. If the Liberals lost ground after 1984, they were still imaginable as a party of government. Most critical is that they were no longer the *only* imaginable party of government. Even the "third" party, the NDP, could at least dream of power (and actually experience it in certain provinces). Its typical share by the 1980s was close to two-thirds the share returned by the next larger party. The NDP may have been perched on the brink of the inner circle. To the older parties, especially the Liberals, this might be an upsetting fact, an indication that their hegemony was still incomplete. But the NDP threatened neither a strictly partisan conception of politics nor the Westminster system. And in many ways, the NDP was already in the inner circle, whether of parliamentary procedure, of media access, or of finance.

The 1988-93 transition
The resilience must have been more apparent than real, as the system collapsed in 1993. What voters did to bring the collapse about is shown in table 3, which depicts

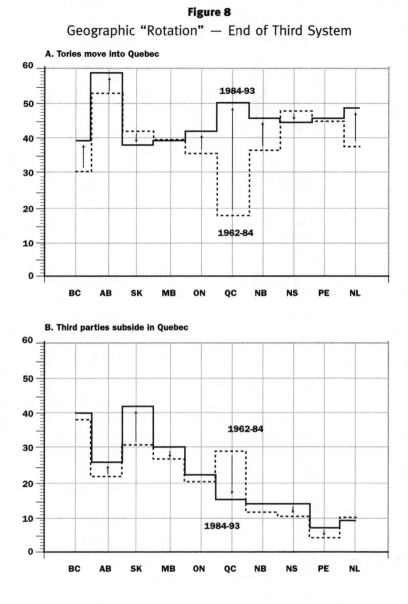

Figure 8

Geographic "Rotation" — End of Third System

A. Tories move into Quebec

1984-93

1962-84

BC   AB   SK   MB   ON   QC   NB   NS   PE   NL

B. Third parties subside in Quebec

1962-84

1984-93

BC   AB   SK   MB   ON   QC   NB   NS   PE   NL

the flow of voting and non voting between 1988 and 1993.[43] Rows denote behaviour in 1988 and columns, behaviour in 1993. "Behaviour" includes nonvoting ("Abstain"), being too young in 1988 but coming of age by 1993 (the row labelled "Entering"), and dying between 1988 and 1993 (the column labelled "Leaving"). Percentages sum to 100 across rows, that is, within 1988 groups. Take, for example,

Table 3

Turnover 1988-93

1988	PC	Lib	NDP	Reform	Bloc	Other	Abstain	Leaving	1988 Distribution
PC	23.1	19.2	1.4	22.1	10.7	1.8	12.5	7.1	28.1
Lib	6.2	57.4	1.0	9.1	2.4	1.0	13.9	9.1	20.9
NDP	3.8	22.6	24.1	11.3	5.3	6.8	19.5	6.0	13.3
Reform	0.0	0.0	0.0	71.4	0.0	0.0	14.3	7.1	1.4
Bloc	0.0	0.0	0.0	0.0	0.0	0.0	0.0	0.0	0.0
Other	0.0	11.8	2.9	3.5	68.2	2.9	7.1	0.1	1.7
Abstain	7.4	19.4	2.3	6.9	6.9	1.8	53.9	2.8	21.7
Entering	8.5	29.2	3.1	5.4	16.2	3.1	36.9	–	13.0
1993 Distribution	11.0	28.5	4.8	12.9	8.8	2.5	25.8	5.5	100.1

Note: Percentages sum to 100 across rows.

the top left cell, which indicates that of 1988 Conservative voters, 23.1 percent stayed with the Conservatives. The next cell along indicates that 19.2 percent of 1988 Tories shifted to the Liberals. On the 1988 "Abstain" row, the largest concentration of 1993 partisans, 19.4 percent, lies in the Liberal column, and among 1988 abstainers a Liberal vote was nearly three times as likely in 1993 as any other vote. But most likely of all, at 53.9 percent, was to abstain again. And so on. Note finally that percentages also appear along the bottom and right margins. The right, or row, margin gives the distribution across all alternatives for 1988. The bottom, or column, margin does the same for 1993. Including percentages for nonvoting categories makes party shares seem smaller than we are accustomed to.[44]

Start with the party that commonly gets lost in discussion of 1993, the Bloc. The Bloc conjoins two rather different electoral streams. One is sovereignist and this stream flows mainly from outside the federal party system entirely. The other is disgruntled Tories, some of whom, presumably, are also sovereignist.

Of newly eligible voters, over 16 percent supported the Bloc, almost *twice* the Bloc share in the full electorate. Of voters eligible in 1988 but who abstained that year, almost seven percent chose the Bloc, the only party that attracted such voters at almost the same rate as in the whole electorate.[45] Together, these new voters constitute over 40 percent of all Bloc supporters.[46] We must suppose, however, that much of this mobilization is to federal elections rather than to elections as such. Many new Bloc voters are old political hands, willing to turn out in provincial politics where sovereignty has been a voting option since the 1960s but unable to assert the option in federal politics until this year.[47]

This interpretation is reinforced by two other pieces in the puzzle, voters inscribed for 1988 as New Democrats or as "others." About five percent of 1988

New Democrats defected to the Bloc. As relatively few 1988 New Democrats lived in Quebec and thus were even eligible to shift to the Bloc, this statistic suggests that virtually the entire 1988 Quebec NDP vote switched to the Bloc. Similarly, two-thirds of 1988 "other" voters shifted to the Bloc. "Other" party voters were not numerous, of course, but most were in Quebec, and most supported the Parti Rhinocéros. The near-unanimity of this defection strongly implies that both the Rhinos and the Quebec NDP were parking spots for sovereignists.

Among the two big, old parties, only the Conservative party was a truly significant source of Bloc support. A 1988 Tory was over four times as likely as a Liberal to vote Bloc, such that former Conservatives supplied over one-third of the total Bloc vote. This exchange was strictly one way, of course. Had these voters stayed with the Conservative party, the Tory share would have been about three points larger in table 3's accounting, or over 20 percent among active voters, rather than the 16 percent the party actually received.

Now to Reform. If the party did make net gains from demographic turnover and from exchange with abstention, as a new party it could hardly do otherwise. But just over five percent of newly eligible voters supported Reform, a much smaller share than Reform's share in the full electorate. About 7 percent of 1988 abstainers voted Reform, also under the whole-electorate share. Altogether, new voters accounted for only about one-sixth the Reform total.

The prime source of Reform support was the Conservative party. A Conservative was twice as likely as any other 1988 partisan to move to Reform. In part, this reflects the fact that 1988 Conservatives were highly likely to defect, somewhere, anywhere. But 1988 New Democrats were even more likely to leave their party, yet their rate of movement to Reform in particular was nowhere near as great. It might seem significant that New Democrats were slightly more likely than Liberals to go to Reform, but this truly is an artifact. The critical thing is that New Democrats, like Tories, were very likely to defect. Among defectors, former New Democrats were the *least* likely to vote Reform: 14 percent of defecting New Democrats went to the new party, as compared with 20 percent from the Liberals and 30 percent from the Conservatives.[48] Ideological proximity was clearly the dominant fact, then, and proximity — more properly, distance — kept the overwhelming majority of New Democrats out of the Reform camp. This is all the more striking in light of the fact that NDP voters, disproportionately concentrated in the West, were more likely to encounter viable Reform candidates than almost any other kind of 1988 partisan was. Reformers, thus, are mainly former Conservatives.[49]

As the Tory vote shattered, the old system shrank. The same is true on a smaller scale for the NDP vote. But a counter-trend also burns through table 3. Some of the fragmentation of the old Tory and NDP vote contributed to consolidation of the old system's remains. A 1988 Tory was almost as likely to switch to the Liberals as to Reform, and twice as likely to go Liberal as to go Bloc.[50] For 1988 New Democrats the Liberals were by far the biggest draw, such that almost as many voted Liberal as stayed with the NDP.[51] That so many Liberals are former Conservatives and New Democrats must be kept in mind when discussion turns, below, to the future of the system.

Fragmentation, consolidation, and policy

From table 3 it should be obvious why the "United Alternative" had so much strategic appeal on the political right. As most Reformers were former Tories, it seemed natural to patch up the quarrel. But table 1 gives one hint of the barriers to this. Notwithstanding old affinities, latter-day Reformers disliked the Conservative Party intensely, about as much as they did the Liberals. The Conservative-Liberal disliking gap may have narrowed between 1993 and 1997, but the Reform-Conservative gap did not. And the feeling was mutual. Conservative voters found Reform/Alliance much less acceptable than they did the Liberals, and between 1993 and 1997 the gap only widened. In 1997 and 2000 Tories even preferred the NDP to Reform/Alliance. This is not a landscape that favoured consolidation.

Figure 9 stylizes the policy differences that underpinned this enmity. The figure is based on questions in the 1988 and 1997 Canadian Election studies, that ask respondents first what they see as ideal policy in a domain and then where they think each party stands. For example, respondents were asked how much they thought should be done for Quebec, with alternatives ranging from "much more" to "much less." They then were asked how much each party wants to do, with the same response alternatives. Response to the Quebec questions defines the horizontal axis in each panel.[52] The vertical axis captures each decade's central economic issue. For the 1980s, this is the closeness of Canada-US ties, prompted by the Canada-US Free Trade Agreement. In the 1990s, the issue is taxing and spending, welfare-state spending in particular. Points on the graph indicate average positions for respondents in each region (squares) and for their perceptions of parties (crosses), simultaneously on both dimensions. The panels differ subtly, so that each can bring out a different point. In panel A, regional differences outside Quebec are glossed over. Instead respondents in and out of Quebec are distinguished by party, the better to dramatize the old system's incoherence and, thus, its explosive potential. In panel B, respondents are distinguished not by party, but more finely by region to make a point about Reform, in particular.

For 1988, the horizontal axis captures a central fact of the history that produced that decade's party system: on Quebec, all three old parties adopted essentially the same position. This is how respondents saw the parties, and this is how the parties actually behaved, notably as all three endorsed the Meech Lake Accord. Given that the accord had the express purpose of making an earlier constitutional settlement

Figure 9
Voters, Parties and Policy

A. 1988

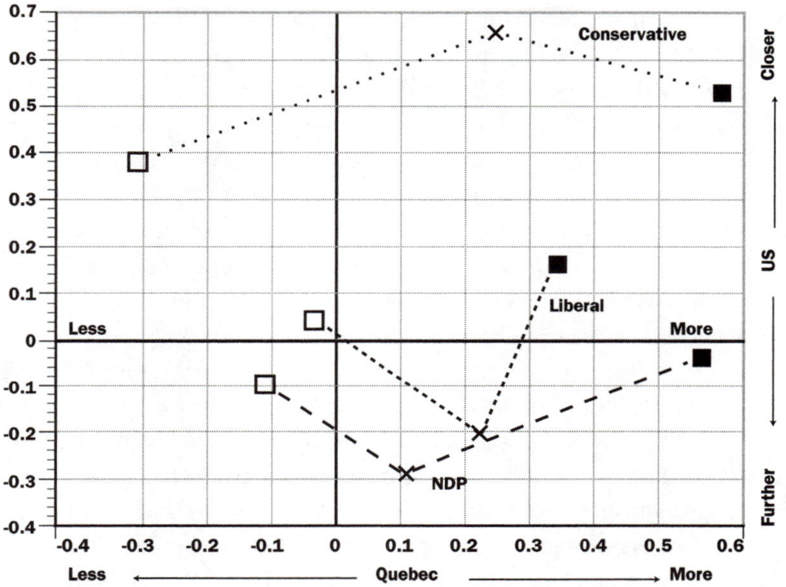

B. 1997

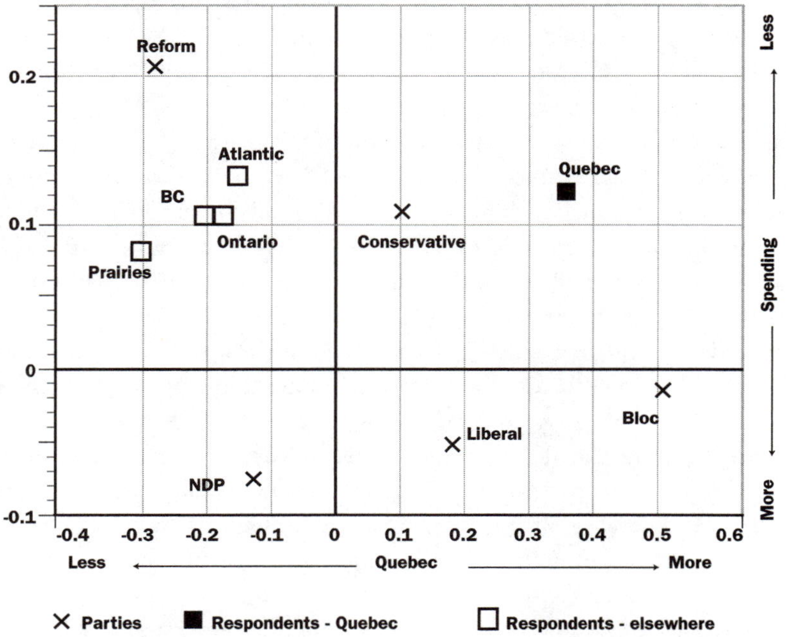

✕ Parties ■ Respondents - Quebec ☐ Respondents - elsewhere

acceptable to Quebec, it makes sense that respondents saw all three parties as leaning mildly toward that province.[53] For the Conservatives, commitment to the accord was the final step in the process captured by figures 6 and 8. Roughly the same was true of the NDP, for whom a credible commitment to Quebec was essential to breaking into the inner circle. But this consensus left the system ripe for invasion, with Reform already on the horizon.

Most vulnerable to invasion was the Conservative party, for the horizontal distance between the party and its own supporters could hardly have been greater. Figure 9 reflects the peculiar incoherence of the electoral coalition assembled by Brian Mulroney in 1984. But then, all parties contained some of this incoherence. Certainly, the NDP was almost as vulnerable as the Conservatives were. The Liberals too were divided along this line, although the distance between its camps was relatively small.

But the 1988 election did not turn on the Quebec-Canada dimension. Reform might have primed the issue but the party was still very new and, in any case, gaps among the old parties were huge on the other, unquestionably important issue, Canada-US relations. Party by party, Quebec and non-Quebec supporters were almost indistinguishable, and for the Conservatives and NDP, closely coincident with their own party's position. By staking out this pole, the Conservative Party made the cost of right-wing defection prohibitive. The NDP might have done the same but for the ability of John Turner's Liberals to close on them.[54] For the parties as a system, the centrality of free trade arguably delayed a reckoning.

The reckoning arrived in 1993. The Bloc's emergence on the far pro-Quebec side of the spectrum is, obviously, a critical part of the story. It burst onto the scene precisely as a reflection of the collapse of the Meech Lake Accord. Its mere existence, tying down a large fraction of the Quebec electorate, narrows the field for pan-Canadian coalition building. Reform, of course, anchored the other pole on the Quebec dimension, as it also did for the spending dimension. On the Quebec issue, Reform in 1997 sat right where the typical Tory outside Quebec sat in 1988. On the same issue, Reform in 1997 may also have been closer to the typical 1988 New Democrat than the NDP itself was that year.[55] Indeed, Reform seems ideally located with respect to all respondents outside Quebec in 1997. On the horizontal dimension of panel B, Reform is right in the thick of the various regions, with only the NDP as a serious rival.

But concentration on the Quebec issue misstates a key part of Reform's appeal. Panel B makes clear that the West, Reform's geographic base, is *not* peculiarly impatient with Quebec. British Columbia is indistinguishable from Ontario, as only the limitations of graphical presentation force the two apart. The Prairie provinces are the polar region, to be sure, but among the Prairie provinces, Alberta is not the polar one; rather it is the most like BC. Yet Alberta and BC were the heartland of Reform. Although within each province (Ontario no less than the West), Reform supporters were clearly distinct from Liberals and Tories, Western voters with a given orientation to Quebec were much more likely to vote Reform than a voter in Ontario, not to mention in Atlantic Canada, with the same orientation. Part of Reform's appeal, we must conclude, was almost purely sectional. To many voters its appeal was as the party of the West, the West that "wants in."[56]

This is another way in which Reform was the Bloc's mirror image. Whether or not the Bloc is irrevocably committed to full sovereignty for Quebec, its mere existence represents a repudiation of pan-Canadian schemes of linguistic accommodation. Quebec's peculiar claim may still be as the francophone heartland, but the fact now remains that what once may have been linguistic demands are now couched in the rhetoric of jurisdiction and place. And if the Bloc is the party of one region, Reform, in the minds of many of its supporters, was the party of another region. For some Reform supporters, this may have been the essential thing.

Where Do We Go From Here?

Within the existing rules of the game, we need to consider two paths for the system's further evolution. One is consolidation of the Right. At the elite level, this seemed to occur with the merger of the Progressive Conservatives and the Alliance in late 2003. We should not dismiss the possibility that pursuit of this alternative might only fragment the Right even more, however. The other path concerns the Left. As the popular vote on this side of the spectrum coalesced only in the 1990s, it is reasonable to ask if this consolidation can be maintained. If the system cannot move back toward effective two-party politics, the precondition for the distinctive virtues of the FPTP electoral formula, then the question of structural reform is squarely on the table.

Consolidation of the Right?

The explosion of the Conservative Party's electoral coalition did not alter the geographic logic that preoccupied Tory strategists into the 1980s. Figure 9 makes clear that such a strategy does not require abandonment of basic conservative economic principles. On some economic questions, indeed, a non-centrist strategy is still probably the winning one.

The problem is that economic ideology was not the only thing, not even the most important thing, driving the votes of the Conservative Party's erstwhile base. Bear in mind, first, that some of the old Tory coalition fell to earth as the Bloc. Sovereignists mobilized into federal politics by the Bloc probably have little interest in renovating the rest of the federal party system. Quebec fugitives from the Conservative party were not attracted to that party in the first place by its economic ideology. Nor are they likely to be attracted by a decentralist conception of the federation that does not also involve recognition of Quebec's special place. Right off the top, then, a consolidation strategy bearing the earmarks of Reform must write off a significant fraction of the original Conservative base.

That said, Reform's base was one obvious place to start rebuilding the Right. Reform's great strength was its geographic focus, and this bastion yielded a significant parliamentary presence. At the same time, Preston Manning's bold move to dissolve Reform into the Alliance recognized that Reform's weakness was the flip side of its strength: Reform was seen as too regional. The merger of 2003 also reflected this logic. But both Manning's attempt in 2000 and Stephen Harper's attempt in 2004 to create a more inclusive party under their own leadership turned the lesson of history upside down. History shows that parties have effected dramatic interregional moves. Figures 6 and 8 document two in the Conservative party's recent history. A third example also stands out from the historical record: the move by the Liberal Party into Quebec in the late 19th century. Each move involved an existing party dramatically raising its credibility in a region of erstwhile weakness by choosing a new leader from the target region, Laurier in 1887, Diefenbaker in 1956, and Mulroney in 1983. This is precisely the opposite action to Mr Manning's in 2000 and Mr. Harper's in 2003-4. Rather than take an existing party and add a new leader from a target region, they tried to hold on to leadership and absorb a target party. In the realm of appearances, Stephen Harper may succeed where Preston Manning failed. But he may also find that under his leadership the new Conservative Party will be just old Reform/Alliance by another name.

The Conservative Party faced a subtly different imperative. Although the Conservatives did need to diversify the geography of their appeal, their appeal was already quite diverse, and this fact remained the Tories' great strategic promise. To realise the promise, they needed not so much to widen the appeal as deepen it. But what did this mean? It might have meant a more full-blooded economic and fiscal conservatism, the sort telegraphed by Jean Charest at the start of the 1997 campaign, then seemingly abandoned.

But such appeals might have alienated one of the key potential pillars of a renewed Conservative party, soft nationalists in Quebec, whose presence in the Tory caucus, 1984-93, pulled it to the left. We have noted already that had the Conservative party been able to hold these voters in 1993, it would probably have outpolled Reform. Few seats would have accrued, but the votes were still important in the field of moral claims. No less important, these votes, even as potential, figured in the larger credibility game. Quebec may not be the pivot for government that it once was, but its seats remain critical. Weak though they were, the Conservatives were still the only party other than the Liberals with "binational" potential. This must be part of why, according to table 1, the Tories were most Liberals' second choice. Of course, many of those Liberals were former Tories.

Inside Quebec, though, the Tories were boxed in between hard federalists and hard sovereignists, each with a geographic bastion. Quebec Tories mirrored the party's strategic predicament for the country as a whole: appeal that was wide but not deep. Deepening the appeal might have required a quite full-blooded nationalist position on Quebec-Canada relations. Such an appeal was unlikely to wash outside Quebec, however, precisely as so many former non-Quebec Tories who all along repudiated national-unity politics had a right-wing party close to them on this issue .

And neither a Quebec-focussed appeal nor an artfully pan-regional one was likely to attract those Westerners for whom Reform's peculiar appeal was sectional. This is bound to be a problem for the reunified Conservatives. If a future leader is a non-Westerner, western supporters of the former Reform/Alliance may bolt. To an important degree, Reform was latter-day Social Credit, and a post-Reform rump born in reaction to reunification need not govern to survive. Social Credit was never more than an Alberta, later Alberta-plus-interior-BC, party, yet it was stronger as a parliamentary presence than the CCF right down to 1958. This testifies to a logic that could sustain a post reunification rump. If Social Credit, or the CCF/NDP for that matter, could think of themselves as affecting policy by their mere presence, why could a Reform survivor not do the same? Social Credit did disappear, of course, but the reasons are telling. Although its former supporters were absorbed into the regionally inclusive Conservative party, it is not obvious that they joined *because* the Conservative party was regionally inclusive. Rather they joined a party that, in the person of John Diefenbaker, crafted a self-consciously western appeal, and the final collapse of western Social Credit into the larger party occurred *after* the Tories lost power. That John Diefenbaker bequeathed his successors a party poised closer to the brink of power than it had been for years may have made its western supporters feel good about that party. But the final compromises necessary actually to deliver power were too readily portrayed as a betrayal.

In sum, the landscape on the Right seems fraught with incompatibilities. A strategy to deepen the Tories' appeal in Quebec may have foundered in that province even as it alienated still more voters elsewhere. The Alliance's broadening out from the Reform base had no resonance in Quebec and yet risked undermining whatever the Alliance inherits of Reform's specifically sectional appeal. This may also describe the effect of the ultimate merger of the Alliance with the PCs. Indeed, the 2004 election strongly hints at this. The sectionalism of the Bloc and Reform should remind us that the landscape in question, the former Tory vote, is not just something that can be summed up as the "Right," differentiated only by gradations of conservatism.

Fragmentation of the Left?

As table 3 shows, a significant fraction of the old NDP base enlisted in Liberal ranks. Why this happens remains to be analysed. Some of the story probably involves the discrediting of NDP claims to ideological distinctiveness by the bitter experience of power in the recession- and deficit-ridden early 1990s. Some probably was strategic, motivated by a desire to smite the Tories. The two motives were probably complementary. But in each motive lie the seeds of possible deconsolidation.

If the point of consolidation was to gain power for a broadly acceptable centre-left formation, just how far left the Liberals lean should matter to their supporters on the NDP flank. Indeed, the 1997 election was a warning signal from this very place. The 2000 election may indicate that the warning was heeded. In 1993, such signalling would have seemed an undisciplined self-indulgence, given the need to drive the old Conservatives from power. Is it now necessary to consolidate to keep their reincarnation from power? If the complete reunification of the Right is next to impossible, then union of the Left is not so manifestly necessary.

As always, much depends on geography. If fragmentation of the Left mainly transfers seats from the Liberals to the NDP, then Liberal majority governments will simply give way to Liberal minority ones. There is no reason to think that coalition government will become the norm, as the Westminster system perfectly embodies a logic that makes all players prefer single-party minorities to multiparty majorities.[57] Each party can reasonably hope that the next election will decisively improve its fortunes; that is the promise embodied in table 2. At the same time, leaders who know their electoral history — littered with the wreckage of parties that entered formal coalitions — rightly fear too close an entanglement with other parties. If minority government becomes the norm, the Liberals need not be utterly dependent on the NDP for a working majority. So long as the opposition remains fragmented, a Liberal government will usually be able to choose its allies issue by issue.

The geography of fragmentation will not necessarily be so favourable. Far from boosting NDP numbers, fragmentation of the Left vote may only convey seats to the Right, especially to the extent that the Right has succeeded in consolidating its own vote. But then, the more credible the threat of a united Right, the more united the Left is likely to remain. In a sense, the Left has a luxury the Right does not. The Left does seem more coherent than the Right, in that the landscape spanned by the Liberals and NDP admits continuous, fine-grained distinctions. Boundaries on the dimension can move according to circumstances. NDP supporters remain, as Mackenzie King described their CCF predecessors, "Liberals in a hurry."

More generally, the Canadian system seems to have reached a point where only the Liberals are truly feasible as a single-party government. The historical record suggests that that has been true for decades, perhaps since 1896. This makes Brian Mulroney's feat of winning two majority victories and governing as if he meant it all the more stunning. But it was an act of hubris, and the punishment in the end was correspondingly brutal. To say that only the Liberals are feasible is not to say that a majority of Canadians always feels disfranchised. In fact, the Liberals exemplify the "Condorcet winner," the option that defeats all comers in straight fights. Table 1 makes clear that the Liberals are the near-universal second choice, where they are not the first choice. If each alternative takes the Liberals on alone, it is bound to lose. In this sense, Liberal victories are not accidents of the electoral system. The system has distorting effects, but it does not as a rule yield the "wrong" winner.[58]

This fact about the Liberals also helps explain the fragmentation of the rest of the party system. For Canadian voters, unlike opposition party elites, the stakes in elections may have gone down. The rest of the system is not so fragmented that only Liberal candidates can win. But the fact that the Liberals are now the only party that can win means that most of the time the government will be broadly acceptable. Greater opposition vote fractionalization is now also acceptable, so long as its geography permits some translation of opposition votes into seats. The Liberals now stand revealed more starkly as what they probably were all along, Canada's equivalent of India's Congress Party, at least the Congress of the first 40 years after Indian independence.[59]

Parties like this can be defeated only by ends-against-the-middle strategies. Such strategies are intrinsically hard to carry off and so are rare. When they succeed, the resulting governments are unstable or their electoral bases, unsustainable. This explains the longevity of Liberal governments and the chequered aftermath of the occasional Tory bout in power. Now such bouts seem even more remote.

Structural reform?

A Liberal government, even a minority one, indefinitely in power is an unhealthy prospect in a democracy. Given that the Liberals are broadly acceptable to many voters — at least as a second choice — we are unlikely to see riots in the streets soon. Passion may still erupt on the left and right of the system, as with Reform in 1993. But the government can probably absorb most initiatives in the realm of policy, where those initiatives have real backing or where they are connected to shoring up the margins of the Liberal coalition. In this sense, Reform had an impact in the palpable rightward shift of the whole spectrum in 1993. The 1997 election, aided by the end of deficit politics, nudged the government, if not the whole system, leftward.

But the lowering of the stakes and the infeasibility of alternatives, opposite sides of the same coin, may be a key reason for the apparent withdrawal from electoral politics signaled in figure 4.[60] As symptom or as the thing itself, demobilization of a significant fraction of the electorate should not be passed over lightly. Under the existing structure, the prospect for renewal in participation and enthusiasm seems as remote as the prospect for party alternation in power.

But that is the point. If for most groups, indirect impact on policy is better than nothing, actually holding office is still critical. If office did not matter, no party would form a government as a minority. If office matters, offices should circulate, and circulation is a missing element in party politics at the millennium. We may finally have reached the point where structural reform can no longer be staved off. If the content of these reforms is the subject for other papers, two things are strongly implied by the analysis in this one. First, proposed changes should promote *circulation* of parties through office, not necessarily as single-party governments. The weakness of the existing system, manifest long before the 1990s, was its peculiar manner of circulation: none for extended periods, then powerful retribution on the usual governing party, the Liberals, retribution which in the long run only made things worse for the short-run beneficiary, the Conservative Party. The system should probably be a more sensitive register of opinion change even as it reduces the likelihood of cataclysm. All this is to say that the system probably must become more proportional. How it does so is the second implication of this paper. Most of the time, the parliamentary parties will have no obvious stake in structural reform. Incumbents are usually, by definition, beneficiaries of the existing rules. Proposals for reform thus must be *opportunistic.* Some of this may be in timing, in searching for moments when some parties already enjoying footholds can move up under new rules. We can imagine, for example, an ends-against-the-middle strategy in electoral reform, where parties that can improve under new rules extract electoral reform as the price of supporting a minority government. Or vote-seat translations under FPTP may become just too unpredictable even for Canada's historically risk-acceptant parties.[61] Sometimes the old game can be sustained no longer, and the only way for old players to survive is to change the game.

Notes

This paper could not have been written without the support, direct and indirect, of Canadian Election Studies investigators from 1988 to 2000, André Blais, Henry E. Brady, Elisabeth Gidengil, Richard Nadeau and Neil Nevitte. They share in the genesis of many thoughts represented in this paper as my own. I am also grateful for earlier comments by Lisa Young, Stephen Harper and Paul Howe. In the end, I am responsible for all errors of fact and interpretation, not to mention offences against the English language.

1. A detailed justification of the specific periods to 1984 can be found in Richard Johnston, André Blais, Henry E. Brady and Jean Crête, *Letting the People Decide: Dynamics of a Canadian Election* (Montreal: McGill-Queen's University Press, 1992), chap. 2.

2. The two minority governments with smaller bases were formed in 1962 (Diefenbaker) and 1979 (Clark).

3. Outright: Ontario (101 seats), Quebec (26), Manitoba (6), and British Columbia (6 in 1997, 7 now); almost: Newfoundland and Prince Edward Island (4 each).

4. For the first identification of the honeymoon, see Richard Nadeau, "L'effet lune de miel dans une contexte parlementaire: le cas canadien," *Revue canadienne de science politique*, Vol. 23, no. 3 (September 1990), pp. 483-97. For a more general analysis of government popularity, with evidence from the 1970s to the 1990s, see Richard Johnston, "Business Cycles, Political Cycles, and the Popularity of Canadian Government, 1974-1998," *Canadian Journal of Political Science*, Vol. 32, no. 3 (September 1999), pp. 499-520.

5. The 1917 election appears to the naked eye as the last of the old two-party elections, but it is equally well viewed as foreshadowing the fragmentation to come. The very formation of the Unionist coalition and the split in Liberal ranks reflected the inability of Liberals and Conservatives to contain all the divisions of Canadian life.

6. Figures 1 and 3 take a small liberty with the historical record by treating Reform as the Opposition in 1993 as well as in 1997. Reform enjoyed the second largest vote share throughout this period, and all along it has been the most serious alternative to the Liberals as a party of government.

7. So much so that, even though 1945 gave the Conservatives their smallest vote share for the whole 1935-57 period, it also gave them their largest seat share.

8. The index used here was first proposed in Michael Gallagher, "Proportionality, Disproportionality and Electoral Systems," *Electoral Studies*, Vol. 10, no. 1 (March 1991), pp. 33-51. Arend Lijphart, *Electoral Systems and Party Systems: A Study of Twenty-Seven Democracies, 1945-1990* (Oxford: Oxford University Press, 1994), chap. 3, argues convincingly that this is the best overall indicator of disproportionality.

9. New Zealand no longer uses FPTP, so that comparison is now of strictly historical interest. For evidence on the FPTP systems as well as many proportional representation ones, see Lijphart, *Electoral Systems and Party Systems*, appendix B.

10. The measure was first proposed in Markku Laakso and Rein Taagepera, "'Effective' Number of Parties: A Measure with Application to West Europe," *Comparative Political Studies*, Vol. 12, no. 1 (April 1979), pp. 3-27.

11. Estimation is by ordinary least squares regression (OLS). The standard error of the slope is 0.005 and the adjusted $R^2 = 0.92$.

12. The best treatment of these propositions is Gary W. Cox, *Making Votes Count: Strategic Coordination in the World's Electoral Systems* (Cambridge: Cambridge University Press, 1997). See especially part II ("Strategic Voting") and part III ("Strategic Entry").

13. The exception, which may only prove the second-system rule, was the period just before 1945. Poll evidence and provincial results between 1943 and 1945 frightened the government and stimulated considerable policy innovation, and its 1945 vote was weak. But much of what ultimately happened electorally was only further fragmentation of the opposition.

14. For quantitative estimates of the difference, see Lijphart, *Electoral Systems and Party Systems*.

15. Johnston, "Business Cycles," compares governments' interelection popularity, as indicated by the Gallup poll for the 1974-98 period, and argues that the fragmentation of opposition in 1993 changed the basic dynamics of popularity to the government's apparent advantage.

16. See the discussion in Richard Johnston, *Public Opinion and Public Policy: Questions of Confidence* (Toronto: University of Toronto Press, 1986), chap. 2, and in Richard Johnston, "Canada" in Byron E. Shafer (ed.), *Postwar Politics in the G-7* (Madison: University of Wisconsin Press, 1996).

17. The data for figure 5 come from the *International Institute for Democracy and Electoral Assistance* (IDEA) Web page for Canada (http://www.idea.int/vt/regionalview.cfm?Country Code = CA).

18. The absolute number ostensibly registered grew between 1988 and 1993 by almost exactly the same value as the growth in the estimated voting age population. This implies that every newly eligible voter was registered, or the arithmetic equivalent thereof. If we discount the 1993 registration figure by the average pre-1993 ratio of registration to eligibility, turnout for 1993 creeps up just over 70 percent.

19. A significant decline registers even before the 1990s, but this seems to be an artifact of the 1949 and 1953 elections, in which registration was strikingly high. With those two elections removed from the series, no 1945-93 downward trend in the ratio of registered to age-eligible voters appears.

20. If the drop is administratively driven, this could reflect either teething difficulties in the transition or a more basic flaw in the logic of the new system. That the change does reflect administrative practice rather than outside demographic forces is not, in any case, in contention here. My concern is simply to flag the issue.

21. Data for other countries comes from the IDEA Web site. See note 17 above.

22. The most recent statement and a useful source of references to his earlier work and to its major critiques is Ronald Inglehart, *Modernization and Postmodernization: Cultural, Economic, and Political Change in 43 Societies* (Princeton: Princeton University Press, 1997).

23. Neil Nevitte, *The Decline of Deference* (Peterborough, ON: Broadview Press, 1996) applies the Inglehart thesis to Canada.

24. Harold D. Clarke and Nitish Dutt, "Measuring Value Change in Western Industrialized Societies: The Impact of Unemployment," *American Political Science Review*, Vol. 85, no. 3 (September 1991), pp. 905-20; and James A. Davis, "Review Essay: Paul R. Abramson and Ronald Inglehart, Value Change in Global Perspective," *Public Opinion Quarterly*, Vol. 60, no. 2 (summer 1996), pp. 322-31, are especially telling critiques.

25. Kitschelt's account of the left is *The Transformation of European Social Democracy* (Cambridge: Cambridge University Press, 1994), and of the right, *The Radical Right in Western Europe: A Comparative Analysis* (Ann Arbor, MI: University of Michigan Press, 1995).

26. Hermann Schmitt and Sören Holmberg, "Political Parties in Decline?" in Hans-Dieter Klingemann and Dieter Fuchs (eds.), *Citizens and the State* (Oxford: Oxford University Press, 1995), Vol. 1 in the "Beliefs in Government" Series (Max Kaase, Kenneth Newton, and Elinor Scarbrough, series editors), chap. 4.

27. Stefano Bartolini and Peter Mair, *Identity, Competition and Electoral Availability: The Stabilisation of European Electorates 1885-1985* (Cambridge: Cambridge University Press, 1990).

28. Ola Listhaug and Matti Wiberg, "Confidence in Political and Private Institutions," in Klingemann and Fuchs (eds.), *Citizens and the State*, chap. 10. See especially figures 10.1, 10.3, and 10.4. We cannot reject the possibility that high governmental turnover is as much a symptom as a cause of political distrust, but the Listhaug-Wiberg graphics lean to the opposite interpretation. Particularly striking is the variance in political trust by turnover within European subcultures. For instance, measured trust levels in Denmark, a country with high government turnover, are closer to those in Italy than to those in Norway, an historically stable system.

29. Richard Topf, "Electoral Participation," in Klingemann and Fuchs (eds.), *Citizens and the State*, chap. 2.

30. Estimates are based on OLS regression analysis for elections from 1935 to 1988, inclusive. Adjusted R^2 for the equation is 0.86. Standard error for the Liberal vote coefficient is 0.17; for the Conservative coefficient, it is 0.11. Each coefficient has less than 1 chance in 10,000 of being the product of random covariation. Each coefficient indicates the effect on seat share of a unit shift in one party's vote share, holding the other party's vote constant. In fact, the two-vote shares vary inversely with each other, as one would expect of two parties historically in such close competition. The regression coefficient of the Tory on Liberal vote share is -0.94, an essentially one-to-one relationship. Note, however, that the adjusted R^2 = 0.60, indicating plenty of slack in the relationship, the substance of which is discussed in the body of the text below. The conversion of percentage-point shifts into seat shifts is just crude arithmetic. In a House of 300 seats, a percentage-point shift is 3 seats. Since 1935 the House has grown from 245 to 301 seats, whence my rounding in multiples of 2-3 seats.

31. For illustrations of the small-party logic, see Alan C. Cairns, "The Electoral System and the Party System in Canada, 1921-1965," *Canadian Journal of Political Science*, Vol. 1, no. 1 (March 1968), pp. 55-80. On the logic over the full range, see Richard Johnston and Janet Ballantyne, "Geography and the Electoral System," *Canadian Journal of Political Science*, Vol. 10, no. 4 (December 1977), pp. 857-66). Both articles illustrate arguments first made in Seymour Martin Lipset, "Party Systems and the Representation of Social Groups," *Archives européenes de sociologie/European Journal of Sociology*, Vol. 1, no. 1 (1960), pp. 50-85.

32. The system unquestionably has another unfortunate geographic effect: it exaggerates regional differences in strength, making a party look stronger where it is strong and weaker where it is weak. See Cairns, "The Electoral System and the Party System."

33. The tilt toward the Liberals reflects their stranglehold on nonfrancophone seats. Note that figure 5 masks some of the party-specific variation just described, as the figure focuses on the *government* share, regardless of the party. So the massive swing from the Liberals to the Conservatives in 1984, for example, instead appears as continuity, with Quebec's share of government seats dropping slightly.

34. On this, see David Sankoff and Koula Mellos, "La régionalisation électorale et l'amplification des proportions," *Revue canadienne de science politique*, Vol. 6, no. 3 (September 1972), pp. 380-99, who compare Quebec provincial elections with Ontario ones as well as with Canadian, British, New Zealand, and US ones. See especially table 2, "Propriété des distributions des comtés."

35. From 1935-88, the median number of Quebec seats won by the government was 58 and the median number of seats required for a majority was 134, hence a majority winner typically needed about 76 seats from other regions.

36. Charles Boix, "Setting the Rules of the Game: The Choice of Electoral Systems in Advanced Democracies," *American Political Science Review*, Vol. 93 no. 3 (September 1999), pp. 609-24, argues that because of their primary concentration in Quebec, Canadian francophones are one of the few ethnic minorities in the world that is better off under FPTP than under PR.

37. The westward shift should not be exaggerated. Recent change is still dwarfed by that from 1896 to 1911, which in effect called the West into existence as a political region. By 1911 Saskatchewan was the third largest province, a

position it held until the 1951 census. Much of the postwar change has been redistribution within the region, and the West's overall share actually shrank from the 1930s to the 1970s. Only since the 1970s has the region's overall share grown.

38. This overstates the true Conservative seat position, as it includes the artifactually high 27 percent of seats won in 1945 on the period's lowest vote share. The Liberal vote share dropped precipitately that year, on a temporary fractionalization of the total vote. In the other four elections the Conservatives averaged under 17 percent of seats.

39. In part, Liberal strength reflected the accession of Louis St. Laurent to Liberal leadership, as, before 1993, having a leader from Quebec was worth 13 points in Liberal share. See Richard Nadeau and André Blais, "Explaining Election Outcomes in Canada: Economy and Politics," *Canadian Journal of Political Science*, Vol. 26, no. 4 (December 1993), pp. 775-90. From 1935 to 1945, however, third-party voting was more notable in Quebec than anywhere else east of Manitoba. Uncoordinated independent candidacies were common in 1935 and 1940, and in 1945 there emerged the Bloc Populaire Canadien, provoked by the First World War and a conscription crisis. Although this bloc anticipates some aspects of the later one, in that it articulated a forward-looking and secular vision of Quebec, it was a one-election phenomenon. By 1949 and the accession of St-Laurent, almost all the third-party vote in Quebec disappeared, yielding to lopsided two-party politics.

40. If we accept that the normal pre-1957 Conservative vote in Quebec was closer to 30 percent than to 20 percent, figure 5 understates the real drop in the Quebec Conservative share.

41. The gains in Alberta and BC were more appearance than reality. Tory shares after 1984 were squarely in line with Conservative strength in those provinces at the end of the 1962-80 period. The whole-period line is dragged down by weaker (in the case of BC, much weaker) shares of the 1960s.

42. This paragraph begs two qualifications. First, Quebec nationalism *did* have an outlet before 1984: the Social Credit Party, and the absorption of the Social Credit vote into the Conservative coalition in 1984 was part of the latter's preemption of Quebec nationalism. Social Credit was not a vehicle for the forward-looking variant of Quebec nationalism, however. Second, the Tories did not emit obviously nationalist signals in the run up to 1984. Indeed, one of Brian Mulroney's first tests as leader was to align his party with the Liberal Party's rights-based, official languages agenda in relation to Manitoba.

43. Respondents' 1988 behaviour is based on their recall questions in the 1993 wave of the 1992-93 Canadian Referendum and Election Study. For more detail on construction of the table, see André Blais and Elisabeth Gidengil, "Constructing a Flow of the Vote Table," Université de Montréal, mimeo, 1995.

44. It is tempting to say that shares here are of the *whole electorate*, but that is not quite true. Note that voters now dead are part of the 1993 total, just as voters not yet of age are part of the 1988 total. If it seems odd to count this way, doing so is necessary to make the accounting system consistent.

45. In comparison, look at the percentage voting Liberal, 19.4. Although an absolutely larger percentage, former abstainers are much less likely to vote Liberal than the electorate as a whole.

46. The basis of this claim follows. New voters are 13 percent of the 1993 total, and the Bloc's 16.2 percent of that 13 percent makes new-voter Blocquistes 2.1 percent of all 1993 voters. Former abstainers constitute 21.7 percent of all 1993 categories, and the 6.9 percent of these who vote Bloc thus are 1.5 percent of the 1993 total. The sum, 2.1 plus 1.5, is 3.6 percent of all categories. Dividing this sum by the total Bloc percentage, 8.8, yields 3.6/8.8 = 0.41, or about 40 percent of the Bloc vote.

47. Table 3 indicates that the turnout dropped from 1988 to 1993, but it masks the fact that in Quebec, the turnout grew, reflecting this mobilization of sovereignists.

48. These percentages are calculated by omitting from the denominator all respondents who stayed with their 1988 party.

49. Given the power of ideological distance, should we be amazed that any New Democrats moved to Reform? In fact, the NDP has always exchanged voters with the most distant party on the left-right scale, which is to say that party turnover in Canada is routinely intransitive. This reflects the fact that it is controlled by at least two policy dimensions, on one of which the NDP and Conservatives or Reform are not polar opposites.

50. This defection took place both inside and outside Quebec, such that *within* each subelectorate, the Liberals were not so peculiarly important.

51. This pattern is not just a reflection of the sheer bulk of Ontario, where NDP switches to

the Liberals might have been especially numerous. Even in the West, where Reform is most viable, the Liberal Party was by far the main destination for ex-New Democrats. Only in Alberta did NDP defectors to Reform outnumber those to the Liberals. In Alberta, Reform was so overpoweringly attractive that any other pattern was next to impossible. Even so, relative to the respective drawing power of Reform and the Liberals, in Alberta NDP movement was still disproportionately to the Liberals. In any case, the number of 1988 New Democrats in Alberta was minuscule. The big Western NDP battalions were in BC, Saskatchewan, and Manitoba, and in those provinces the Liberals were as differentially attractive to former New Democrats as they were in Ontario.

52. In the 1988 study, the object was labelled "French Canada," but in 1997, it was called "Quebec." Evidence from 1993, when both versions were employed as a test, suggests little difference in the response evoked.

53. Outside Quebec, respondents saw the lean as more than mild; inside Quebec, they did not see it as a lean at all. The mean perception splits the difference.

54. For speculation on why it made sense for the Liberal Party to stray so far from its supporters' location, see Johnston, et al., *Letting the People Decide.*

55. These observations are only suggestive. They require that the Reform location be projected from panel B to panel A, perhaps a questionable practice, and then horizontal distances compared.

56. A few further comments on the basis of Reform support need to be made. Elisabeth Gidengil, André Blais, Richard Nadeau, and Neil Nevitte, in "Making Sense of Regional Voting in the 1997 Federal Election: Liberal and Reform Support Outside Quebec," *Canadian Journal of Political Science*, Vol. 32, no. 2 (June 1999), pp. 247-72, argue that, although Westerners have roughly the same mean position on Quebec-Canada relations, opinion on this issue makes a bigger difference to the Reform vote in the West. That is hard to square with my claim that the vote differences are about the same within these regions. The discrepancy may be between the bivariate graphical account that underpins my statement and the multivariate one that underpins theirs. Neil Nevitte, André Blais, Elisabeth Gidengil, and Richard Nadeau (*Unsteady State: The 1997 Canadian Federal Election* [Don Mills, ON: Oxford University Press, 2000], table C.4), confirm the importance of West-focused regional alienation, however. Did Reform represent a more generalized alienation from party politics? The answer is yes. For 1993, Reform was only weakly distinguished this way, much less than the Bloc, according to Richard Johnston, André Blais, Henry E. Brady, Elisabeth Gidengil, and Neil Nevitte, in "The 1993 Canadian Election: Realignment, Dealignment, or Something Else?" presented to the 1996 annual meeting of the American Political Science Association. In 1997, Reform became more distinct, as cynicism about politics evidently diminished in the other party groups, according to Blais et al., *Unsteady State*, figure 4-4 . There is, in sum, much work still to do in understanding post-1993 party politics, but most of the work lies off the path of this paper.

57. On this see Kaare Strom, "Minority Governments in Parliamentary Democracies: The Rationality of Non-Winning Cabinet Solutions," *Comparative Political Studies*, Vol. 17, no. 2 (July 1984), pp. 199-227.

58. It *can* yield the "wrong" winner, to be sure. This was probably the case in British Columbia in 1996, or Ontario in 1990, and probably describes many Tory federal victories in the twentieth century.

59. The comparison is not idle. Canada and India have always stood as the great challenges to the apparent logic of FPTP. In the Canadian case, it traditionally sufficed to refer to local two-party consolidation, with different parties standing as front-runners in different places. India was harder to solve. William H. Riker, "The Number of Political Parties: A Re-Examination of Duverger's Law," *Comparative Politics*, Vol. 9, no. 1 (October 1976), pp. 93-106, addressed both the Canadian and Indian cases. For Canada, he concentrated on geography. For India, he proposed that the key was Congress's centrist position, which made it the Condorcet winner. Now we see that his argument also applies to Canada, and may have all along.

60. Nevitte et al., *Unsteady State*, attribute two percentage points of the turnout difference between 1997 and the pre-1993 average to competitive factors. Theirs is probably a lower-bound estimate.

61. Boix, "Setting the Rules of the Game," argues that incumbent parties' calculations of risk are historically the central factor in electoral reform.

Part B
Electoral Reform

2

Changing the Canadian Electoral System

Louis Massicotte

Introduction

Canada belongs to the minority among the established democracies (together with Britain and the United States) that have kept the first-past-the-post electoral system used in the nineteenth century. Most of the other constitutional polities of Europe that had a plurality or a majority (two-ballot) electoral system at that time later switched to proportional representation (PR) or to a mixed system.

In these countries, plurality or majority formulas were criticized primarily because they resulted in national parliamentary outcomes that did not closely reflect the votes cast for each party. In our federally minded country, the debate over the electoral system is predictably dominated by a different concern: preserving the cohesion of the federation by ensuring that federal political parties, especially the governing party, include elected members from all regions.[1]

This is not, however, the only argument for electoral system reform. Some have been concerned with the failure of the existing system to provide parties with representation corresponding to their electoral support in the country as a whole, while in recent years others have advocated PR as a device that would increase the representation of women in Parliament.[2] Recently it has been argued that given existing party alignments, first-past-the-post condemns Canadians to decades under Liberal governments for lack of alternatives, and is driving down electoral turnout.

Some form of proportional representation has usually been advocated as a remedy to these problems, though other formulas like alternative voting or second ballots have also been advocated, if less frequently. This paper takes up the debate, assessing the merits of different electoral systems in the Canadian context and analyzing the current prospects for reform. We begin with a review of the chief arguments raised against the existing electoral system.

Problems with Canada's Current Electoral System

Regional polarization

Regionalism has been a central feature of Canadian federal elections at various points in the country's history. This has taken two forms. First, building on the perception that a region was disadvantaged by policy decisions of the federal government, political parties have emerged with a strictly regional agenda and electoral support in one region only. Second, even political parties with a more national perspective have received quite uneven support in the country's regions, at times sweeping some while being shut out in others.

Some degree of electoral regionalism can be found in most democracies, whether unitary or federal, either because a few regionalist parties have been represented in parliament for a long time, or because some regions tend to support a specific party more than do others. Yet the extent of electoral regionalism, measured on the basis of *seats* won by parties, is higher in Canada than in Germany, Australia, Switzerland, Spain and even Belgium.

In the 2000 general election, all but three of Ontario's 103 seats went to the Liberals. The latter, however, won the most seats in only four other provinces: Newfoundland, Prince Edward Island, New Brunswick and Manitoba, as well as in the three territories. Elsewhere, the Canadian Alliance held a majority of seats in British Columbia, Alberta and Saskatchewan, the Bloc Québécois was leading (by a very small margin) in Quebec, while no party was leading in Nova Scotia. Further, the sectional nature of one of these parties was emphasized by the fact that the Bloc Québécois fielded no candidates outside Quebec. The Canadian Alliance, this time, had candidates in all but one of the Quebec ridings; in 1997 the Reform Party had fielded only 11 candidates in Quebec's 75 ridings (in 1993, it had none). Electoral regionalism in 2000 was less acute than than it was in 1997, when each of the five parties was leading in at least one province, but it was nevertheless a strong factor.

Regionalism was also manifest in both the 1979 and 1980 elections. There were no regional parties at that time, but the Liberals were practically obliterated in the Western provinces while the Tories failed to win more than a handful of seats in Quebec. Even before that, the tendency of voters in each region to back different parties had, at times, been a source of alarm for commentators. Writing about the 1921 election, for example, an historian commented: "the political map of Canada had been transformed into a Balkan nightmare...a jigsaw of isolated tribes, merchant guilds, and husbandsmen."[3] In 1917, the country had emerged bitterly divided from an election focused on conscription, with Laurier's Liberals gaining 62 of Quebec's 65 seats but only 20 of the 170 seats in all other provinces.

To a large extent, electoral regionalism is an undeniable fact of Canadian life and cannot be eradicated simply by modifying electoral rules. However, the first-past-the-post system has exaggerated this regionalism by amplifying both the strengths and weaknesses of parties in different regions. For example, the Liberals' quasi-monopoly over Ontario seats is based on slightly more than half of the popular vote (51.5 percent), while they won few seats in the four Western provinces with 20.7 percent to 32.5 percent of the vote. The Canadian Alliance's virtual sweep of Alberta's seats is based on 58.8 percent of the vote, while their respectable 24 percent score in Ontario brought only two seats. In Quebec, the strength of the Bloc Québécois (38 of 75 seats, against 36 for the Liberals), conceals the fact that the latter were actually leading in the popular vote by a margin of 150,000 votes (44 percent versus 40 percent).

The existing electoral system has not created regionalism. However, in recent years it has rewarded parties with a strong regional appeal, and disadvantaged weaker, nationally-oriented parties that attract votes more evenly from one region to another. With almost as many votes as Reform, the Progressive Conservatives won many fewer seats in 1993 and 1997 because their vote was more evenly spread among regions.

An immediate consequence of this situation is that forming a regionally representative cabinet becomes more difficult, insofar as the governing party has few or no elected members in some provinces. Party caucuses are regionally skewed, and the policies adopted by governments may discriminate against unrepresented regions, or at least are vulnerable to such accusations. This process is somewhat self-perpetuating, since caucuses dominated by members from specific regions may slow down policy changes designed to widen support for the party in other regions.

Fairness

Fear of regional polarization and of its adverse consequences on Canadian unity has remained the driving concern among reformers. Yet Canadian election results are also vulnerable to the standard criticisms routinely raised elsewhere. Since 1921, federal elections have produced majority governments 15 times out of 23, yet in only three cases (1940, 1958 and 1984) has this been based on a majority of the popular vote. The governing Liberals' majority rested on 41 percent of the national vote in 1993 and 2000, and on a mere 38.5 percent of the national vote in 1997. Further, the electoral system at times has altered the rank-ordering of party strength. In 1993, the Bloc Québécois reached Official Opposition status while coming fourth in the popular vote. In 1979, Joe Clark formed a minority government just shy of majority status, yet his party had scored only 36 percent of the vote against 40 percent for the Liberals, whose popular support was heavily concentrated in Quebec. Results like these highlight that the plurality system is not only unfair in amplifying the representation of the leading party, but also because it sometimes gives power to a party that does not even have the support of a plurality of the electorate.

There is some polling evidence that a growing number of Canadians feel it is unacceptable that a party can form a majority government without winning a majority of the vote. In a survey from 2000, 49 percent considered such an outcome unacceptable, 29 percent found it acceptable, and 23 percent had no opinion. Ten years earlier, in a similar survey, the respective figures were 39 percent, 34 percent and 27 percent.[4]

First-past-the-post makes it more difficult for new parties to emerge given that they have little chance of success unless their support is spatially concentrated. Supporters of PR argue that political debate would be enriched by the presence in the House of Commons of new political forces like the Greens.

Plurality systems are also accused of driving down electoral turnout, insofar as the supporters of a minority party in specific districts, knowing in advance that their chances of winning are slim, may choose to abstain. By the same token, supporters of the party that clearly dominates in a district may also conclude that voting is a waste of time. There is empirical support for this argument, as turnout tends to be higher in countries that have proportional systems.[5] The steady decrease in the turnout at federal elections to 69 percent in 1993, 67 percent in 1997 and 61 percent in 2000 — down from a postwar average of 75 percent — lends greater salience to that dimension of the issue. It is difficult not to see some correlation between the monopolistic position of the Liberals in Ontario in recent years and the fact that in 2000 only 58 percent of the voters, in a province where the turnout is traditionally high, went to the polls.

Under-representation of women

Women, who represent more than one-half of the total population, currently constitute only one-fifth of the members of the House of Commons. As the percentage of women sitting in legislatures elected by proportional representation tends on average to be higher, many scholars have identified single-member districts as an obstacle to female candidates. The rationale is that multimember districts require parties to field lists of candidates, making it easier to ensure gender balance on the ticket (and possibly ethnic and linguistic balance too). With single-member districts, parties tend to select candidates that fit the prevailing stereotype of the politician as a middle-aged male.

Equal gender representation in the House of Commons could also be achieved by keeping first-past-the-post but switching to *dual* member districts, each electing one male and one female member, with each voter casting one ballot for each seat. Though this would solve the problem of women's under-representation, it has not been advocated so far for Canada as a whole. A scheme of this sort was put forward for territorial elections in Nunavut, but was rejected in a referendum held in May 1997. The main reasons for its rejection seem to be that it would have prevented women from eventually outnumbering men in the Assembly and would have forced women to stand against other women.

Democratic alternation

The Liberal Party has been described as one of the most successful parties in the democratic world, having been in office of three-quarters of the years since 1896. Years of rule by another party, in practice by the Conservatives, have been comparatively few and far-between. There is no evidence that the first-past-the-post system is or has been significantly biased in favour of the Liberal Party as such. Liberal dominance in Parliament has reflected their lead in the popular vote, and any party commanding a similar lead would likely have reaped the same rewards.

Richard Johnston has argued that the eruption of both the Reform Party and the Bloc Québécois in 1993, combined with the precipitous decline in Conservative and New Democratic fortunes, has created a context that precludes any alternation in office for the foreseeable future. The two strongest alternatives to the ruling Liberals have little chance of making gains outside their respective bailiwicks, and indeed the Bloc has no intention of expanding beyond Quebec. While they are more nationally-oriented, the Tories are hampered by the impact of the Mulroney legacy. Should the Tory party vanish completely, polling evidence suggests that its supporters, in defiance of the view that the Tories and Reform are ideologically close, would mostly go to the Liberals.[6] The result is that there is virtually no alternative to the Liberal Party, each of the challengers combining enough negatives to be seen as unelectable. Johnston interprets the downward trend of voting turnout in the 1990s as a symptom that electors are exiting from the system because the alternatives seem unpalatable.[7] This was written, of course, before the merger between the Canadian Alliance and the Progressive Conservatives (an updated version of Johnston's analysis appears elsewhere in this collection).

The Case Against Electoral Reform

Most political scientists who have taken a stand on the electoral system have come down on the side of reform. Yet there is no unanimity, and various points of the case for electoral reform have been challenged.

No panacea for regionalism

The argument that first-past-the-post increases regional cleavages in Parliament is empirically strong, but the inference that a reformed electoral system would solve the problem has not gone unchallenged. Some critics have argued that the problem lies with the depth of regional tensions and the strength of regional parties more than with the electoral system. As Richard Katz has put it, "the fundamental problem is not how voter preferences are translated into a seat distribution in the House of Commons, but the distribution of the preferences themselves."[8] Others have pointed out that regional polarization comes and goes: the image of a country sharply and increasingly divided on regional lines that was suggested by the 1979 and 1980 elections was swept away in 1984 when Brian Mulroney won a majority of votes and seats in every province and territory. The acute electoral regionalism revealed by the 1921 election had similarly vanished after a few elections with the gradual demise of the Progressives.

It is also argued that Canadian prime ministers have dealt with the problem by appointing to the cabinet senators from unrepresented regions, and that the predominance of a specific region within the government caucus does not necessarily ensure that this region will automatically carry the day on every issue. As John Courtney has noted, even strong cabinet representation does not preclude the rise of regional alienation, as exemplified by the growth of Reform at a time when the cabinet included strong ministers from the West, or by the rise of the Bloc Québécois (and of separatism) under prime ministers from Quebec.

Problems with the alternatives

Opponents of electoral reform have also targeted the alternative formulas put forward. Proportional representation brings fair representation to political parties, but also generates many undesired consequences: political fragmentation, coalition or minority governments, cabinet instability, and changes of government unsanctioned by the electorate. It facilitates the emergence of new parties, but some of these could be extremist or farcical. Mixed systems also necessitate the coexistence in the House of locally elected and regionally elected members: might not the latter be branded as second-class MPs, or, on the contrary, as the privileged few who have little constituency work to do and owe their position to their high standing with the party brass?

Questionable effects on voter turnout

The argument that the first-past-the-post system drives turnout down and ensures the perpetuation in office of the Liberals is not flawless. It is true that the average turnout at Canadian federal elections is lower than in most democracies, and the plurality system may be partly responsible for that. However, over the past two decades turnout has declined in most democracies, including those where PR prevails. Declining turnouts can more plausibly be traced to the decline among Western publics of trust in politicians and institutions, a trend that became acute in the early 1990s.

No greater alternation in government

Finally, there is little evidence that PR guarantees the alternation of parties in office. Indeed, it arguably does the opposite by making it easier for some parties to rise, only to be shunned by others as unacceptable coalition partners because of their alleged extremism. At the same time, it does not encourage opposition parties to fuse or to conclude alliances in order to offer a credible alternative. This can mean that the same group of centrist parties stays in power for a long time. There are plenty of examples of democratic PR countries that have been governed without interruption by the same party or coalition of parties for decades.[9]

Alternation in office can be achieved if parties opposed to the "ins" join hands in order to offer a credible alternative, and the plurality system provides them with a powerful incentive to do this. This point has been given greater weight by the December 2003 merger between the Progressive Conservatives and the Canadian Alliance. There were important differences between the two parties that led many Tories to object to the fusion. The likelihood in the fall of 2003 that both parties might be nearly eradicated by the Martin Liberals contributed mightily to this development. It still remains unclear (in early 2004) whether the new Conservative Party of Canada will attract all the electoral support previously given to its component parts.[10] Nevertheless, under the plurality system parties that are ideologically akin to each other are strongly encouraged to hang together in order to avoid being hanged separately.

Alternatives to the Present System

One of the chief problems faced by reformers is that Canadians are not very familiar with other electoral systems. Plurality rule has prevailed continuously at both the provincial and federal levels since the beginning of elections in Canada, except in three Western provinces, where alternative voting and/or proportional representation through the single transferable vote were tried and later discarded, the last one in 1956.[11] The foreign country with which

Canadians are most familiar, the United States, also uses a plurality system. In addition, alternative electoral systems are more complex than first-past-the-post, a feature that makes them more difficult to sell.

There are many types of electoral systems, though they fall broadly into four categories: *simple plurality* or first-past-the-post, as in Britain and Canada; *majority systems*, i.e., systems demanding more than one-half of the popular vote in a district in order to be elected; *proportional representation*; and *mixed systems* that combine proportional representation with either a plurality or majority system.

Majority systems

Under first-past-the-post a candidate may be elected with a very small proportion of the vote, provided the remainder of the vote is divided among the other candidates, all scoring less individually than the leading candidate.[12] Majority systems are attractive for those who wish to keep single-member districts but want to raise the threshold for a member to be elected.

There are two basic types of majority systems: alternative voting and the two-ballot system. The latter, used in France, is the more prevalent of the two internationally. In this system, the candidate, at the first ballot, needs a majority (more than 50 percent) of the popular vote in order to be elected. If no candidate reaches that threshold, a second and final ballot is held one or two weeks later. Then, two different rules may apply: either the candidate winning a plurality of the vote (as in first-past-the-post) is elected, or the competition is restricted to the two leading candidates on the first ballot, one of whom will necessarily be elected (this is known as a "run-off"). The first rule prevails in French legislative elections, while the second applies in most countries having a directly elected president.[13]

In the 2000 Canadian election, about half of all the seats were won with more than 50 percent of the vote.[14] In 1997, the corresponding figure was about one-third. If a majority had been demanded for election in the 1997 contest, a second ballot would then have been necessary in almost 200 seats. Much would have depended, then, on the second preferences of voters and on alliances between the parties.

Second ballots, if they are to be held in many districts, entail a substantial increase in the cost of elections, at least for polling day. The alternative (or preferential) voting system, guarantees that a candidate will be elected with a majority of the vote, and with less expense. Voters are required to rank candidates on the ballot paper by marking "1" beside the name of the candidate they prefer, "2" beside their second choice and so on. On election night, only first preferences are counted. Candidates obtaining more than 50 percent of first preferences are elected, and other preferences are not examined. Should no candidate reach that threshold, however, the weakest candidate is eliminated and the second preferences marked on his or her ballots are transferred to the remaining candidates. This process is continued until a candidate reaches a majority of the vote. Alternative voting has been in force in Australia since the end of World War I. Though few other countries now use the system, it was in force for some time in three Western Canadian provinces for provincial elections.[15]

Alternative voting guarantees that winners will be backed by a majority of the vote in their respective districts, as does the two-ballot system provided the second ballot is a run-off between the two leading candidates. Otherwise, it does little to reduce the vote-seat distortions found in plurality systems. The chief advantage is to allow ideologically close but formally distinct parties to escape obliteration by combining their vote behind a single candidate.

What would have been the outcome of the 1997 election if an alternative voting system had been used? That a counting of subsequent preferences would have been needed in almost two-thirds of seats suggests at first sight that the outcome might have been substantially different, and that the Liberals' weak majority in the House would have been jeopardized, especially by an exchange of preferences between Reformers and Tories in Ontario. However, a simulation conducted recently found otherwise.[16] Projecting second preferences on the basis of the second choices of voters (using data from the Canadian Election Study), Bilodeau found that these would have altered the result in 31 ridings out of 301. The number of Liberal seats would have jumped from 155 to 173, while the number of Tory seats would have increased from 20 to 27. The representation of all other parties would have been smaller: 47 Reformers instead of 60, 36 Bloc Québécois members instead of 44, and 17 New Democrats instead of 21.[17]

The province-by-province results of that projection suggest that regional polarization would have been somewhat reduced, with the Liberals making substantial gains in Alberta and British Columbia (at the expense of Reform) and in Quebec (at the expense of the Bloc). However, neither Reform nor the Tories would have made any gains in Ontario, where the Liberals would have kept every one of their 101 seats. Further, the distribution of seats would not have been any "fairer," that is proportional to the popular vote; with 38.5 percent of the vote, the Liberals' share of seats would have increased from 51.5 percent to 57.5 percent.

Proportional representation systems
While the mechanics of PR are complex, the basics are relatively simple. PR requires electoral districts with more than one member, preferably at least four. In each district, the number of votes cast for each party is divided by a quota, so that the "cost" of a seat is about the same for each party.

PR systems fall into two categories: list systems (by far the most common form) and single-transferable-vote systems (STV). The latter, conceived by Thomas Hare and advocated by John Stuart Mill, has been ardently promoted in English-speaking countries, so far with little success, but is the only variant of PR that has been used on occasion in Canada.[18]

The accuracy of representation depends mostly on the number of seats in each district (the higher the number, the more accurate), but also on the specific technique used for distributing seats (the highest-average technique tends to magnify distortions and provide a "bonus" to the stronger parties, while the Ste-Laguë and largest-remainder techniques produce more accurate distributions). Some countries also provide for national seats to top up the district results, so as to increase proportionality.[19]

Proportional representation is normally associated with more fragmented legislatures, as it is easier for a small party to win seats, and with the absence of a majority for a single party. As such, it often leads to coalition governments or minority single-party governments.

Mixed systems

Mixed systems combine PR with a plurality or majority system. A few basic combinations can be identified.[20] The two most common are *superposition* (or parallel) systems, now typified by Japan, and *corrective* systems. The latter are in place in Germany, New Zealand, Scotland and Wales, and were proposed for Britain by the Jenkins Report in 1998. Superposition systems combine plurality or majority in single-member districts with PR in larger multimember districts. Thus there are two sets of legislators, local and regional. Such is also the case in corrective systems, the crucial difference being that PR seats are distributed among parties so that the total number of seats (local and regional) won by each party approximates its percentage of the popular vote. Corrective systems result in proportional outcomes, but this is achieved while still retaining single-member districts for about half of all legislators. This is why such systems are officially known as "personalized PR" in Germany, and as "mixed-member proportional" (MMP) in New Zealand. In contrast, superposition systems do not result in outcomes that are significantly more proportional.[21]

A survey, conducted in the mid-1990s, of all countries with working parliaments found 59 using the plurality rule, 25 with a majority system (either two-ballot or alternative voting), 56 using PR, and 25 using a mixed system.[22] The number of countries using mixed systems has increased dramatically in the 1990s.

Among other electoral formulas, the majority system must be ruled out as an alternative by anyone trying to respond to the criticisms of first-past-the-post cited above. A clear lesson from comparative studies is that the outcomes produced by majority systems are no more proportional than those produced by first-past-the-post, and are sometimes even less so, as was amply confirmed by the projection of the results of the 1997 Canadian election using the alternative vote.

Mixed systems have been most often advocated in Canada as alternatives to the existing system, because they offer the advantage of adding some dose of PR while keeping the single-member districts familiar to Canadians. However, numerous and substantially different variants have been put forward.[23]

What Impact Would PR Have on the Canadian Political Process?

This section explores the likely consequences of proportional representation for crucial features of the Canadian political system. The focus is on two options — full-fledged PR or a German-style mixed system — because they alone have any chance of both producing fairer results and addressing problems of regional polarization, low voter turnout and the under-representation of women.

"Full-fledged PR" is envisaged here as an electoral system where seats are allocated to parties in proportion to their vote in four to 10-seat constituencies.[24] A "German-style system" means a mixed electoral system where about half of MPs are elected in single-member districts; other seats are allocated so as to make the total distribution of seats proportional to the votes cast for each party. Both formulas would result in proportional outcomes, the chief difference being that a German-style system would retain a sizable contingent of members from single-member districts.

PR would have a direct impact on the shape and size of electoral districts, the work of members of the House of Commons and the representation of political parties and minorities. But it would also likely alter the way cabinets are formed and operate, their composition, their relationship with both Houses of Parliament, and the position of the prime minister. The federal-provincial balance might be modified as well. We should make no mistake about it: together with responsible government and disciplined parties, the first-past-the-post system is one of the three most crucial variables that have shaped Canada's Westminster system of governance, both federally and provincially, and replacing it with PR would likely have sweeping consequences.

Not all the potential consequences of PR can be anticipated. We can determine what the result of previous elections would have been, assuming voters would have voted the same way. Such exercises are helpful, but the conclusions that can be derived from them are somewhat fragile, insofar as we cannot know what the distribution of the popular vote at future elections will be. It is even more difficult to anticipate with certainty the impact of PR on Canada's system of governance, which will depend on decisions made by a myriad of political actors.

In these areas, the experience of countries where PR has been operating for generations is relevant, though it should not be transposed slavishly. The real world of PR encompasses dozens of countries, from the inauspicious cases of Italy and Israel to the more reassuring examples provided by Germany and the Scandinavian countries. We should resist the temptation to systematically assume rosy scenarios, if only because the occasionally wild expectations of reformers have often been shattered by the actual operation of the systems they ardently advocated.[25]

A more representative Parliament

Parliament, meaning here the House of Commons, would be more representative, insofar as the number of seats won by political parties would more closely match their electoral support. The number of political parties represented in the House would probably be higher than it is now, not necessarily because PR would lead to the fragmentation of existing parties, but because the threshold of admission for new movements like the Greens would be lower. The range of political views represented in Parliament would be broader, and would include viewpoints that Canadians might find innovative and engaging as well as some they would find objectionable, should any of these gather significant support.

Existing minority parties whose electoral support is widely spread would no longer be disadvantaged compared with parties whose electoral support is equivalent in size, but concentrated in specific areas. This would have worked to the benefit of the Progressive Conservatives before they merged with the Canadian Alliance, and would also benefit the New Democrats.[26]

Countries with PR systems normally have a higher proportion of women in legislatures than countries with plurality or majority systems, which has led many activists and scholars to advocate PR as a kind of affirmative-action measure to guarantee the presence of more women legislators.[27] It is untrue, as some have argued, that the first-past-the post system blocks women's access to Parliament. The number of women in the House of Commons now hovers around 20 percent, a significant increase compared with the all-male House elected in the 1968 election. Significant variation in the number of women among PR legislatures sheds some doubt as to whether PR alone guarantees the presence of women legislators. This led the Jenkins commission to conclude in its 1998 report that the evidence linking PR to women MPs was "not overwhelmingly strong."[28] Much depends on the extent to which political parties give priority to the inclusion of women on their slates of candidates. In the short term, PR in Canada would likely lead to more women in Parliament, though the percentage is likely to increase in the future whichever electoral system is used.

Certain ethnic and cultural groups would lose the advantage they now arguably derive from their concentration in some smaller metropolitan ridings. On the other hand, they might have some of their own included on party PR lists. Failure to do so by a major party would probably be controversial.

Less regional polarization in Parliament

PR would ensure that party caucuses include some representatives from most major provinces, provided, of course, they secure some minimum electoral support there. More specifically, PR would break the Liberals' present monopoly over Ontario seats, which was a crucial factor in their back-to-back majority victories in the 1990s.[29] It would allow the new Conservative Party of Canada, while losing some seats in the west, to gain seats in Canada's largest province and to some extent shed the image the Reform Party had of being a purely Western party. Barring a major ideological realignment, it is unlikely, if PR were introduced, that the Bloc would be interested in even running candidates outside Quebec, or that the Conservatives would secure more than a handful of seats in Quebec.

PR would provide all parties but the Bloc Québécois with more regionally balanced caucuses. It would become more difficult for Ontario or Quebec MPs to secure the inflated one-third of the ruling party caucus that the Quebec Tories achieved in 1988, the one-half that the Quebec Liberals achieved in 1980, or the two-thirds that the Ontario Liberals enjoyed in 1997.

This, in turn, would encourage parties to develop policies more palatable to all regions rather than engaging in "Churchill strategies." On election night, regional variations would be accurately reflected in the distribution of seats, rather than being exaggerated, as was the case in 1979, 1980 and 1997. This consideration was a major factor in the decision taken in Belgium in 1899 to introduce PR, and was successful for a long time in reducing the polarization that existed previously under a majority system between Flemish Catholic and Walloon Liberal or Socialist areas.[30]

PR would resolve the deep-seated problem of regional polarization in federal elections, a phenomenon the Pépin-Robarts Commission claimed was a harbinger of the break-up of federations.[31] After the 1984 election, many thought regional polarization was dead following Brian Mulroney's selection as Tory leader, following John Turner's as Liberal leader, and following the former's sweeping victory with a majority of both votes and seats in every province and territory. Yet this appears to have been a short interlude, with polarization resurfacing later with a vengeance.

The results of the 2002 German election illustrate very well how regional polarization can be reduced by PR. The Social Democrats won almost 57 percent of single-member district seats (elected, as in Canada, under first-past-the-post rules). Without the addition of corrective seats, the opposition Christian Democrats would have been shut out in no fewer than six of Germany's 16 *Länder*. In the second largest *Land*, Bavaria, the ruling party would have won a single seat out of 44. The use of personalized PR resulted instead in the Social Democrats winning 27 percent of Bavarian seats, while the Christian Democrats were able to win seats in every *Land*.

This is not to say that PR will solve the crisis of Canadian federalism. The strong presence of a region within the federal executive, bureaucracy and judiciary does not necessarily dampen aspirations for regional autonomy, as shown by the rise of separatism in Quebec over the past 30 years. Many regional champions expect far more than mere inclusion in federal decision-making circles. However, the presence of a sizable group of cabinet ministers from these regions is likely to weaken their case: we can only imagine how disenchanted with federalism Quebecers would have been if their presence in the federal cabinet had been as weak for one or two decades as it was for a brief time after the 1957 and 1979 elections.

Less emphasis on constituency work for MPs
Would PR change the job description of MPs? Here, the two PR systems should be distinguished. Full-fledged PR would substitute large, multimember districts for smaller, single-member districts. German-style PR would mean — assuming the total number of seats in the Commons remained around 300 — that half the MPs, possibly more, would continue to be returned from single-member districts, but that these districts would be twice as large as existing ones. The PR members would likely be returned from province-wide districts, except in Ontario and Quebec where the creation of regional "top-up areas" would probably emerge as the most appropriate solution.

In both cases, the job description of MPs would be affected, but to different degrees. If all MPs were elected in larger multimember districts, they would find it more difficult to control their district associations than they do now with smaller, single-member district associations. Campaigning might become more onerous, unless candidates from each party informally decided to focus on a portion of the district. Constituency work, an activity which absorbs much energy and enhances the self-esteem of many MPs, would be affected by PR. In a full-fledged PR system, members would no longer be the sole district MP, but would face competition, within a wider territory, of other MPs from their own or other parties. There is no guarantee that within a wider district all areas would be equally covered, since most or all MPs could end up residing in a major urban centre. In mixed rural-urban districts, residents of outlying areas might be less likely to have a member close at hand. This is not a major problem in most PR countries, because constituency casework is a less prevalent practice.

A German-style system would maintain the close relationship between MPs and their enlarged constituencies, but would create a second layer of representation. As such, it is open to the often-made (but rarely substantiated) charge that mixed systems produce two warring "classes" of MPs. How the two categories would interact cannot be predicted with absolute certainty, but it is worth pointing out that in the two dozen countries with mixed systems, no serious tensions are reported.[32] In Germany, the chances for MPs to make it into the cabinet are not significantly affected (positively or negatively) by the way they were elected. A powerful reason for this is that the vast majority of list MPs are actually defeated constituency candidates who, once elected, open constituency offices and meet with voters in order to enhance their chances of being reselected as constituency candidates at the next election.

No less party discipline
Currently members are constrained by party ties, and some, together with many observers of Parliament, find party discipline too constraining and are pushing for a higher number of free votes. Would PR lead to a relaxation of party discipline?

Little change should be expected on that front. There is no clearcut correlation between party discipline and single-member district systems, as exemplified by the contrast between the US House of Representatives and the Canadian House of Commons. In the former, parties exhibit much less cohesion at congressional roll-calls than members of other legislatures, a pattern of behaviour that has prevailed for over a century.[33] In Canada, the same electoral system now coincides with relatively tight party discipline, yet our parties were much less cohesive during the second half of the nineteenth century.[34]

There is no reason to believe that individual MPs would have much more freedom and clout if PR were introduced. Disciplined parties appear to be the norm in all democratic countries except the United States, irrespective of the electoral system used.[35] Party discipline is no less stringent within Canadian governing parties in minority than in majority situations.[36] Indeed, at times it has been more stringent in the former. The practice in PR countries is for interparty negotiations to take place at the cabinet level, with MPs from all sides expected to accept the outcomes reached by their leaders. If the electoral fortunes of candidates rested on their party-determined position on party lists, parties would arguably be in an even better position to exact conformity from their followers in parliament. Further, MPs breaking with their respective parties would have more difficulty getting re-elected as independents in substantially enlarged districts.

It should be added that under the parliamentary reform announced by Prime Minister Martin, party discipline might be significantly relaxed in the future, irrespective of the electoral system used.

No more single-party majority governments

If the past is any guide, single-party majority governments like those we have had for most of our history would likely become exceptional. The experience of PR countries suggests that single-party majority governments would become rare interludes in a long succession of minority and coalition governments. Indeed, in countries where coalition government is the norm, it is not infrequent for a party having secured a majority on its own to maintain its earlier alliance with smaller parties, in anticipation of a return to the standard pattern.

Though Canadian parties have some experience of single-party minority governments (eight of the 24 elections held since 1921 have produced such outcomes), the latter would probably not become the standard government formula. So far, they have been resorted to as a temporary expedient by parties, in the hope that the ensuing election would produce a majority. The latter scenario is plausible with the first-past-the-post system (three elections[37] since 1921 resulted in a majority for the incumbent minority government), as gaining only a few percentage points of the popular vote may well be enough to reach a majority of seats. Under PR, this is unlikely.

The experience of PR countries also suggests that coalitions would be more frequent than minority governments. For the years 1945 to 1987, Laver and Schofield found an almost two-to-one ratio in European cabinets.[38] In this regard, much would depend on the constitutional rules governing cabinet formation. It is easier for minority governments to be formed and to endure if no formal vote of investiture in parliament is required for a new cabinet to be appointed. By the same logic, mechanisms like that provided by s. 49 of the French Constitution, whereby cabinets can be censured by the Assembly only by an absolute majority of its membership, with the votes in favour of censure being the only ones to be counted (which means that abstentions are implicitly counted as supporting the cabinet), would facilitate the survival of minority administrations.

If coalitions became the norm, Canadians would find little guidance in their own parliamentary history as to how to operate them. Ottawa's experience with coalitions is uninspiring, being limited to the Borden Unionist coalition of 1917-20. Ontario had a coalition of United Farmers and Labour under Drury (1919-23). British Columbia was ruled by a coalition of Liberals and Conservatives from 1941 to 1952 under John Hart and afterwards Byron Johnson. Saskatchewan had a Tory-dominated "cooperative" coalition during the Depression years under Anderson (1929-34), while a Liberal joined the NDP cabinet following the inconclusive 1999 election. Bracken's long premiership in Manitoba included a lengthy period of coalition government. An encouraging feature is that most of these coalition governments lasted for the full life of a legislature.

Despite our own limited experience in this field, coalition government is well entrenched in most democratic countries, including some with majority systems like France and Australia, and Canadians could derive inspiration from the practices that have been developed elsewhere.[39]

Less durable cabinets

Our experience with minority governments (as opposed to coalitions) strongly suggests that if these became the norm under a PR system, governments would be less durable. Since 1867, minority governments in Ottawa have lasted an average of less than 20 months, compared with more than 50 months for majority governments. There is no reason to believe that minority governments, if they were formed in a PR context, would be any more lasting.

As our experience with coalition governments in Ottawa is quite limited, we must turn to the experience of other countries to see whether coalition governments would survive longer. In their study, Laver and Schofield found single-party minority governments to have lasted an average of 19 months in office, compared with 33 for minimal winning coalitions and 45 for majority governments.[40] There was no evidence that coalitions had become more durable over time.[41] True, one can cite examples of cabinets in PR countries lasting for the full duration of a legislature, of heads of governments serving aggregate terms comparable to those served by many Canadian prime ministers,[42] or even of coalitions lasting for decades (like the Swiss four-party coalition that has run the country for the last 40 years). Yet the possibility remains that party fragmentation, coupled with the presence in Parliament of parties deemed "extremist" and systematically shunned as coalition partners, can combine to produce a succession of short-lived governments. Cases like Israel, Italy, the French Fourth Republic and Finland, where governments have on average been short-lived,[43] are not necessarily typical of outcomes under PR, but they are possible.

Coalitions are inherently more fragile than single-party majority governments and are more likely to break up during the life of a parliament or to lead to early elections. When an unpopular decision has to be made, it is tempting for the junior partner to withdraw support in the hope of escaping voters' vengeance. When an unforeseen issue arises, coalition partners may find their respective positions irreconcilable and dissolve their partnership.

It is difficult to gauge how Canadians would react to this new pattern of parliamentary politics. Criticisms have been voiced in recent decades about governments having too much power, the executive dominating Parliament and the prime minister behaving like an elected monarch.[44] PR would likely make governments more fragile, but this may be what many Canadians actually want, especially if it means governments are more willing to listen and compromise. It is striking that Australia, the country where the working of the Westminster model arouses the least opposition, is also the only one where the power of the ruling party or coalition is checked by a PR-elected second chamber rarely controlled by the government party or coalition.

Weaker prime ministers

In the long run, PR would probably erode the authority of the prime minister within cabinet. At present, prime ministers enjoy a very strong position and are acknowledged to be far more than *primus inter pares*. Compared to their counterparts in Britain, Australia and New Zealand, Canadian prime ministers have stayed longer in office and have been immune (so far) to cabinet or caucus revolts,[45] probably because their status as party leaders derives from elected delegates at a party convention or direct election by party members, rather than from a caucus decision.

Jean Chrétien's August 2002 announcement following pressure from his caucus and the party rank-and-file that he intended to retire in early 2004 does not really alter the picture. There are very few precedents in Canadian history, and Chrétien amply proved over the ensuing months that even a lame-duck prime minister can make important decisions in defiance of his caucus. This predominance also results from the prime minister's position as leader of the sole ruling party and from the existence of crucial powers commonly acknowledged to be personal prerogatives of the prime minister, like recommending the convocation or dissolution of Parliament, and making appointments to the bureaucracy, the judiciary and the Senate.

These prerogatives, if unaltered under Prime Minister Martin's reform proposals, would survive intact in a minority, single-party cabinet, though the more precarious position of the cabinet as a whole would affect their use. In coalition cabinets, many ministers would belong to a party other than the prime minister's and would have more complex loyalties. The list of the prime minister's personal prerogatives is then likely to diminish. In the long run, junior coalition partners are unlikely to tolerate appointments to the bureaucracy, the Senate or the bench being made secretly by a single individual. They are likely to insist on some kind of sharing of order-in-council appointments. They might even have a veto on the prime minister's appointment.[46]

Inasmuch as prime ministers wield too much power, PR would likely make our cabinet system more collegial and less monarchic in its operation and style.

The relationship between election results and government formation

It has been argued that first-past-the-post empowers the electorate to select rulers "directly," since elections normally result in a clear majority for one party with a recognized leader and clear policy positions, instead of leading to negotiations between parties as to what kind of coalition will be formed, who will lead it and what that government will do.

There is much truth in this argument, though most of the time a "clearcut" outcome reflects the will of only a plurality of the electorate. However, malapportionment of electoral districts or excessive concentration of a party's vote in some districts at times lead to majority governments that do not even rest on a plurality of the popular vote, as was the case for a while in Quebec and British Columbia. This unquestionably amounts to a serious distortion, some would say a denial, of the voters' will.

Under PR, voters would have a less direct say in government formation than they now do. Governments would be formed after the election through negotiations between parties, taking into account, of course, each party's respective strength. Leaders may state in advance of polling day with which party they would ally — or not ally — but there would be no legal obligation for them to do so. There does not appear to have been any systematic survey determining to what extent, in PR countries, parties make such pre-election commitments. In the absence of party statements on their coalition partners, the feeling may develop among the electorate that the people's role at elections amounts merely to "redistributing the cards" between political elites, while the most crucial decision of forming a government is in practice transferred to the latter. An even worse scenario can be imagined, where pivotal parties choose to ally with other parties in defiance of their own pre-election public statements (as occurred in New Zealand in 1996) or even to switch sides in the middle of the life of a parliament (as the West German Liberals did in 1982).

An encouraging consideration is that in these two cases, the "slippery partner" suffered losses in the ensuing election, thus deterring many politicians who would be tempted to emulate this behaviour.

No evidence that governance would be worse

It is still largely accepted in Canada, especially among political elites, that the first-past-the-post system, while distorting to some extent the representation of parties in Parliament, should be maintained because the stable and effective cabinets it produces ultimately ensure better governance.

Most Canadian elections have resulted in majority governments. Parliaments with no single-party majority have been typically short interludes managed by a single-party administration biding its time before it could call another election in the hopes of securing a majority. Except in the 1920s and in the 1960s, there have been a few back-to-back minority parliaments that might have entrenched minority governments or coalitions as standard government formulas. Since 1980, no election has failed to return a majority government.

In such cabinets, decisions can be made quickly. It is easier to reach consensus within the confines of a cabinet composed of people belonging to a single party. Policies that are unpopular in the short-term but advantageous in the long run can be pursued. The conventional wisdom, then, is that our present system produces firm and decisive leadership. For many Canadians, this is to be equated with good governance.

Until the 1970s, this was the accepted wisdom among students of comparative government. The Westminster system was widely acknowledged to be the most successful variant of parliamentarianism. After all, it originated in one of the most powerful countries in the world, one where democracy had successfully withstood the challenges of the interwar period.

However, more recent literature casts serious doubts on the governance advantages that supposedly derive from single-party majority governments. Simple assumptions that were deemed self-evident and accepted without question, have recently been tested and found wanting. The argument advanced by perceptive observers of French politics before 1958 like André Siegfried and Raymond Aron, namely that cabinet instability, while perhaps exposing a country to ridicule, is less harmful for governance than many assume, has been restated. There is, it turns out, no statistical evidence that economic growth in majoritarian countries is higher, or that inflation and unemployment are lower. On the whole cabinets are more stable in majoritarian countries than in PR countries, but there is no evidence that cabinet durability results in better governance outputs.

Arend Lijphart, for one, has attacked the conventional wisdom that assumed the existence of a trade-off between accurate representation and good governance.[47] Lijphart reaffirms that PR coincides with a more accurate representation of parties in the legislature, a higher proportion of women, and a higher electoral turnout. He does not deny that executive durability is higher in countries with majoritarian electoral systems. Rather, he presents evidence that PR countries do not perform less well than countries with plurality systems on a number of important indicators. On average, countries with plurality systems have a lower incidence of political riots, but a higher incidence of political deaths than PR countries. On crucial economic indicators like economic growth, inflation and unemployment, countries with majoritarian systems do not, on average, outperform PR countries. In other words, there is evidence that PR leads to less durable executives, but no evidence that durable executives produce better policies. Indeed, some data point to the opposite conclusion. "Majoritarian governments," Lijphart writes, "may be able to make decisions faster than consensus governments, but fast decisions are not necessarily wise decisions."[48]

Lijphart's conclusions are an important milestone in the age-old debate between supporters of PR and advocates of majoritarian systems, a debate that had become largely repetitive by the 1980s. His findings are grounded on the analysis of as many as 36 stable democracies, small and large, while the conventional wisdom tended to focus excessively on a few large and dysfunctional PR countries. Methodologically, they are based on factual quantitative indicators rather than on impressionistic evidence. To date, no systematic rebuttal has been provided by supporters of the Westminster model.

Other recent works have also offered a more positive assessment of governance under nonmajority administrations. Kaare Strom has analyzed the workings of minority governments in 15 democratic countries in the period from 1945 to 1987. He found that minority governments (either coalitions or single-party governments) were frequent, accounting for almost 35 percent of all cabinets formed. Looking at the performance of minority governments, he concluded that "contrary to conventional wisdom, minority governments do not perform particularly poorly in office. While minority governments are less durable than majority coalitions, they fare better at the polls and resign under more favourable circumstances. [They] perform best in those political systems where they are most common, and least well where they are most rare."[49] Following a more detailed examination of minority governments in Italy and Norway, he concluded that "at least in these countries, minority governments are just as effective as majority coalitions."[50]

The thrust of this analysis is that many Canadians' instinctive preference for majority governments and distaste for coalitions or minority governments rest on shaky foundations. Even if cabinets were shorter-lived than they now are, it is far from certain that Canada's governance would perforce be negatively affected.

The federal/provincial balance

Any examination of the consequences of introducing PR federally must take into account the fact that Canada is a federation with powerful provinces and a strong secessionist movement, where federal-provincial relations tend to be conducted in an adversarial mode. Indeed, in 1983, former Clerk of the Privy Council Gordon Robertson described Canada as "the most quarrelsome" among major federations, and this remains true today.

Would a succession of short-lived administrations in Ottawa, facing strong single-party majority administrations in the provinces, hamper the stature of the federal government? It is difficult to derive significant insights from the experience of other federations because the same electoral system tends to prevail at both levels in federal countries, either because such congruence is constitutionally mandated (as in Austria) or because the federal and state legislatures have freely opted for the same kind of system, as in Switzerland.[51] This pattern is probably due to the assumption that electors will be overwhelmed by the existence of two systems using different rules and criteria to elect national and state legislators.

It is not, however, necessarily the case that PR would result in less assertive federal cabinets in the field of federal-provincial relations. It is true that Ottawa's most prolonged succession of minority administrations (1962-68) coincided with a more accommodating attitude with the provinces, as exemplified by the pensions deal of 1964, the abortive Fulton-Favreau formula which granted *every* province a constitutional veto, or the establishment of the Royal Commission on Bilingualism and Biculturalism. But it is also true that Trudeau's attitude toward provincial governments does not appear to have been markedly more accommodating while he was heading a minority cabinet from 1972 to 1974, as exemplified by his energy policy. Further, Mulroney's very large majority in the Commons during his first term coincided with one of the most accommodating eras in federal-provincial relations, which included the mothballing of the National Energy Program and the negotiation of the Meech Lake Accord. One is tempted to conclude that in this field much more depends on the character and beliefs of the federal prime minister than on the extent of his or her support in the Commons.

Even if federal cabinets were weaker, however, this might be counterbalanced to some extent by an increase in their representativeness. More broadly-based federal cabinets might weaken the claim of some premiers, when facing a federal cabinet including no minister from their own province, to be the true spokesperson for provincial interests. William Irvine, one of the leading advocates of PR in the late 1970s, argued that PR, by increasing the representativeness of the federal government, might spare Ottawa massive transfers of powers to the provinces.

Quebec and francophones

How would PR affect francophones in general and Quebec in particular? PR would not change the proportion of Quebec seats, which would remain governed by section 51 of the *Constitution Act, 1867*. However, it would alter the shape of political representation in that province and others. Bakvis and Macpherson have documented the fact that Quebec's "block vote" made a substantial difference to the outcome of many Canadian elections throughout the 20th century.[52] This resulted not only from the sheer weight of Quebec seats (between 25 and 29 percent of the total, depending on the election) but also from the fact that Quebecers tended historically to support massively a specific political party, thus enhancing the chances of that party forming the government. An extreme illustration of this occurred in 1980 when all but one of Quebec's 75 seats went to the Liberals, allowing this party to form the government despite trailing in all other provinces combined. For the next four years, more than half of the ruling party caucus came from Quebec. While the Liberals' share of the vote in Quebec was already high (68 percent), only the first-past-the-post system could translate it into 98.6 percent of the seats. In this sense, PR would reduce Quebec's clout — or for that matter the clout of any major province engaging in block voting to the extent Quebec did until 1984.

Before rushing to the conclusion that PR would hamper Quebec, two notes of caution must be added. First, block voting is a risky game, as any region which puts all its eggs in the same basket may secure two kinds of results: either strong representation within the winning party (as Quebec usually got) or very weak representation, as in 1917, 1957 and 1979. In the latter scenario, a region will find itself with a limited number of cabinet seats or must rely on expedients like ministers sitting in the Senate, which in retrospect does not seem to have been an effective substitute either for Quebec (1979-80) or for the Western provinces (1980-84). PR, on the other hand, would guarantee each major party a minimum number of seats from Quebec and would substantially reduce the likelihood of the province being severely underrepresented in cabinet.

Second, one might doubt whether massive one-party contingents from Quebec will be frequently elected again. The Liberals' historic dominance of federal elections in Quebec rested during the 1970s and the early 1980s on the decision of supporters of Quebec sovereignty to stay away from the federal arena. This factor appears to have contributed strongly to Trudeau's lopsided victories, at a time when the PQ was doing well on the provincial scene but was unwilling to divert its energies to federal elections. Many PQ supporters abstained, deliberately spoiled their ballots, voted for fringe parties like the Rhinoceros Party, or dispersed their vote more or less strategically among the Conservatives, the Créditistes, the New Democrats or even the Liberals.

Since 1990, supporters of Quebec sovereignty have had their own party on the federal scene, fully backed by their provincial allies. A return to Liberal ascendancy in Quebec and the election of massive Liberal contingents from that province appear unlikely unless the sovereignty option vanishes completely from the Quebec political scene. The most likely scenario for the near future is that the electorate in Quebec will remain fragmented and that there will continue to be a substantial number of Bloc Québécois members in the House of Commons.

PR would have been helpful to the Bloc Québécois had it existed in the 1970s, but would likely be detrimental to the Bloc now. First, it would eliminate the advantage the Bloc derived in 1993 and 1997 (but less so in 2000) from the division of the federalist vote between the Liberals and the Progressive Conservatives. It would increase the likelihood of prominent Quebec federalists being elected in heavily francophone areas, thus undermining the Bloc's claim to speak for Quebec's francophones. PR would also diminish a handicap that afflicts the Liberals and benefits the Bloc, namely the excessive concentration of Liberal support in English-speaking areas of Quebec. This phenomenon, which is replicated to an even higher degree on the provincial scene, largely explains why the Bloc won a majority of Quebec seats in 2000 while trailing the Liberals in the popular vote, and why in 1997 the near equality between the Bloc and the Liberals in the province (37.9 percent vs. 36.7 percent of the vote respectively) was not matched in terms of seats (44 Bloc vs. 26 Liberals). The massive majorities won — and thus votes wasted — by the Liberals in western Montreal provide the explanation.

On the other hand, PR might reduce the likelihood of francophones being elected from provinces other than Quebec. The reasoning here is that PR implies much larger electoral districts, and much would depend on the willingness of parties (not only national leaders, but also local activists) to include French-speaking candidates on top positions on their lists. For example, under its present boundaries and linguistic profile, Ottawa-Vanier can be expected to return a francophone MP, but the same result would be less certain in a larger constituency including the whole city of Ottawa and its satellite communities, where francophones make up about 10 percent of the population. If New Brunswick were a single PR constituency electing 10 members, Acadian representation could also be reduced, depending on decisions made by parties while preparing their lists of candidates. By this reasoning, a German-style mixed system, by keeping single-member seats, would help to preserve the representation of Acadians.

The role of the Senate

Two important constraints influence the impact of the Senate on the political process. The first, that Senators are appointed rather than directly elected, diminishes the clout of the Senate insofar as most Canadians believe it is illegitimate for a chamber so constituted to oppose the government on major issues. This would not be affected by PR. The second constraint depends on whether the Senate is dominated by the government or the opposition: experience suggests that the Senate is much more likely to be assertive when the government has no majority "up there," as exemplified by the behaviour of

Senators from 1984 to 1990 and to a lesser extent from 1994 to 1996. As long as the Senate continues to be made up almost exclusively of members from both traditional parties, coalition governments including those parties can expect a cooperative attitude from Senators. Coalitions excluding those two parties can expect a rough time in the Senate until they have appointed enough of their own in that chamber. It is likely, furthermore, that junior coalition partners will sooner or later insist on some share of Senate appointments, thus leading to a more broadly representative Senate than is presently the case.

The Governor General

Governors General are appointed and may be dismissed by the Queen at the personal request of the prime minister. Their political influence is extremely modest, notably because most elections produce clearcut results, and because even in minority contexts, refusing to follow the prime minister's advice in the use of the reserve powers is assumed — rightly — to be highly risky. In coalition cabinets, junior partners might challenge the right of the prime minister to personally recommend appointments to Rideau Hall.

Would PR, by multiplying hung parliaments, provide an opportunity for the governor general to play a more active role in the selection of the prime minister, as parliamentary presidents have in some PR countries? Probably not. The trend in the latter, including New Zealand, is for party leaders to negotiate among themselves, and for the head of state to be informed of their conclusions and to act accordingly. Unlike hereditary monarchs or directly or indirectly elected presidents, the governor general may be dismissed by the Queen at any time on the recommendation of the prime minister. This should dampen any temptation by the governor general to act as a referee, either in cabinet formation or with regards to the dissolution of Parliament.

The judiciary

The relative position of the judiciary in the Canadian political system would not be directly affected by PR, as it derives from constitutional provisions. The only possible influence has to do with the appointment of judges. Junior coalition partners would probably insist on having a more decisive input in judicial appointments or on a more open selection procedure involving public hearings by Commons committees.

No threat to the survival of democracy

Some still fear that PR would endanger the very survival of democracy. A quick succession of short-lived cabinets might give the public the impression that anarchy prevails at the highest level of the state, and the country could become a laughingstock abroad. At worst, the working of parliamentary government under PR might be unfavourably contrasted by the public with the firm and decisive leadership of earlier monarchs or dictators, thus discrediting democracy itself.

The argument that PR can lead to democratic breakdown, quite popular in the 1940s and 1950s, is now discredited, though it may have some validity for emerging democracies.[53] This argument was inspired by an analysis that focused excessively on the experiences of Weimar Germany and interwar Italy. It overlooked the fact that in many PR countries, like Switzerland, the Low Countries and Scandinavia, democracy survived quite well the challenges of the interwar period. A recent survey of historical works on democratic breakdowns during the interwar period revealingly makes no mention of PR.[54]

Scenarios for the Introduction of PR

In what kind of circumstances can we foresee PR being introduced in Canada? So-called "rational-choice models" assume that PR will be accepted when the party or parties in power reach the conclusion that this system will work to their advantage. This has been the case, notably, of ruling parties that were anticipating oblivion at the next election under a plurality or a majority system. PR could also, however, be imposed on politicians by the voters through a referendum. Finally, one can imagine PR being forced on Parliament by court rulings.

The Parties

In early 2001, when the first version of this chapter was published, it seemed highly unlikely that the Liberal government would reform the electoral system on its own initiative, or would do so under the pressure of opposition parties or following a referendum. While opposition parties represented in the Commons had shown some interest for the topic, as expressed by the adoption of resolutions at national conventions, none had pressed very far for a reform of the electoral system. Policy statements by opposition parties revealed at least some awareness that a problem existed and should be addressed one way or the other. However, they had to be taken for what they were: stands couched in fairly general terms that may or may not be implemented once in office.

The introduction of PR by the existing Liberal administration still appears unlikely. Despite the sympathy Pierre Trudeau expressed for some dose of PR after his temporary retirement as Liberal leader in 1979, the Liberals have subsequently shown no interest in the matter, even during the period (1980-84) when the paucity of their representation in the Western provinces was perceived as a serious problem. Indeed, Liberal backbenchers at that time even resisted the introduction of PR for an elected, though not very powerful, Senate. Presently, the trade-off that PR would produce between a weaker Liberal representation in Ontario and a stronger Liberal representation elsewhere is unattractive for Ontario Liberals, as it seemed in the early 1980s for the then strong contingent of Quebec Liberals. Those Liberals whose chances of election would be enhanced by PR are simply not in Parliament to make their case, while those who would be adversely affected by it now dominate the Liberal caucus. Electoral system reform was debated twice in the House of Commons in recent years (in February 2001 and September 2003): in both debates Liberal backbenchers expressed strong opposition to the idea.

However, circumstances are changing. Under their new leader Jack Layton, New Democrats are giving higher priority to the electoral system than before. In September 2003, Lorne Nystrom, MP, proposed that a referendum be held in order to determine whether Canadians wanted to replace the existing electoral system and that a commission be appointed to devise a new system. The motion was opposed by the ruling Liberals and (more surprisingly) by the Progressive Conservatives, but was supported by all other three parties. One can imagine the Liberals losing their majority in the Commons at a subsequent election, while remaining the strongest party, and being forced to conclude some kind of alliance with the New Democrats. The latter have announced their intention to exact the introduction of PR in exchange for their support. Whether Liberals would accept a change of that magnitude is uncertain — because PR would make perennial the stronger bargaining position enjoyed by smaller parties — but the pressure will be strong.

The referendum route

The circumstances that led to the introduction of MMP (mixed-member proportional system) in New Zealand and of a mixed system in Italy have led many supporters of PR to envisage a different scenario, whereby voters would force PR on a reluctant but thoroughly discredited political class. In New Zealand, two referendums held in the early 1990s, the second binding on Parliament, established that the public preferred MMP to the existing plurality system and other alternatives, and despite its own misgivings the government of the day had no choice but to comply. In Italy, voters took advantage of the popular initiative — and of the discrediting of politicians following the *tangentopoli* scandal — to trigger a referendum on the elimination of the PR element in the Senate's electoral system, thus forcing parliamentarians to review the electoral systems for both houses.

The New Zealand scenario, which is also advanced in Britain, is unlikely to prevail in Canada as long as the Liberals keep a majority in Parliament, because of their reluctance to provide supporters of PR with a golden opportunity to argue their case with the public and possibly to win. No referendum can be organized without the concurrence of members of Parliament. The existing *Referendum Act* provides only for referendums on questions "relating to the Constitution of Canada," and even if this wording was stretched so as to include a (non-binding) referendum on PR, the approval of a majority of members of both Houses must be obtained for such a question to be asked. The holding of a referendum might be a concession demanded by a smaller party in a minority Parliament in exchange for its support. Should the Liberals be reduced to a minority position, a promise to hold a referendum on the issue might well become the only way for the Liberals to survive in office.

The Italian scenario is even more unlikely because there is no federal provision allowing citizens to force the holding of a referendum by way of petition. If such a provision existed, as in British Columbia, the introduction of PR would become a possibility. Two crucial variables would condition the effectiveness of the procedure: the number of electors required for a petition to be successful, and whether Parliament would be bound by the result of the referendum (as in Switzerland for constitutional amendments) or would be left free to enact or reject the measure approved by the people.

A Charter challenge

A final scenario is the imposition of PR by the courts, in response to a Charter challenge. At first sight, the Charter of Rights and Freedoms seems silent on the issue; the only mention is in section 42(1)(a) of the *Constitution Act, 1982*, which calls for "the principle of proportionate representation of provinces in the House of Commons prescribed by the Constitution of Canada." This, however, refers exclusively to the redistribution of seats among provinces, not to the representation of parties in the House.

Yet the "right to vote" guaranteed by section 3 of the Charter was given an unexpectedly broad meaning by a British Columbia court in 1989 in the *Dixon* case. The court held that it encompassed a "right to equality of voting power" that would be violated by blatant disparities in the population of electoral districts, an approach later upheld (though qualified) by the Supreme Court of Canada. The argument might be made, then, that if the right to vote is breached by serious malapportionment of electoral districts that dilutes the voting power of ridings with above-average populations, it is also breached by an electoral system that provides electors who vote for smaller parties with little or no representation.

Nobody can predict how this kind of argument, presented in a more elaborate way, would fare in court. Yet this avenue for change exists and is described in greater detail in another article in this collection (see David Beatty's chapter later in this section).

Recent decisions in the provinces have increased the pressure for electoral system reform at the federal level. The Charest Liberal government elected in Quebec in April 2003 announced after its election that it would stick with its pre-election commitment to introduce an MMP-type system within two years of its election. The McGuinty Liberal government elected in Ontario the same year has promised to hold a referendum on the issue. New Brunswick has created a nine-member Commission on Legislative Democracy. In Prince Edward Island, a one-person commission, following extensive public hearings, has recommended in December 2003 the introduction of MMP. British Columbia has followed a very original course of action by creating a Citizens' Assembly composed of randomly selected interested citizens. The assembly must debate the issue and decide in favour of an alternative to be submitted to the people in a referendum that will take place at the same time as the next election. The incumbent government has agreed to accept the referendum result as binding if at least 60 percent of the voters province-wide and a majority in 60 percent of the ridings support the assembly's proposal. All these developments suggest that reform is likely to be tried in a few provinces first before being introduced for federal elections, a rather familiar pattern in Canadian political development.

Another interesting development is the creation in recent years of grassroots organizations dedicated to electoral system reform, like Fair Vote Canada, the Mouvement pour une Démocratie Nouvelle in Québec, Fair Voting BC, and Every Vote Counts in Prince Edward Island. The Canadian Law Commission has also ordered studies and was expected to report in the spring of 2004 on the issue. Never since the 1920s has electoral system reform been so widely discussed in Canada, which increases the pressure on Ottawa to either appoint a commission or to hold a nonbinding referendum.[55]

Conclusions

There is no perfect electoral system, as evidenced by the continued use of both PR and of majority or plurality systems in established democracies, as well as by the spread throughout the 1990s of mixed systems that try to secure the best of both worlds. It is significant, however, that unlike the 1950s, PR systems rarely come under fire nowadays, whereas plurality systems and the Westminster model are frequently challenged, sometimes successfully, in the established democracies where they are used.

On balance, in this country and at this time, the benefits of PR outweigh the disadvantages. Party caucuses would become more balanced regionally, no region would appear to have an overwhelming say within the government party, and the formation of regionally representative cabinets would be facilitated. The chief downside, that large electoral districts would be less suited to constituency work as Canadian MPs have traditionally practiced it, could be offset to a large extent by opting for a German-style mixed system, with 50 percent or 60 percent of members elected in single-member districts.

Our cabinet system would be profoundly transformed by PR. Party elites, rather than the straight will of a plurality of the electorate, would select the government. Single-party majority governments would largely disappear and coalitions would become the standard government formula, though the formation of single-party minority governments would not be ruled out. Cabinets would be less durable, and prime ministers would lose some of the dominance they now enjoy.

Contrary to a widely held view, there is no evidence that PR would necessarily lead to a poorer economic performance or to bad governance more generally. Governments would devote more time to cabinet discussions in order to reach agreement between coalition partners, but the decisions so arrived at might prove to be wiser than some decisions taken impulsively by a prime minister after minimal discussion in cabinet.

Notes

1. Major contributions in this vein are Alan C. Cairns, "The Electoral System and the Party System in Canada, 1921-1965," *Canadian Journal of Political Science*, Vol. 1, no. 1 (March 1968), pp. 55-80; W.P. Irvine, *Does Canada Need a New Electoral System?* (Kingston: Queen's Studies on the Future of the Canadian Communities, Monograph no. 1, 1979); John C. Courtney, "Reflections on Reforming the Canadian Electoral System," *Canadian Public Administration*, Vol. 23, no. 3 (fall 1980), p. 427-57.

2. See for example Donley Studlar, "Will Canada Seriously Consider Electoral System Reform? Women and Aboriginals Should," in Henry Milner (ed.), *Making Every Vote Count: Reassessing Canada's Electoral System* (Peterborough: Broadview Press, 1999), pp. 123-32.

3. Ralph Allen, *Ordeal by Fire: Canada, 1910-1945* (Garden City, NY: Doubleday and Co., 1961), p. 235.

4. This finding is included in Paul Howe and David Northrup, "Strengthening Canadian Democracy: The Views of Canadians," *Policy Matters*, Vol. 1, no. 5 (July 2000).

5. See Mark N. Franklin, "Electoral Participation," in Lawrence LeDuc, Richard G. Niemi, and Pippa Norris (eds.), *Comparing Democracies: Elections and Voting in Global Perspective* (Thousand Oaks, CA: Sage, 1996), p. 226.

6. Neil Nevitte, André Blais, Elisabeth Gidengil, and Richard Nadeau, *Unsteady State: The 1997 Canadian Federal Election* (Don Mills: Oxford University Press, 2000), pp. 15-16.

7. Richard Johnston, "Canadian Elections at the Millenium," *Choices*, Vol. 6, no. 6 (September 2000).

8. Richard S. Katz, "Electoral Reform Is not as Simple as It Looks," in Milner (ed.), *Making Every Vote Count*, p. 108.

9. We can cite Sweden, where Social Democrats occupied the premiership uninterruptedly from 1932 to 1976, except for a few summer months in 1936; Italy, where Christian Democrats dominated all cabinets from 1945 to the mid-1990s; and Switzerland, which has been ruled by the same coalition of parties — and the same party balance within the government — since 1959. In Belgium, the Catholic Party has been almost continuously in office since 1884, either alone or in alliance with other parties. In Spain, the Socialist Party governed from 1982 to 1996 under the same premier.

10. Actually, it did not. The new Conservative Party under Harper secured 30 percent of the vote, while the combined support for the Canadian Alliance and the Progressive Conservatives in 2000 was 37 percent.

11. The limited vote, a plurality formula that tries to ensure representation for the minority party in multimember districts by granting to each voter a number of votes less than the number of seats in the district, was also tried briefly for electing Toronto repesentatives to the Legislative Assembly of Ontario in 1886 and 1890.

12. In the 1997 Canadian federal election, one member was elected with 28.9 percent of the vote. In 1944, in a provincial election held in Quebec, a CCF candidate was elected with 21 percent of the vote. Once in Papua New Guinea, where first-past-the-post applies in a highly fragmented electorate, a candidate was elected in a district with as little as 6.3 percent of the vote.

13. See André Blais and Louis Massicotte, "Direct Presidential Elections: A World Summary," *Electoral Studies*, Vol. 16, no. 4 (December 1997), pp. 441-55.

14. The number of members elected with 50 percent of the vote or more was 104, including 58 Liberals, 29 Reformers, 11 Bloquistes, 3 Conservatives and 3 New Democrats.

15. More precisely, alternative voting was in force in Manitoba's rural districts from 1924 to 1955, in Alberta's rural districts from 1924 to 1956, and province-wide in British Columbia for the 1952 and 1953 elections. In 1923, a serious attempt was made to introduce alternative voting for Ontario's rural districts (coupled with a proportional system for urban districts). It failed because a filibuster by the Opposition led the premier to call an early election, which he lost.

16. Antoine Bilodeau, "L'impact mécanique du vote alternatif au Canada," *Canadian Journal of Political Science*, Vol. 32, no. 4 (December 1999), pp. 745-61.

17. Independent candidate John Nunziata would have been elected in both scenarios.

18. STV was in force in Manitoba for provincial elections between 1920 and 1955 (in Winnipeg only) and also in Alberta for the election of MLAs from Calgary and Edmonton from 1926 to 1956. Since either the plurality rule or alternative voting were in force at the same time in rural single-member districts, both provinces, in fact, used a mixed system consisting of two distinct electoral systems in different areas.

19. For a more complete description of the mechanics of the various electoral systems, see André Blais and Louis Massicotte, "Electoral Systems," in LeDuc, Niemi and Norris (eds.), *Comparing Democracies*, pp. 49-81.

20. Louis Massicotte and André Blais, "Mixed Electoral Systems: A Conceptual and Empirical Survey," *Electoral Studies*, Vol. 18, no. 3 (September 1999), pp. 341-66.

21. A survey of the outcomes produced by the various types of mixed electoral systems, using Mackie and Rose's index of proportionality (from 0 to 100, with a higher score meaning a more proportional result) found an average index of 80.5 for superposition systems, much less than the index for plurality systems (87) or majority systems (84). In contrast, the average index for corrective systems was 91.8, quite close to the index for PR systems (94). See Louis Massicotte and André Blais, "Mixed Electoral Systems: A Conceptual and Empirical Survey," paper presented at the XVII World Congress of the International Political Science Association, Seoul, 1997, pp. 10-11.

22. André Blais and Louis Massicotte, "Electoral Formulas: A Macroscopic Perspective," *European Journal of Political Research*, Vol. 32, no. 1 (August 1997), pp. 107-29. Plurality systems tend to be found in former British colonies, and on the North American, Asian and African continents. Among established democracies, PR is more widespread than the first-past-the-post system, though the latter tends to prevail in larger countries.

23. A sample includes: David Elton and Roger Gibbins, *Electoral Reform: The Need is Pressing, the Time is Now* (Calgary: Canada West Foundation, 1980); Ronald G. Landes, "Alternative Electoral Systems for Canada," paper presented at the 1980 meeting of the Canadian Political Science Association, Montreal, June 2, 1980; Irvine, *Does Canada Need a New Electoral System?*, pp. 52-58; W.P. Irvine, "Power Requires Representation," *Policy Options*, Vol. 1, no. 4 (Dec. 1980/Jan. 1981), p. 22; W.M. Dobell, "A Limited Corrective to Plurality Voting," *Canadian Public Policy*, Vol. 7, no. 1 (winter 1981), pp. 75-81; R. Kent Weaver, "Improving Representation in the Canadian House of Commons," *Canadian Journal of Political Science*, Vol. 30, no. 3 (September 1997), pp. 473-512.

24. Full-fledged PR here refers to list systems, but the effects of STV would be quite similar. The chief difference is that in the latter, voters have more freedom to choose from among the various slates of candidates sponsored by each party, though in practice few do so.

25. For example, New Zealanders were promised the best of all worlds in the early 1990s when the introduction of the mixed-member proportional system (MMP) was under debate, and this, combined with almost universal scorn for the existing political class, contributed to the victory of MMP in two referendums. A few years later, the actual operation of MMP had proved so disappointing, even to some of its advocates, that public opinion turned sharply against it, and New Zealand began to be cited as an example of the drawbacks of PR, to the point where people forgot about the real improvements it made in the area of representation. The successful operation of MMP in the 1999 election, however, might swing public opinion back in favour of it again.

26. In 1993, the Reform Party and the Bloc Québécois, with 18.7 percent and 13.5 percent of the vote, respectively, secured 52 and 54 seats, while the Progressive Conservatives, with 16.0 percent, got only 2. The Bloc reached Official Opposition status while ranking fourth in terms of popular vote. It should not be overlooked that the Bloc fielded only 75 candidates and Reform 207, while the Conservatives had candidates in all 295 ridings.

27. See Wilma Rule, "Women's Underrepresentation and Electoral Systems," *Political Science and Politics: PS*, Vol. 27, no. 4 (December 1994), pp. 689-93.

28. Lord Jenkins of Hillhead (chair), *The Report of the Independent Commission on the Voting System* (London: HMSO, 1999), para. 39.

29. Since 1993, Ontario has been a one-party province in terms of representation in the House of Commons, with the Liberals sweeping all but one of Ontario's 99 seats (1993) and all but two of 103 seats (1997), though the Liberal share of the Ontario vote did not exceed 53 percent in either case.

30. Belgium initially had a two-ballot majority system in multimember districts. In the 1894 election, before PR was introduced, the Catholic Party won all the seats in Brussels and 71 of the 72 Flemish seats, but only 14 of the 62 seats in Wallonia. See Xavier Mabille, *Histoire politique de la Belgique* (Brussels: CRISP, 1986), p. 194. This result illustrates how little a two-ballot system can do to mitigate regional polarization.

31. Canada, *Task Force on Canadian Unity (Pépin-Robarts): A Future Together: Observations* *and Recommendations* (Ottawa: Ministry of Supply and Services, 1979), p. 105.

32. See Massicotte and Blais, "Mixed Electoral Systems," pp. 341-66.

33. See David W. Brady et al., "The Decline of Party in the U.S. House of Representatives, 1887-1968," *Legislative Studies Quarterly*, Vol. 4, no. 3 (August 1979), pp. 381-407.

34. Louis Massicotte, "The Rise of Party Cohesion in the Canadian House of Commons 1867-1945: A Descriptive and Comparative Summary," paper presented at the Third Workshop of Parliamentary Scholars and Parliamentarians, Wroxton College, Oxfordshire, UK, August 1998; Joseph Wearing, "Tweaking the Whips: Modified Rebelliousness in the Canadian House of Commons," paper presented at the Third Workshop of Parliamentary Scholars and Parliamentarians, Wroxton College, Oxfordshire, UK, August 1998.

35. Jean-Claude Colliard, *Les régimes parlementaires contemporains* (Paris: Presses de la Fondation nationale des sciences politiques, 1978), pp. 210-16.

36. Louis Massicotte, "Bridled Workhorses: Party Discipline in Committees of the Canadian House of Commons," paper presented at the annual meeting of the Canadian Political Science Association, St. John's, Newfoundland, June 1997.

37. The elections of 1958, 1968 and 1974 provided an incumbent minority government with a majority of seats.

38. Michael Laver and Norman Schofield, *Multiparty Government: The Politics of Coalition in Europe* (Oxford: Oxford University Press, 1990), p. 70.

39. See, for example, Jonathan Boston, *Governing under Proportional Representation: Lessons from Europe* (Wellington: Institute of Policy Studies, University of Victoria, 1998).

40. Laver and Schofield, *Multiparty Government*, p. 152. The median duration of minimum winning coalitions (35 months) was higher than the mean.

41. Laver and Schofield, *Multiparty Government*, pp. 148-49.

42. For example, Tage Erlander served as prime minister of Sweden without interruption from 1946 to 1969, a period (23 years) that exceeds that served by Mackenzie King, Canada's longest-serving prime minister. In recent years, Felipe Gonzalez was premier of Spain for 14 years, while Helmut Kohl led Germany for an uninterrupted 16 years.

43. From 1945 to 1995, there were 42 cabinets in Israel (starting from 1948), 46 in Finland and 55 in Italy. The French Fourth Republic saw 28 cabinets in its 13 years of existence. See Jaap Woldendorp, Hans Keman, and Ian Budge, "Party Government in 20 Democracies: An Update (1990-1995)," *European Journal of Political Research*, Vol. 33, no. 1 (January 1998), pp. 125-64.

44. See Donald J. Savoie, *Governing from the Centre: The Concentration of Political Power in Canada* (Toronto: University of Toronto Press, 1999).

45. One was attempted against John Diefenbaker in 1963, but failed.

46. Australian political history offers at least two examples of this. After the 1922 election, the Country Party, whose support had become a precondition for the continuation in office of the Nationalist Party government, insisted not only on an almost equal number of cabinet ministers, but also blackballed incumbent Prime Minister Hughes, thus obliging the Nationalist Party to select a new leader as prime minister. Similarly, in 1967-68, following the death of Liberal Prime Minister Holt, Country Party Leader John McEwen vetoed the appointment of William McMahon as prime minister, on the grounds that McEwen did not trust him personally.

47. Arend Lijphart, "Democracies: Forms, Performance, and Constitutional Engineering," *European Journal of Political Research*, Vol. 25, no.1 (January 1994), pp. 1-17; and *Patterns of Democracy: Government Forms and Performance in Thirty-Six Countries* (New Haven and London: Yale University Press, 1999).

48. Lijphart, "Democracies," p. 12.

49. Kaare Strom, *Minority Government and Majority Rule* (Cambridge: Cambridge University Press, 1990), p. 238.

50. Strom, *Minority Government and Majority Rule*, p. 238.

51. See Louis Massicotte, "Federal Countries, Elections in," in R. Rose (ed.), *International Encyclopedia of Elections* (Washington, DC: Congressional Quarterly, 2000), p. 101-4.

52. Herman Bakvis and Laura G. Macpherson, "Quebec Block Voting and the Canadian Electoral System," *Canadian Journal of Political Science*, Vol. 28, no. 4 (December 1995), pp. 659-92.

53. André Blais and Stéphane Dion, "Electoral Systems and the Consolidation of New Democracies," in Diane Ethier (ed.), *Democratic Transition and Consolidation in Southern Europe, Latin America and Asia* (London: Macmillan Press, 1990).

54. Thomas Ertman, "Democracy and Dictatorship in Interwar Western Europe Revisited," *World Politics*, Vol. 50, no. 3 (April 1998), pp. 475-505.

55. See F. Leslie Seidle, *Electoral System Reform in Canada: Objectives, Advocacy and Implications for Governance.* Ottawa: Canadian Policy Research Networks. Research Document F/29 Family Network, October 2002.

3

The Alternative Vote

Tom Flanagan

I have to express a degree of agnosticism about comparing the merits of electoral systems. Fifty years of theoretical research deriving from the Arrow General Impossibility Theorem has demonstrated that there is no perfect method of aggregating votes into a collective choice. The criterion of perfection is the "Condorcet winner," that is, the option that would be preferred to all other options in a series of pairwise comparisons. For example, in a three-way choice among options a, b, and c, there might not be a majority for any of the three. But a would be the Condorcet winner if a majority preferred it to b and to c. As such, a is the rational choice for the voting group, for a majority of its members prefer no option over a.

All voting methods that reach a determinate outcome are capable, under some conditions, of picking an option other than the Condorcet winner, that is, reaching an outcome that, to a majority of the group, is less preferred than one of the other available options. Proportional representation (PR) is an exception, but only because it does not pick a winner at all, at least in the sense of selecting a government or a prime minister. Proportional representation only composes a legislature, which then provides a backdrop against which party leaders negotiate the composition of a government; and a coalition put together in this way could well fail to be a Condorcet winner if presented to the voters. Would the voters of Austria have preferred the coalition of the People's Party and the Freedom Party, which party leaders gave them after the election of 1999, to a coalition of the People's Party and the Social Democrats? We will never know because the people never got to vote on that choice, but there is no reason to assume that the coalition that took power was actually a Condorcet winner.

If theoretical analysis shows that no electoral method is unambiguously superior to all others, common-sense reflection leads to the same conclusion. Great Britain uses first-past-the-post (FPTP) or single-member-plurality voting; France uses a two-stage run-off; Australia uses the alternative vote (AV) for its House of Representatives; Ireland uses the single transferable vote; the Netherlands uses the list form of proportional representation; Germany uses the so-called mixed-member-proportional system; and Japan used the single non-transferable vote until the 1996 election, when it switched to a parallel combination of PR and first-past-the-post that does not give as proportional an outcome as the German model. Although each of these seven countries has a different electoral system, all have been highly successful for the last 50 years. They have had their ups and downs, to be sure; but by world standards they all enjoy political stability, democratic government and a productive capitalist economy underwriting a high standard of living. I conclude that the success of liberal democracy depends on other factors that all these countries have in common: respect for the constitution; adherence to the rule of law; extension of the franchise to all adults, including racial, linguistic and religious minorities; and protection of property rights. In this tableau, the electoral system is clearly a secondary factor.

Secondary factors, however, are not necessarily unimportant factors. Although any country may succeed or fail with any electoral system, the choice of electoral system does have important consequences for the political system. It affects the number of political parties and their bases of support, the way in which the parties compete or cooperate with one another during election campaigns, and the way in which they behave when they are in government or in opposition. Although no electoral system is demonstrably the best as a general proposition, it is quite possible that a certain electoral system will be better suited than others to the needs of a particular country at a particular stage in its history.

That is the context for pondering electoral reform in Canada. Although Canada is a highly successful country, it has recurrent problems of political fragmentation, which many scholars, from Alan Cairns onward, have plausibly traced to reliance on first-past-the-post voting. Would another system work better, if not in general, at least for Canada at this point in our history?

To seek an appropriate remedy, we must first be clear about the nature of the malady. Like Richard Johnston, I see Canada's enduring political problem as a tendency for political parties to fragment along linguistic and regional lines, thus exacerbating regional and linguistic tensions and even encouraging separatist movements. This tendency was apparent as early as 1885, with the formation of

Honoré Mercier's Parti National as a reaction to the hanging of Louis Riel, and again in 1911, with the entry of Henri Bourassa's Nationalist League into electoral politics. Then came the era of Western-based parties, with the entry into federal politics of the Progressives in 1921 and Social Credit and the Co-operative Commonwealth Federation in 1935. Finally we have the events of recent history, with the creation of the Reform Party of Canada in 1987 and the Bloc Québécois in 1990. Each time a new party emerged, one or both of the historic parties, the Conservatives and Liberals, lost a large bloc of regionally or linguistically concentrated voters. The Conservatives have been more battered than the Liberals, but the latter have also suffered huge losses at times, such as in 1921, when they lost the western farm vote to the Progressives, or 1984, when the francophone voters of Quebec switched *en masse* from the Liberals to the Conservatives, as a dress rehearsal for the creation of the Bloc Québécois.

A century of splitting old parties along regional and linguistic lines and creating new ones gave us the 1993-2003 five-party federal system, in which only the Liberals had the breadth of support necessary to win an election. Although they commanded only about 40 percent of the vote in a five-party contest, they were undoubtedly a Condorcet winner in that period. Polling data on voters' second choices made it clear that none of the other four parties could have come close to beating the Liberals in a two-party contest. In that sense, the fact that first-past-the-post voting gave the Liberals over half the seats with only 40 percent of the popular vote was not really unfair; rather, it reflected their underlying strength as a Condorcet winner.

Yet all was not well. Even if the Liberals were a Condorcet winner in the five-party configuration, it was unhealthy to have only one potential winner. A party that can always count on winning is likely to become unresponsive and even corrupt. Indeed, by the late 1990s, the "usual operation" of Jean Chrétien's Liberals had started to resemble the unrestrained cronyism of the PRI in Mexico and the Christian Democrats in Italy in their heyday.

The underlying cause of this tendency toward political fragmentation is the imposition of a parliamentary form of government with disciplined parties upon a sprawling, diverse country. In contrast, the American executive does not require the support of the legislature to remain in power, and thus political parties do not need to be as disciplined as Canadian parties. Republicans and Democrats coming from various parts of the United States and holding divergent views on many issues can cheerfully coexist within their respective parties, because there is no need for party members to vote the same way all the time. Canada could deal with the fragmentation of political parties by adopting an American-style system based on the separation of powers; but after two centuries of parliamentary government, most

Canadians would regard such action as extreme and even treasonous. Tinkering with the electoral system is a less drastic remedy.

The problem, to repeat, is the tendency of Canada's parties to split along linguistic and regional lines. Because it levies heavy penalties upon small parties, the first-past-the-post electoral system tends to discourage fragmentation in general. But it has one exception that actually encourages fragmentation in Canada's case: New parties with regionally concentrated support can thrive for long periods of time by playing to the voters in their territorial base. In this respect FPTP may not be the best electoral system for Canada.

Proportional representation, as proposed by Nick Loenen, Henry Milner, Louis Massicotte and many others, would recognize the tendency toward fragmentation and carve it in electoral stone. New parties would crowd in to join those already represented in Parliament. The Greens would almost certainly surmount any reasonable threshold for representation, as they have in many other PR countries. The new Conservative Party might well split along lines of cleavage between fiscal and social conservatives, or western and eastern supporters. The Liberals might also split if — to take only one example — pro-life Catholic voters concluded they might have more influence as a separate party than as a largely submerged voting bloc within the Liberal Party. If Canada adopts PR, all future governments will be coalitions of two or more parties — perhaps even minority coalitions dependent on other parties for their survival, as has been the case in New Zealand since adoption of MMP.

The style of politics engendered by PR would be novel for Canada. I am sure we could adapt to it and perhaps even prosper with it, but I am not sure that Canadians should make such a radical leap of faith when less sweeping alternatives are available — alternative voting (AV) as practiced in Australia and the two-stage run-off as practiced in France. Because these two so-called "majoritarian" systems would have much the same practical effect, I will concentrate here on AV, which is in effect a temporally condensed run-off.

Under AV, most things are the same as in the FPTP system to which Canadians are accustomed. The ridings retain the same boundaries and are still represented by a single person, whom residents of the riding can regard as their own member of Parliament. Voters still vote for candidates representing parties rather than for parties as such; no party members are appointed by and represent only the party apparatus. Moreover, Canadians are already familiar to some degree with the alternative vote. A few older citizens may remember it from the 1950s, when it was still in use in provincial elections in Manitoba, Alberta and British Columbia. Others have encountered it in recent years in the process of nominating candidates for election campaigns or choosing a party leader. Even those who have not encountered AV will be aware of the run-off method, which has been widely used for the same purposes and which is, as noted above, both logically and practically similar to AV.

AV differs from FPTP only in one respect as far as the voter is concerned. Instead of putting an X before the name of the favoured candidate, the voter is required to rank all the candidates from first to last, marking them 1, 2, 3, etc. (Some versions of AV allow the voter to mark only the first choice, or to stop ranking anywhere before the bottom, but these refinements need not be discussed here.) When the ballots are counted the first time, only the first choices are tabulated. A candidate who receives 50 percent plus one or more of the first count is declared elected at that point. If no one has a majority, the candidate with the lowest number of first preferences is removed, and all those ballots are transferred to other candidates based on the indication of second preference. The process of recounting, elimination and vote transfer is repeated until someone emerges with a majority, at which point the victor is declared and the election ceases. With paper ballots, the process can take several hours, or even a couple of days; but if Canada ever modernizes its voting technology, computers could do the recounting almost instantaneously.

If one party is overwhelmingly dominant, or if two big parties compete with each other, AV will give much the same results as FPTP; but in multiparty races, AV opens up a new world of possibilities for cooperation. Political parties can retain their separate identities, organizations and programs while forging electoral alliances with each other by "exchanging preferences," as the Australians call it. Ever since the end of World War I, when AV was introduced, the Liberal Party and the National (previously Country) Party have been encouraging their supporters to vote first for their own candidate but to rank the other party's candidate second. In this way, a Liberal can vote Liberal, and a National can vote National, without guaranteeing a victory for the Labor candidate. If the Labor candidate trails after the first count, then the Liberal or National candidate will win on the second count. If the trailing candidate is Liberal or National, most of the transferred ballots will go to the other; and the Labor candidate will win only if he gets a majority on the second count. The net effect is to allow the Liberal and National Parties to run an effective electoral alliance without splitting the vote so that Labor wins a majority of seats.

Over time, the Liberals and Nationals have taken their cooperation quite far, so that they usually sit in a joint caucus, both in government and in opposition, and negotiate a joint platform at election time. The cooperation is sometimes looser, and it has occasionally broken down altogether, as in 1973, when the two parties fell out with each other during a spell in opposition. But the system also allows cooperation and exchange of preferences to be re-established, which happened in time for the 1974 election.

If AV had existed in Canada in the five-party period of 1993-2003, it would have been easier for the Reform Party/Canadian Alliance and the Progressive Conservatives to deal with each other. Without having to merge, they could have tried to form an electoral coalition on the Australian model. Each party could have run as many candidates as it wanted (though common sense advises against opposing your partner's incumbents), while ameliorating the vote-splitting effects of competition by "trading preferences" with the other party. That is, Reform could have advised its voters to rank the PC candidate second on the ballot, and the Tories could have advised their voters to do the same with the Reform candidate. There would have been some leakage on both sides; voters are not sheep who always act exactly as they are advised. The leakage, however, might well have been balanced by the addition of new supporters who would have seen the coalition as a potential governing alternative to the Liberals.

What about the Bloc Québécois? AV would have done nothing to bring that party into a coalition with Reform and the Tories, but it would have operated in another way to dampen the separatist threat. In the polarized politics of Quebec, the BQ, as the only separatist party, won many seats with a plurality of the vote as the Liberals, Tories, Alliance and NDP split the federalist vote. Even without forming explicit coalitions, it seems likely that many federalist voters in Quebec would have ranked the BQ last and would have given their higher preferences to other federalist parties. Separatist sentiment was too strong for the BQ to be frozen out altogether, but it probably would not have won as many seats under AV as it did under FPTP.

As with PR, the long-term result of bringing AV to Canada would probably be a preponderance of coalition governments. Under PR, however, governing coalitions are put together by party leaders after elections have taken place, whereas under AV the coalitions are formed before elections and the voters get a chance to choose between them. Coalitions tend to be long-lasting, so the voters become familiar with them. In these respects, AV gives voters a higher degree of control over politicians than PR does.

The objection that AV does not yield proportionality between the percentage of popular votes and the percentage of seats a party wins is certainly true. Its operation in this respect is closer to FPTP than to PR. Those to whom proportionality is the highest political value should choose one of the many varieties of PR rather than AV.

In my view, however, proportionality is a purely abstract value of little importance in the real world of politics. I believe what is important is to have governments capable of taking decisive action when needed and to give the voters an effective choice between governing coalitions. For Canada, what is particularly important is to create a political vehicle that can alternate with the

Liberals in government. If a single party can do that, well and good; but the historical record of political fragmentation in this country suggests that such a party will be difficult to create and probably short-lived if it does emerge.

By allowing separate parties to retain their distinct identities while forming effective electoral coalitions, AV offers Canada a way out of its historic difficulties. The theoretical properties of AV, its long record of encouraging electoral coalitions in Australia, and the similar effect of the closely related run-off system in the French Fifth Republic — all suggest that the alternative vote could play midwife to the birth of a new coalition broad enough to win an election.

AV is based on an understanding of practical problems, modest in scope, only incrementally different from past practice, and easily rescinded if it does not live up to expectations. It is the sort of reform that a cautious people like Canadians could agree to undertake.

Notes

The author expresses personal views in this chapter and does not purport to speak for Mr. Harper or the Conservative Party.

4

Three Dimensions of Justice for Evaluating Electoral Systems

Jean-Pierre Derriennic

There are two major reasons for changing Canada's electoral system. The first has long been recognized: by making parliamentary representation impossible for parties that are in the minority locally, it amplifies conflicts amongregions. The second has developed in the last ten years or so: a single-member electoral system generates an increasing number of perverse effects the further the party system moves from a simple two-party model.

There are, furthermore, two main obstacles to any electoral reform. The first is that the new electoral system must be adopted by a parliament elected under the old rules. Even if a reform is desirable for the population as a whole, it is not usually so for the party in government. If the latter manages to convince itself that it would gain in the medium term from a reform, this will not be true for each of its members of Parliament, as reform will make it less likely or even impossible for some of them to be re-elected. The second obstacle is related to the fact that many citizens tend to think of voting procedures as only technical matters, exaggerating their complexity and underestimating their political consequences. Politicians who claim to be able to explain the effects of free trade to voters believe that it is impossible to explain to them the impact of a new electoral system, even though the latter effects would be much less uncertain. They themselves often pretend, moreover, not to understand anything about these effects.

I therefore consider it important to set out the technical aspects of different electoral systems as clearly as possible, to show that they involve simple enough mechanisms and to demonstrate how much their political consequences can differ. It is above all important to show that these consequences bring principles into play. The technical aspects of electoral systems will certainly never arouse great passion among the masses, but there may be a small chance of transforming these underlying principles into public concerns, as happened in the past in relation to the undoubtedly less important issue of party funding.

The choice of an electoral system is often presented as a trade-off between fairness and effectiveness, the former being viewed as equity in the distribution of elected officials between the political parties and the latter as the possibility of effective decision-making. This is perhaps not the best way to characterize the problem nor to make its importance understood. Equity among political parties is but a secondary value that must only be respected to the extent that it contributes to a more fundamental value: equality among citizens.

Therefore, at least three dimensions must be considered in determining whether or not an electoral system is just. To what extent does it help to encourage or compel those in government to concern themselves equally with the interests of all those being governed? To what extent does it permit the consideration of all opinions that are politically pertinent, or as many of these as possible? To what extent does it provide for the removal of governments without violence (which was for Karl Popper the central function of democracy)?

The first two dimensions are complementary. The third transects the other two. The electoral system that appears to be most equitable is worthless if it does not allow for any effective decision. And the most vital decision in a democracy is not to choose leaders, which citizens always do somewhat blindly, but to remove them from office, without risk to life and limb, when they have demonstrated that they are, or have become, useless or dangerous. On this last point, Popper is undoubtedly right to apply to politics the central reasoning of his philosophy of science. Falsity is more easily recognized than truth, and we get closer to the truth by successively eliminating the theories that have been demonstrated to be false. Similarly, one can never know with certainty what those in government will do, nor whether their decisions will have beneficial effects. It is easier to know what they have done and what disasters they have caused, before deciding to remove them and replace them with a new team whose incompetence or harmful character have not yet been demonstrated.

There is wisdom in this minimum conception of democracy, from which Popper arrives at a strong defence of the single-member-majority or, more exactly, single-member-plurality (first-past-the-post) system as being the only one that allows citizens to reject a government decisively. However, this is undoubtedly an exaggerated conclusion. Rulers, like scientific theories, should not be eliminated in any which way, subject only to the restriction that removal be done without violence. This is why the other two dimensions of fairness must be brought into play — equality among citizens and the consideration of all pertinent opinions.

The first-past-the-post electoral system is profoundly questionable from the perspective of equality among citizens. The electoral weight of these citizens depends on whether they live in more or less populated constituencies. This shortcoming is well known. While impossible to eliminate altogether, this imbalance can be reduced by changing the boundaries of constituencies on a regular basis so as to reduce demographic differences.

However, this voting procedure brings with it a second, much more serious, inequality between citizens. It results in what could be called "localism," a discrimination between people based on where they live. The power that a voter has is proportional to the probability that he or she is a marginal voter, the one whose vote determines the outcome of the election. This probability is significant in constituencies where the result is very close; it is insignificant where the gap between the parties is very wide. Since the parties often know ahead of time which constituencies are already lost or won, they focus their efforts on the ones that are most hotly contested. This may influence their electoral strategies, which is perhaps not so serious. However, this may also influence their way of governing. It would hardly be advantageous to buy voters with taxpayers' money if it were necessary to buy them all, as those who lose out would be just as numerous as those who stood to win. But patronage becomes an effective political strategy if, using the money of all taxpayers, it is enough to buy only some of the voters, that is, those who live in the few constituencies where the outcome of elections is decided. This is one of the reasons why our governments provide firms and associations with innumerable grants that have little economic or social justification. Priority should be given to denouncing localism-based discrimination in an eventual judicial challenge to Canada's current electoral system.

This phenomenon disappears altogether in voting without geographical districts, such as referendums, direct elections of heads of state (but it is huge in the case of the indirect election of the president of the United States through the electoral college system), nationwide proportional systems, and certain mixed compensatory PR systems. The principle of equality of citizens is much better respected under these systems, since the probability of being a marginal voter is the same for everybody. Localism-based discrimination becomes weaker in elections with proportional representation, in which there are fewer "wasted" votes — those that do not serve to elect anybody. The objection often made to proportional systems, however, is that they achieve equality through impoverishment, as they give nearly the same influence to all voters, but an influence that in the aggregate is much weaker than that provided by a first-past-the-post system.

With the alternative vote (sometimes also called "preferential" or "transferable" vote), voters can indicate an order of preference for candidates rather than a single preference for one of the candidates. This system greatly reduces the number of wasted votes as those who want to vote for a candidate who has absolutely no chance of winning can give their second or third preference to a candidate from one of the major parties. By eliminating triangular elections, which can be won with approximately one third of the votes, the legitimacy of results is reinforced. It reduces but does not eliminate localism-based discrimination among voters. This can only be completely eliminated through a proportional system.

The principal merits of the alternative voting system relate to the second dimension of fairness identified above, the consideration of all pertinent opinions. Popper's reasoning is that the least-bad government is obtained through trial and error, by giving citizens the possibility of quite easily removing incompetent or unfair governments. The first-past-the-post system and the bipartisan model sometimes offer this possibility, when the two opposing parties are aligned with the major political views among the population. However, the same mechanism gives citizens very few means to encourage or compel these parties to change should they become inflexible or incapable of dealing with the political issues of the day. In fact, citizens who create a new party because they are dissatisfied with the party that has hitherto represented them initially increase the chances of victory of the party that is furthest from their preferences. This was the experience of the Labour Party in Great Britain in the early twentieth century, the Liberal Democrats in the 1980s, and the Reform Party in Canada recently. This thus has an extremely powerful deterrent effect on partisan innovation.

With a system of proportional representation, there is a danger that citizens will always be governed by the same more or less centrist parties, according to coalitions that can vary slightly at each election without causing any of the parties to leave power. With a first-past-the-post system, citizens sometimes have to choose between two evils: either trying to change the party system, accepting the risk that the parliamentary system will be dysfunctional for a few decades, or remaining long-term prisoners of an unsatisfying party system. Alternative voting offers an elegant solution to this problem which Canada has had for about a decade. Alternative voting applied to single-member constituencies would have the following effects. The probability that one party would form the majority in the House would not decrease and could even increase for the big middle-of-the-road parties, which are more adept at drawing in second preference votes. The chance that minor parties would elect members would not increase and could even decrease. But since voters would no longer have to worry about wasting their votes, the minor parties could get a greater number of votes, including in constituencies where they have no chance of winning. These parties could thus play a more important role in the public debate. The major parties would have to take more account of the positions defended by the minor parties, because they would know how many of their candidates were elected owing to the second preferences of voters whose first preference was going to such a minor party. Founding and developing a new party would be less difficult and would no longer work primarily in favour of the major party whose views are most at odds with those taking the initiative.

With alternative voting, voters can avoid being confined to a simplistic choice, without sacrificing effective decision-making. It should not be considered as a technical matter that is recommended according to the circumstances, but, like the secret ballot, as an ethical rule made necessary out of respect for the intelligence of citizens and their freedom.

It is important to understand that the basic mechanism of the alternative voting system, which consists in allowing the voter to express his or her multiple, ordered preferences, can be adapted to any type of electoral system, whether single-member-majority or proportional. It is highly likely that in all cases alternative voting improves the electoral system on to which it is grafted.

If a single-member system is considered necessary in order to have members who are close to the population and stable government majorities, there is no excuse for preserving the current voting procedure rather than allowing voters to cast a vote that is more complete, balanced, and which involves fewer risks of perverse effects. In Canada, alternative voting would correct one of the two major disadvantages of our current system — the uncertainty that results, in a multiparty situation, from a large number of local triangular elections won with not much more than one third of the votes. This results in a dual risk, that is, either the same party will remain in power for a very long time, or a party that has been clearly rejected by more than half of the population will still be able to form a government. Alternative voting would not upset our political life or the composition of the House of Commons. It would only give us more legitimate electoral results, since all the members of Parliament would be elected with a majority of the votes cast, along with more viable and influential minor parties, major parties that pay more attention to the opinions of their voters, and a less stagnant political life.

If one form or another of proportional representation is considered desirable, to put an end to the amplification of conflicts among regions or for other reasons, alternative voting is still possible. The simplest method would be to ask voters to indicate their order of preferences, no longer among individual candidates but among lists of candidates presented by the parties. Used in this way, alternative voting would have two main advantages.

The first advantage would be to make a very moderate proportional representation more legitimate. The main criticism made of proportional representation is that it results in too many political parties, which may become a cause of government instability. To limit this disadvantage, either a minimum threshold of votes could be imposed in order for a party to elect representatives (for example, 5 percent, 10 percent or even 20 percent of all votes), or quite small constituencies could be drawn (for example, with three to five seats). Thus there would still be wasted votes, though many fewer than in a first-past-the-post system. In such a system, it would be entirely appropriate to allow voters to vote freely for their favourite minor party and to indicate their subsequent preferences for the major parties. In this way, they would not have to make strategic calculations before voting, and the minor parties which are unable to elect members would be ensured greater participation in public debate.

The second advantage of alternative voting in proportional representation is that it would usefully influence alliances between the parties. Proportional representation tends to give rise to a multiparty system, which often makes coalition governments necessary. In some countries (Weimar Germany, France's Fourth Republic, Turkey or Israel), these coalitions have been unstable or paralyzed, and scandalous in the eyes of many citizens. In other countries (Netherlands, Spain, Germany or contemporary France), these coalitions are ideologically coherent, predictable and approved by the voters. Alternative voting gives voters the means to make their opinions known on acceptable alliances and to reject parties that do not take those opinions into account. Consequently, if a proportional system is adopted, it will still be useful to graft a form of alternative voting on to it as an antidote to incoherent government coalitions.

An alternative voting formula can also be used with a mixed electoral system, either to elect members in single-member constituencies, which was recommended by the Jenkins report in Great Britain, or to enhance the proportional dimension of the vote, or to do both at once.

One of the most successful combinations of moderate proportional representation and alternative voting is the "single transferable vote" used in Ireland. It allows voters to indicate both their order of preferences for the parties and for the candidates presented by the parties in constituencies that have at least three seats. This system allows voters to vote judiciously and intelligently. It encourages stable coalitions and the major middle-of-the-road parties without completely depriving the minor parties of the possibility to participate in political life. It should be of great interest to those who think that party discipline has become excessive and that voters should have more influence over the choice of persons who represent them. In Canada, it would make it possible to do away with the amplification of conflicts between regions resulting from our current electoral system.

Other innovative combinations of moderate proportional representation and alternative voting are possible. In an article published by *Policy Options* in November 1997, I described a system that would not be any more complex than that of Ireland and that would make it possible to achieve three objectives that are often considered incompatible: to give voters an effective influence over the choice of the persons, and not only the parties, who represent them; to eliminate the amplification of conflicts among regions; and, nevertheless, to maintain the probability that one party would obtain a majority in the House of Commons — a probability at least as high as that which exists today.

To obtain this type of result, it is important to stop confining voters to a simplistic choice and allow them to express multiple preferences. Any electoral reform should include alternative voting, through which the best compromises can be reached between the equality of citizens, the diversity of their opinions and the effectiveness of decision-making processes.

5

New Zealand Adopts PR

Paul Harris

New Zealand's change to the mixed-member proportional (MMP) system of electoral representation reveals the kinds of complex interactions of events, personalities and pressures that are present in any major public policy process. Ultimately, politicians found that they had — directly and indirectly, wittingly and unwittingly — unleashed forces they thought they could control but found they could not. Once the change had occurred, they found the political game had new rules to which they had to adapt. Some adapted successfully, others did not.

In 1998 Keith Jackson and Alan McRobie published a detailed history of New Zealand's change to MMP.[1] I agree with most of their analysis and their conclusions, and I recommend their book to anyone looking for more detailed information than I can provide here. I should emphasize that this paper presents a personal view of the way New Zealand's change to MMP came about, and is not necessarily the view of the Electoral Commission on which I served. I should add that the process of electoral reform in New Zealand was the result of our country's unique circumstances, and it is for others to decide for themselves what aspects of our experience may be relevant to their own situation.

So why did New Zealand change from the first-past-the-post system (FPTP) it had used since 1913 to MMP? Three sets of factors were particularly important: election results, the Royal Commission on the Electoral System and the political context. In what follows, I shall outline each, describe the reform process and our three MMP elections, and then say something about current public attitudes to MMP. I shall conclude by briefly discussing the outlook for MMP.

By the late 1930s Labour and National had emerged as New Zealand's two major parties. No minor parties made much electoral impact until the mid-1950s when Social Credit began to gain some support, although probably largely as the result of protest votes. In the eight general elections from 1954 to 1975, Social Credit gained an average of nine percent of the vote, but won only one of the 653 seats it contested. As Labour had done when it was a struggling new party under FPTP, Social Credit advocated proportional representation.

The 1978 election was an important milestone in New Zealand's journey toward MMP. Labour received 10,000 more votes than National, a margin of 0.6 percent of the total number cast, but won just 40 seats compared to National's 51. This convinced many in Labour that FPTP was biased against it. Social Credit won 16 percent of the nationwide vote and one seat, but what was important was that some members of a major party began to share Social Credit's concern about FPTP.

After the 1978 election a parliamentary committee was established to inquire into various aspects of electoral law and administration. For reasons that are not entirely clear, its terms of reference included whether there should be any change to the voting system. The committee decided that there was not a strong case for a change and by majority rejected a proposal from the Labour members that a Royal Commission should be appointed to carry out an authoritative re-examination of New Zealand's electoral system, including the voting system.

That proposal became part of Labour's policy at the 1981 election. When National again won more seats than Labour with fewer votes, some Labour MPs grew more determined to review the electoral system when next in government. Social Credit's difficulties were again clearly evident: although it won 21 percent of the nationwide votes, it won only two of the 92 seats.

Within seven months of its victory at the 1984 election, the new Labour government established an independent nonpartisan Royal Commission to conduct a wide-ranging inquiry into electoral matters. The commission's report, *Towards a Better Democracy*, was published at the end of 1986 and contained two unanimous recommendations about the voting system.[2] First, to the surprise of the major parties and the delight of the smaller parties, and after a careful assessment of the strengths and weaknesses of FPTP and alternative voting systems, it recommended that FPTP should be replaced by the system used in Germany, which the commission called "mixed-member proportional" or MMP.

The commission's second recommendation was crucial to subsequent events. It said that the final decision about whether or not to change from FPTP to MMP should not be made by Parliament but by the people in a binding referendum held after a period of public debate. This recommendation was based on a number of considerations. First, a new *Electoral Act* passed in 1956 provided that certain provisions, including the voting system, could only be changed by a vote of 75 percent of all MPs or by a majority of votes cast at a referendum. Second, the Royal Commission believed that major constitutional changes should only be made by referendum. Third, New Zealand had long experience with referendums. Triennial "General Licensing Polls" on liquor licensing were held from 1911 to 1989, usually at each general election. Other referendums had been held on gambling, compulsory military training and whether the term of Parliament should be increased from three to four years. For each nonlicensing referendum, Parliament passed a special act to authorise the holding of the referendum, stating the question to be asked and specifying the procedures to be followed (usually drawing on those in the *Electoral Act*).

At the time, it seemed very unlikely that the Royal Commission's recommendations concerning a change to MMP would be accepted. Neither Labour nor National supported a proportional voting system, although a few MPs in each party did support a change, including Geoffrey Palmer, Labour's deputy leader. In the mid-1980s, there was no significant public interest in electoral reform.

Over time, however, it became more and more difficult for politicians to ignore the issue. A lobby group, the Electoral Reform Coalition (ERC), had been formed in mid-1986 to promote proportional representation. It was greatly assisted by having unanimous and clear recommendations from a nonpartisan and authoritative body which had carefully considered the arguments for and against electoral reform. After some internal debate, the ERC agreed to focus on MMP as the only alternative to FPTP and on the Royal Commission's recommendation for a referendum as a clear and overtly democratic process by which the decision should be made.

Although it was not well-resourced, the ERC managed to keep the issue of electoral reform on the political agenda throughout New Zealand by the effective use of the techniques of grass roots political activity. Its efforts were given a significant boost in a live television debate during the 1987 election campaign, when one of the ERC's leaders extracted a clear undertaking from the prime minister that Labour would hold a referendum on electoral reform. It was later revealed that the prime minister had misread his briefing notes and that such a referendum was not Labour policy.[3]

In my view, however, the most crucial factor in New Zealand's change to MMP was changing public attitudes to politics and politicians. It gradually became clear that a major shift in those attitudes had occurred from about the mid-1970s to the late 1980s and then into the early 1990s. The prime minister from 1975 to 1984 (who was also finance minister throughout that period) dominated politics through a strong and combative style of leadership which clearly demonstrated the Executive's control of Parliament. Then the new Labour government elected in 1984 came to be regarded as having deceived the voters, first by imposing a radically different model of economic and state-sector management without notice and against widespread public opposition, and then by not significantly changing course after being re-elected at the 1987 election despite undertakings to do so. Labour's refusal to honour its leader's election undertaking to hold a referendum on electoral reform was seen as further evidence of the disconnection of political representatives from those they were meant to represent. The public saw politicians as unwilling to extend the free market model they readily applied elsewhere to matters where their own interests were at stake.

Although the Royal Commission's report had been published before the peak of popular discontent with the Labour government, those looking for ways to reassert popular and parliamentary control over governments soon began to use its recommendation for a referendum on MMP as a means of doing so. The ERC and other advocates of electoral reform found an increasingly receptive audience. The strength and political importance of this public opinion combined with calculations of political advantage to the point that the election manifestos of all major and minor parties at the 1990 election included a promise to hold a referendum on the voting system.

In fact, the new National government elected in 1990 decided that it would hold two referendums. The first would be a stand-alone referendum to establish whether there was a popular desire for a change to the voting system and, if so, which of four "reform options" voters preferred — the single transferable vote system, the alternative or preferential vote system used to elect the Australian House of Representatives, MMP, and the supplementary member system (which is similar to MMP except that only list seats are allocated proportionally rather than list seats being allocated to parties so that there is an overall proportional allocation of all the seats in Parliament, as under MPP). The government said that if a majority of those voting in 1992 supported change, there would be a second binding referendum at the time of the 1993 general election at which voters would choose between FPTP and the reform option receiving the most support in the first referendum.

The first referendum was held on 19 September 1992 — coincidentally the 99th anniversary of the day universal suffrage was granted to New Zealand women. Parliament passed specific legislation for the conduct of the referendum and did not impose campaign spending limits.

The government appointed and funded an independent ministerial panel chaired by the Chief Ombudsman to carry out a neutral public information campaign concerning the referendum and the four reform options. However the panel faced a major problem because of the lack of detail about how each of the alternative systems would be implemented — whether, for example, they would include the Royal Commission's recommendations for an increase in the number of seats in Parliament to 120 or for the abolition of the electorate seats reserved for Māori.

The ERC had been promoting MMP since the Royal Commission reported six years earlier. It virtually had the field to itself, since the opposition to electoral reform was relatively muted and unorganized. Some politicians from both major parties tried to defend FPTP, but soon found that their efforts tended to increase support for reform. The public mood had become even more distrustful of politicians, since the National government elected in 1990 was regarded as continuing Labour's reforms and as having broken some of the specific promises it had made to the voters. Some voters began to ask whether there were any real differences between the two major parties. Although there was a good deal of public interest in the referendum, the political climate in 1992 was not conducive to a dispassionate debate on the merits of FPTP and the reform options.

Although voters were expected to favour a change in the voting system and to prefer MMP as the preferred alternative to FPTP, the margins of victory were completely unforeseen. In a turnout of 55.2 percent of registered voters:

- 84.7 percent voted for a change to the voting system
- 70.5 percent voted for MMP
- 17.4 percent voted for the single-transferable-vote system
- 6.6 percent voted for the preferential-voting system
- 5.6 percent voted for the supplementary-member system

The leader of the Opposition commented immediately after the referendum: "The people didn't speak on Saturday, they screamed."[4]

The second referendum was held in November 1993 in conjunction with the general election. Parliament passed two *Acts* after a select committee had considered submissions from the public. The first, concerning the conduct of the referendum, was similar to that for the 1992 referendum. The second was a new *Electoral Act* to implement MMP. It would automatically replace the old electoral law if the official result of the 1993 referendum showed that a majority of voters did in fact support a change to MMP.

Few politicians became actively involved in the debate in 1993 and the major parties did not state policies on the issue. However the ERC no longer had the field to itself. A new group, the Campaign for Better Government (CBG), was formed in May 1993 to oppose the change to MMP. The CBG was seen as supported by business interests and, being extremely well-resourced compared to the ERC, it was able to run a professional advertising campaign opposing MMP. Public support for MMP began to decline markedly after the CBG began its campaign. Late in the passage of the new *Electoral Act* that would implement MMP, the CBG unsuccessfully argued that a change to a new electoral system should require the approval of a majority of registered voters, not just a majority of those who voted.

Once again, an independent panel was appointed to carry out a neutral government-funded programme of public information about the options at the 1993 referendum. Because the panel had a detailed law on MMP it could be specific on the details of both FPTP and MMP. Based on its regular survey research, the panel concluded that at the time of the referendum there were roughly equal levels of public knowledge of the main features of FPTP and MMP.[5]

Polling just before the referendum also showed approximately equal levels of support for FPTP and MMP. Because the 1993 referendum was held in conjunction with a general election, the turnout (85.2 percent of registered voters) was much greater than it had been at the 1992 referendum. The referendum resulted in a narrow but decisive public endorsement of MMP, by 54 percent to 46 percent.

Once the result of the 1993 referendum was known, preparations for MMP began in earnest. Parliament's *Standing Orders* were revised, a major review was undertaken of the ways the public service would carry out its responsibilities under multiparty governments, and the governor-general publicly clarified his role in relation to government formation. Political parties had to review their structures and establish new candidate selection procedures for MMP. The reduction in the number of electorate seats from 99 under FPTP to 65 under MMP meant there were hard-fought selection contests among some incumbent MPs of the same party.

Two factors underlined the urgency of these preparations. First, because of the reduction in the number of electorate seats, electorate boundaries had to be completely redrawn before an MMP election could be held. That task was completed in April 1995. Second, the National government had been re-elected in 1993 with a majority of one seat (which it held by 54 votes).

The timing of the first MMP election became increasingly uncertain. MMP would obviously improve the electoral chances of small parties, and new parties began to be formed, both inside and outside Parliament. In the two years before the 1996 election, 13 of the 99 MPs left their former parties to join established parties or to form new ones. As a result, the form of government changed from single-party majority government to a majority coalition in September 1994, then to a minority coalition in May 1995, then to a single-party minority government (August 1995), then back to a majority coalition (February 1996), and finally in March 1996 — seven months before the first MMP election — to another minority coalition.[6] Although these changes passed largely unnoticed by the public, they provided the public service and Parliament with invaluable pre-MMP experience of a multiparty majority and minority government. Nevertheless, through skillful political management and because of the parties' need for time to prepare for an MMP election, the National-led government survived in its various forms until the first MMP election was held in October 1996.

This election went relatively smoothly, although there was some criticism of the extra time it took on election night to get provisional results under the new system. Six of the 21 registered parties which contested the party vote at the election won seats, including two parties not previously elected to Parliament (although one had been formed through defections). Official turnout was 88.2 percent of registered voters, compared to 85.2 percent in 1993. A total of 7.6 percent of all the party votes were cast for parties which did not win seats in Parliament.

As expected, no party won a majority of seats at the election. The government formation process after the election was unsettling for the public. New Zealand First was the pivotal party, and it decided to conduct parallel coalition negotiations with National and with Labour (which would also have needed support from the Alliance Party). Contrary to many expectations, after nine weeks of negotiations, New Zealand First decided to form a coalition with the National Party. A very detailed coalition agreement was signed on 11 December 1996, the day before the law required the new MMP Parliament to meet for the first time and exactly 10 years to the day since the members of the Royal Commission on the Electoral System signed the letter of transmittal of its report to the Governor-General.

The period from 1996 to the 1999 election marked another stage in New Zealand's transition to MMP. The National-New Zealand First coalition ended in August 1998, but National continued to lead the government to full term with the support of newly-independent MPs (some of whom had been members of New Zealand First) and ACT New Zealand. These and other defections from parties provoked considerable public and political resentment.

Twenty-two parties contested the 1999 general election and seven parties won seats (the Green Party was elected to Parliament in its own right whereas in 1996 it had been part of the Alliance Party). Official turnout declined to 84.8 percent of registered voters — the lowest since the mid-1970s. A total of 6.0 percent of all the party votes were cast for parties which did not win seats in Parliament.

Labour and the Alliance had been discussing a possible coalition for 18 months before the 1999 election, and shortly after election day they announced an agreement to form a two-party majority coalition government based on provisional election night results in which the Green Party narrowly failed to win any seats.[7] Once final election results confirmed that the Green Party had won seven seats, the Labour-Alliance government was reduced to 59 of the 120 seats, and the Greens agreed to support the government on confidence and supply while remaining outside the government.

Within two years, however, internal dissension within the Alliance came to a head, ostensibly over the government's support for the "war on terrorism," and became so serious that the party split. Ironically, the passage of the anti-defection legislation (discussed below) meant that the party's MPs were forced to remain together for parliamentary purposes, even as the party leader and some of his parliamentary colleagues were supporting the formation of a new party (the Progressive Coalition) to contest the 2002 election.

The Prime Minister cited the wasting of parliamentary time over the Alliance's internal difficulties as the major reason why she decided to hold a general election in late July 2002 rather than the expected time of October or November. Other factors, however, were also thought to have influenced her decision: favourable opinion polls seemed to offer Labour a chance of winning a majority of seats in its own right, the National Party had not gained traction following the election of a new leader in October 2001, and there was some speculation that the economy would begin to slow later in 2002.[8]

Seven of the 14 parties that contested the 2002 election won seats, with the Progressive Coalition supplanting the Alliance.[9] The election was, however, notable on several counts:

- levels of voter enrolment reached a record 94 percent of the estimated age-eligible population;
- the turnout of 77 percent of registered voters was the lowest for a century;
- the National Party's 21 percent support (27 seats) was the lowest since the party's formation in the 1930s;
- the proportion of party votes cast for parties which did not achieve representation dropped further to 4.9 percent;
- a late surge in support for United Future New Zealand (8 seats) meant that the Labour (52 seats) and the Progressive Coalition (2 seats) were able to form a minority coalition government with support from United Future rather than having to rely on the Green Party (9 seats) — a welcome result for Labour since there were fundamental policy differences between it and the Greens concerning genetic modification.

Prior to the breakup of the Alliance, party alignments and MMP politics in general seemed to be more or less settled after an unexpectedly long transition period since 1996. The period since the 2002 election has again held out that prospect, with parties regarded as left or centre-left (Greens, Progressive Coalition, Labour) facing those regarded as centre-right or right (National and ACT, plus probably the populist NZ First party). United Future sits between these groupings, seeing itself as a genuine centre party available to support governments from either the centre-left or the centre-right according to the voters' verdict. Although there are policy differences — sometimes fundamental — among the parties within each grouping, the experience of three elections under MMP has begun to establish those groupings as the basis of alternative governments. Each general election therefore establishes which of the groupings is ascendant (although that was not clear-cut in 1996) and sets the relative bargaining power of the parties necessary to form a government that has the confidence of the House.

Two other matters arising out of New Zealand's change to MMP should also be noted. First, the defections (or "party-hopping") that allowed a National-led government to survive after the end of the National-New Zealand First coalition in 1998 so angered opposition parties and the public that one of the first bills introduced by the new Labour-Alliance government after the 1999 election sought to prevent any further occurrences. The bill was opposed by the Green Party but was passed in late 2001 with the support of NZ First. It will expire on the day of the next general election, which is expected to be held in 2005.

In its final form, the amendments mean that the seat of any electorate or list MP becomes vacant if the MP ceases to be a parliamentary member of the party for which he or she was elected to Parliament. This will occur in the following circumstances:

- if the MP notifies the Speaker that he or she has resigned from their party or wishes to be recognised in Parliament as an independent or as a member of another party; or
- if the party leader notifies the Speaker that the leader "reasonably believes that the member of Parliament concerned has acted in a way that has distorted, and is likely to continue to distort, the proportionality of political party representation in Parliament as determined at the last general election" (section 55D(a), *Electoral Act 1993*), and that at least two-thirds of the party caucus agree that the leader should notify the Speaker accordingly.

No party-hopping has occurred since this legislation was passed. As noted above, however, it caused some difficulties for the Labour-Alliance minority government before the 2002 election. It has also been invoked by the parliamentary leadership of the ACT party following expulsion from the party of a list MP who is facing criminal charges. That MP is contesting the application of the legislation to her circumstances and the matter is before the courts at the time of writing.

Secondly, the act to implement MMP required a parliamentary select committee to be appointed to review MMP after the second election under the new system. That committee was established in April 2000 to report by June 2002 on the following specific matters:

- the law relating to setting general electorate boundaries;
- the legal provisions relating to Māori representation;
- whether there should be a further referendum on changes to the electoral system and, if so, which proposals should be put to the voters and the timing of such a referendum;
- the appropriate number of MPs, taking account of the results of the non-binding citizens initiated referendum held with the 1999 general election (in which 82 percent of those voting supported a reduction in the number of MPs to 99);
- the extent to which party lists have resulted in better representation of women;
- the effectiveness of MMP in relation to representation of Māori and ethnic minorities.

All parliamentary parties were represented on the 10-member committee, except NZ First, which declined an invitation to participate or to make submissions. The committee was chaired by the Speaker and sought public submissions on its terms of reference. In establishing the committee, however, the House imposed a decision-making rule similar to that used in the Business Committee of the House:[10]

Select committees as a general rule make decisions by a simple majority vote. The MMP review committee, however, was established under different decision-making rules. The committee was charged with making recommendations that may have major constitutional and political significance. The House therefore directed members to reach conclusions on the basis of unanimity, or if this was not possible, near-unanimity, having regard to the numbers in the House represented by each of the members of the committee. The chairperson was directed by the House to be the judge of whether unanimity was possible and, if not, whether a sufficient degree of near-unanimity had been reached for the committee to reach a conclusion. These changes to normal committee operating procedures were made to ensure a fair process for the smaller parties

represented on the committee who, because of their size, are more likely to be outvoted, and to avoid 'bloc' voting by a majority.

The effect of this rule was to make major change "highly improbable,"[11] and so
it proved. The Committee reached unanimous agreement on five issues, all for
the status quo, and near-unanimity that closed national lists should continue.[12]
Although no changes were made to MMP as a result of the committee's work,
Church and McLeay comment that this "might not have been the worst possible outcome. Electoral systems take time to become established and legit-
imated, and it was surely far too soon to contemplate major changes to MMP."[13]

The change to MMP has revealed that there is a general lack of public understanding among New Zealanders of their parliamentary democracy. For the first
time in recent years, there has been systematic research on New Zealanders' understanding of their system of government, along with attempts to increase that
understanding. The research reveals that New Zealand is similar to other democratic countries in having significant gaps in public knowledge about electoral and
parliamentary matters (particularly among young people, women, Māori and ethnic minorities). Although little systematic research is available, it seems too that
there were similar levels of ignorance of the previous FPTP system.

Experiences since the 1996 election have clearly affected public attitudes to
MMP. One public opinion poll shows that, when given a choice between FPTP
and MMP, the majority prefers MMP around the time of a general election but
prefers FPTP in-between elections.[14] Other polling shows, however, that support for MMP is higher than support for FPTP when respondents can choose
other voting system options.[15]

Moreover, survey research also shows that the major influences on New
Zealanders' views on MMP are their attitudes to recent and current governments elected by the system. Most people make these judgements irrespective
of the basic features of the system (which in many cases they may barely understand) or its merits or consequences as an electoral system rather than as an
entire system of government. There are also suggestions that MMP may have
been "oversold" in that some members of the public had unrealistic expectations of what a change in the electoral system could achieve.

The referendum victory that brought MMP came just seven years after the
Royal Commission recommended its adoption. In their history of the change to
MMP, Keith Jackson and Alan McRobie conclude that, from the points of view
of the major parties, the introduction of MMP was "reform by misadventure"
and was "no copy-book model of how reform can be achieved."[16] On the other
hand, MMP's victory was an unambiguous reassertion of popular sovereignty
against the wishes of the major parties. Despite the difficulties of isolating caus-

es in any complex process, it is difficult to avoid the conclusion that the most important factor in the adoption of MMP was the mood of those who felt betrayed by the actions of successive governments of different parties from the mid-1980s to the early 1990s. MMP is one of only two of New Zealand's "adventures in democracy" that occurred "in response to significant public demand and after an intense period of debate," the other being the introduction of women's suffrage a century earlier.[17] All the signs are that the future of MMP will depend more on public attitudes to what MPs, parties and governments do than on their attitudes to the mechanics of the electoral system.

Notes

1. Keith Jackson and Alan McRobie, *New Zealand Adopts Proportional Representation: Accident? Design? Evolution?* (Aldershot: Ashgate, 1998).

2. Royal Commission on the Electoral System, *Towards a Better Democracy, Appendices to the Journals of the House of Representatives*, H.3, 1986.

3. Jackson and McRobie, *New Zealand Adopts Proportional Representation*, pp. 46-48.

4. Stephen Levine and Nigel S. Roberts, "The Referendum Results: 'The People Screamed,'" in Alan McRobie (ed.), *Taking it to the People? The New Zealand Electoral Referendum Debate* (Christchurch: Hazard Press, 1993), pp. 57-67.

5. Electoral Referendum Panel, *Report on the Public Information Campaign Organised in Conjunction with the Electoral Referendum Held on 6 November 1993*, Appendices to the Journals of the House of Representatives, E.9A, 1993.

6. Electoral Commission, *The New Zealand Electoral Compendium*, 3rd ed. (Wellington: Electoral Commission, 2002), p. 185.

7. Jonathan Boston, "Forming the Coalition between Labour and the Alliance," in Jonathan Boston et al. (eds.) *Left Turn: The New Zealand General Election of 1999* (Wellington: Victoria University Press, 2000), pp. 239-75.

8. Stephen Church, "Going Early," in Jonathan Boston et al. (eds.), *New Zealand Votes: The 2002 General Election* (Wellington: Victoria University Press, 2003), pp. 33-38.

9. *The New Zealand Electoral Compendium*, pp. 66-67, 168-75.

10. MMP Review Committee (New Zealand House of Representatives, *Inquiry into the Review of MMP*, Appendices to the Journals of the House of Representatives, I.23A, 2001, p. 10; available at www.clerk.parliament.govt.nz//content/20/mmprevw.pdf

11. Stephen Church and Elizabeth McLeay, "The Parliamentary Review of MMP in New Zealand," *Representation*, Vol. 39, no. 4 (2003), p. 249.

12. MMP Review Committee, *Inquiry into the Review of MMP*, p. 11.

13. Church and McLeay, "The Parliamentary Review of MMP in New Zealand," p. 253.

14. Deborah Hill Cone, "Electors yet to Be Won over by the Merits of MMP," *National Business Review*, December 5, 2003, p. 15.

15. Jack Vowles, Jeffrey Karp, Susan Banducci, and Peter Aimer, "Public Opinion, Public Knowledge, and the Electoral System," in Jack Vowles et al. (eds.), *Proportional Representation on Trial: The 1999 New Zealand General Election and the Fate of MMP* (Auckland: Auckland University Press, 2002), p. 163.

16. Jackson and McRobie, *New Zealand Adopts Proportional Representation*, p. 336.

17. Neill Atkinson, *Adventures in Democracy: A History of the Vote in New Zealand* (Dunedin: University of Otago Press, 2003), p. 237.

6

Making Democracy Constitutional

David Beatty

Political scientists have been writing about the inequities of Canada's election laws for a very long time. Alan Cairns's pathbreaking essay, documenting how the *Canada Elections Act* has exacerbated regional tensions in the country, was written in 1968. A decade later, in 1979, William Irvine published his internationally acclaimed book, *Does Canada Need a New Election System*, in which he highlighted these and other discriminatory effects of election laws, (known as the single-member-plurality (SMP) or first-past-the-post (FPTP) system), that award representation (seats) in Parliament and our provincial assemblies to those who win the most votes in geographically defined constituencies.

Since then, many others have added their names to calls for a re-evaluation of the laws we use to translate votes cast in an election into representation in Parliament and our provincial assemblies. All of the more recent studies confirm the biases that Cairns and Irvine had identified against smaller, issue based parties like the Greens and established national parties, like the NDP (and more recently the Progressive Conservatives), whose supporters are spread across the country but which have no realistic hope of winning an election. They also show that our election laws make it much more difficult for women (and members of minority groups who are not concentrated geographically) to stand as candidates and claim their fair share of seats in the legislative and executive branches of government.

The unfairness of election laws that give representation in legislatures only to candidates who win the most votes in geographically defined constituencies is widely understood in other parts of the world. Canada, along with the UK, France (from whom we inherited our political traditions), India and the United States, is one of the few "free and democratic" societies that still conduct their elections on a rule of winner-take-all. A number of countries, including New Zealand, South Africa and Japan have recently scrapped their FPTP laws in favour of systems based on the principle of proportional representation (PR). Even the United Kingdom and France now elect their representatives to the European Parliament on the principle of proportional representation.

In contrast with the spirit of reform that has flourished in other countries, the established institutions of Canadian politics have been embarrassingly resistant to change. So much so that, when Brian Mulroney's Conservative government set up the Lortie Commission on electoral reform in 1989, proportional representation was deliberately kept off the agenda. Even the NDP, whose representation in Parliament would be greatly enhanced if the *Canada Elections Act* were based on the principle of proportional representation, has been unwilling to mount a sustained campaign for reform largely because a few of its provincial cousins have been shameless beneficiaries of the current regime.

Our history suggests it is unlikely that, left on their own, either of the elected branches of government is capable of initiating meaningful electoral reform. Canadian politics has so far not had the benefit of the sorts of serendipitous and seismic events that have precipitated structural changes in the way votes are counted and representatives selected in other parts of the world. If proportional representation is ever to come to Canada, it seems, the third branch of our government — the courts — will have to insist on the change.

The idea that judges could order such a sweeping reform of the way Canadians govern themselves is not as radical as it might first appear. The Supreme Court of Japan, which is widely regarded as one of the most cautious and conservative courts in the world, actually declared three national elections to be unconstitutional before the Japanese government adopted a modified system of proportional representation for the two houses of its National Diet.

Even the most deferential theories of judicial review insist courts should be vigorous and unforgiving in ensuring that laws that define the processes and institutions of politics are held to the highest constitutional standards. Even constitutionalists who believe courts have no business second guessing governments when it comes to social and economic policy, think they do have a duty to police the processes by which representatives are elected to ensure that they are as fair and even-handed as possible. As our own Supreme Court put it in a recent judgment, "it is precisely when legislative choices threaten to undermine the foundations of...democracy...that courts must be vigilant in fulfilling their constitutional duty to protect the integrity of [the] system."

In strictly legal terms, a constitutional challenge to the *Canada Elections Act* (or any provincial elections act) is surprisingly simple and straightforward. All of the major inequities that political scientists have identified in election laws that use the principle of winner-take-all constitute clear violations of either the right to vote (section 3) and/or the right to equality (section 15) that are guaranteed in the Charter of Rights.

The Supreme Court of Canada has characterized the right to vote as one of the Charter's most important guarantees ("one of the touchstones of a free and democratic state") from the very beginning. In its seminal ruling in the *Saskatchewan Electoral Boundaries* case, the Court reflected at some length on what the right to vote should be understood to mean and concluded that its overarching purpose was to ensure the equal and effective representation of every citizen in the country. Relative parity of voting power, the Court said, was a pre-condition of the kind of effective representation that section 3 of Charter guarantees. More recently, in its decision in *Figueroa*, the Court told Parliament that section 3 imposes an obligation on it "not to enhance the capacity of one citizen to participate in the electoral process in a manner that compromises another citizen's parallel right to meaningful participation in the electoral process."

When they are measured against a principle of "equal, meaningful representation," it is hard to imagine how any of our federal or provincial election laws would be able to meet the test. The evidence that has been collected by political scientists since Cairns's, seminal work is overwhelming. It shows our election laws do more to frustrate than further the goals of parity of voting power and meaningful representation of each and every citizen in the country. The fact is that, in virtually every federal and provincial election that has ever been held, some significant number of Canadians can make the claim that their votes were seriously undervalued and they did not receive as effective representation of their political principles and ideas as their numbers, and the representation of others, warranted.

The biases and distortions that Cairns wrote about more than 30 years ago have continued to manifest themselves in more recent elections and, if anything, have gotten even worse. In the last four federal elections, the differences in the value of votes cast for the major parties far exceed the differentials between urban and rural ridings that the Supreme Court approved in the *Electoral Boundaries* case.

In the *Saskatchewan* case, the Court ruled that the province's election law did not violate the right to vote even though some urban ridings had almost twice as many voters as the most sparsely populated rural constituencies. The Court recognized that the value or weight of a rural vote was double that of a ballot cast in an urban riding, but it concluded the disparity was justified because, in its opinion, the effective representation of the most isolated parts of the province required a differential of that size.

In our recent federal elections, the value or weight of a vote cast by a supporter of a Liberal, Bloc or a Reform/Alliance Party candidate has been as much as five, 10, even 30 times greater than a ballot that was marked for the Progressive Conservatives or the New Democrats. On occasion, including two recent elections in Quebec and BC, the distortions have been so severe that the party that won the largest share of the popular vote actually lost the election!

Undoubtedly the most egregious disparities occurred in the 1993 federal election when a Progressive Conservative vote counted for next to nothing. Even though they received more votes than the Bloc Québécois and almost as many as Reform, they only won two seats while the latter got 54 and 52 respectively. In effect, supporters of the Progressive Conservative Party got a seat in the House of Commons for every 1,093,211 votes while the Bloc elected a member of Parliament for every 34,186 votes they received. In terms of electing representatives to give voice to their opinions and points of view, Bloc votes were worth 30 times more than ballots that were marked for Progressive Conservatives.

In the 1993 and 1997 elections, the fortunes of the Progressive Conservatives improved slightly, but the disparities remained shockingly large. In 1997 the Progressive Conservatives held less than half the number of seats occupied by the Bloc Québécois, even though they received almost twice as many votes. In 2000, a Conservative vote was still three times less valuable than a vote for the Bloc.

Voters who support the New Democrats have suffered a similar devaluation of their votes since the birth of their party, as the CCF, in 1935. Although the prejudice to the party has never been as extreme as what the Progressive Conservatives endured in 1993, they have frequently received less than half the number of seats that they would have won had their votes been weighted equally and in 1993 they would have elected three times more MPs if their votes had carried the same weight as the Liberals. Moreover, supporters of the party who live in Quebec have practically been denied any representation in Parliament even in elections when their share of the popular vote in the province has been as high as 15 percent.

Not only are the deviations from parity among supporters of different parties much greater than they were between urban and rural voters in the *Saskatchewan Electoral Boundary* case, neither can they be defended on the basis that they ensure minority groups more meaningful representation, as the preferential treatment of rural voters did in that case. Unlike the disparity of voting power between rural and urban ridings, the inequalities that are caused by the rule of winner-take-all frustrate rather than foster more effective representation of millions of voters. Those who support national parties like the New Democrats, and more recently the Progressive Conservatives, that have no realistic chance of winning an election, never get the representation they deserve. People who vote for small, issue-based parties like the Greens, get no representation at all! In terms of the number of representatives their votes have elected to the House of Commons, supporters of all of these parties have had far less influence in the legislative process and the formation of public policy than Canadians who cast their ballots for the Liberals, the Bloc and the Alliance/Reform.

The fact is that voters who want to back smaller parties like the Greens do not "have a genuine opportunity to take part in the governance of the country through participation in the selection of elected representatives" as the Supreme Court has said they must. Environmentalists do not have as much input into government policy in Canada, as in other parts of the world, precisely because of the way our election laws aggregate their votes. Half a million Canadians voted Green in the 2004 election, but they have no right to speak in any legislative debate.

In addition to the various ways in which our federal and provincial election laws infringe the right to vote of many Canadians, it is also the case that they offend the Charter's guarantee that every person is entitled to the equal benefit and protection of the law, especially in their treatment of women. The fact that women are consistently elected in significantly smaller numbers in elections conducted under laws that are based on the principle of first-past-the-post than under those that use the principle of proportional representation, constitutes a clear violation of the Charter's proscription of discrimination on the basis of sex that is impossible to defend.

In its landmark ruling *Law v. Canada*, the Supreme Court identified the central purpose of the Charter's guaranteeing every Canadian the equal benefit and protection of the law to be "to prevent the violation of [a person's] essential human dignity...through the imposition of disadvantage, stereotyping, or *political* or social *prejudice*" (emphasis added). In considering whether a law discriminates in the way section 15 was meant to proscribe, the Court said reference should be made to a variety of factors including (i) any pre-existing disadvantage endured by those who are prejudiced by the law and (ii) the nature and scope of the interest that is adversely affected.

When Canada's election laws are measured against the test the Supreme Court laid down in *Law*, they fall well short of the mark. Women currently occupy roughly one seat in five in the House of Commons and Provincial Assemblies and that is the highest that it has ever been. By comparison, depending on the time frame that is used, anywhere from two to four times more women have been elected to national assemblies that use the principle of proportional representation. In countries where both systems are used, such as Germany, New Zealand and Australia, women are elected in significantly greater numbers to seats that are not attached to any geographic area than to those that are.

Deliberately designing an election system in a way that systematically results in such underrepresentation of women compounds their "disadvantage" and demeans their "dignity" as persons. Women suffer both in their opportunity to do public service and be elected to our most important governmental institutions and, instrumentally, to the extent that their underrepresentation contributes to the enactment of laws which do not fairly reflect their interests and priorities.

The interests that are prejudiced by our election laws implicate our most basic ideas about how we govern ourselves. There is no social institution that is more fundamental or of greater political significance than Parliament. By making it much more difficult for women to claim their fair share of seats in the House of Commons and provincial assemblies, our electoral laws deny half the population a "basic aspect of full membership in Canadian society." Election laws that impose barriers that inhibit the election of women (as well as aboriginal people and other geographically dispersed minorities) perpetuate a stereotype (of women's traditional role in society) and constitute a profound affront to their dignity and self respect.

To prove that a law violates the Charter, a case must pass through two stages. At first, the onus is on those who say their constitutional rights have been violated to make their case. If, as seems certain in a challenge against any of our election acts, this hurdle is cleared, the case moves on to the second phase, and the onus shifts to the government to justify why a law that does not respect people's constitutional rights should be allowed to remain on the books.

Those who are inclined to defend our current electoral system invariably make the argument that FPTP is a better method of counting votes than PR because it makes for more stable and therefore more effective governments. They say FPTP is more likely to produce majority governments and "foster a strong political centre," which is important in a country like Canada that is so linguistically and geographically diverse.

Although the claim that FPTP is conducive to stronger and more durable governments is still popular in some political circles, it is unlikely to be well received in the courts. Two fundamental problems stand out. Legally, in *Figueroa* the Supreme Court was very emphatic that election laws can't be enacted for the purpose of promoting majority governments because that privileges one group of voters and their parties over others. Empirically, the argument that FPTP does a better job than PR in facilitating the formation of strong, stable governments is flatly contradicted by the facts.

The truth is that many countries including Germany, the Netherlands, Norway and Sweden, which use the principle of proportionality in their election laws, have enjoyed long histories of incredibly stable and effective government. Elected on a mixed system of SMP and PR, German governments led by

Adenauer, Brandt, Schmidt and Kohl have been among the most stable and effective in the free and democratic world.

If election laws are deliberately designed to encourage the proliferation of political parties — by, for example, allowing parties with only a tiny fraction of the total vote (1 or 2 percent) to claim representation in a legislative chamber — instability in government is certain to become part of the system. That is what has happened, for example, in Israel. The experience of Germany and the Scandinavian countries (that use higher — 5 percent — thresholds) proves, however, that laws based on a principle of proportional representation don't have to have such negative effects.

Our own experience confirms that the capacity of FPTP laws to foster all-inclusive majorities and counter factionalism has been greatly exaggerated. In election after election, the way the *Canada Elections Act* requires votes to be counted has resulted in Parliaments dominated by regionally concentrated parties that accentuate and aggravate the fissures and fault lines that cut across the country. Our history proves FPTP is more an antagonist than an ally of a "strong political centre" and the unity of the country more generally.

When our country's election laws are analyzed through the lens of the Charter, their constitutional frailties stand out in stark relief. Regrettably, however, the strength of the argument that all of our country's election laws are blatantly unconstitutional does not mean Canadians can expect fair elections soon. The Constitutional Test Case Centre in the Faculty of Law at the University of Toronto has launched a constitutional challenge to the *Canada Elections Act* in the Ontario Superior Court of Justice on behalf of the Green Party of Canada, but it is unlikely to be heard for a year. If the case proceeds in the usual way, it will take at least another two to three years to make it to the Supreme Court. Beyond that, it is almost certain the Court would give Parliament an additional year or two to study the different models of proportional representation that exist in the world and choose one that is most suitable to our constitutional traditions and needs.

The wheels of justice can grind slowly, but it is important to be clear that the case doesn't need to take this long. The government has the power to refer important constitutional questions directly to the Supreme Court as it has with its proposed legislation on same-sex marriages. If it exercised its prerogative in this case we could be reasonably certain that Paul Martin's government would be the last to be elected without the support of a majority of the citizens in the country.

Only the selfish interests of the Liberal Party are served by requiring the issue to be debated in front of three different courts instead of one. The national interest would be better served if the government asked the Supreme Court to rule directly on the constitutional status of the *Canada Elections Act.* Scarce resources would be saved, and everyone's attention could be focused on the more important question of what particular model of proportional representation will work best for us. Rather than tying the issue up in the courts, and allowing the lawyers to drag on a debate about relatively simple and straightforward questions of constitutional law, ordinary Canadians, through their elected representatives, could become actively involved in the critical research and policy work that needs to be done.

Referring the case directly to the Supreme Court would be a very powerful way for our new prime minister to show he really is committed to democratic reform. It would finally allow Parliament to have the debate about the fairest way for Canadians to choose their elected representatives that Brian Mulroney censured more than fifteen years ago. How Paul Martin instructs his legal team to respond to the Green Party's case will tell us whether he thinks of himself as a Canadian or a Liberal first.

7

Getting from Here to There: A Process for Electoral Reform in Canada

Matthew Mendelsohn and Andrew Parkin
(with Alex Van Kralingen)

This paper leaves aside the question of whether electoral reform is needed and instead considers whether reform is even possible in Canada. As many observers have pointed out, the biggest obstacle to reform is that the political party with the power to initiate change — the governing party — almost certainly will have been rewarded by the quirks of the existing system. Nothing is likely to turn advocates of proportional representation into defenders of the status quo faster than seeing their party win an unexpectedly large parliamentary majority on the basis of 40 percent of the popular vote.

This conventional wisdom, while containing a good deal of truth, would be more convincing if it weren't for the fact that several established and stable liberal democracies — notably New Zealand, Italy, Japan and the United Kingdom (at both the sub- and supranational levels) — have made changes to their electoral systems in recent years. In these countries, a way was found to encourage reluctant political leaders to embrace reform. It is therefore instructive to review these cases briefly and to identify the conditions that facilitated change in order to see what lessons they offer advocates of electoral reform in Canada. Following this review, we will propose a process for reform that includes a referendum to ratify change, but embeds the referendum in a larger mechanism of citizen participation.

In Japan in the 1980s, the Recruit scandal, which involved widespread financial corruption, damaged the careers of many leading Japanese politicians. But much of the blame for the scandal (named after the Recruit Corporation) fell on the electoral system itself and the factionalism and hypercompetitiveness that it bred. In 1988, in the scandal's aftermath, an advisory committee was set up to examine various aspects of the electoral system. In 1990, it produced a report that recommended a mixed electoral system similar to the one found in Germany.

The scandal produced a large number of defections from the Liberal Democratic Party (LDP) that had governed Japan uninterrupted since 1955. These deserters formed a variety of new parties, many with the words "new" and "clean" in their names, all of which featured electoral reform as a prominent plank in their democratic reform agendas. It is certainly possible that they made these promises not out of a genuine commitment to reform but to avoid the electoral retribution that was likely to befall the LDP. This fact, however, high-lights the importance of genuine popular interest in electoral reform: it compels self-interested parties to take up this gauntlet. The new parties did very well in the subsequent elections in 1993, while the LDP dropped 10 points to 37 percent of the vote. After several unsuccessful attempts at putting together a package that would satisfy all coalition members, in 1994 a compromise was finally reached that had three-fifths of the seats elected through first-past-the-post and the remaining two-fifths elected using proportional representation in 11 regional blocks. That compromise was enacted into law in 1994 and the first election under the new rules took place in 1996. Postelection negotiations resulted in a coalition government made up of the Liberal Democrats, the Social Democrats and Sakigake (one of the new parties formed before the 1993 election).

In New Zealand, the Labour Party won more votes than the National Party in the 1978 and 1981 elections, but on both occasions the National Party formed the government. In these two elections, the third party, Social Credit, received first 16 percent and then 20 percent of the national vote, but won just one seat, and then two seats. Although this very high disproportionality clearly put the issue of the electoral system on the agenda for the supporters of the Social Credit, it was the back-to-back losses for Labour that incited it to include in its election platform a promise to appoint a Royal Commission that would consider electoral reform. When Labour won in 1984, it made good on its promise. The Royal Commission examined a wide range of issues and eventu-ally recommended the adoption of a German-style mixed system. As is all too common in such cases, the Labour government then took no action. During the subsequent election campaign of 1987, it promised to hold a binding referen-dum on the issue in its next mandate, but this promise was not honoured. The opposition National Party then attempted to capitalize on Labour's broken promise by making its own promise to hold a referendum, even though the opposition leader, James Bolger, personally opposed PR.

When the National Party was elected in 1990, it largely followed through on its promise, holding an advisory referendum that included two questions: a first asking whether voters wished to retain the existing first-past-the-post system and a second asking which of four reform options voters would prefer, if reform were to occur. Voters overwhelming rejected the existing system (85 percent), and a substantial majority (70 percent) chose the Royal Commission's recommendation of a mixed system, a result that highlights the importance of a recommendation from a credible, neutral source. Fifty-five percent of voters turned out to cast a ballot, a respectable result considering that the referendum was only advisory and no simultaneous election was being held. The results of the 1992 advisory referendum prompted a binding 1993 referendum that asked voters to choose between the new system and the status quo. Voters opted for change by a relatively close margin (54 to 46 percent), with 85 percent of the electorate turning out to vote. One reason for the closeness of the result was that opponents of the changes, backed by big business, were able to outspend proponents by about 10 to one.

The New Zealand process is instructive. The Royal Commission's legitimacy put pressure on the government to act and provided the public with a credible voice to which they could turn for a trusted recommendation. The process also featured what can be described as cascading referendums, in which the voters were asked three separate questions (one including four options) over a period of 14 months. On the face of it, voters made reasonable and informed choices on the usually arcane topic of electoral reform.

In Italy, electoral reform was facilitated by the *referendum abrogativo*, which provides Italian voters with an opportunity to overturn legislation that has been passed by Parliament. In order to initiate a referendum, 500,000 signatures must be collected within a period of 90 days. In the wake of widespread public belief that the country's political parties were rife with corruption and unable to reform themselves, a petition drive in 1991 succeeded in provoking a referendum to strike down parts of the existing electoral law. The initial drive for a referendum was led in part by sitting deputies who did not like the existing system — a fact that highlights how the referendum abrogativo allows dissident parliamentarians to circumvent government leaders.

In the 1991 referendum, 96 percent of voters approved the change. The turnout was 62 percent. The result was a severe reprimand to the existing system and a strong mandate for change. Parliament, however, responded by making only small changes to the existing system. The 1992 election therefore featured continued debate on electoral reform, and for the first time voters were offered the possibility of voting for a party list where all members were committed to more ambitious changes to the electoral system. Following the election, in which the party committed to reform did quite well, a second petition drive was launched and qualified easily. In the ensuing referendum in 1993, 83 percent of voters expressed support for radical reforms to the electoral system (the turnout was 77 percent). This time, Parliament felt compelled to act.

Several points about the Italian experience stand out. First, the referenda passed so overwhelmingly in part because the public attributed the corruption within the parties in large part to the electoral system itself. Second, the presence of the *referendum abrogativo* — an institution which allows voters to strike down existing legislation but not draft their own — was key. The referendum allows those outside the government and the legislature to initiate change. It also produces an ongoing dialogue between the general public, those sponsoring the referenda, existing politicians, the courts (which rule on the legality of referendum questions) and parliament, which, as we have seen, responded to the first referendum by passing moderate reforms, only to be rebuffed again in a second referendum. Finally, because the party elites (or partiocratzia) were in such wide disrepute, many of them felt compelled to make proposals to democratize aspects of the political system, even if they did not want to abandon the country's existing form of PR. For example, Bruno Craxi, the leader of the Socialist Party, called for the direct election of the president. Such proposals stimulated debate about the overall need for change and by so doing gave the issue of electoral reform a higher profile than it might otherwise have had.

The UK currently offers a classic example of how a party's interest in electoral reform can cool once it finds itself in office with a healthy parliamentary majority. After its election victory in 1997, the Labour government appointed an Independent Commission on the Voting System, but after the commission's report it backed away from its pledge to hold a referendum on proportional representation. Electoral reform nevertheless has occurred in the UK since 1997. The new assemblies in Scotland and Wales are elected under a form of PR, and so are the UK's representatives to the European Parliament. Admittedly in the case of Scotland and Wales, it was not a case of changing the electoral system but of putting a new system in place where none previously existed — which highlights the importance of opportunities afforded by rare moments of regime change or constitutional reform. In the case of elections to the European Parliament, the switch to PR can be viewed as a concession that Labour chose to make in order to gain credibility with reformers within the party and among the Liberal Democrats, the third-largest party in the House of Commons.

The Liberal Democrats have played the key role in advancing the debate on electoral reform in the UK. Like many third parties, they are heavily penalized under the first-past-the-post system. Moreover, they not only favour PR but have vigorously championed the cause and state categorically that a referendum on the issue is the sine qua non of their participation in any coalition government. As some recent election campaigns have at one stage or another been close enough to make a hung parliament a realistic outcome, the media have tended to pick up on the issue of electoral reform, pressuring the Labour and Tory leadership to take a stand.

In the absence of a major constitutional or regime change (such as Quebec secession or the creation of new assemblies in Scotland and Wales), the factors that persuade politicians to accept change are quite easy to identify but difficult to reproduce on demand.

The Italian and Japanese systems were beset by major scandals or institutional paralysis that could be credibly blamed on the electoral system. In both cases, existing parties began to disintegrate over issues of corruption and the need for democratic reform. The result was the emergence of new and legitimate parties within the legislature making credible commitments to change.

Thus it appears that unpopular political leaders, recessions, or general declines in confidence in the government are not sufficient conditions for change. Moreover, an even more serious crisis of confidence may not be sufficient if it is attributed to one individual or party: The crisis of confidence must be severe, must be attributable to a deeper problem linked with the electoral system, must force parties to take a stand in favour of reform, and, in the process, must provoke the public to become interested in the issue.

In Japan and Italy, electoral reform was linked with other issues of democratic reform. This too appears to be an enabling condition for reform. By itself, electoral reform can be a technical and arcane issue. But when presented as part of a broader package of democratic reforms, and linked to such other issues as campaign finance reform, it is more likely to capture the public's interest and support.

In New Zealand, Labour Prime Minister David Lange's promise to hold a binding referendum was made inadvertently during a campaign debate, while Japanese Prime Ministers Noboru Takeshita and Sosuke Uno acted in the heat of scandal to initiate political reform and appoint an advisory committee on the electoral system. In both countries, political leaders later tried to downplay their commitments. But the act of badgering a leader during a crisis or an election campaign into promising some kind of process was an important first step in securing reform in both countries.

Debates about electoral reform led by political parties are fueled by self-interest: There is, not surprisingly, a close correlation between parties' positions on the need for change and their expected benefit from any new system. Governing parties usually get a bonus in first-past-the-post systems, as do regionally concentrated smaller parties, while smaller parties with widely distributed support suffer most. Disproportionality and unfairness occur in many countries, however, and yet do not trigger electoral reform. But in New Zealand, the fact that one of the two major parties was consistently punished by the electoral system was an important factor contributing to change. By the time the Labour Party formed a government in 1984, many of its leading figures had concluded that reform would be in the party's interest. The Liberal Party of Quebec is similarly penalized by that province's electoral system: in both 1994 and 1998, the party received about as many votes as the Parti Québécois but lost the elections (in terms of seats) by wide margins. Similarly, in BC, the Liberals lost the 1996 election to the NDP despite winning a greater share of the popular vote. These experiences go a long way to explaining why the Liberal parties in both provinces, now that they are each in government, have decided to seriously examine electoral reform.

Change can take time. In Japan and New Zealand, it took five to seven years from the time of the formation of a commission until new legislation. It took under four years in Italy, but this was due to the use of the citizens' initiative, which struck down the existing legislation and forced the government to act. During these lengthy processes, much can go wrong to derail progress. Even so, the reform agenda can be advanced if certain parties and political leaders make clear public commitments to reform. In Canada, it is therefore very important that parties which stand to benefit from PR make unequivocal promises regarding electoral reform, and make a referendum on reform the sine qua non of their participation in any future minority government. Activists should insist that these promises be highlighted rather than buried in election platforms, and they should remain vigilant and active within political parties to keep these issues alive, especially after the parties come to government. Leaders of smaller parties should raise the issue in televised leaders debates and try to force other parties to respond. As we saw in the Japanese case, it is only when a large coalition of opposition parties got together, all with ironclad commitments to reform and a shared belief that the public is interested and expects these commitments to be honored, that the systemic inertia against change can be overcome.

One other option is available to reformers, at least in the provinces of Saskatchewan and BC. In these provinces, citizens have the power to initiate referendums on issues of their choice. While the existing rules make it difficult to successfully launch a referendum (something that no doubt explains why none has been held to date) the possibility of a citizen-initiated referendum on electoral reform does nevertheless exist. In exceptional circumstances — for instance, should one provincial party win every seat in the legislature — the public may be sufficiently mobilized to make the gathering of the requisite number of signatures a very real possibility, particularly with the help of party organizations that have been penalized by the existing system. (In fact, exactly such an attempt was made in BC after the 2001 election, which saw the Liberals capture all but two seats. The Green Party, which won an historic 12 percent of the popular vote but no seats, led a petition drive to force a referendum on electoral reform, but its efforts to collect the requisite amount of signatures fell short.) As in the Italian case, change is more likely to come from outside established political parties than from within. And once changes occur at the provincial level, changes to the federal system become more plausible.

Suppose a Canadian government – either of its own accord or under pressure — did decide to initiate a process of change, what should this process look like? We argue that it should have three goals in addition to change itself: to inform the public; to focus the debate and narrow the choices; and to provide opportunities for citizen participation in setting the agenda, defining the options, and making decisions. While it is important that voters make the final choice of how (if at all) to change the electoral system, the referendum must be just one part of a larger package of public consultation.

The process should begin with the formation of a commission of inquiry, charged with examining options for electoral reform and the likely effects of each option in the Canadian context. We argue, however, that the commission of inquiry should itself be embedded within a larger and more participatory citizens' forum on electoral reform. The citizen's forum would be charged with two tasks. The first would be debating and approving the mandate of the commission of inquiry; the second, debating its findings and amending and approving the options to be put to the people in a referendum on electoral reform. As was the case with the Australian people's convention on the future of the monarchy, the citizens' forum would be made up of both appointed and elected members. All registered political parties (including those currently without representation in parliament) would be allowed to appoint a certain number of members, while elected members would be chosen by the public, either by postal ballots or via the Internet. This would ensure that many of the key voices in the debate about electoral reform — notably those from minor parties that hold few or no seats in the House of Commons — had some input.

Why a citizens' forum? Greater and more meaningful citizen participation in the making of key political decisions is both a public priority and an important feature of a maturing democracy. It is not enough to allow citizens to testify before public commissions or even to vote in referendums. Public hearings allow for an airing of views but provide citizens with no chance to participate in the deliberations that shape the commission's recommendations. And if citizens are called upon to vote on options that they have had no say in shaping, they can end up feeling more frustrated with the political process than they were before the referendum.

A citizens' forum would help to educate the public about the issue of electoral reform. This process of public education must start long before a referendum campaign is held; if not, risk-averse voters are likely to reject change simply for want of information. Public awareness and interest in electoral reform would be raised initially when elections for members of the citizen's forum are held. Citizens could inform themselves further by tuning into televised coverage and web casts of the forum's proceedings. And they would learn even more by noting the stands taken on the issue by leading public figures participating in the forum.

A citizens' forum would enhance the credibility of the process in two key ways. First, it would help to make it less partisan. The involvement of the forum in shaping the commission's mandate and its recommendations would make it less likely that the process would be seen as being driven by the governing party with a view to advancing its own interests. Second, the process would be seen as less exclusively "top-down" in nature. While most of the forum members would be political leaders of one sort or another, public involvement throughout the process would discourage the public from dismissing the proposal as merely an elite project to benefit those in power.

The question of the mandate of the commission of inquiry is especially important. It is not surprising that the Independent Commission in the UK recommended a mild form of PR — a mixed system in which at least 80 percent of MPs would continue to be elected in individual constituencies on a first-past-the-post basis — given that under its terms of reference it had to choose a system that combined the objective of "broad proportionality" with those of "the need for stable Government" and "the maintenance of a link between MPs and geographical constituencies." Whether or not a future Canadian commission will favour one or another form of PR will also depend on its initial terms of reference. Under our proposal, the government would suggest the commission's mandate, but that mandate would be debated, amended and approved by the citizens' forum before the commission began its work. This would help to ensure that the government could not overtly rig the commission's mandate in a way that favoured its own interests.

The second function of the citizens' forum would be to debate the commission's findings and amend and approve its recommendation for a referendum question. Essentially, this means adding a step between the release of the commission's report and the approval of a referendum question by Parliament. Again, the rationale is clear. First, it would ensure that a wider range of interests had some input into the selection of those options that would be put to the public in a referendum, thus making it somewhat more difficult for the government and larger parties to write a referendum question that offered voters only a "soft" option for reform. Second, it would help to ensure that the commission's findings received more public attention and were subject to greater public discussion. Third, when recommendations for reform emerged from these highly public processes, it would be more difficult for governments to escape action.

Finally, we turn to the referendum itself. Throughout this paper we have taken it as a given that no serious change can be made to the electoral system without its being approved by referendum. But one referendum may not be enough. Unless there is a more or less unanimous view that only one type of new electoral system is appropriate for Canada, the government should be prepared to hold more than one vote, so that voters could choose from a "short list" of different options. For instance, the public could be given the option of choosing among the status quo, the option recommended by the commission and approved by the majority of the citizens' forum, and an option recommended by the government. The model here is the sequential referendums on the future of Newfoundland held in the late 1940s: the first round was used to eliminate the least popular of three options, and the winning option was determined in the second round.

This is not the same as a "never-endum" in which voters are asked to revisit the same question. Instead, we take citizens seriously as responsible decision-makers. Differences between contending electoral systems are profound and important. Canada would look very different if elections were conducted under a mixed system or under the single transferable vote. There is no reason why Canadian citizens should not be given the chance to decide which type of new system they prefer, rather than being given a single "take it or leave it" option for reform. To do otherwise risks reproducing the result of the Australian referendum on the country's head of state, where a reformist public voted for the status quo simply because it did not like the only option for change that it was offered.

Postscript

Since we initially wrote this piece, there has been significant activity in many Canadian provinces on electoral reform. The Liberal Party of Quebec, recognizing that they have been hurt by the first-past-the-post system, has appointed a minister specifically charged with changing the electoral system. A draft bill is expected in 2004. In New Brunswick, a full scale examination of democratic practice is being undertaken by a committee established by the legislature. The committee has until the end of 2004 to, among other things, recommend if a change to the electoral system should be made. In PEI, Norman Carruthers, a retired provincial chief justice, was appointed to head the PEI Commission on Electoral Reform. After consulting with Islanders, his final report was submitted in 2004. At this point, however, further government action seems unlikely. In Ontario, the government has committed itself to a public dialogue on electoral reform and have appointed a minister who is committed to the idea.[1] In Yukon, a senior advisor on electoral reform has been appointed to observe the deliberations of the BC Citizens' Assembly on Electoral Reform (discussed below) to assess whether a version of this process should be conducted in the Territory.

Perhaps most importantly, in the context of the argument we presented above, is the innovative Citizens' Assembly on Electoral Reform established by the government in BC. The assembly is formed of 160 British Columbians who were initially contacted at random, who subsequently presented themselves at regional meetings, and who finally were chosen from among those present at these meetings by lot. Its mandate is to learn, deliberate and consult the public about electoral systems and possible changes to the first-past-the-post system in BC. If the assembly recommends change, it will be charged with writing the referendum question that will be put before voters in the provincial election of May 2005.

The specific form taken by the BC citizens assembly is different in some ways from that of the citizens' forum we proposed above. It has a larger mandate — in effect combining the citizens' forum and commission of inquiry we proposed into one body — and it is entirely composed of citizens chosen by means of a process that involved a crucial element of random selection. These differences in structure, however, are overshadowed by the similarity in purpose to what we put forward, namely, the establishment of a process that includes members of the general public and that would ensure that any referendum on electoral reform occurs only as a final step of a larger exercise that encourages citizen participation, public education, deliberation and nonpartisanship.

Much can go awry on the way to reform. Whether governments will have the political will to move forward and confront many of their own sceptical elected members on an issue that is not terribly high-profile remains to be seen. However, if change is successful in some provinces, this may create momentum in others, and perhaps even at the federal level, where change is even more important because of the severe regional distortions and disproportionality that occur in some federal elections.

Notes

1. Matthew Mendelsohn has been appointed deputy minister and head of the Democratic Renewal Secretariat charged with developing the process for electoral reform in Ontario.

8

Is Talk of Electoral Reform
Just Whistling in the Wind?

John C. Courtney

An electoral system does not exist in a vacuum. It is part of an evolved and integrated set of institutional arrangements that together make up a larger and infinitely more complex political system. Collectively and with the passage of time, those institutional arrangements establish the framework within which public policy is formulated, political accountability is maintained, and public expectations about elections, parties and candidates are shaped. In consequence of those expectations, voters and parties make strategic electoral choices, parties and party systems take shape, and representative and governing institutions operate.

To call for the reform of the electoral system, to speculate about the presumed benefits that could be claimed to flow from a different electoral system, and to imagine how an altered method of voting would play out in Canada is one thing. But to do so without first considering the larger institutional context and the expectations that would be created under a different set of electoral rules is quite another. The standard maxim about well-intended reforms leading to unintended consequences should serve as a warning here. As Bert Rockman of the University of Pittsburgh reminded his American political science colleagues not long ago, "yesterday's reform often is today's problem."

It is idle to speculate about reforming an electoral system (an instrument of government I define as an essential "representational building block" of a liberal democratic state) without first determining the conditions to be met before any changes can be adopted. If an electoral system is to be reformed, certain critical variables must first be in place. The purpose of this paper is twofold: to remind us of the institutional and constitutional framework within which any electoral system must operate in Canada and to describe briefly the conditions that must first be met before electoral reforms can be put in place in this country.

At their most basic levels, the parliamentary and federal systems together have served since Confederation as the essential institutional contexts within which parties have developed and electoral outcomes have been determined. Barring some major and unforeseen event, that will continue to be the case well into the future. Within those parliamentary and federal arrangements, the problems of plurality elections in Canada that are typically identified by observers for special comment derive from the degrees of "fairness" and "representativeness" of electoral outcomes for parties, voters and regions. Those terms cast a wide net. They range from concerns that are essentially representational, such as those expressed by Alan Cairns more than three decades ago about the tendency of our electoral system to produce sectionalized and potentially nonintegrationist federal cabinets and parliamentary caucuses, to attacks on grounds of democratic theory about the perverted allocations of votes into seats that are seen as "unfair" to some regions, parties and voters.

Whatever alternative or modified electoral system may be agreed to in the years ahead, it must be one that is compatible with Canada's larger parliamentary, federal and constitutional systems. On the governance side of the reform equation a different electoral method must ensure the continuation of certain fundamental cornerstones of our parliamentary system. This should hold true even if coalition governments of two or more parties become the governing norm as a consequence of electoral reform. What are Canada's essential constitutional principles? At their most basic level they include cabinet secrecy and solidarity, Commons confidence votes on issues of critical public policy, responsible government and (however shopworn this concept may have become) individual ministerial responsibility.

Regardless of the changes that may be made to the electoral system, these constitutional and parliamentary pillars of Canada's political system should be neither fundamentally altered nor discarded in favour of some as yet untried and unfamiliar ones. Our constitutional-federal-parliamentary systems have deep roots in this country. Collectively they are the source of our entire machinery of government. They have contributed to and helped to shape our political culture, the expectations that the electorate holds about the political process and parliamentary government, and the internal organizational and authority structures of the parties. Too much is at stake both constitutionally and institutionally to contemplate changes to the electoral system that might compromise or endanger the carefully crafted set of arrangements we have established to govern ourselves. Thus, the fundamental principle that must be adhered to in the search for alternative methods of election is that whatever system is eventually settled upon must be compatible with our constitutional, federal, and parliamentary systems.

On the representational side, the range of considerations is no less important than on the governance side. Representational considerations are, in a sense, more complex than governance ones, or at least they have become so in the past two decades or so. The advent of identity politics, in which women, aboriginals and ethnocultural groups have made powerful representational claims, has the potential of making the issue of electoral reform a particularly salient one for many who now feel disadvantaged by plurality voting. So too has the move toward direct democracy helped to reshape representational practices. The appeal of such plebiscitary vehicles as referendums, recall, initiatives and, in the case of national and provincial party organizations, universal membership votes, has been unmistakable. The creation first of the Reform then of the Alliance parties speaks to that issue.

Identity politics and direct democracy can be expected to impact negatively on the age-old accommodative model of Canadian parties if parties see a different electoral system as offering a different set of strategic options and if they choose to fashion their respective support bases around a narrow range of social, linguistic, racial or regionally concentrated supporters. New institutional arrangements, we need scarcely remind ourselves, bring with them new incentives and strategic options. Should electoral changes come to pass this could fundamentally alter or bring to an end the transnational-brokerage-party model first crafted by Macdonald and Laurier. It is true that the broadly based catch-all party has become an exception on the national political scene in the past few elections. But we need to be mindful of the possibility that its recent exceptionalism, which surely owed much to the peculiar workings of the plurality vote system at a time when the governing Conservative Party essentially imploded over its constitutional initiatives and its perceived public policy slights of Western Canada, could in fact get worse under a reformed electoral system.

Every electoral system offers its own set of incentives. For truly national parties intent on winning office under the plurality system the most obvious of these incentives has been to create and maintain the "big tent" within which interregional, linguistic and social differences could be accommodated. Whatever reforms are introduced to Canada's electoral system should not encourage parties to abandon that option in order to pursue other more narrowly or sectorally based ones that, in turn, would be destructive of the larger national political community in Canada. The leadership style favoured by Mackenzie King owed much to the incentives that first-past-the-post offered parties competing for electoral support. We should not set out to construct an electoral system that would all but rule out the continuation of that accommodative approach to national political leadership.

Representation has a practical as well as a theoretical base in our political system. Practical representational concerns of MPs will no doubt become part of the background discussion of any move to reform the electoral system. For example, for Canada to change its method of electing members of Parliament to, let us say the mixed-member proportional system of Germany or New Zealand, several fundamental institutional readjustments would have to be made that would in practical terms hold little appeal for many MPs. Principal among these would be the need to redraw electoral boundaries around substantially larger ridings. If only one half of the Commons were to continue to be elected from single-member constituencies, the size of the ridings from which they would be chosen would effectively double — both in population and territory. This would hardly be a selling point for electoral reform for members, candidates and party organizers who already complain of constituency workload and geographically over large ridings.

Although there is currently considerable interest in electoral reform in several provinces, debate over electoral reform in Canada has been episodic. It has not followed a consistently upward-moving trend line growing in intensity from one election to the next. The issue all but disappeared from public view at the federal level when, as in 1968 and 1984, elections produced majority governments whose levels of popular support and parliamentary representation were not wildly incommensurate, the governing party enjoyed a measure of electoral and parliamentary support from all regions, and the opposition parties saw their shares of seats more or less reflect their shares of votes.

But interest in reforming the electoral system has re-ignited whenever, as has been the case most strikingly since 1993, popular votes were not converted into seats in a fair and reasonable manner, the regions sensed a heightened alienation from the centre and found comfort in singling out the plurality electoral system as a major contributor to that alienation, and the shares of Commons seats of several parties bore little relationship to their respective shares of popular votes. It is that stage of re-ignited debate that we are now in. Even so, the intensity of and interest in the current debate over plurality voting in Canada so far falls short of matching that of the 1920s when the question of reforming the electoral system was first addressed on a major scale in Parliament and several provincial legislatures.

There could be little doubt by early 2004 that the "electoral reform issue" had once again heated up in Canada. A spirited House of Commons debate had taken place at the end of the previous year on an Opposition member's motion to hold a national referendum on proportional representation. Although defeated by the government in a vote of 144 to 76, the motion was the first to make it to the floor of the Commons since the 1920s. Several conferences sponsored by major public policy institutes had been held on electoral reform over the previous half-decade. Websites, electoral reform organizations such as Fair Vote Canada, and Internet chat groups were created to encourage public discussion of the topic. A year after the Green Party of Canada launched a court challenge against plurality voting in 2001, the Law Commission of Canada and the Canadian Policy Research Networks released discussion papers on electoral reform. Possibly of greatest significance was the fact that five provinces (Prince Edward Island, New Brunswick, Quebec, Ontario and British Columbia) had by early 2004 undertaken investigations of various kinds to explore alternative methods of election. Other provinces may follow suit.

It should come as no surprise that the question of electoral reform has surfaced at the provincial level. Federalism lends itself to a measure of "test-tube" experiments conducted by its component units. Provinces are, by definition, less heterogeneous, less complex, and smaller in both population and territory than the country as a whole. Accordingly, they have a greater capacity to innovate and, should they so wish, to change some of the fundamentals of their system of government. With time, the successful innovations are sometimes adopted by the other jurisdictions. Canada's provinces have a demonstrated history of having been the first order of government to initiate fundamental changes to several key elements of their electoral systems. Manitoba led the pack in granting the vote to women in 1916 and, forty years later, in passing legislation guaranteeing that electoral districts would be redrawn periodically by independent commissions. In 1964 Quebec became the first Canadian jurisdiction to adopt election expenses legislation, and several of the provinces granted the vote to status Indians well before Ottawa did in 1960.

The results of recent provincial elections proved to be the catalyst that brought electoral reform to the forefront in several provinces. Plurality voting, most strikingly when more than two parties compete in an election, has a tendency to convert votes into seats in a capricious manner. Not unusually the party gaining a majority of an assembly's seats wins no more than a plurality of the popular vote. Sometimes, as happened in Quebec in 1966 and again in 1998, the party forming the Official Opposition actually receives more votes than the party winning office. At various points in their history most provinces could point to election results that were decidedly "lopsided" even though the popular vote was far closer than the composition of the assemblies would suggest. That was recently the case in both British Columbia and Prince Edward Island. In BC the Liberals won all but two of the 79 seats in the 2001 election with 58 percent of the votes cast, and in Prince Edward Island the

Conservatives, with the same level of support as the BC Liberals, won all but one of the Island's 27 seats. The combination of such results and the work of several organizations created with the stated objective of promoting electoral reform ("Every Vote Counts" in PEI and "Fair Voting BC" in British Columbia) soon captured the attention of the media and the politicians. The result was the establishment in several provinces of committees (or, in the case of British Columbia, a "citizens' assembly") to look into alternative methods of election.

The irregular nature of the debate in the past over our electoral system is important to note, for it suggests that Canadians have not shared a profound or deep-seated distrust of plurality voting *per se*. Rather, theirs can be characterized as having been a tempered, spasmodic and election-driven response to particularly egregious instances of inequitable conversion of votes into seats. With few exceptions, calls for electoral reform have been most numerous, as they were following the last three federal elections, whenever parliaments were elected with vote/seat ratios that were clearly skewed by parties and regions. Canadian history is littered with examples of newspaper articles, letters to editors, scholarly studies and conferences in which academics, members of the media and civic-minded individuals have called for electoral reform. Their irregularity, however, demonstrates that concern about the electoral system has been circumstance-driven rather than primeval or deeply philosophic.

To a considerable extent these well-intended, though periodic, initiatives in the past have amounted to little more than whistling in the wind. Why? Because several fundamental conditions have not been in place that collectively would have to have been met before changes to the electoral system could be made.

A basic condition of the reform of any representational building block is that until such time as the governing elites accept the case for modifying it, changes cannot take place. There is no evidence of any measurable level of support for electoral reform among Canada's governing elites at the federal level at the present time. Such reform proposals as are made come from some, but by no means all, Opposition members or, as in the case of the Greens, parties without elected members. The probability of a government agreeing to changes at the present time is low, for reform can scarcely be said to work to their advantage. With few exceptions, governing parties at both the federal and provincial levels have benefited from plurality voting, with the result that on the issue of reforming the method of election by which they won office governments' self-interest has outweighed the public interest as defined by electoral reformers.

What could change that is a series of unstable, possibly coalition or minority single-party governments in which minor parties successfully bargain for electoral reform. Alternatively, as was the case in New Zealand in the early 1990s, profound public dissatisfaction with and disdain for politicians and parties, following on the heels of an influential and respected commission of inquiry examining alternative electoral methods and recommending one, could be the catalyst needed to prompt the principal political actors to accept changes to the electoral system.

At the moment, neither of these alternatives is in the works in Canada. There are several reasons for this. The Liberal government, including the prime minister, shows little interest in electoral reform. Paul Martin has singled out several aspects of Canadian government under the general rubric of "democratic deficit" that, he contends, need to be changed. The electoral system is not one of them. There have in the past been no Canadian equivalents to New Zealand's "agenda-setting" public interest groups on electoral reform, although such relatively new organizations as Fair Vote Canada are gaining a measure of serious attention. The level of public dissatisfaction with the electoral system and politicians has yet to reach the level that it did a decade ago in New Zealand. As well, Canada's equivalent to New Zealand's commission on electoral reform (the Lortie Commission) evinced not the slightest inclination to move away from plurality voting.

If a continuing and manifestly general dissatisfaction with plurality voting were present amongst the Canadian electorate, and if there were widespread agreement on a single alternative espoused by a respected national commission of inquiry, that would be, as they say, a "no-brainer." Those conditions would properly lead to genuine and far-reaching demands for electoral reform that those in government would ignore at their peril.

But is the case for electoral reform as compelling when the principal arguments for reform derive from periodic dissatisfaction with the results of a particular election or set of elections as expressed by a limited number of individuals (academics, occasional Opposition members and the print medium)? Without extensive and profound disapproval on the part of the electorate with the current system, coupled with general agreement on an acceptable alternative to plurality voting, the push for electoral reform in Canada is likely to fall on deaf government ears. Given the abundance of alternative proposals bandied about in Canada over the recent past, ranging from German-style MMP elections, through alternative voting, run-off elections and single transferable votes, to two-member-plurality elections, it is fair to say that agreement on a preferred option to the current system is some distance away.

There are two institutional and territorially bounded filters through which our current plurality vote system works. The first is the single-member electoral district, the second, federalism. Both constitute important representational institutions for the periodic reallocation of federal seats among the provinces, the designing of district boundaries, the aggregating of votes, and the eventual determination of election winners and losers.

A study in the *American Political Science Review* by Carlos Boix (1999) compared electoral reform at the federal level in a number of countries. It concluded that at the federal level Canada is not naturally predisposed to electoral reform because of a complex interrelationship between its federal system and the geographical distribution of its citizens by language groups. Canada is a territorially large federation in which the two principal linguistic groups are geographically concentrated — francophones predominantly in Quebec and anglophones predominantly in all other parts of the country. Unlike several European countries, Canada's principal social cleavage is not distributed more or less evenly across the country. If it were, that would serve as a powerful inducement to replace plurality voting with a more proportionate electoral scheme designed to protect the linguistic minority and to guarantee it a measure of parliamentary representation. As that is not now the case, nor is it likely to become so in the foreseeable future, the geographic distribution of the two dominant language groups and the federalized institutional structure within which their electoral choices are aggregated collectively lend no support to the case for a reformed electoral system at the present time.

Chart 1 highlights the principal conditions that need to be met before Canada's electoral system can be changed to some as yet undetermined, non-plurality voting system. Of those, the support of governing elites and the agreement on a single alternative to the current system are clearly the most essential. Others, such as the support of other agencies, academics, the press and the like, as well as the extraparliamentary resources that might play a pro-reform advocacy role in the debate over moving away from plurality voting, are obviously important to shaping public and elite opinion. As valuable as they may be, they are not as critical to the exercise as the government leaders who play the vital constitutional and decision-making role on such questions.

The obstacles to reform are, for the most part, attitudinal on the part of both the politicians and the general public. Leading politicians on the government benches do not, so far at least, favour change, and the electorate has, for the most part, shown little interest in the issue. Federalism may not be either a hindrance or a help on this issue, though Boix's analysis serves as a reminder that the geographic distribution of voters along a key demographic variable helps to explain why reform has so far gained relatively little public support federally.

If federalism offers any lessons at all on the question of electoral reform that would need further exploration, it is that for varying lengths of time in the twentieth century two of the three Prairie provinces and British Columbia used nonplurality electoral systems before reverting, once again, to the plurality vote. What were the reasons that these provinces abandoned their respective experiments? Does the answer confirm that "far away pastures look greener" and that

Chart 1

Reforming Canada's Plurality Vote System:
What Would It Take?

Variables	Present to what extent?
Support for change from:	
Media	Moderate but intermittent
Public	Low to moderate but intermittent
Academics	Several supportive of change
Commissions	No support from the Lortie; provincial underway
Public interest groups	Some active federal and provincial groups
Government agencies	Elections Canada not proactive to date
Courts	No decisions yet on method of election
Elected officials	Low support on government side; moderate to high among Opposition parties
Agreement on an alternative	No; numerous alternatives proposed
Resources on which to draw	Some academic research No influential pro-reform commissions of inquiry at the federal level
Obstacles	Politicians' self-interest Public ambivalence Unease about implications for government stability
Impact of federalism	Negative in terms of concentration of linguistic minorities Positive if provincial test tubes are created and reformed electoral institutions are successful

a return to plurality voting offered something that the more proportional schemes had failed to deliver to the three provinces? That certainly was part of the argument that led Manitoba to return to plurality voting in the 1950s.

In sum, given both the absence of a single alternative strongly favoured by an electorate seriously disaffected with plurality voting and the failure to date of governing elites to have embraced the cause of electoral reform, the chances of adoption of a reformed electoral system for federal elections would have to be judged as low at present.

The expression "reforming the electoral system" has a pleasant ring about it. It suggests improvement, progress and an ultimately fairer and more democratic electoral system for all citizens. There is no doubt much in the debate over Canada's electoral system that confirms the inherent justice of the attempt to alter Canada's method of election. But equally it is essential to understand fully that no electoral system is neutral. How it distributes votes into seats ultimately affects the composition of institutions and the content of public policies. Accordingly, the relationship between the constitutional principles and institutional framework, on the one hand, and the representative and electoral systems, on the other, deserves full consideration before the plurality system is modified. This paper has argued as well that certain basic variables must first be in place before the electoral system can be reformed. Until those tests have been met, a reformed electoral system in the federal arena in Canada remains largely a speculative academic question and, possibly, the latest in a long list of "whistling in the electoral winds" exercises in Canada.

Part C
The Broader Debate

9

From Enumeration to the National Register of Electors: An Account and an Evaluation

Jerome H. Black

Introduction

As with most processes designed to regulate aspects of political life, the decision to establish a particular voter-registration regime entails making significant choices. In one sense, the task can be portrayed as a mechanical endeavour, the need to select from among alternative methods, each of which strikes a different balance between guaranteeing that qualified citizens have unimpeded access to the vote, on the one hand, and ensuring the integrity of the voting process by guarding against voter fraud, on the other. Registration approaches also differ in their degree of support for certain secondary, but nonetheless important, functions of the electoral system, such as allowing for the mobilization of voters by providing parties with lists of electors. Registration systems also vary along other key dimensions, such as operational costs and the quality of the resulting lists. While such considerations are often regarded as establishing appropriate criteria for evaluating the performance of different registration regimes, they can also be thought of as objectives that the process might be expected to meet. The selection of a registration method, however, can also be understood within a more philosophical context where central principles and values establish a priority as to the most important purposes that the chosen approach should serve. Characterizing the decision in this way follows from the recognition that in attaching a greater weight to particular objectives, different registration regimes elevate some principles to a higher status than others.[1]

A key principle underlying Canada's approach to registration for federal (and most provincial) elections for much of the twentieth century, and around which there seems to have been a strong consensus, was that the state should assume the onus of ensuring that all eligible citizens were listed as electors.[2] This belief was manifested in the country's postwrit or election-specific enumeration approach, through the practice of carrying out a door-to-door canvass that used enumerators who determined and recorded eligible voters. The resulting compilation, carried out once the writs had been issued and used solely for the election at hand, became the preliminary list of electors. Typically, there would be several visitations for those initially missed or not at home, and while at some point the onus shifted to the uncontacted (and thus unlisted) individual to take some minor steps to become registered, the dominant thrust of the approach amounted to a reaching out on the part of the state — literally to the doorsteps of the citizenry. With the state assuming the initiative, the effort required or "costs" incurred by the individual were quite minimal.[3] Moreover, in employing a virtual army of enumerators (e.g., about 110,000 enumerators were used for the 1988 election), the massive canvassing effort was able to capture a very high proportion of the eligible population.[4] It also served to enhance inclusion, particularly since it drew into the political process the kinds of individuals, such as the young, the poor and those with little formal education, who otherwise would be less likely to take the initiative to participate.[5] This proactive approach, which was the essence of enumeration, worked to augment voter turnout among all segments of society and thus mitigated a natural tendency toward participation inequality in electoral politics.

The fact that registration was undertaken just before an election also served to ensure that currency and accuracy would characterize the registration information compiled. Close sequencing resulted in a reasonably up-to-date list of electors identified at their current addresses and, consequently, preliminary lists that contained a minimum number of errors, either of exclusion (eligible voters not listed) or of inclusion (ineligible voters listed). Thus, enumeration captured those who had changed residence, an important characteristic in a country with a high mobility rate, as well as new citizens who were constantly entering the electorate along with the newly age-eligible. The timely nature of postwrit enumeration also meant that the false listing of those who had emigrated or passed away was kept to a minimum.

This model, with state initiative at its core, had come to define Canadian tradition, and moreover constituted, as Boyer notes, a practice that was unique in the world.[6] While he goes on to point out that a major criticism of the approach is its prolongation of the campaign (because of the time requirement of enumeration), Boyer also states that the "most telling recommendation for it is that approximately 98% of all eligible voters are registered."[7] He also cites, with apparent approval, Ward's own positive verdict on the approach, including how the Canadian experience has "furnished conclusive evidence that the making of voters lists is a proper state function."[8] For his part, Qualter also sees virtue in a system that generates an up-to-date and accurate list of electors and does so, moreover, "at relatively low cost."[9] Courtney and Smith make the strongest and most carefully constructed case for the traditional system, highlighting its advantages not only in absolute terms but also relative to alternative approaches. They too emphasize the ability of the enumeration method to reach out to all kinds of individuals:

> Enumeration possesses the potential for incorporating those with special needs into the eligible electorate. These include electors in hospitals and prisons, those with physical and mental disabilities, and the homeless, the poor and the illiterate. For such people, a system that depends upon self-registration may well have a repressive effect on their willingness or capacity to be included on the list of electors. (p. 433)

They also believe that the personal contact inherent in enumeration can be beneficial in and of itself:

> A system that places the onus for registration on the state rather than on the citizen and that is coupled with door-to-door enumeration serves as a personal reminder by the community of the positive value that it places on electoral participation by its citizens. The approach of a pending election is heralded through human contact. (p. 433)

While not all academics have embraced enumeration as the ideal model,[10] the greater emphasis on its merits is certainly part of a broader consensus that has existed about its value as a uniquely Canadian institution.

More to the point, enumeration had long stood the test of official scrutiny and reflection, including evaluation against other methods of registration. As recently as 1986, a *White Paper on Election Law Reform* reaffirmed a preference for the traditional system as opposed to either permanent-list forms of registration or annual enumerations.[11] Though the white paper identifies some problems with enumeration, including the increasing difficulty some returning officers were having finding competent enumerators, these were spelled out in the context of recommendations designed to remedy these problematic aspects. Moreover, the report lists the main arguments typically offered on behalf of alternative approaches. The advantages of a permanent voters list, for example, are cited as being a shortened campaign period and the elimination of both the "duplication of effort at the three levels" of government (realizable through computerization) and the confusion of voters caught up in overlapping registration efforts. Overall, however, the recommendation to maintain enumeration was forceful and strongly justified. Compared to a permanent-list approach, it was regarded as a less costly method. Moreover, it was argued that a permanent list "would not necessarily be more accurate, more complete or more up-to-date than the present enumeration system unless strict controls or compulsory registration were imposed,"[12] and would be unacceptable to Canadians concerned about the threat to privacy entailed in the maintenance of permanent records. It seemed, then, that support for Canada's traditional system of enumeration was solid.

Ten years later, however, the postwrit enumeration system was abandoned. It was replaced by a permanent-list approach based on the compilation and maintenance of a voters register. Bill C-63,[13] which received Royal Assent on December 18, 1996, mandated the implementation of the new system for all electoral events (elections, by-elections and referendums) at the federal level. The National Register (formally, the National Register of Electors) was subsequently established following a final door-to-door enumeration that was carried out in April 1997, which, in turn, generated the preliminary lists for the ensuing June election.[14] The legislation also reduced the minimum period of an election campaign from 47 to 36 days.[15]

The National Register itself was established as an "automated database" containing the name, gender, date of birth and address of each Canadian citizen eligible to vote. Given that the standing expectation is for about 20 percent of the listed information to alter each year as a result of address changes (16 percent), new 18-year-olds (2 percent), new citizens (1 percent) and deaths (1 percent),[16] regular updating of the permanent list is regarded as being imperative. This is done by incorporating new information from federal departments, particularly the Canada Customs and Revenue Agency and Citizenship and Immigration Canada, as well as provincial motor registration and vital statistics agencies. The system is also designed to incorporate voting lists from other jurisdictions. The commitment to maintain the register in as up-to-date fashion as possible distinguishes this approach as an "open" or "continuous" permanent-list form.[17] So too does the commitment to provide ample opportunities for unlisted individuals to register during an official revision period and on voting day itself. These latter opportunities are vital because no updating process can sufficiently track and record the enormous number of demographic and eligibility changes that constantly occur.

What happened? Why was enumeration, given its strong official endorsement as late as 1986, replaced by a permanent list? The question has even greater import considering that the changeover occurred fairly quickly, indeed within a remarkably short time frame, given that a major "representational building block," to use Courtney's words,[18] was at stake. Moreover, the change was part of a 1990s trend that witnessed five provinces adopt their own registers, joining British Columbia, which had (exceptionally) long relied on a permanent list.[19] Accounting for the switch in registration regimes at the national level is one of two principal and interrelated tasks undertaken in this paper. The other is to evaluate the performance of the new system in facilitating the electoral participation of Canadians.

In examining these two dimensions, this paper follows up on an earlier project[20] that provided some initial exploration in both areas. That effort, in fact, identified most of the antecedent factors that appeared relevant for a rudimentary understanding of the changeover in registration regimes. The current contribution provides a more systematic account of what happened and, in the process, outlines the major developments that unfolded over the period in question. Beyond this descriptive aspect, an emphasis is placed on the role played by Elections Canada and the chief electoral officer in implementing the new system. This portrayal consists mainly in considering what motivated the agency to take the lead in pressing for change and, as well, the kinds of arguments it advanced in order to convince other major actors about both the need for, and the benefits of, such a switch. These aspects are dealt with in Part I. Part II similarly follows up on the earlier study, which had identified the main issues and criteria that are relevant for comparative assessments of the two methods of generating voters lists. In the current study, the emphasis is placed on the implications for voter turnout in Canada, exploring these in connection with participation levels among both the general population and the poorer and less established segments of society (what is characterized as equality of participation). The growing concern over decline in voter turnout and nonvoting in Canada provides an important justification for such a focus. Moreover, one of the key conclusions drawn in Part I is that relatively limited attention was given to the possible consequences the changeover might have for the electoral participation of Canadians. This sets up the central question explored in Part II: whether the alteration in registration methods has resulted in reduced voter turnout. The paper closes with a reiteration of the main conclusions, some reflections on their implications and a discussion of issues and possibilities in the development of the new regime.

Part I: Replacing Enumeration with a Permanent List

The preliminary study, designed to frame relevant questions for this more extensive work, identified most of the factors that had a bearing on the changeover in regimes and, as well, indicated that many of them operated in such a way as to reinforce each other's influence.[21] They included increasing concern over difficulties with the enumeration system and a sense that a permanent list would resolve these, while at the same time delivering the additional advantage of cost savings and a shorter campaign period. Achieving economies was an especially attractive prospect in a climate wherein neoliberal principles, centred on fiscal conservatism and a scaling back of government, continued to gain ascendancy. This new environment was also characterized by a concern to reduce duplication of effort and expenditures in the federation, so that the prospect of shared voters lists, and thus even more savings, added to the appeal of a permanent list. A more immediate factor was the close sequencing of the 1992 referendum on the Charlottetown Accord and the 1993 general election. This proximity allowed for the use of the 1992 lists, outside of Quebec at least, in the 1993 election, establishing a precedent for the "reuse" of lists[22] and thereby helping to legitimize the argument for a permanent list. Also consequential was a 1992 recommendation by the Royal Commission on Electoral Reform and Party Financing (RCERPF, or Lortie Commission) to move toward a register, albeit a provincially based one.[23] The 1989 auditor general's report was additionally identified as having relevance insofar as it motivated Elections Canada to integrate new computer technology into its operations, upon which any successful and cost-effective permanent list would ultimately depend. Finally, Elections Canada and Chief Electoral Officer Jean-Pierre Kingsley were characterized as being strongly supportive of the change.

Independently, Courtney has since provided his own brief account of the reasons for the advent of a permanent list, but he is more explicit in identifying the near-perfect alignment of pressures and motivations that culminated in the change.[24] He does so by drawing upon some fundamental aspects of organizational-innovation theory, particularly the propositions that innovation is most likely to occur when motivation is strong, the obstacles to change are weak and resources are available to overcome any obstacle. Based on information gained from interviews, he writes:

> There was at the time (1) strong support from the prime minister (Jean Chrétien) and a conviction on the part of important political handlers in the prime minister's office (such as Jerry Yanover) that change was highly desirable; (2) a notable absence of political opposition to the change in Parliament and indifference on the part of the public and media to the issue; and (3) ample resources to overcome such obstacles as there might have been. Those resources included Elections Canada's identification of a set of problems with the existing system packaged together with a proposed solution to those problems; the Lortie Commission's qualified endorsement of a move away from

door-to-door enumeration; the high priority accorded the legislation's speedy passage by the minister responsible for election administration [Herb Gray] and by the cabinet generally; and the attraction that the claims about the cost savings held for the parliamentarians.[25]

Courtney also points out, and rightly so, that the switch was facilitated by a consensus surrounding a single alternative. The fact that some provinces supported and were interested in future co-operation also served to expedite change.[26]

In short, both studies understand the alteration in voter registration regimes (and as well the relative quickness of the change) as resulting from a matrix of forces and events that pushed in the same direction; moreover, these converging factors operated without much in the way of countervailing pressures. Cast at this level, the explanation for the changeover is fairly straightforward and hardly a mysterious affair. Still, as both accounts are quite brief, there is a clear need for more extensive documentation. A chronological analysis helps to meet this need, while also affording an opportunity to specify the essential differences between the two registration approaches and review the kinds of arguments and claims that can be made on behalf of each. A chronological and descriptive narrative also meets the second objective of Part I, namely to document the key role played by Elections Canada, including the chief electoral officer, in engineering the changeover. To anticipate, it is maintained that the agency and Chief Electoral Officer Kingsley were pivotal in two ways. First of all, they took advantage of opportunities within an evolving political context from the mid-1980s to the early 1990s in which reform of the electoral process was under serious and active consideration. While the developments associated with this period can themselves be seen as certainly having some relevance for the eventual emergence of a permanent-list system, their impact is largely due to the mediating efforts of Elections Canada. As the agency committed itself to the idea of a register, it gave expression and shape to these background forces and made them more pertinent and weighty. Elections Canada was also pivotal in a second sense, as they subsequently embarked upon a strategy to demonstrate the technical and economic feasibility of a permanent list in order to sell the idea to elected officials. Moreover, they did so at an opportune time, when both government and the main opposition parties found the arguments for change especially compelling and indeed self-serving.

The backdrop to change: the white paper, two reports and the Royal Commission on Electoral Reform and Party Financing

The idea of a change in the registration regime gained momentum during a period of broad reflection and debate on Canada's electoral law. Prompted by concerns about the inappropriate and outdated nature of current legislation and practice, especially in light of new Charter-based realities and lags in the use of new technology, a consensus developed around the need to countenance reform in many areas, though not in the electoral system itself. The 1986 white paper and the RCERPF were both products of, and in turn contributed to, this context of questioning and the contemplation of change. At the same time, they differed considerably in the conclusions they drew about replacing the enumeration system. Two other reports, discussed in a moment, also helped define this period, and these too made reference to registration matters.

The white paper's impact on subsequent developments is probably best understood as being an indirect one. While it did initiate debate on reform in many key areas, in the particular case of voter registration it ended up, as already noted, reaffirming a commitment to enumeration. Still, it did list some of the potential benefits associated with a permanent list and indicated the changes that would be needed to make it a more feasible and acceptable alternative. As well, the white paper alluded to the chief difficulty with the enumeration system, one that had been slowly developing over the years — a shortage of qualified enumerators.[27]

The chief electoral officer's 1989 statutory report[28] can be similarly identified as having reinforced the general sense as to the need for reform without making any direct contribution to the idea of substituting the enumeration system. While it acknowledges the shortage of qualified enumerators as a problem by listing the various discretionary measures that returning officers had to take in the 1988 election, at no point does it call the enumeration approach itself into question, and it certainly makes no mention of replacing it. The concern with the need for reform in other areas is, however, very much in evidence. Chapter 2, "The Crisis in Election Administration," succinctly lists the various issues and pressures that were threatening to overwhelm the agency (pp. 9-12). One of these was the challenge of adopting new computer technology, a task made more difficult by understaffing and outdated legislative arrangements. At the same time, the report indicates that some steps had been taken in the use of computers and office automation, including during the 1988 election.

The auditor general's report, also issued in 1989, acknowledged these developments but regarded them as insufficient.[29] It emphasized that far too much work was still being done manually, particularly with regard to enumeration and revision, and that even in those areas where computers were being employed disparate software programs were being used. The message, strongly conveyed, was that Elections Canada needed to become more efficient and to seek economies through a greater reliance on information technology and standardized software. The report pushed the case further by noting that computerization could result in additional cost reductions through the development of common procedures with other jurisdictions and the sharing of both information and tasks. It also recognized Elections Canada's difficulty in finding enumerators, though it provided no further commentary in this regard. Still, in urging the agency to embrace fully technology and computerization and, as well, to engage in co-operative endeavours with other jurisdictions, the auditor general's report may have contributed to the change that eventually occurred. After all, it was generally understood that the only way that a permanent-list approach could be rendered sufficiently cost-effective, and thus have a chance of being considered seriously, was through the use of automation to handle the necessary large-scale data collection and data management tasks. As will be discussed below, the report apparently served as a catalyst in moving Elections Canada to embrace technological change.

The RCERPF, without doubt, provided the most extensive commentary and analysis on enumeration and its possible replacement by a register. Its impact is evident in the way that it added to the general climate for change and, more specifically, enhanced the legitimacy of a permanent-list approach as a serious alternative to enumeration. Indeed, the RCERPF was, in fact, required as part of its mandate to report on "the compiling of voters lists, including the advisability of the establishment of a permanent voters' list."[30] In the end, it proposed moving toward a register-based system. This added considerable momentum to the notion that change was desirable, and certainly the commission's arguments and recommendations were often employed (though at times in a selective fashion) and became frequent points of departure and reference in the discourse of those supporting a shift.

More particularly, the RCERPF's main analysis and conclusions on voter registration are spelled out in two chapters of volume 2 of its final report, one dealing with the enumeration system (chapter 1, "The Registration of Voters"), the other with the permanent-list approach (chapter 4, "A Register of Voters"). The significance of the former is the concrete expression it gave to the scale of the decline in the quality of the canvassing effort: "The critical issue that was raised time and again at our public hearings and that has been acknowledged by election administrators, federally and provincially, as an increasingly serious problem over the past two decades, is the number of voters who are missed by enumeration" (p. 7). The issue was regarded as having two main components. One difficulty involved the predicament that enumerators faced accessing voters at their residences. This was attributed to occupational and lifestyle changes, such as more women entering the labour force and jobs requiring more travel, all of which meant that fewer individuals were at home when enumerators called. Also noted were problems accessing multiple-unit buildings where policies restrict door-to-door contact of residences. Furthermore, it was argued that in some urban areas "personal safety makes some voters, especially the elderly and those who live alone, unwilling to respond to unannounced callers" (p. 9). The commission acknowledged that while these were not necessarily new concerns, they were nonetheless of increasing importance and that "taken together, they make a census-type count of voters more difficult than in the past" (p. 9). Similarly, problems accessing special-needs groups such as the hearing impaired, the illiterate, those who do not speak English or French, and immigrants "who may be hesitant to respond to callers representing the state given their experiences in their country of origin" were identified as having "increased substantially in both absolute and relative numbers over the past two decades" (p. 9).

The second difficulty — a more serious one that had been the subject of increasing commentary over the years — was the shortage of competent enumerators. Here, too, more women entering the labour force was a factor, since it meant that fewer individuals were available to take up enumeration duties. Personal safety concerns in urban centres "have also taken their toll" (p. 9). Moreover, candidates and political parties, which have the right, in the first instance, to nominate enumerators, had become increasingly unable or unwilling to do so. The supply of enumerators was further constrained by statutory requirements limiting appointment to qualified voters residing in the constituencies.

Importantly, chapter 1 also went on to make recommendations for improving the quality of the enumeration process by addressing these problems. These included the earlier appointment of enumerators, the appointment of "supervisory enumerators," the selection of enumerators from all registered constituency associations and from community associations, a lowering of the minimum age to 16 and, in areas where safety was not a concern, the employment of one enumerator instead of two. These measures would no doubt have gone a long way toward resolving the problems identified, and some were put in place for the 1993 election (although enumeration was not required outside of Quebec). Still, judging from comments by the proponents of a register, it was the problems of enumeration, not their recommended solutions, that stood out most in this part of the RCERPF's report.

The chapter on register systems (chapter 4) was even more influential, simply because it did indeed end up recommending that a permanent register be adopted for federal elections — although arguing that this would be affordable only if federal authorities were to rely on provincially maintained lists. The particulars of the commission's advocacy on behalf of a register can be thought of as involving multiple (and overlapping) types of argumentation and commitments. One stressed how it would be possible to ensure that a register could be guided by some of the principles associated favourably with enumeration. This essentially entailed a commitment to maintain the principle that "registration should primarily be a state responsibility" (p. 113), along with the long-standing orientation to facilitate access to the voting process. Thus, the commission saw revision and election-day registration as being integral components of the overall process, in effect establishing the approach as an open-list system offering multiple opportunities for voters to become registered.[31] In practical terms, of course, these provisions would be necessary to compensate for the expected gaps in the register's coverage and lack of up-to-date listings of potential voters stemming from eligibility and demographic changes.

Another line of argumentation underscored the distinctive benefits of a permanent list. Principal among these was the advantage of a shorter campaign — because canvassing would no longer be necessary. This segment of the argument built on a brief section in another chapter (chapter 3, "Administering the Vote") that began by noting that a shortened campaign was seen as a major advantage of a register, favoured as it was by most intervenors before the commission (p. 77). Proponents of a shortened campaign typically claimed that "Canadians are overexposed to politics and lose interest as a result" (p. 79), that it would reduce administration costs and that it would make it easier to recruit campaign help. Opposition came from those in large ridings and from small parties with fewer campaign workers.

The case for change also involved the reiteration, often by implication, of the problems with enumeration. One point given particular emphasis was that a shared voters list would avoid the confusion of overlapping enumeration by the different levels of government. Maintaining that co-operation with other jurisdictions would bring down the overall costs of registration exemplified another critical line of argumentation, namely, addressing the concerns that had in the past surrounded the adoption of a permanent-list approach (such as its greater costs relative to enumeration). The claim that provincially maintained lists could be employed was regarded as being even more important for the idea that a register could be economically feasible. In this regard, the commission could point to its own research for backing (pp. 125-32). Other research findings, it claimed, indicated that the high quality of the stored registration information, another long-time concern with a permanent-list approach, could be ensured.

Yet another reservation about permanent lists centred on fears that citizens might have about state intrusion and the loss of privacy. In response, the commission suggested that a "high-quality voters register" could be established and maintained without the need to access confidential information in government databases (p. 124), that registration could be kept voluntary, without voters having to relinquish the right to list themselves for a particular election, and that the current legal restrictions limiting the use of lists for electoral purposes could be extended, along with the implementation of appropriate administrative and technical safeguards.

A final line of reasoning involved challenging the idea that what some regarded as distinctive benefits of the enumeration system would not necessarily be lost in the move to a register. In response to the argument that voter interest could decline without personal contact with enumerators as representatives of the state, the commission suggested (but without any supporting evidence) that the extensive campaign activity would itself produce sufficient stimulation. In a somewhat similar vein, it asserted that "a shorter election period would not diminish the time available to conduct a campaign at the local level" (p. 123) — candidates and parties would get the preliminary lists of voters earlier since they would be automatically produced from the register.[32]

Putting Elections Canada into the picture

While it is clear that the next focal point in the narrative is Elections Canada, there are several possible ways of inserting the agency into the analysis relative to this background of significant discussion and the urging of change. One possible interpretation would be to take its subsequent role and specific advocacy of a permanent list as deriving from, and responding to, these developments in the broader environment. Another vantage point, and the one adopted here, attributes more autonomy and proactivity to the agency and, in fact, places it at the centre of an explanation of the changeover. In essence, it appears that Elections Canada was already motivated to give serious consideration to the idea of a register and, in effect, capitalized on the greater receptivity to such a change that was being engendered. This included taking advantage of the contribution that was made by the RCERPF in enhancing the legitimacy of the idea of a new registration method.

Such a perspective finds substantiation, in part, by the demonstration that the causal nexus between the RCERPF's advocacy of a register and subsequent developments is weaker and much less direct than might be expected. Key to this characterization is the commission's recommendation of provincially maintained lists. This was simply a nonstarter for Elections Canada, and, indeed, it is difficult to imagine that the agency would ever take such a suggestion seriously, given that provincial processes and eligibility requirements differ too widely to allow it to meet its obligation for standardization and a national outlook. There is also, of course, the play of ordinary bureaucratic politics and federal-provincial considerations that suggest that the agency would have been reluctant to cede direction of the registration process. Co-operating with the provinces was one thing, yielding control was quite another. A key discussion document that would later emerge from Elections Canada makes this point in plain language:

Elections Canada has a pan-Canadian need for complete, accurate and current electors lists. Federal electoral eligibility requirements provide a common denominator amongst federal, provincial and territorial jurisdictions. Elections Canada is, therefore, well positioned to assume the role of leadership.[33]

Still, this did not stop the agency from repeatedly dwelling on the commission's sanctioning of a permanent-list approach as a critical source justifying a switch in registration regimes.

The initiatives that Elections Canada undertook well before the RCERPF tabled its final report (in February 1992) constitute even more persuasive evidence that the changeover was only diffusely and tenuously the result of the commission's work; more to the point, they indicate the agency's predisposition toward the adoption of a permanent-list approach. In part, these steps suggest a determined response to the growing recognition that Elections Canada needed to exploit new technology, especially computer-based technology. Still, the tight sequencing of these initiatives and corresponding developments strongly indicates that these measures were put into place with the larger goal of developing a list well in mind.

Specifically, by-elections as early as 1990 provided the agency with an opportunity to, in its own words, "test customized software for the computerization of the lists of electors."[34] That experience provided the basis for a March 1991 commitment to use procedures that had already been developed (known as Elections Canada Automated Production of Lists of Electors, or ECAPLE) to produce voters lists on a broader scale. The first opportunity to do so came in October 1992 with the referendum vote on the Charlottetown Accord, in the 220 ridings outside of the province of Quebec (which had opted to supervise the referendum under its own rules). Even if the computerized lists were drawn up in conjunction with an enumeration, this large-scale use of automation was a significant step on the road to a permanent list. More to the point, it was what Elections Canada not only believed but, as well, what it planned for. The goal was to have the finalized 1992 voters list serve as the basis for the preliminary list for the next general election, expected in 1993, thus eliminating the need for another enumeration. This would allow the agency to claim a relevant precedent in moving toward a register, since list reuse is the core principle of such a system. In practical terms, it would allow Elections Canada to point to the acquisition of necessary experience and make more concrete the ways in which the foregoing of a door-to-door canvass would save money.

The forward thinking of the organization in this regard is quite apparent. A specific provision in the 1992 *Referendum Act* allowed for reuse of the voters list for up to one year following the nationwide consultation on the Charlottetown Accord. Moreover, this intent was certainly not disguised by Elections Canada. In his report on the referendum, the chief electoral officer made it quite clear what he had in mind for the future and the importance of computer automation in achieving that objective.

> Implementation of the ECAPLE system for the referendum was an investment in the future. The system played a key role in making possible the re-use of the official lists of the referendum as preliminary lists for the 35th general election, as was foreseen in the *Referendum Act*, and its continued use offers potential for savings in future electoral events at the federal, provincial and municipal levels.[35]

Kingsley's report on the 1993 election is even more forthcoming and elaborative of what the larger objective was, and indeed includes a chapter appropriately titled "Preparing for a Continuous Register of Electors."[36] The preface to this chapter is interesting not only for its summary statement about the commitment to a register, but also for the way in which it justifies that commitment, illustrating several of the interpretations discussed above:

> In its report of February 1992, the Royal Commission on Electoral Reform and Party Financing recommended that Elections Canada investigate ways of reducing duplicated efforts among election administrators at the federal, provincial/territorial, and municipal levels, especially in the compilation of the voters list. From the number of submissions to the Royal Commission and the number of letters to Elections Canada, it is clear that methods better than door-to-door enumeration must be found to prepare the voters lists. Some form of a continuous register, that is, a voters list that is maintained and updated on a regular basis, seems to be the obvious solution. (p. 130)

As will be seen, Kingsley, in an interview with the author, confirmed an even earlier commitment to a permanent-list approach on the part of Elections Canada.

By itself, the fact that the chief electoral officer was personally strongly in favour of a change in registration methods is no minor detail. Indeed, it appears that if Elections Canada was at the centre of the process of bringing about a switch, Kingsley was its epicentre. His public reports and pronouncements, as well as his comments during the interview,[37] provide plenty of evidence of the leading role that he played. This is not to suggest that the idea originated with Kingsley. By his own admission, it was one that had been bandied about within

Elections Canada before he took over, and certainly it is fathomable that over the years there would have been much "institutional reflection" on registration matters, increasing as enumeration came under intensifying scrutiny. Rather, what is a simple but nevertheless vital point to understand about Kingsley is that, as the top official, he came to hold a sturdy personal commitment to a permanent list not long after assuming the post in February 1990, and he clearly pushed for its implementation as soon as circumstances permitted. Indeed, it is difficult to imagine the register coming into force as quickly as it did without his enthusiastic commitment to a new approach and without his guidance in focusing the agency's efforts in that direction.

The formal record, including Kingsley's statutory reports on the 1992 referendum and the 1993 election (both issued in January 1994), is replete with substantiating evidence and cannot possibly be read without immediately grasping the strength of the commitment to a register-based approach. A few years later, in April 1996, Kingsley would appear before the Standing Committee on Procedure and House Affairs, welcomed by the chair to discuss "his favourite project, the registry of elections."[38] In October, Herb Gray stood in the House to move that Bill C-63 be referred to that same committee, commenting: "This bill stems from the report of the Royal Commission on Electoral Reform and Party Financing, the Lortie Commission, and from the recommendations made by the Chief Electoral Officer."[39]

In the interview with the author, Kingsley corroborated the evidence on his central role, and he also helped to shed light on some important details that, in turn, reinforce the perspective that privileges the impact of the agency in the overall scheme of things. Clearly, he had thought about the possibility of a register early on. When he first arrived at Elections Canada, the Lortie Commission was in full swing, but by his own admission Kingsley initially concentrated on the problems associated with the lack of automation and standardization in drawing up voters lists for the 1988 election. Even before the RCERPF released its report, he had laid the groundwork for the development of ECAPLE for use in the 1992 referendum. At one point in the interview, he allowed that the notion to push for a register had come to him early on but that his staff warned him that "you can't go too far too fast." At other times, he talked about how, while he gave particular direction to the development of the register, it was an idea that had been "percolating" for a while in Elections Canada: "A damned good idea whose time had come" was how he described it. That it was his initiative to reuse the 1992 list is another important marker of Kingsley's early conviction; indeed, he indicated that he would have preferred to see amendments to the *Referendum Act* permitting the re-employment within two years, not one, presumably to enlarge the window of opportunity for establishing the reuse precedent. Certainly, he was unambiguous in communicating the importance of a consecutive application of the list and of its forming the basis for testing a permanent-list system.

Kingsley's claims about the primary reasons that drew him early on to the notion of a register are also consistent with other available information about how the process unfolded. He spoke of being motivated by the growing problems with enumeration and, as well, the need, as a general matter, to develop automated and standardized procedures; these were, of course, the kinds of arguments that were being widely made to justify a change in registration approaches. He also identified possible future benefits in areas such as cartography. Interestingly, he did not spontaneously mention cost considerations, which, as will be seen, came to figure prominently in arguments that were being marshalled on behalf of a register. Only when directly asked about their role did he give them some relevance, indicating that as a career civil servant he was always interested in saving money. Still, he did maintain that "Cost is a factor; it is not a driving factor." He also said he "might have had second thoughts" had the research demonstrated that the new system would cost more.

Two other factors, the idea of sharing data with the provinces and the "benefit" of having a shortened campaign period, were also not offered upfront as having primary relevance. Again, only when specifically probed about each did he indicate that they were "important secondary" considerations. Sharing does save the taxpayer money, he readily acknowledged, but it was up to the provinces to use the data. His only elaboration with regard to campaign length was to suggest, interestingly enough, that the Lortie Commission was mistaken in concluding that a 40-day campaign is possible even with enumeration; only a register, Kingsley maintained, can reduce the period to under 47 days.

His broader comments on the RCERPF reinforce the argument made above about its lesser or its more indirect impact on the emergence of the register. Kingsley even went so far as to assert, in rather blunt language, that the RCERPF's support for a provincially based approach had a negative impact on the movement toward a register: "It hindered the work of Elections Canada because it created for some provincial electoral bodies a form of tacit recognition of their centrality; some saw it as being in their hands." In fact, if the interview provided a sense that any report deserves to be singled out for having influenced his thinking and developments within Elections Canada, it was the auditor general's report, which had sharply criticized the agency's sluggishness in embracing new technology. This jolt to the agency appears to have engendered a commitment to catch up technologically and indeed, judging from Kingsley's demeanour and actions, to go much further than that.

This point merits emphasis and helps make a larger argument that the eagerness for the project was part of a broader vision, no doubt shared by Kingsley and others in Elections Canada, that the agency needed to embrace technological change and innovation unreservedly. The development of a computerized list was only one way that Elections Canada could position itself in the forefront with regard to the use of the most sophisticated technology available; other areas included digital mapping, voting by telephone, electronic voting (or "smart cards") and voting machines (including touch-screen equipment) in ballot booths.[40] A computerized voters list would fit well with and indeed facilitate these innovations. In short, it is probably fair to say that a "culture of technology" gripped Elections Canada and that the exploitation of information technology became an operating and self-evident norm. This outlook represented a conscious break with the past and with an orientation that had been criticized in the auditor general's report; by adopting the very latest in automation and other technology, the agency would be heeding the imperative to "modernize," a word that Kingsley repeatedly used as he endeavoured to promote the switchover.[41]

Beyond establishing ECAPLE, Kingsley and the agency took other concrete steps that reveal an eagerness to move expeditiously toward instituting a register. A steering committee was struck on October 20, 1993, with a mandate to "act as a coordinating body, within Elections Canada, with respect to communicating and encouraging the development of A Continuous Register of Electors."[42] By the spring of 1994, the in-house "Discussion Paper on a Continuous Register of Electors" was produced, intended to provide a "*high level overview* of the concept of the Register."[43] The document provides background commentary about registers, including the experiences of other countries, but the bulk of the treatment and its overall tone make it quite clear that what was at issue was not whether a register would be established but rather the timing and the modalities of *how* it might be brought to fruition.[44] No consideration whatsoever was given to the possibility of retaining enumeration and handling its shortcomings through remedial measures; instead, the emphasis was squarely on the need for change. To this end, there was the by now familiar litany of complaints surrounding enumeration and the advantages and opportunities that a register could confer.

Other important themes further reveal the goal-oriented nature of the document. One chapter, for instance, dealt with design considerations and some administrative and technical matters that would need to be taken into account in establishing a register (e.g., how the register might be structured, data quality considerations and the like). Perhaps most important of all was the chapter "Strategic Avenues," which dealt with the issues and obstacles, including political ones, that needed to be addressed. One section, headed "Political Will," pointed out that "politicians need to be educated about the current problems and potential solutions in a cross-jurisdictional perspective" (p. 28). The document concluded, confidently, that "key arguments support the initiation of a process that will lead to the creation of a shared Register of Electors" (p. 33).

The next step involved the steering committee setting up a special project team, in late 1994 or early 1995,[45] charged with examining "the costs and benefits of a register, extensive work on new processes and procedures, evaluation of sources for updating data, consultation with potential partners, and feasibility assessment."[46] One year later, in December 1995, sufficient work had been done to allow the chief electoral officer to present the team's main findings to the House of Commons Standing Committee on Procedure and House Affairs at an in camera meeting.

The project team's report, *The Register of Electors Project: A Report on Research and Feasibility*, began circulating in the spring of 1996. It declared unequivocally that study and analysis had shown that a national register was "both feasible and cost effective" (p. 5). Other assertions were set forth as additional "main conclusions." A few of these reiterated familiar themes such as how the register would allow a reduction in the election period from 47 to 36 days. Another identified the most appropriate existing sources for keeping the register up-to-date and argued that a "targeted reliability level of 80%" for the register could be maintained, meaning that the derived preliminary list would have the correct addresses for an estimated 80 percent of eligible voters. This figure was judged as "the level necessary to conduct an electoral event" (p. 5). The report also confirmed current support and future interest by other electoral agencies for a shared national register and as well dealt with the kinds of legislative changes that would be required for its creation. Finally, a key conclusion highlighted fiscal savings. While the implementation of a register at the next election would cost about the same as carrying out an election under enumeration (in large measure because a final enumeration would be necessary), each subsequent contest would allow for savings (a "cost avoidance") of $40 million, and even more as other jurisdictions joined in (p. 6).[47]

Beyond these specifics, the report's general tone reflected what had by then developed into the set strategy for selling the register, and one rooted in the logic employed by the Lortie Commission, namely, taking the problems and limitations of the enumeration approach as a point of departure, demonstrating how a permanent-list system would both ameliorate those difficulties and provide further benefits, and finally, pointing out how traditional concerns attendant with a permanent-list method could be surmounted. The latter included the argument that the voters list could indeed be effectively maintained and kept up-to-date. It was even pointed out that "electoral information would be of higher quality, because preliminary lists of electors would be produced over time and not in the tight time frames currently required during an electoral event" (p. 17).

The report also addressed the long-standing concern over invasion of privacy and confidentiality of the information that electors provided, and in several ways. First of all, it proclaimed privacy and confidentiality as core standards that had helped guide the research; this was part of the commitment to ensure that the register would preserve "certain principles and characteristics of the Canadian electoral system." There were also indications that the project team had reviewed the treatment of privacy concerns in other jurisdictions, and there were references to how there had been continuous consultations with the federal Privacy Commissioner's Office (p. 21); indeed, there was an acknowledgement that a "privacy advisor" from the office had participated in many of the workshops (p. 7).

The politics of change[48]

However one might characterize Elections Canada's packaging of arguments and background research to make a case for a register, it is abundantly clear that the government bought the package. Its support of an altered registration process and abbreviated campaign period is indicated most obviously by the legislative priority it attached to the changeover. On October 21, 1996, a little over half a year after the release of *The Register of Electors Project*, Bill C-63 was given first reading. The legislation moved fairly quickly through the House, receiving a third reading on November 26. The government's firm support of the initiative is further evident in the selection of Herb Gray, who was House leader and solicitor general, to shepherd the bill through the chamber. Courtney similarly notes (in passing) this turn of events as being reflective of the government's determined backing and, importantly, adds that his interviews suggested firm specific support from Jean Chrétien and the Prime Minister's Office. Political support was apparent not only from within the executive, however. It was also forthcoming from legislators as a whole. Indeed, the Standing Committee on Procedure and House Affairs had signalled its approval even before the formal release of the *The Register of Electors Project* report, when members were briefed by Kingsley in December 1995. While that session, it will be recalled, was held behind closed doors, the minutes of subsequent meetings dealing with the draft legislation make it clear that there had been widespread endorsement for the register at that earlier gathering. Moreover, in the report itself the committee was characterized as having "concurred in the value of moving to a register system, enthusiastically supported the approach proposed for its implementation, and agreed that Elections Canada should immediately prepare a report in the form of draft legislation to begin to develop the administrative mechanisms and systems needed to use a register in the fall of 1997."[49]

What is the basis of this political support? Why was the changeover given such an easy political ride? Courtney does not elaborate on what, specifically, may have motivated Chrétien, his ministers and his political advisers to embrace the change, but presumably they accepted the long-standing argument that a permanent list would resolve old problems and bring new benefits — among which the prospect of curbing expenditures would have had special appeal. While the costs associated with running the registration system had always been one of the criteria for evaluating the relative merits of different approaches, registration economics came to play an even larger role as neoliberal principles became more widespread and entrenched during this period and as the Chrétien government became convinced of the need to reduce the state's financial burden. In short, as the costs of the registration system came to be evaluated within a climate of economic restraint, the notion that a permanent voters list could save governments and taxpayers money would have generated a positive response in many quarters.

Federal-provincial politics were no doubt also a consideration. At one level, the fact that some provinces had signalled their interest in co-operating with Ottawa enhanced the prospect of the federal government using provincial sources to update the register and cut overall costs through shared voters lists. Another amenable development, alluded to earlier, was the adoption at that time of permanent lists by a growing number of provinces. On a more political level, however, Ottawa's ability to point to provincial interest and possible involvement, in an era when cross-jurisdictional conflict was more common than not, provided it with a focal point for federal-provincial co-operation and success. It also served to illustrate that concrete steps were being taken to end overlap and duplication of effort on the part of the different governments,[50] a fixation that had been intensifying as part of a general process of "rethinking government" designed to render its operations more efficient and cost-effective.[51] Thus federal-provincial co-operation meshed with savings as significant explanatory factors driving support for the register.[52]

The appeal of a reduced campaign period must have also been politically attractive to key politicians and their advisers. While most proponents of a shorter campaign touted its virtues by making the specific argument that administrative costs would be curbed or by offering the more diffuse notion that Canadians would be spared the tedium of an overly long contest, behind the scenes it may well have been understood that a condensed campaign would serve the re-election interests of an incumbent government — especially one that commanded a substantial lead in public opinion polls and that faced a sharply divided opposition. Even in the absence of hard evidence for a direct link between campaign length and incumbency success,[53] the government likely realized that any lead it held would be harder to overcome in a compressed campaign period.[54]

The main opposition parties were no doubt also aware of this Liberal advantage, though they merely alluded to it in the House.[55] With the Liberals still leading in the polls and an election imminent, the worry was that hasty implementation would indeed give the governing party an advantage.[56] This is the chief reason why the opposition parties ultimately voted against the legislation. Indeed, the government used time allocation to end debate and expedite passage, ignoring opposition protests that there had been insufficient consultation and that there was no "real reason" to rush the process. There were also the obligatory and predictable add-on complaints, such as that the bill did not go far enough in the context of what was regarded as other areas in need of consideration. The Reform Party wanted additional deliberation on the subject of having fixed elections and the establishment of recall procedures, and also urged debate on removing the subsidies and tax concessions to political parties.[57]

From the other direction, the Bloc Québécois pushed for a stricter election finance regime, specifically one that mimicked Quebec's more regulated approach. That said, the opposition protest was driven mostly by the timing of the process and its hurried implementation of the new registration approach. As has already been pointed out, the Standing Committee on Procedure and House Affairs as a whole had been supportive of the idea of change from the very outset, and throughout the legislative proceedings the two main opposition parties continued to signal their fundamental agreement with the principles of establishing a permanent list and a shorter campaign.[58] Reform MPs on the committee and in the House were openly enthusiastic about the possible cost reductions that would be realized from the changeover (and, to a lesser extent, content that a source of minor patronage would be removed for the dominant Liberals), while, for its part, the Bloc continued to take its lead from developments in Quebec where the provincial government was in the process of establishing its own voters register. Mention might be made as well that opposition members, as incumbent politicians contemplating their own personal re-election campaigns, likely also regarded a shorter campaign as an attractive feature.

In short, the fact that Reform and the Bloc ultimately voted against Bill C-63 does not contradict the essential portrayal that the major political forces were lined up on the same side. Moreover, in retrospect, given their political outlooks, it is not at all surprising that there was support for the permanent list on the benches opposite the government. This is, of course, one of the implications of what was the most prominent feature of the political era, the collapse of the traditional party system, characterized by devastating losses by the New Democratic Party and, especially, the Progressive Conservative Party, and their replacement by Reform and the Bloc. The two older parties were virtually invisible in the debate, as they were in Parliament generally, and, of course, lacking status as "recognized parties," had no representation on the Standing Committee on Procedure and House Affairs.

The executive, the Liberal Party and the two main opposition parties were clearly neither invisible nor irrelevant as part of the defining political environment that ultimately produced the National Register. Obviously, their endorsements, and particularly the backing by the government, were essential ingredients, and it is significant that these forces were all arrayed on the same side as the process unfolded. However, their impact, even if convergent in nature, was subsequent to the initiative demonstrated by Elections Canada and the engineering efforts that agency made to develop and sell the case for change. The early steps that Elections Canada took, already documented, are especially relevant for appreciating its prior impact with reference to these political forces. Reinforcing this interpretation of causal sequencing is the virtual absence of any evidence suggesting that these political actors, all of whom fared well in the 1993 election, had signalled any pre-existing preferences for a change in the registration system. Especially important in this regard is the lack of any mention of registration reform in the Liberals' famous "Red Book," which set out campaign pledges in numerous areas.[59] Another timing-sensitive point is apparent when one recalls that the agency established its all-important steering committee with the mandate, again, "to act as a coordinating body, within Elections Canada, with respect to communicating and encouraging the development of A Continuous Register of Electors" on October 20, 1993, that is, even before the 1993 election campaign had drawn to a close.

In sum, the argument here is that both government and opposition responded positively to Elections Canada's initiative because the change was politically and economically favourable and because it was in the interests, both partisan and otherwise, of the main parties to go along. No doubt, much of what was pitched to the elected officials and their advisers by Elections Canada reflected its appreciation of which arguments, explicitly made or perhaps merely implied, would be most effective. In this sense, the organization not only capitalized on amenable circumstances as it took up the cause of a register, but actively championed it as well.

Number of options on the table: one

John Courtney makes the simple, though important, point that the process of change became easier in the absence of debate on what might replace enumeration. Consensus among those seeking change that the only acceptable alternative was some form of "open" permanent list no doubt helped concentrate opposition to enumeration in favour of a register. A broader take on Courtney's observation might be that this consensus effectively ended up precluding the option of reforming enumeration. As it was, the reflection and discussion that surrounded registration reform tended to be narrowly focused. A more encompassing consideration might have done more to stress the relative strengths of enumeration and to include an analysis of the possibility of reforming the canvassing-based process to meet what were regarded as its limitations. Such a stance would not have been completely at odds with the conclusions of the Lortie Commission, which did, of course, offer important recommendations for improving the enumeration system, even as it favoured the move to a (provincially based) register.

However, the weight of the recommendations was undermined not only by the RCERPF's advocacy of a permanent list, but also by the limited analysis that it had conducted as it drew critical conclusions about the functioning of the enumeration method. This is the case that Courtney and Smith make in their RCERPF-sponsored background publication.[60] While admitting that the shortage of qualified enumerators had been a problem, they state that it was not a particularly new difficulty, that there was no hard evidence that it had increased in magnitude and that it was in any event a circumscribed matter involving some, but hardly all, urban polls. Courtney and Smith also wonder if enumeration problems, especially overlooked voters, could indeed all be linked to the failure to find sufficiently qualified enumerators. Importantly, they point out that 85 percent of the returning officers were new in 1988 and that their inexperience could easily have resulted in the inadequate training of enumerators. In addition, they observe that the pressure to begin the campaign quickly was "another practical constraint on efficiency that is quite separate from the quality of personnel" (p. 363). They also list other factors, such as inadequate pay, as explanations for the shortfall in qualified enumerators.

Courtney and Smith also raise questions about the evidence justifying a move toward a shorter campaign. While the commission was no doubt impressed by the large number of interveners who identified a shorter campaign as one advantage of a permanent list, it is unclear whether this sentiment spread much beyond the context of its proceedings. The two authors admit that although there had been some concern about campaign length in the recent past (and presumably this is what led to the reduction from 60 to 50 days), their sense of the matter is that it continued to be a fairly minor preoccupation. After reviewing statutory reports, newspaper commentaries and Elections Canada's publication *Contact*, they conclude: "In a list of problems and shortcomings of Canada's voter registration system, the length of the campaign to which enumeration contributes, must be ranked low" (p. 371).

It would appear, then, that the RCERPF's limited research into the problems of enumeration is one of the specific ways in which the commission contributed to the ascendancy of the permanent-list idea, which Elections Canada benefited from as it began to sponsor a federally controlled permanent list. The absence of a comprehensive assessment, one that included research-based solutions to the problems of enumeration, made it easier for the agency to take those difficulties (and the supposed benefits of a shorter campaign) as its launching point. It then had only to demonstrate that the substitution of a permanent list would resolve those problems. Of course, the fact that the agency's research agenda did not itself include any analysis of a revamped enumeration process is even more indicative of a very early preference for a complete overhaul. Note as well that Elections Canada's general strategy of selling the idea of a register served the same purpose — to keep all other options off the table.

Participation and participation inequality: limited attention

Elections Canada's research agenda was, unfortunately, also circumscribed in another important way: relatively little concrete consideration was given to the impact of a permanent-list approach on electoral participation, including equality of participation. To be sure, there was a formal commitment to the idea that any new system would need to work to facilitate the vote. Indeed, appearing before the Senate as it considered Bill C-63, Kingsley articulated six principles that had guided thinking about the development and maintenance of the register, pointing out that the RCERPF's own deliberations had been framed in these same principles. The first three centred on the need to ensure that the state would continue to assume primary responsibility for registration, that potential voters would be given postwrit opportunities to register and that the new system would function as effectively as the enumeration system — meaning that levels of coverage and accuracy would be equivalent to those achieved through enumeration. The remaining guidelines centred on concerns about privacy, confidentiality and the right not to participate in the process.[61]

These principles are comparable, though not identical, to the orienting standards that were spelled out in *The Register of Electors Project*.[62] The first three of these similarly identified state initiative and voter access as guiding principles. The fourth pledged to respect electors' privacy and the confidentiality of their personal information. A fifth posited the need to locate reliable data sources, in order both to minimize the costs of developing and maintaining the register and to avoid "any further imposition on Canadians in gathering personal information." Finally, there was a commitment to investigate the matter of sharing the register's data with other jurisdictions.

The main point is that nowhere in that key report was there any note of concern about the possible negative effects on voter participation that might ensue from the implementation of a permanent list. Short of a population register that would serve as the basis for a voters register or a system of mandatory registration, neither of which was seriously considered (and understandably so), the permanent-list method as envisaged could never match the effectiveness of the state-initiated enumeration approach in facilitating regististration. It is true, of course, that once they are inscribed in the National Register, voting would be a relatively easy matter for the overwhelming majority of Canadians who do not move between electoral events. Nevertheless, for the many who do change addresses, particularly if they move out of their original constituency (see below), some action would be required to correct their registration information. The newly eligible, especially those turning 18, would need to do even more to register in the first instance. Without denying that with the new regime in place Elections Canada has made it as easy as possible for individuals to become properly registered, and as well granting that, from an objective perspective, the amount of effort required to do so is quite minimal, the reality nevertheless remains that individuals still need to exercise some initiative. And, again, everything that is known about the facilitation and inhibition of participation would anticipate a drop in participation as these demands, modest as they may be, are placed on the prospective voter. Given the circumstances and the demographics involved, the negative effect is likely to be accentuated among those who frequently move, such as renters and poorer persons, as well as among those entering the electorate. Many such individuals are already less prone to vote, which is why there have long been disparities in turnout across social categories. A registration regime that demands some action on the part of such individuals may very well run the risk of creating even larger gaps. Unfortunately, such concerns about diminished participation and participation equality, arguably the main disadvantages associated with the new system, were largely ignored in the extensive research and discussion that framed the understanding and arguments about the impact of a regime change.[63]

But what of the fact that matching the "effectiveness" of enumeration was set out as one of the criteria that the new system had to meet in order to be considered acceptable? In particular, *The Register of Electors Project* claimed that its background studies had shown that a new permanent-list approach, drawing upon a variety of sources to establish the register and keep it reasonably up to date, and, furthermore, incorporating an enhanced revision process, could in the final analysis equal the coverage and accuracy levels realized through enumeration. Does this not, then, constitute relevant research about matching the data quality of the old system, and thus respond to criticism that participation was not a priority? One obvious problem with such a rebuttal is that a larger array of revision opportunities is just that — opportunities — and individuals would still need to take advantage of them. In other words, it is precisely the rebalancing of the registration exercise toward a heavier emphasis on revision that is at the heart of the new system. Therefore, to demonstrate that compensating opportunities could be put in place, without, at the same time, an analysis of how easy or difficult it would be for citizens, particularly specific categories of them, to avail themselves of the opportunities constitutes a very incomplete form of analysis.

The notion that the research into data quality might be taken as evidence of a concern about participation is also weakened by the low threshold that Elections Canada set for itself as it defined what the agency needed to achieve in order to meet the pledge of matching enumeration's coverage and accuracy. This point merits some unpacking. *The Register of Electors Project* claims that the research showed that "a register could be maintained between electoral events at a targeted reliability level of 80%, the level necessary to begin conducting an electoral event, by importing electronic data from existing sources" (p. 5). This percentage represents all eligible voters expected to be listed at their correct address as the register generates the preliminary lists. Importantly, it is "based on the 1993 experience of successfully conducting an election using an unmaintained one-year-old list that had declined to an average of 80% level of reliability" (pp. 25-26). This benchmark, then, has its origins in the reuse of the 1992 list one year later, without modification — that is, without additions or purgings — and in the knowledge that 20 percent of the electorate is affected by demographic changes over the course of a given year (16 percent address changes, 2 percent new 18-year-olds, 1 percent new citizens and 1 percent deaths). The intent, of course, was to have revision and election-day registration provide the opportunities for the needed corrections and additions.

There are two points to make regarding the 80-percent reliability figure. First, it was perhaps given more credence than might be warranted simply because the 1993 election with which it was associated was deemed by Elections Canada to have been "successfully conducted." Without challenging that summary characterization — establishing the overall success of an election, from an administrative perspective, is surely a complex undertaking – the attribution still required detailed substantiation. It would be insufficient to merely state that an unprecedented number of people registered during the revision period and on voting day; indeed, it would be strange had this not occurred given that an outdated list was used in most of the country and election-day registration was a new arrangement. An analysis that explored how easy or difficult individuals found it to register, how many did not do so because of registration problems and the like, would have provided the basis for a more convincing claim about success. Second, and more importantly, 80 percent is the target for a list unmaintained over a one-year period. However, Elections Canada had from the outset committed itself to a strategy whereby the list would be updated regularly, certainly multiple times within any given 12-month interval. Thus meeting the target of 80 percent amounted to a lesser challenge. Still,

Elections Canada has not exceeded that comparatively modest goal by a large margin. Estimates of the data quality of the National Register since June 1998 have generally ranged from 80 to 83 percent.[64]

Part II: The Impact on Participation

In evaluating the consequences associated with the change in registration method, the greatest emphasis is placed here on the electoral involvement of Canadians. Such a focus is in keeping with the tradition in Canada of considering the facilitation of voter participation as the primary objective of a registration regime. As was noted above, however, Elections Canada ended up paying less attention to participation concerns than it ought to have done as it developed the case for the adoption of a register. This raises the question of whether or not its limited focus on participation has resulted in any negative outcomes.

The fact that voter turnout in Canada has dropped so precipitously in the last few elections is another reason why an emphasis on participation is warranted. Up until the 1988 contest, voter turnout over the postwar period averaged around 75 percent and while this figure is low relative to turnout in most other long-established democracies, Canadian turnout did not drift noticeably upwards or downwards over the period.[65] A dramatically new pattern, however, has been established over the course of the last three elections. Participation, as officially recorded (votes cast as a percentage of registered voters), dropped to 69.6 percent for the 1993 election, underwent another decline to 67.0 percent for the 1997 contest and then plummeted to 61.2 percent for the 2000 election. The last figure was the subject of much commentary, not only because it helped confirm the negative trend since 1988, but also because it established a new record for the worst turnout ever documented in a federal election, eclipsing the record low of 63 percent set in 1896. Not surprisingly, the drop in electoral participation has been regarded as being serious enough to prompt a fair amount of soul-searching as to its meaning for the nature and legitimacy of Canadian democracy.[66] Chief Electoral Officer Kingsley appears to have had this in mind when he mused aloud about the possible wisdom of instituting compulsory voting in Canada.[67]

There has also been a considerable amount of scholarship vested in understanding why more and more Canadians are voting less and less.[68] While a variety of factors have been identified as contributing to lower turnout levels, much of the analysis has focused on generational effects, particularly the influx into the electorate of young voters who are less interested in and less knowledgeable about politics than their predecessors, and noticeably less inclined to participate than their similarly aged counterparts of earlier generations.[69] This phenomenon is also a source of participation inequality, insofar as turnout disparities have increased across age categories.

What bearing might the changeover in registration regimes have had on the lower levels of participation observed in recent elections? Has it had some impact, even of a secondary kind, on the post-1988 decline in voter turnout? The suggestion has, in fact, already been made that the move to a register can be ruled out as an explanation for the drop in turnout observed in the last three elections, simply because the decline began well before the new system came fully into effect with the 2000 election.[70] This idea finds additional support in the observation that voter turnout has declined in many other countries as well, so perhaps the Canadian experience is simply part of a broader trend.[71]

Still, such a line of argumentation does not by itself foreclose the possibility that the National Register of Electors played a role in lowering turnout in the 2000 election; it could be that turnout would have been higher were it not for the operation of the new registration process. Moreover, if this is true then it is conceivable that the change in registration regimes contributed, however modestly, to the decline in electoral participation at least across the 1997 and 2000 pairing of elections.

Perhaps a case could even be made that the move to a permanent list is relevant for understanding some of the broader post-1988 decline. After all, the 1993 election was conducted, outside of Quebec, on the basis of a registration process that had some of the hallmarks of a permanent-list approach.[72] The reuse of the year-old 1992 list meant a correspondingly heavy reliance on revision and polling-day registration to handle subsequent changes and additions, which might have resulted in lower participation because of the greater effort involved in registering. As for the 1997 election, it was, of course, preceded by the last enumeration held before the formal adoption of the National Register. However, as discussed below, that particular canvassing effort did not conform exactly to standard or ideal practices, which leaves some room for doubt about its interpretation vis-à-vis the facilitation of voting.

As will be seen, the extent to which the implications of the change in registration regimes can be linked to broader patterns of turnout decline (in addition to whatever impact it may have had in the specific 2000 election) depends, in part, on the approach taken to characterize the dependent variable. Two sorts of measures are available to gauge the registration-participation relationship: the standard turnout measure defined by votes cast as a percentage of registered voters, and eligibility measures. The latter allow for investigation of the variability in the "coverage" of the registration process as it has a bearing on the overall turnout rate. With registration as a necessary condition for voting, turnout is naturally decreased as large numbers of adult citizens are excluded from the lists. Put differently, eligibility measures, by benchmarking the number of votes cast relative to the number of eligible citizens, index voter turnout while taking into account the operation of the registration regime.

Official turnout in 1984-2000

The utility of the turnout measure defined by votes cast as a percentage of registered voters stems from its status as the official measure, as published by Elections Canada, for documenting voter turnout in the country and, of course, from its long-time use by students of Canadian elections. Its pertinence here, however, arises from its value as an index of participation when the focus is on how easy or difficult it is for those *already* registered to follow through and cast their vote.

In this regard, it is pertinent to recall the near-truism that the level of participation is inversely related to the amount of effort required to carry out the activity in question. This leads to the expectation that a smaller proportion of those registered under a permanent-list method will vote compared to the traditional postwrit enumeration system. This follows simply because the compilation of the voters list afresh and in close proximity to the election translates into situations where individuals are more likely to be listed at their current address and to have received the subsequent information they require in order to cast their ballot; put differently, the timeliness of the postwrit enumeration process implies fewer listing errors and other problems requiring action. In contrast, permanent lists (at least those based on a volunteer system) cannot match this level of currency, because they cannot track and instantaneously record Canada's high level of population mobility; consequently, the register's preliminary list will contain a large number of individuals listed at outdated addresses.

The need for remedial action, or lack thereof, on the part of electors is not the only way of understanding how registration effects may influence participation. Under the traditional system, personal contact with enumerators on the doorstep may very well have acted as a stimulus enhancing the probability that individuals vote beyond their existing predispositions to do so. Under the new regime, it seems unlikely that receipt of a card, even one that contains the correct information, will in itself make much of a difference. A more certain case can be made for the importance of contacting in connection with the canvassing efforts of parties and candidates. In their study of the 2000 election, Blais et al. determined that, all things being equal, "the likelihood of voting increased by five percentage points when someone had been contacted by a political party."[73] However, electors who are improperly recorded on the register are less likely to be mobilized by the parties; they risk being missed during the course of the campaign because the parties rely heavily on the preliminary lists.[74]

That said, it is somewhat problematic to draw inferences about registration effects for the entire period in question on the basis of the official voter turnout measure. (As will be seen, the specific 2000 election lends itself to a more certain investigation of the link between registration circumstances and turnout.) The fluctuations in voter participation across the elections in question are influenced by so many factors, including generational replacement, that it is nearly impossible to attribute specific effects to the registration circumstances in which individuals found themselves. The challenge of drawing inferences is compounded, ironically enough, by the errors of inclusion that attend the permanent-list approach, mainly because of the delay in purging names (those individuals who are no longer part of the electorate because they have emigrated or passed away) and in correcting duplicate listings (those individuals who have reregistered following a move but are listed at their former address as well as their current one). These inaccuracies make it difficult to sort out how much the declining turnout figures reflect the problems faced by registered electors as they sought to participate and how much is due to the existence of "impossible voters" picked up in the denominator of the turnout measure.[75]

However, one registration-based effect can be discerned in connection with the standard measure: the surplus names and redundant listings have created the appearance of a lower level of participation than actually prevailed. The artificially deflated turnout figures that result are not a particularly attractive by-product of the permanent-list method, as Canada's lower-than-average turnout rates hardly need to be exaggerated.

This inflationary effect is demonstrated in figure 1 by showing the turnout rates for the last five elections as officially reported and as adjusted, drawing upon existing information and research that provide the basis for estimating (and thus subtracting) extra names and listings. It is quite apparent that the adjusted figures do transform the pattern of decline over time. Information is not available, it should be noted, to modify the official turnout figure of 75.3 percent for the two postwrit enumeration elections in 1984 and 1988. This is unfortunate because, even though in those elections the registration process was done from scratch and in close proximity to the election, there were no doubt some errors of inclusion — such as students being redundantly registered by their parents in their home constituency. That said, the number of errors would have been far less compared to what transpired in connection with list-based elections.

For the 1993 election, the official turnout rate is 69.6 percent and the corrected figure is 72.9 percent, which is the average of two near-equal estimates of similar magnitude, one (72.7 percent) derived from Elections Canada's reckoning of the number of duplicates and deceased on the final voters list,[76] the other (73.1 percent) taken from an independent analysis carried out by Blais et al.[77]

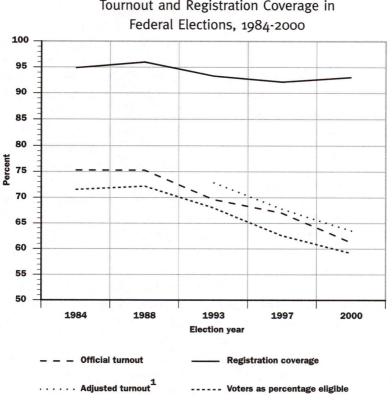

Figure 1

Tournout and Registration Coverage in Federal Elections, 1984-2000

Percent

100
95
90
85
80
75
70
65
60
55
50

1984   1988   1993   1997   2000

Election year

– – – Official turnout   ——— Registration coverage

· · · · · · Adjusted turnout[1]   - - - - - Voters as percentage eligible

Source: Official turnout figures taken from reports of the chief electoral officer. Other figures taken either directly or calculated from Elections Canada, Statistics Canada, IDEA and other sources.
[1] Surplus names and duplicate listings removed from the total number of individuals registered (1993, 1997 and 2000 elections only).

The reworked percentage suggests a more modest impression of the magnitude of turnout decline between 1988 and 1993; indeed the new figure is not far from the 75-percent benchmark and is well within the range of variation around that norm. The drop in participation really began in earnest with the 1997 election. The adjusted figure for that contest, using Elections Canada's estimates of surpluses,[78] is 67.8 percent, which represents a quite substantial five-point drop from 1993. This compares with a decline of only 2.6 percent based on the official, unadjusted tallies. The fact that the corrected figure lies within a percentage point of the unadjusted one (67.0 percent) reflects the fact that the 1997 election, based largely on a canvassing effort within two months of voting day, had fewer errors of inclusion.

The drop in turnout associated with the 2000 election would also appear to be "real." The official turnout rate plunged to 61.2 percent, a decline of almost six points (5.8 percent), while the adjusted figure of 63.6 percent (again calculated using Elections Canada information)[79] still represents a substantial four-point drop (4.2 percent). Nonetheless, the difference between the official and reworked figures — about two and a half points — is far from trivial and rivals in magnitude the adjustment made for the 1993 election. The recalculated figure itself takes into account an estimated 614,000 duplicates on the final list of voters and 177,000 individuals who had passed away since being inscribed on the National Register.

The other comment to make about the adjusted figure for 2000 is that its acceptance would remove that election from the record books as having the lowest turnout ever, allowing the 1896 contest to once again claim that dubious honour. Still, no amount of adjustment can alter the fundamental fact that voter decline in recent elections is real and deserves the attention it has received as a prominent feature of contemporary political behaviour in Canada.

Coverage and eligibility in 1984-2000

Typically, the number of individuals who meet the statutory age requirement is taken to denote the pool of eligible voters. In traditional immigrant-receiving societies, however, it is advisable to use citizenship as well as age to circumscribe the eligible population. Two versions of such measures are relevant here, a more important one that allows for direct measurement of the coverage achieved by the registration method by dividing the number inscribed by the number eligible, and a second, derivative measure that relates votes cast to the potential number of eligible voters.

In both cases, the same orthodoxy specifying an inverse relationship between the requirement of individual initiative and participation also anticipates less coverage (and less voting) in the new system relative to the traditional one. The state's more decidedly proactive approach in the past meant that eligible voters had to do little to get their names on the voters list. Moreover, the fact that the compilation of names was carried out in close proximity to election day meant that new 18-year-olds and new citizens were more likely to be included. By contrast, those not already on the permanent list would need to take some action, however minimal, to be included on the electoral rolls. Furthermore, being unregistered, these individuals are also more likely to be overlooked in the campaigning efforts of parties and candidates.

The adjusted registration data can be retained as the analysis shifts to consider what conclusions might be reached about coverage (and thus participation) differences over the same 1984-2000 period.[80] Of prime interest is the comparative performance of the enumeration and list systems in capturing the optimal number of eligible voters. The information needed to estimate the eligible population in terms of age and citizenship comes mainly from Elections Canada and Statistics Canada. Because these population figures are estimates,[81] as are the adjusted registration statistics for the last three elections, coverage rates are best considered in broad juxtaposition with one another rather than as precise point estimates. Of course, the fact that elections in the 1984-2000 period were carried out based on either enumeration or permanent-list principles allows for the comparison of coverage rates using the two methods. The enumeration elections of 1984 and 1988 were followed by reuse of the 1992 referendum voters list for the 1993 election (again, outside Quebec), by an enumeration process for the 1997 election and finally by a full application of the National Register in 2000.

The top graph line in Figure 1 indicates that coverage did decrease over the last three elections but not in a pattern that suggests that the decline is strictly associated with list-based methods.[82] Coverage dropped nearly three percentage points after the 1988 election and, importantly, did not rise with the enumeration-based contest in 1997. For 1984 and 1988, the registration effort is estimated to have reached 94.9 percent and 96 percent, respectively, of the eligible population. Inclusion decreased to 93.3 percent for the 1993 election, dropped further to 92.2 percent in 1997 and then rose slightly to 93.1 percent in 2000.

Taking these statistics at face value, the interpretation must be that coverage declined noticeably in the last three elections and that neither registration method was able to match previous levels. There is, moreover, a plausible basis for such a conclusion, and it involves two characterizations. One would be that the permanent lists performed as expected and ended up capturing fewer individuals than the enumeration method had been able to do in 1984 and 1988. The second would involve acknowledging that the employment of enumeration in the more contemporary period can no longer equal its past achievements. This latter conclusion, of course, would square with the argument of diminishing quality and coverage that had been put forward as a reason for abandoning enumeration. Indeed, in his official report on the 1997 election,[83] the chief electoral officer pointed out that there were challenges in getting the political parties to supply a sufficient number of names for enumerators and that returning officers had, as a consequence, to turn to other sources. No exact figures are cited, though the report does go on to specify that there were problems finding enough enumerators in the west end of Toronto and in Newfoundland (p. 45).

Without wishing to dispute the reality of this shortage as a factor, it remains unclear whether enumeration problems, per se, were solely or even largely responsible for the relatively lower coverage level recorded in the 1997 election. Other factors — not necessarily associated with the application of the enumeration method — could have been equally or more important. In this regard, it is significant to note that elsewhere, Kingsley's report on the 1997 general election calls attention to the "intense activity" that the agency entered into within the tight time frame they had following the passage of Bill C-63: "While revising manuals and forms to reflect the latest amendments to the Act, we also had to provide the necessary training for returning officers and their key staff in preparation for the last enumeration" (p. 42). More importantly, the report goes on to note that, because of redistribution, three-quarters of the 271 returning officers who were to oversee the final enumeration were new appointees and, moreover, that their selection had been a slow process:

> Because of the delays in the appointment process, despite the training efforts of Elections Canada, many returning officers did not have time to assimilate the many manuals and procedural guidelines for their tasks before they plunged into an enumeration and election. (p. 42)

Insofar as these time pressures might have had a bearing on the quality of the registration effort — and common sense suggests that they must have had, at some level — then attributing the low coverage in 1997 to a shortage of enumerators (and other enumerator-elector contact problems) is not such a straightforward matter.

There are additional grounds for questioning whether the coverage rate in that election can be taken as a valid indicator of a generally diminished capacity on the part of the enumeration method. One piece of evidence, interestingly enough, comes from the 1993 election. In that year, Elections Canada regarded the enumeration drive that had been carried out in Quebec — an effort that arguably more closely conformed to standard enumeration practices — as a great success. Indeed, in its report the agency boasts that it managed to reach 98 percent of Quebec's eligible population.[84] It gives no information on how that figure was derived or how this high level of coverage was achieved,[85] but such a figure by itself more than suggests that enumeration could still, in the early 1990s, be carried out quite effectively.

The registration process bound up with the last enumeration featured not only tight time frames, riding redistribution and the slow appointment of returning officers; at least two other elements involving deviations from normal enumeration practice may have contributed to the decreased coverage. First, in two provinces — Prince Edward Island and Alberta – there were no enumerations; instead, Elections Canada purchased the final lists of registered voters that had been generated for the preceding provincial elections, held in April 1996 and March 1997, respectively. Given the numbers of eligible voters involved, the use of Alberta's list is particularly troubling. Not only was that list several months old by the time the election took place (in June), but it was a product of the province's register-based system, which, in turn, had been based on a November 1996 general enumeration. Thus, the purchased list was susceptible to error, and to the extent that there was a substantial number of errors of exclusion (presumably, as a function of Alberta's rapid population growth), this could have been a source of the lower coverage. Second, the enumeration process carried out in the rest of the country took place slightly earlier than usual, leaving room for further slippage. Instead of taking place between 35 and 29 days before the election (as had been the case in Quebec for the 1993 election), the final April enumeration was carried out between 53 and 47 days ahead of voting day. While this change extended the lag time by a mere two and one-half weeks, it would have resulted in some individuals being missed. To be sure, each of these deviations by itself would be expected to play only a minor role in explaining the lower overall coverage, but together their cumulative impact could be significant in a context where additional factors were at play.

If these facts suggest that adequate coverage is still possible with enumeration, Elections Canada might, in rebuttal, point to the evidence of enumeration-like problems with the 2000 election in the context of its "targeted revision" efforts. Targeted revision is a process by which a pair of agents call on residents in specifically designated areas during the second week of the election period. "In general, they concentrated on recently developed areas such as new subdivisions, areas known for high mobility, including clusters of apartment buildings and student residents, and institutions such as nursing homes and chronic care hospitals."[86] This process, which is very much akin to enumeration, is, of course, intended to compensate for the limitations in coverage and currency associated with maintained lists. Altogether, about 515,000 additional addresses were targeted in this manner. "The targeted revision exercise provided effective coverage of high-mobility areas," concluded the report on the 2000 election.[87] In making the point about coverage problems with enumeration, however, Elections Canada could have emphasized that 29 percent of the addresses called upon failed to produce a response at the doorstep, even after two visits (at which time a mail-in package was left). Later, when asked about the possibility of a return to the traditional system, Kingsley did use this statistic to illustrate the problematic nature of enumeration.[88] In rebuttal, it could be pointed out that, given the areas that were designated, a 71-percent rate of contact is actually quite impressive and, moreover, a subset of those who were not at home or did not answer their door ended up registering by taking advantage of the mail-in package that had been left. Indeed, the statistic might even be taken to suggest the value of a three-visit canvass (at appropriately altered times) for certain special areas, with the routine two-visit mode used elsewhere. Clearly, the other point to make is that coverage in the 2000 election would have been lower without targeted revision.

In short, there may be some reason to believe that the use of list-based approaches contributed, however modestly, to the recent decline in electoral coverage (and participation). Key to this interpretation is seeing the 1997 election as constituting only a weak test of the coverage achieved with enumeration. Still, a more prudent perspective at this juncture would be to see this only as a possible inference. A more certain one is that coverage under the new regime has been inferior to what enumeration was able to achieve in the past. Therefore, the commitment on the part of the advocates of a permanent-list approach to maintain the high levels of inclusion that had long characterized Canadian registration practice has not yet been fulfilled.

Turnout and eligibility

Finally, and for the sake of completeness, figure 1 shows the overall participation rate by relating the number of votes cast to the number of eligible voters. Since this measure captures both registration coverage and voting behaviour, it is to be expected that it records the lowest percentages across all elections. And, of course, it also picks up the declining coverage that has occurred as well as the fact that fewer Canadians have been voting. In the 1984 and 1988 elections, 71.5 and 72.2 percent of the eligible population voted, while in 1993 only 68 percent did so; the figure falls off sharply to 62.5 percent for the 1997 contest and drops again, to 59.2 percent, in 2000. However it is measured, participation in Canadian federal elections has clearly been declining.

The 2000 election

The evidence is much clearer on the impact — a negative one, to be exact — of the new registration process on voter turnout in the 2000 election. That contest is of prime importance, of course, because it was the first one to be held with the new regime well in place. The National Register had been functioning for nearly three and a half years when it was used to generate the preliminary voters lists. Now, therefore, its performance as an open-list system, based on the incorporation of a continuous flow of updated elector information, can be meaningfully assessed. A focus on that contest does require, however, stepping back somewhat from making strong distinctions in the analysis of participation effects according to whether or not an individual was registered. This is because a large number of people were in "in between" situations, such as having their name listed, but at an old or incorrect address. Apart from these "incorrect" registrations, factors such as receipt of a voter information card and manner of receipt would have made a difference. Nevertheless, it is possible to demonstrate that the less than ideal registration circumstances in which many individuals found themselves — including, most fundamentally, not being registered at all when the preliminary voters lists were generated — had an inhibiting effect on participation.

A variety of information sources allow for this conclusion. To begin with, there was ample media coverage of the campaign that focused heavily on the administrative aspects of the election, including various concerns about the nature and functioning of the new registration system. There were also reactions by MPs, particularly members of the Standing Committee on Procedure and House Affairs, as they had an opportunity to conduct a post-mortem on the election by questioning Kingsley directly. As well, Elections Canada carried out its own "post-event" analysis of the voter registration process in addition to other aspects of the election.[89] Its summary report, in turn, draws upon survey-based information taken from, among other individuals and organizations, 60 randomly selected candidates who ran for registered parties, 20 selected "representatives of registered political parties,"[90] 259 returning officers and 49 academics who had signalled their interest in electoral matters. The report also cites some (summary) results of national surveys, including one conducted by Ipsos-Reid on behalf of Elections Canada. As will be seen, that data set is used extensively as a basis for an independent analysis of the registration process and its impact. While the statistical work provides the most convincing, and certainly the most generalizable, evidence on registration effects, the disparate sources of information essentially converge in producing a characterization of the new system as having operated in such a way as to have inhibited voter turnout.

Media commentary
There is nothing surprising or new about the fact that the media chose to focus heavily on the problems surrounding the registration and voting processes and did not dwell so much on those aspects that worked well. Certainly, past elections governed by the enumeration method were not immune to critical reports that emphasized voters being missed in the canvassing effort, being given the wrong information about where to vote or confronting long queues in the polling stations. Still, the heavy and persistent media scrutiny of the difficulties and irregularities in the 2000 election is quite striking. The following excerpts from a sampling of different newspapers are fairly representative of the tone of newspaper coverage right across the country:

> Electors receiving their voter registration cards should avoid the temptation to toss them into a heap of unread mail. Many local residents are noticing their cards list them as voters in the wrong riding, despite the fact they may have lived in the same place for decades. *Fredericton Daily Gleaner* (November 9)

Glitches in the country's computerized list of federal electors are angering voters in various parts of the city. And their situations mirror similar problems across the country as the National Register of Electors makes its debut in this federal election. Some voters, particularly those in new housing developments, are not on the list at all, others have received faulty voter cards and still others have seen their cards go astray to old addresses. *Hamilton Spectator* (November 15)

The new system has created chaos in some constituencies, with angry voters objecting that they have received Elections Canada cards with wrong information, that they haven't received cards or that they got more than one. *Edmonton Journal* (November 21)

There were widespread reports of futile attempts by voters to register on the list for the first time, as well as reports of wrong addresses for voters and even incidents where deceased citizens were still on the list. *Vancouver Sun* (November 24)

Voting across the country was marred by glitches yesterday as polling stations opened up to four hours late and one in 10 Canadians arrived ready to cast their ballots only to find their names were not on the official voters list. *National Post* (November 28)

One of the specific themes taken up in the print media, but picked up as well by the broadcast media, was the confusing nature of Elections Canada's television advertisements informing the public that they had to be listed in the National Register in order to vote. Clearly, the agency wanted as many people as possible to register during the revision period in order to avoid logjams on polling day, when it would still be possible to register. The exact wording of the message was, "If you're not on the voters' list, you can't vote. No, you can't." What transpired, of course, was that many individuals who did not receive a voter information card concluded (wrongly) that they would be unable to vote. Similarly, some of those who received a card bearing the name of another person (e.g., the previous occupant of their dwelling) reached the same determination.

Parliamentary scrutiny
The advertising campaign received even more intense criticism from members of Parliament on the Standing Committee on Procedure and House Affairs, who had their first postelection opportunity to quiz the chief electoral officer and his staff formally on March 1, 2001. Kingsley, who indicated that he had

personally approved the advertisement, at first defended it, but yielded – "Okay, what we're going to do is revise the ad"[91] — after persistent challenges by one parliamentarian. That MP, John Reynolds of the Canadian Alliance, who was also the lead-off questioner, began on a broader note by quoting from Elections Canada's performance report for 1999-2000, including positive developments with regard to the National Register, but then went on to say:

> Now, it all sounds great, but at one other meeting before you got here, we heard that just about every member on this committee has had a problem. As the whip of the party, I have a bunch of notes from members who have real problems...I had lots of complaints...from constituents, in that they just weren't on the list.[92]

No doubt Reynolds's annoyance was compounded by the fact that his own name had been erroneously left off the list.

Michel Guimond of the Bloc Québécois began by signalling his sense that there were some general problems with the way in which the election had been conducted, promised more queries at a second meeting and went on to ask about Elections Canada's updating arrangements with Quebec. Still, he did feel the need to make a general comment on the register: "On page 9 of your document, Mr. Kingsley, you stated that, 'The register met our expectations for the most part.' I beg to differ slightly."[93]

Libby Davis of the NDP was the next opposition MP to speak, and she was unequivocal in her condemnation:

> I find it ironic that the information we've had presented today — these graphs and slides and so on that make the national registry look like a success story, even though there are some problems — is vastly different from the experience we actually had on the ground. I consider all of us, as MPs, as the real experts in this matter...Within our own caucus, I know the first thing we talked about when we got back here was what happened on election day. Everybody had incredible stories of concerns and situations that took place.[94]

She went on to cite the specific problem of "discrimination against poor people and aboriginal people," making it clear that, to her way of thinking, not only did the permanent-list method depress turnout in general but it had an especially debilitating effect on less favoured groups.

The theme of participation inequality was sounded even earlier in the hearings by a Liberal MP, Carolyn Parrish, who first of all wondered if she needed to change her position as a supporter of the register:

As a great advocate of a national registry, I have lived to eat my words. We had a rough time in this election. We also had a rough time with the national registry in the 1999 [Ontario] provincial election. I don't expect perfection, and I think it'll probably take several elections to get this thing ironed out and cleaned up, so I'm not going to throw the baby out with bathwater quite yet.[95]

Her worry that the new registration method had a negative effect on turnout and equality were practically the next words out of her mouth:

I'm more concerned about the voter turnout than I am about anything else. I think the voter turnout was poor. A low voter turnout disenfranchises the poorest and most disenfranchised people in society to start with. I think it was really good for the blue-haired ladies who have lived in my riding for 60 years, because they were on the voters list, they had property, nobody hassled them, and they were fine. The teenagers didn't get to vote, nor did new immigrants, people who had moved recently, or the poor. Generally, society doesn't give a damn about those people, but I do — even if they vote NDP.[96]

While it is unclear how much of this criticism Kingsley expected to hear, he cannot have been surprised by the concerns voiced about the particular situation of young people. In preliminary remarks to the committee, his top official responsible for the National Register, Rennie Molnar, readily identified this gap in coverage as an area in need of significant improvement. Molnar allowed that only an estimated 30 percent of eligible youths had been registered when the lists were first generated (with a final registered level of 55 to 60 percent).[97] Kingsley himself had been quoted several times during the campaign as lamenting the fact that a huge majority of the estimated 400,000 Canadians who had turned 18 during the year had not registered in spite of Elections Canada's outreach program; after all, all they had to do, he emphasized, was to sign a "confirmation of information" form and mail it back to the agency.[98] To summarize, there is no disagreement that the permanent list came up short with regard to registering newly age-eligible voters.[99]

Elections Canada's post-mortem

The agency's own assessment, drawn from the elite sources already mentioned, does not hide the difficulties experienced with the new registration regime. Its *2000 General Election Post-event Overview* notes that "a majority of candidates and political party representatives indicated a low degree of satisfaction" with the preliminary lists of voters generated by the National Register (p. 7) and that for their part returning officers reported having "to deal with widespread or major complaints about the preliminary lists of electors, indicating that the accuracy of the lists did not meet their expectations" (p. 7). Academics were described as seeing no difficulty with the registration procedures, though some "indicated that the process unduly put the onus on electors and required too much initiative from them, especially those who were less involved or interested in the first place" (p. 7). Candidates and political parties apparently were "neutral about most aspects of voter registration," but when opinions were given "they generally reported low satisfaction rates, particularly with registration at advance polls and on polling day, with the targeted revision process and with the accuracy of revised lists of electors" (p. 8).

The Ipsos-Reid survey[100]

Central to the use of survey data for deriving insights into the link between registration and participation is the single item that was employed to categorize the registration status and circumstances of respondents. The question, structured around people's experiences with the voter information card, merits quoting in full:

> Prior to the November 27th, 2000 Election you should have received a "voter information card." This card is approximately 5 inches by 9 inches and would have provided you with information about the election, including where and when to vote. It also would have had your name and address and told you that you were on the voters list. Which of the following most closely describes your situation?" [READ, ACCEPT ONE RESPONSE].

The response possibilities were as follows (followed by the percentage distribution):[101]

- Your voter information card came in the mail and was correctly addressed to you personally (75.3)
- Your voter information card came in the mail, but there was some personal information that was incorrect (4.5)
- You got a voter information card with someone else's name (2.2)
- You never got a voter information card (14.5)
- You had to make some sort of enquiry (for example, a phone call or e-mail) to get your own voter information card (3.0)

Taken at face value, the responses would appear to support Elections Canada's estimates of the "data quality" of the register. Among the respondents, 75.3 percent indicated that they had received the card with correct information. Presumably, one could add to this figure the 4.5 percent who had received a properly addressed card (or at least correct enough to receive it) even though the card contained some inaccuracies about the elector's personal information. The resulting total of 79.8 percent is not too far removed from the sort of figures that the agency had been generating as estimates of the percentage of individuals listed at the correct address.

At the same time, the survey figures are probably too generous to be taken as corroboration for those data quality estimates. As with most election surveys, the sample probably overrepresented the more interested and informed individuals among the citizenry. This is strongly suggested by the very high turnout level of 81 percent reported by the survey respondents, a figure that is a far cry from the actual level of participation. No doubt this inflation is partly the product of nonvoters falsely reporting having voted, but it could be partly the result of politically engaged and motivated individuals (those likely to be registered and to vote) being disproportionately represented in the sample.

Nonetheless, the survey still managed to capture a significant number of Canadians who were in less than ideal registration situations and who would have needed to undertake some remedial action in order to vote. Among these, the largest category (14.5 percent) comprised people who reported not having received a card at all; presumably these were primarily individuals who were simply not recorded on the National Register. A further 2.2 percent indicated that they had received someone else's card; likely these were mostly individuals who had moved into a dwelling unit previously inhabited by a person who was registered. The ordinary expectation is that remedying these various registration situations would require different levels of engagement and effort. The anticipation is that those with only incorrect personal information would need to take the least action, while those who had received someone else's card would need to make somewhat more of an effort and those who had received no card at all would have to take the most steps to get on the list.[102]

As will be seen below, there is support for characterizing these registration situations in this way, but it is also clear that the response categories are not perfectly homogeneous; it seems that the response alternatives could have been constructed with greater precision. No doubt most of those who did not receive a card were indeed not registered, but a small subset of those listed might have simply failed to receive their card because of address errors. As well, some of those registered might have moved into a dwelling whose previous occupant had not been listed. Similarly, the circumstances of those who received a card addressed to someone else could have varied, some having been already registered at their old address, others not. Furthermore, it is not inconceivable that some individuals did not move at all but received another person's card simply because it was incorrectly addressed. The category comprising those who took the initiative to obtain their voter information card poses another problem from a methodological point of view. In particular, it conflates not being registered — including, presumably, not having received a card — with the taking of subsequent action. This makes the category distinctive because none of the others has purposefully captured the motivation to register. (Subsequent analysis will show that this does indeed make the category stand apart somewhat.) Incidentally, insofar as some of these individuals did not receive a card then this suggests that the nonrecipient level might be higher than 14.5 percent. Finally, judging from media reports, a small subset of those who received a card with incorrect personal information may have been given wrong information about where to vote.

Still, it appears that this ordering of registration statuses, if not ideal, does tap the various situations in which people found themselves, at least in a rudimentary way. Table 1 helps to demonstrate this by displaying how some registration situations are, as expected, more likely to be bound up with certain age and income categories. One premise is that younger and poorer Canadians are more likely to have had suboptimal registration experiences, largely because they are more likely to be renters or to change residences frequently. As anticipated, age exhibits the sharpest pattern with registration status. Among those between the ages of 18 and 24, only one in every two individuals (48.9 percent) received a correctly addressed card with accurate information, and among those between 25 and 34 years old, only two of three (66 percent) had this ideal registration experience. The percentage continues to rise for the next two age brackets, reaching 82.7 percent for those between 35 and 64 and 91.5 percent for those 65 and over. Most of these differences are mirrored in the corresponding percentages associated with the most unfavourable situation, not having received a card. Over one-third (34.5 percent) of the youngest adults and almost one-fifth (19.7 percent) of those in the next age bracket claimed that this was their experience. By contrast, only 10.2 and 3.3 percent of those between the ages of 35 and 64 and those 65 and over, respectively, did not receive a card.[103] Apart from this, younger Canadians were also modestly more likely to take the initiative to register, capturing, it would appear, that comparatively small and exceptional segment of young people with the motivation and interest to participate.

The pattern for income is also as expected, again suggesting that the registration status categories are measuring at least basic differences. Those with an income of less than $20,000 had the least favourable experiences. Among these individuals — the poorest Canadians — 66.7 percent found themselves correctly registered, while 22.6 percent responded that they had failed to receive a card. Registration circumstances are slightly better for those with incomes

Table 1

Voter Registration Status by Age, Income (percent)

Registration status	Age				Income			
	18-24	25-34	35-64	65+	Less than $20,000	$20,000-39,999	$40,000-59,999	$60,000+
Correctly registered	48.9	66.0	82.7	91.5	66.7	73.0	79.0	79.5
Personal information incorrect	5.8	5.8	3.8	3.6	3.5	5.9	5.4	3.3
Received another's card	2.2	5.2	1.3	1.2	3.8	2.8	1.3	1.8
Received no card	34.5	19.7	10.2	3.3	22.6	15.4	11.6	12.7
Took initiative to get card	8.6	3.3	2.0	0.3	3.5	2.8	2.8	2.7
(*N*)	(362)	(483)	(1,280)	(329)	(372)	(597)	(542)	(738)

Source: Based on data provided by Elections Canada from a random telephone survey of 2,500 Canadians conducted by Ipsos-Reid between November 28 and December 11, 2000 . While the survey oversampled individuals between the ages of 18 and 34, the weighted version is used here. According to Ipsos Reid, it is "representative of Canada's age and gender composition in accordance with 1996 Census data."

between $20,000 and $39,999, at 73.0 and 15.4 percent, respectively. Those in the two higher income brackets were also better off with regard to registration, with the corresponding percentages hovering around 80 percent for being correctly registered and 12 percent for failing to receive a card. Finally, and in part overlapping with the above data, part-time and full-time students were also prone to be in registration situations where some remedial measures were necessary. Only 50.0 percent of students found themselves in the ideal registration situation, while 31.2 percent received no card (specific data not shown).[104]

The survey offers additional perspectives on the various registration experiences of Canadians in the last election. An important insight is available from a line of questioning that asked individuals who did not receive a card with the correct information and address whether or not they took any action to rectify their registration status. Those who responded in the affirmative were queried about whether they thought the process was easy or difficult. The data indicate that a substantial proportion of people either failed to act or regarded the process as difficult when they did try to do so. Altogether, nearly one-third (30.9 percent) of those who received a card with incorrect personal information, someone else's card or no card at all did nothing to adjust the irregularity. A further 15.7 percent of these individuals took action but reported that they found the process difficult or very difficult. In other words, nearly one-half of the individuals (46.6 percent) in less than optimal registration circumstances either failed to follow through as hoped for or, if they did, found the process wanting.[105] Table 2 breaks down this figure for the various registration categories: 41.4 percent for those who had only personal information to amend, 44.4 percent for those who received another person's card and 51.8 percent for those who received no card. Roughly, then, inaction and perception of difficulty increased according to the amount of remedial action required. This helps substantiate the value of distinguishing among the categories, imperfect as they are. The data also reveal that there were undesirable registration results even when relatively little remedial action was required.

Table 2 presents results for three other variables that illuminate further aspects of Canadians' reaction to the new regime. All respondents were asked to rate, on a 0-to-10 agree-disagree scale, the flow of information on "how to get on the voters list and about where and when to vote." The results are presented in two ways, with mean scores for the original 11-point measure and percentages for the agree, neutral and disagree (collapsed) portions of the scale. The first item shown asked whether the information on registering and voting was "clear and easy to understand." For the sample as a whole, the response was quite favourable, with more than 8 in 10 people (82.9 percent) agreeing that this was indeed the case (*Mean* = 8.0). Given what was widely reported about the confusing nature of the "Are you on the list" advertising campaign, this perhaps suggests that many Canadians did not, in fact, find it to be confusing (or, at least not consciously so). However, as noted below, there were differences across the various registration situations. On the second item, respondents were less likely to agree that there was "enough information." Only 62.9 percent agreed that they had received sufficient information, while 30.4 percent disagreed (*Mean* = 6.6), suggesting that Elections Canada might have done more in this area. The lowest ratings occur in connection with the third item, which recorded sentiment about motivation, in particular, whether the registration and voter information "encouraged me to vote." Less than half the sample (45.4 percent) replied in the affirmative, while a substantial 37.3 percent indicated disagreement (*Mean* = 5.2). Although it might be argued that some part of this response reflects the low-stimulus (e.g., noncompetitive) nature of the election itself, the question does after all refer to administrative rather than political aspects of the election over which the agency had some control.

The breakdowns shown suggest, not surprisingly, that registration status made a considerable difference in individuals' assessment of the information flow. In general, the more the registration circumstances deviated from the ideal, the lower the likelihood of respondents rating the information as clear and understandable, of sufficient quantity and of having encouraged them to vote. Thus, while 88.5 percent of those who received an entirely accurate card and 85.6 percent of those who received a card with incorrect personal data agreed that the information was clear and understandable, the figure diminishes somewhat (to 77.8 percent) for

Table 2
Correction Process and Attitudes Toward Registration and Voting Information, by Registration Status (percent)

		Registration status				
	All	Correctly registered	Personal info. incorrect	Received another's card	Received no card	Took initiative to get card
(a) Took no action or found correction process						
difficult/very difficult	46.6	–	41.4	44.4	51.8	–
(N)	(528)		(111)	(54)	(363)	
(b) Registration and voting information						
Clear and easy to understand						
Agree	82.9	88.5	85.6	77.8	53.6	82.7
Neutral	6.0	5.1	4.5	9.3	11.1	4.0
Disagree	11.1	6.4	9.9	13.0	35.3	13.3
Mean	8.0	8.5	8.2	7.6	5.6	7.7
Enough information						
Agree	62.9	66.4	64.0	63.0	44.4	59.5
Neutral	6.7	5.5	9.9	7.4	11.4	9.5
Disagree	30.4	28.0	26.1	29.6	44.2	31.1
Mean	6.6	6.9	6.8	6.2	5.0	6.3
Encouraged vote						
Agree	45.4	48.8	46.8	31.5	28.7	50.7
Neutral	17.3	17.7	20.7	25.9	13.5	15.1
Disagree	37.3	33.5	32.4	42.6	57.7	34.2
Mean	5.2	5.5	5.2	4.6	3.6	5.2
(N)[1]	(2,456-76)	(1,849-68)	(111)	(54)	(351-60)	(73-75)

Note: [1]Sample numbers vary because the number of respondents for these questions varied.
Source: See table 1.

those who received someone else's card and tumbles dramatically to 53.6 percent for those who received no card at all (*Mean* = 8.5, 8.2, 7.6 and 5.6, respectively). Clearly, the positive assessment of the quality of the information, seen in connection with the entire sample, does not hold across the board, especially for those who did not get a card. These same individuals were also less likely to respond that they had received "enough information" — only 44.4 percent provided positive replies compared to 63 to 66 percent for individuals in other registration circumstances. Assessments of whether the information encouraged participation also form a pattern, with both receiving someone else's card and not receiving a card apparently making a difference. Of those who received a completely correct card, 48.8 percent indicated that they were encouraged to vote as a result; this is true of only 31.5 percent for those who received another's card and only 28.7 percent for those who received no card at all (*Mean* = 5.5, 4.6 and 3.6, respectively).

In short, these figures reveal that the flow of registration and voter information was regarded as particularly inadequate by those who were most in need of more and clearer guidance, and perhaps stimulation. No doubt, some of the responses could be the result of rationalizing by individuals who were predisposed not to vote and therefore downplayed or did not recall the information they had come across; still, there is no reason to assume that such a phenomenon overwhelms all other interpretations. And, of course, at a basic level it makes sense that individuals who did not receive a card would, naturally, be those most likely to indicate limited informational effects.

What of the counterclaim that these results speak not so much to the principles of the new regime as to the particulars of how the information campaign was conceived and put into place? No doubt, this is true to some extent and future campaigns will likely be designed, recalling Kingsley's pledge, to reflect some progress on the learning curve. Still, it is not entirely inappropriate to view the inadequacies as being inherent elements of the new regime. From the very beginning, after all, the plan to develop and implement a permanent-list system called for a huge effort to be made during the election period to pick up the slack, to capture the very large numbers expected who would not be listed or would be listed incorrectly. In other words, the decision to develop a register automatically raised the stakes and demanded that the greatest priority be given to facilitating the registration of the millions of unlisted or incorrectly listed Canadians. Without effective communication with this population, it is hard to fathom how their participation could be facilitated.

The impact on participation

The most important aspect of the new registry system to explore is, of course, its direct impact on voting in the November 2000 election, and not only in connection with turnout in general but as well the implications that it had for participation inequality across social categories. With regard to the broader dimension, the pertinent question is not so much whether higher registration thresholds led to less voting, since the expectation of some sort of a negative effect is well grounded in the literature. Additionally, there is the plain but important fact that a substantial number of survey respondents reported that they did not regularize their registration circumstances, and thus many of them would not have been able to vote. What is at issue, then, is not whether a relationship emerges (nor, for that matter, whether the causal inference is appropriate[106]), but rather the magnitude of the impact on voter turnout associated with less than optimal registration experiences.

It would appear that registration status indeed exerted a strong influence on voter turnout. Table 3 provides an initial sense of this by setting out the voter participation rates for individuals in the different registration circumstances. Putting aside the category of those who took the initiative to get registered (90.7 percent of whom voted), the effects are conspicuously monotonic. For respondents in the most favourable registration situation — those who received a card with correct information — 88.3 percent ended up voting. Turnout fell, but only modestly, to 82.9 percent, for those who received a card with some incorrect personal information. However, the decline is noticeably greater, down to 72.2 percent, for those who received a card addressed to someone else. Finally, the lowest participation level and the biggest drop across categories occur in connection with those who received no card at all, with barely half, or 51.2 percent, indicating that they had cast a ballot. This represents a huge gap between the two extreme registration situations.

Closer inspection of the data, involving a multivariate orientation, strengthens the inference that registration status had a direct and substantial bearing on lower levels of voter turnout in 2000. A follow-up on the bivariate perspective is necessary to ensure that the results reported above are not masking other effects, including the possibility that they are merely picking up the typical nonvoting habits of certain social groups, particularly the young and the poor (who were, to begin with, also less likely to be properly registered or registered at all). While it can be argued that logistic regression is the more appropriate multivariate technique to employ in light of the nominal dependent variable (voted/not voted), results are shown based on OLS regression techniques because the coefficients generated for the independent variables have a more conventional interpretation (they gauge the increment or decrement in the dependent variable for a unit change in the independent variable in question, net of the other variables included). That said, parallel logistic analyses were carried out for confirmation purposes, and revealed essentially the same effects.[107] The first cut through the data assembled virtually all of the

Table 3

Voter Turnout by Registration Status

Registration status	(%) voting	(N)
Correctly registered	88.3	(1,883)
Personal information incorrect	82.9	(111)
Received another's card	72.2	(54)
Received no card	51.2	(363)
Took initiative to get card	90.7	(75)

Source: See table 1.

demographic variables available in the survey that could potentially exert some influence on voter turnout. The list included age, income, education, employment/student status, gender, province/region of residence, mother tongue, Aboriginal origin and nativity (whether Canadian- or foreign-born). These background characteristics were incorporated as (0/1) dummy variables, as were the primary items measuring registration status: "personal information incorrect," "received another's card," "received no card" and "took initiative to get card," leaving those correctly registered as the reference category.

Only the demographic variables representing the effects of age, education, income and Aboriginal origin proved to be statistically significant and were retained for subsequent, pared down, treatment. The results of this parsimonious approach are shown in Table 4 in three forms or models, the first serving as a baseline by capturing the effects of the demographic variables alone, the second assessing the additional influence of the registration experience measures and the third adding potentially relevant attitudinal variables. As the variables examined in the first two regression runs are all binary, the regression coefficients record the turnout level of the category in question relative to the level of the omitted category. Thus, the coefficient -.31 for those 18 to 24 years of age records a participation gap of 31 points compared to those 65 and over. By itself, that result reiterates the widely documented fact that Canada's youngest adults (i.e., newer "generations") vote at much lower levels. Also as expected is the overall pattern for the set of age variables, which reveals a narrowing voting deficit as age increases. As well, these initial results confirm both income and education as having a bearing on turnout (those who are less well off and less educated vote at lower levels than their more privileged counterparts), though the impact is less than the effect associated with age. The regression coefficient of -.17 for Aboriginal people indicates less participation on their part relative to other Canadians, even after taking age and socioeconomic status into account. Altogether, this small collection of variables explains about

Table 4

Regression Models of Voter Turnout

	Model 1 Baseline: demographic effects		Model 2 Including registration status		Model 3 Including attitudinal variables	
Age						
18–24	-.31	(.030/.000)	-.23	(.030/.000)	-.10	(.027/.000)
25–34	-.23	(.029/.000)	-.18	(.028/.000)	-.06	(.025/.011)
35–64	-.09	(.025/.002)	-.06	(.025/.017)	-.01	(.022/.779)
Income						
< $20,000	-.07	(.026/.005)	-.05	(.025/.035)	-.01	(.022/.684)
$20,000-39,999	-.06	(.021/.006)	-.05	(.021/.009)	-.01	(.018/.758)
$40,000-59,999	.01	(.021/.535)	.01	(.020/.674)	.02	(.018/.185)
Education						
< High school	-.11	(.029/.000)	-.10	(.028/.000)	-.03	(.025/.279)
High school	-.11	(.023/.000)	-.11	(.022/.000)	-.06	(.020/.003)
Some college/university	-.06	(.020/.005)	-.06	(.019/.003)	-.04	(.017/.014)
Aboriginal	-.17	(.041/.000)	-.14	(.039/.000)	-.13	(.035/.000)
Registration status						
Personal information incorrect			-.02	(.036/.534)	-.03	(.032/.333)
Received another's card			-.13	(.050/.012)	-.07	(.044/.101)
Received no card			-.28	(.022/.000)	-.18	(.020/.000)
Took initiative to get card			.08	(.045/.078)	.04	(.040/.306)
Attitudes						
Election interest					.07	(.008/.000)
Knowledge: parties					.04	(.010/.000)
Knowledge: voting process					.08	(.010/.000)
Vote matters					.01	(.002/.000)
Important to vote					.05	(.004/.000)
Constant	1.05		1.05		-.06	
Adj. R^2	.106		.169		.357	
N = 2,218						

Source: See table 1.
Notes: Entries are unstandardized regression coefficients. Figures in parentheses are standard errors and statistical significance levels.

11 percent of the variation in turnout in the sample as indicated by the (adjusted) R^2 statistic of .106.

The level of explanation rises somewhat, to .169, when the variables tapping registration status are incorporated for the second step, signifying that they make an additional contribution in accounting for who does and does not vote. More to the point, the inference attributing an inhibiting effect to registration is sustained in this phase of the multivariate analysis. Clearly, some registration experiences do have a bearing on participation independently of age, education and income (and Aboriginal origin), and, moreover, the most important ones have negative consequences. The largest such effect is associated with not receiving a card, which is clearly indicated by the (statistically significant) regression coefficient of -.28; relative to those who were correctly registered, this registration condition amounts to a substantial 28-point deficit in turnout. For its part, receiving a card addressed to another person translated into a turnout decline of 13 points, also a fairly sizeable impact. There was evidently no effect for those who received cards with only incorrect personal information (-.02). Finally, there was a small positive effect for those who took the initiative to get registered, reinforcing the view that these individuals are distinguished by their motivation.

Factoring in registration also leads to an adjustment of the effects of certain other variables. Note in particular that the coefficient for the lowest age category decreases to -.23 (from -.31), implying that unfavourable registration circumstances were partly responsible for the group's lesser participation, though, of course, a substantial effect associated with that age group persists. Interestingly, the consequences stemming from not receiving a card would appear to be just as detrimental for turnout, if not more so, as being between 18 and 24 years of age.[108] The inference, then, is not only that registration matters, but that it matters a great deal.

This conclusion holds in the face of a third regression model, also shown in table 4, which adds some available attitudinal variables that are typically considered in more comprehensive treatments of turnout. These include a measure of election interest, two knowledge items (one on party platforms and policies, the other on the voting process), one indicator of citizen duty and one tapping vote efficacy.[109] One rationale for including these items is to consider them as tapping the propensity of individuals to be politically engaged, including making the effort to register and vote. Indeed, insofar as they are conceptualized as antecedent variables, then one might wonder whether the primary registration-vote relationships seen so far merely reflect underlying differences in political predisposition.[110]

Not surprisingly, each of these variables has a statistically significant impact on turnout and collectively they ratchet up the level of explanation by a noticeable amount, more than doubling the R^2 to .357. Moreover, most of the coefficients for the previous sets of variables are attenuated with the incorporation of these attitudinal items, implying that they play a part in explaining how the demographic and registration variables have an effect. The biggest drops actually occur for age, with the coefficients for the youngest and next youngest categories weakening from -.23 to -.10 and from -.18 to -.06, respectively, suggesting that lesser levels of interest, knowledge and the like are intervening variables that help interpret the lower voting rate among individuals in these two age groups. For its part, the coefficient associated with not receiving a card is diminished, from -.28 to -.18 (and from -.13 to -.07 for those receiving some-one else's card), indicating that the attitudinal variables do have a bearing on the registration-vote relationship. Still, registration status continues to exhibit a direct and reasonably sizeable effect on turnout. Moreover, the results per-taining to knowledge of the voting process are also helpful in supporting the inference that registration is consequential. As a measure of understanding the administrative side of voting, it has a significant impact on turnout itself; and even when this is taken into account, registration status continues to have rele-vance. In short, experience with registration is important.

The impact on participation inequality[111]

Not only do these results substantiate the argument that the new permanent-list system, in its first full manifestation in the 2000 election, had a debilitating impact on voter turnout, but they also necessarily mean that the negative effects worked to increase participation inequality. One reason why younger people and the poor were less likely to vote in that election was that they found them-selves in more challenging registration circumstances; simply, they were dis-proportionately in categories where a greater degree of effort was needed in order to participate. Additionally, and as noted earlier, because they were less likely to be included on the preliminary list or to be recorded properly at their current address, they were less likely to be stimulated to vote through the can-vassing efforts of parties and candidates. By comparison, older and more afflu-ent individuals tended to be in more amenable registration (and contact) situ-ations. Since participation disparities already exist across these social cate-gories, in part driven by differences in interest and information, the registration system served to magnify the traditional discrepancies in turnout.

The registration process may also have worked to increase the inequalities further, even beyond these situational aspects. It is possible, indeed plausible, that the new regime's inhibiting impact on turnout was not uniform across socioeconomic categories but, rather, exerted a stronger influence in some cases than in others. Such an "interaction effect" is to be expected for younger and poorer individuals because they are less likely to vote to begin with. Generally less motivated and informed than other members of society, they are more sus-ceptible to the operation of contextual effects that make political activity easier or, as in the present case, harder to undertake. Perhaps, as well, this predisposi-tion not to be engaged politically makes the mobilization efforts of the parties all the more critical for their participation; put differently, not being contacted may represent a larger opportunity cost for the young and the less affluent than for other potential voters. In short, the new registration process may well have had a double effect: not only did it put young people and poorer individuals in

Table 5
Turnout by Registration Status and by Age and Income (percent)

Registration status	Age				Income			
	18-24	25-34	35-64	65+	Less than $20,000	$20,000-39,999	$40,000-59,999	$60,000+
Received no card	32.0	49.5	69.7	(63.6)	38.6	42.4	65.1	63.8
Received another's card	(62.5)	64.0	87.5	(75.0)	64.3	81.2	(57.1)	76.9
Personal information incorrect	66.7	85.7	95.8	66.7	61.5	74.3	89.7	95.8
Correctly registered	75.3	80.0	90.5	96.3	84.2	83.9	89.7	91.3

Source: See table 1.
Notes: Figures in parentheses indicate an *N* of less than 12.

certain constraining registration situations, it may have risked enhancing the consequences of that placement.

Table 5 sets out some evidence that suggests this additional inhibiting effect did indeed occur in the 2000 election. Shown are turnout percentages related to registration status, on the one hand, and age and income, on the other. With the registration categories ordered from the least to the most amenable situations, the joint effect of registration and each of the other variables can be readily seen. In the case of age, the turnout rate is extraordinarily low, at 32 percent, for those between 18 to 24 years of age who did not receive a card, but soars to 96.3 percent for those 65 and over who were correctly registered. As a whole, the essentially nonadditive pattern in the data is hard to miss. The disparity in turnout between being correctly registered and not receiving a card amounts to 43.3 percent (75.3 vs. 32 percent) among the youngest group. The gap drops to 30.5 percent among those between 25 and 34 and to 20.8 percent for those between 35 and 64. Interestingly, it actually goes back up to 32.7 percent among those 65 and over; it is unclear whether this is a function of the limited number of cases in some of the cells or if it indicates that older individuals were also susceptible to the impact of registration constraints. Still, the main message from the table with respect to age, and to a lesser extent income, is that the pattern accords with the interpretation put forward that the negative registration effects were stronger for the young and the poor relative to other Canadians.[112]

Conclusion

This investigation into the change in Canada's voter registration regime has been structured by two objectives. One entailed explaining why the traditional postwrit enumeration approach was replaced by a permanent-list system. The significance of the registration method as an integral component of the electoral process, and the need to document and understand new developments in its character and operation, provided a rationale for pursuing this aim; the fact that the canvassing approach in particular had been abandoned added further justification. After all, enumeration had been long-established in the country, had come to define a uniquely Canadian institution and, moreover, ended up being replaced fairly rapidly even though its merits and the overall desirability of keeping the system had been officially reaffirmed as late as 1986. In broad terms, the task of assembling an explanation involved identifying the forces and circumstances, political and otherwise, that pushed in the direction of change. Since most factors worked to support replacing enumeration, in retrospect the outcome was predictable; the subject was nonetheless seen as worthy of study — in order to describe the process of change, emphasize some key points and establish some of the significant linkages among the various contributing causes. At another level of analysis, this paper set out and defended a perspective that privileges the role of Elections Canada and the chief electoral officer as key and proactive elements that deserve most of the credit for the advent of a register. The agency not only took advantage of opportunities within an evolving context of electoral reform to seize the initiative in advocating on behalf of a register, but it then greatly facilitated its adoption by employing an effective selling strategy that stressed the technical and economic feasibility of a permanent list that appealed to the interests of both the government and the main opposition parties.

One point that was emphasized in the account of the changeover was the relatively limited attention that had been devoted to considering the possible consequences for participation, including participation disparities. The exploration of these areas formed the basis of the second objective pursued here. What gave added weight to this focus, of course, is the anxiety that has been building about the decline in voter turnout in the country. By and large, the evidence indicates that the new registration approach has contributed to this decline and has accentuated participation gaps across social groups. Evidence of these negative effects is strongest and most certain in the 2000 election, where the National Register had its first full test. Both qualitative and quantitative types of information were marshalled to demonstrate that a large number of Canadians ended up in less than ideal registration circumstances, which, in turn, served to decrease their likelihood of voting. The impact was particularly heightened for those who did not receive a voter information card, a situation that disproportionately worked to constrain the voter turnout of younger and poorer citizens. The results also suggest that the registration process increased participation inequality beyond these situational aspects.

These results potentially provide the basis for some rethinking about the change in registration regimes, even for contemplating a return to enumeration in order to recapture its advantages in facilitating participation. Such a reversal, however, is clearly not in the cards. Even if concerns have been raised by some MPs and in the media about registration in the 2000 election, such voices have not generated anywhere near the momentum necessary to bring about the status quo ante. More to the point, the same dominant forces and amenable circumstances that converged to bring about the register in the first instance still prevail. Claims about costs and federal-provincial co-operation, the attraction of incumbency advantage and the ongoing commitment to technological change, among other factors, continue to characterize views about the merits of the new regime. Moreover, with the passage of time, the investment and commitment, material and otherwise, that have gone into producing and maintaining the National Register have entrenched it as a central element in the electoral process. The other political reality that mitigates against the possibility of switching back to enumeration is the simple fact that those most affected by the inhibiting effects of the register have the least political clout. The fact that the debate on registration, to the extent that there has been a debate, has been confined to elite circles, and has not at all penetrated public consciousness, has also served to solidify the permanent-list approach.

Interestingly, there is some evidence suggesting that a wider debate, had it occurred, might have led to at least some reservations about a new regime. Two questions on voter registration were posed as part of a national public opinion survey sponsored by the Institute for Research on Public Policy and carried out in the first half of 2000.[113] The second question is more pertinent but it may be useful to note the first one as well; it asked:

> In the past, the voters list was prepared by having enumerators go door-to-door before every election. In order to save money, we now use a list that is updated regularly using government records like income tax forms. Do you think we should go back to using the door-to-door list, or continue to use the government list, or do you not have an opinion on this?

Slightly more than one in two respondents (56.7 percent) indicated a preference for continuing with the list, while only 19.3 percent suggested a return to enumeration. At the same time, it is unclear how much can be read into these responses as an endorsement of the register. Considering that practical experience with a permanent list would not come until the election later that year, it is likely that much of this opinion was "soft"; some people indicating a preference for the new system might have responded unreflectively, being more swayed by the cost-savings reference in the question than anything else. The fact that nearly a quarter of the respondents (23.9 percent) offered no opinion also suggests uncertainty or tentativeness. One wonders what the distribution might have looked like had this question been put to a similar sample just after the November 2000 election. Such curiosity surrounds the second question as well. It was designed to probe which of two principles, economics or participation, should inform the registration approach:

> What do you think is more important, that the voters list be prepared as inexpensively as possible or that every effort is made to include everyone, even if it costs significantly more, or do you not have an opinion on this?

Here, too, a substantial number of respondents, in fact, 30.6 percent, responded that they had no opinion, suggesting a lack of engagement with the issue, though some of these individuals might have had difficulty choosing strictly between the two ideals. Those who did voice a preference were divided about the principle that should prevail but, interestingly, more thought that inclusion (39.6 percent) as opposed to costs (29.7 percent) should be the defining principle guiding the registration process. Rather than make too much of this 10-point difference, perhaps it suffices to note simply that this result at least suggests that Elections Canada will need to do more to meet the desire of many Canadians for greater equality in electoral participation.

Among the factors inhibiting a return to the old registration regime, Elections Canada's unwavering enthusiasm for "its" register probably ranks at the top. At the same time, the agency has not been indifferent to the kinds of concerns voiced in some circles. Indeed, it cannot be. Obviously, it must provide some kind of response, at the very least, to MPs who have spoken out and continue to express reservations about the register's debilitating effects on participation. More importantly, the agency can be expected to take its job seriously and improve the effectiveness of the National Register, and that includes maximizing coverage and accuracy. Ironically enough, with the register firmly in place, the agency can perhaps now afford to pay more attention to participation-linked matters that originally were given little regard.

The chief electoral officer's appearance before the Standing Committee on Procedure and House Affairs on May 7, 2002, provided him an opportunity to discuss the kinds of steps that Elections Canada had recently taken or was contemplating to improve the operation of the register. To begin with, Kingsley pointed out that an agreement had been reached with the Canada Customs and

Revenue Agency to alter tax forms in order to allow individuals who give their permission and confirm their Canadian citizenship to be added directly to the National Register. This option was actually put in place in time for the spring 2002 tax period. While it applies to all eligible voters, the expectation is that it will register mainly young people, especially new 18-year-olds. According to Elections Canada, of the 275,000 people expected to be added to the voters lists through this ticking of boxes, some 225,000 will be young people. Other endeavours have entailed devising communications strategies to make more effective contact with young people in order to encourage their registration. Plans were also afoot, Kingsley indicated, to research coverage, and undercoverage, of key demographic groups such as low-income individuals, using the newly available 2001 census data.

Kingsley also indicated that a review of "address and geography components of the registry" had been launched by returning officers "to ensure that street and place names are spelled correctly in those few places where there are still problems and that electors are in the correct electoral district and polling division."[114] And testing was apparently continuing with regard to the tracking of address changes using Canada Post information and in connection with on-line registration.

The chief electoral officer used his appearance before the standing committee to remind MPs of proposals (requiring legislative changes) that he had set out earlier, in the context of his recommendations following the 2000 general election.[115] One modification recommended in his report, *Modernizing the Electoral Process*, was to make it easier for voters who move from one constituency to another to phone in their corrections, an option that is currently limited to those who move within a constituency (p. 19). (At the same time, enhanced networking among computers would allow officials to remove a listing at a person's former address, thus reducing duplicate listings.) A more general recommendation would make it easier for individuals who take the initiative to register (outside of the election period) by eliminating the need for them to sign a certificate of eligibility (pp. 13-15). Another proposal, if implemented, would enhance the ability of the chief electoral officer "to undertake initiatives to verify, correct and update the Register and to authorize returning officers and others, to conduct such initiatives outside of the electoral events" (p. 16).

No doubt, these measures have the potential to make some difference, though the nature and magnitude of the effects are an open question at this juncture. Some new measures, such as the option of using the telephone to register in a new constituency, would be helpful to individuals with enough interest and initiative to take advantage of them. It is unclear how much the easier option will serve those who lack that interest and initiative. And, as well, not all young people file an income tax return, which is also true of many poorer

Canadians. The effectiveness of identifying areas of undercoverage, especially in low-income locales, would be important but, of course, matters will depend on the thoroughness of the subsequent action taken. Presumably, the intention is to take proactive measures along the lines of targeted revision, which, it will be recalled, entails limited but focused enumeration-like actions carried out during the election period.

What is interesting to note in this regard is that the chief electoral officer's last recommendation quoted above would provide the basis for canvassing measures between election events as well as during revision. Presumably, it would even allow for the possibility of a complete enumeration in off-election years, which would bring the Canadian approach more in line with the Australian model, whereby biennial door-to-door canvassing is used to update the voter register. Closer to home, British Columbia has mandatory enumeration during the third calendar year following an election, and the five other provinces that recently adopted their own registers officially allow for enumeration as well. In the absence of any possibility of turning back the clock, the incorporation of enumeration-like activities in order to balance the registration approach would appear to be the best way to address the coverage inadequacies that seem almost inherent in the current system.[116] Planned and unhurried periodic nationwide canvassing outside of election periods, in conjunction with a substantially expanded use of targeted revision during the election period, would serve to add hundreds of thousands of Canadians to the voters list. Such state-promoted initiatives would have the additional benefit of establishing direct contact with eligible voters, constituting, to quote Courtney and Smith again, "a personal reminder by the community of the positive value that it places on electoral participation by its citizens."[117]

The supplementary use of enumeration measures would naturally add to the cost of registering voters. But this is the trade-off that must accompany any kind of serious commitment to facilitating participation. For the longest time, ensuring unfettered access to the vote was the dominant principle governing the employment of the registration method in Canada. This commitment to access wound up receiving relatively little consideration during the process that culminated in the establishment of the National Register. With very little systematic thought given to what might be lost in terms of participation, the financial savings were accorded more weight than was warranted. It now appears that the time is right to revisit the matter, and to ensure that the discussion and the policy choices reflect the ideal that registration regimes should primarily operate to uphold the key democratic principle of facilitating the participation of all citizens.

Postscript: An Update from Elections Canada

With a federal election looming on the horizon, the author recently communicated with Elections Canada[118] to provide the agency with an opportunity to spell out its current plans with respect to improving the effectiveness of the register. The written response includes an acknowledgement that:

> Elections Canada recognizes that there may be variation between electoral districts or polling divisions and between various groups of electors, according to their demographic characteristics, in the quality of the Register data that are used to produce preliminary lists of electors.

To deal with these variations, the agency is planning two major kinds of endeavours. One involves a mail-out to "over 900,000 people who have turned 18 years of age since the 2000 election." The mail outreach is designed to encourage registration among young people and to increase awareness of the electoral process for those already listed. Many of these individuals will also be contacted in the context of a greatly augmented targeted revision effort, which is the second major thrust. This entails not only increasing the "scale" of the effort but also "improving the methods used to select dwellings." Moreover, these methods "will be expanded to take low income and ethnic diversity into account."

Notes

This paper benefited greatly from the enormous assistance provided by Elections Canada. Many important facets of the analysis, including those that critically examine the agency's role in the development of the National Register of Electors and the permanent list's impact on turnout, would not have been possible without Elections Canada's active cooperation; this included the provision of in-house documents, statistical information and survey material, as well as discussions with key personnel. This paper also benefited from the reflections and suggestions of André Blais, Paul Howe, Richard Johnston and an anonymous referee, and from the research assistance of Chris Anderson.

1. For a brief discussion (with references) of the different objectives and principles associated with alternative registration regimes, see Jerome H. Black, "The National Register of Electors: Raising Questions about the New Approach to Voter Registration in Canada," *Policy Matters,* Vol. 1, no. 10 (December 2000).

2. Histories of voter registration at the federal level in Canada are provided by Norman Ward, *The Canadian House of Commons,* 2nd ed. (Toronto: University of Toronto Press, 1963), ch. 10; J. Patrick Boyer, *Election Law in Canada: The Law and Procedure of Federal, Provincial and Territorial Elections,* Vol. 1 (Toronto: Butterworths, 1987), pp. 416-24; and John C. Courtney and David E. Smith, "Registering Voters: Canada in a Comparative Context," in Michael Cassidy (ed.), *Democratic Rights and Electoral Reform in Canada* (Toronto: Dundurn Press, 1991), pp. 346-58. Provincial and territorial variations are also considered by Boyer, *Election Law in Canada,* pp. 424-25, 452-527; and Courtney and Smith, "Registering Voters," pp. 372-89. A fairly up-to-date listing of the legal provisions governing voter registration at both levels of government is set out in Elections Canada's *Compendium of Election Administration in Canada: A Comparative Overview* (Ottawa: Elections Canada, 2002), part D.

3. One key generalization that can be made about registration systems is that their impact on accessibility for voters very much depends upon whether voters need to take the initiative in order to be registered. See, for instance, Valentine Herman and Françoise Mendel, *Parliaments of the World: A Compendium* (London: Macmillan, 1976), p. 40; and William C. Kimberling, "A Rational Approach to Evaluating Alternative Voter Registration Systems and Procedures," in John C. Courtney (ed.), *Registering Voters: Comparative Perspectives. Report of a Round Table*

on Voter Registration (Cambridge, MA: Center for International Affairs, Harvard University, 1991), pp. 3-11. Illustrative of this fact is the notoriously low registration numbers in most American states, where individuals must assume the major responsibility for registering; see G. Bingham Powell, Jr., "American Voter Turnout in Comparative Perspective," *American Political Science Review,* Vol. 80, no. 1 (March 1986), pp. 17-43. The broader argument and demonstration of how the prevailing institutional features and procedures can alternatively facilitate or inhibit voter turnout is well established in the literature; see, for instance, Robert W. Jackman, "Political Institutions and Voter Turnout in Industrial Democracies," *American Political Science Review,* Vol. 81, no. 4 (December 1987), pp. 405-23; and Robert W. Jackman and Ross A. Miller, "Voter Turnout in the Industrial Democracies During the 1980s," *Comparative Political Studies,* Vol. 27, no. 4 (January 1995), pp. 467-92.

4. Courtney and Smith, "Registering Voters," for instance, report a coverage figure of 95.99 percent for the 1988 election; the estimate was generated by Elections Canada for the Royal Commission on Electoral Reform and Party Financing (p. 451, note 4). They also reference coverage estimates of 97 percent and 95 percent for other periods (p. 421).

5. For a strong statement on how participation inequality translates into unequal political representation and influence, see Arend Lijphart, "Unequal Participation: Democracy's Unresolved Dilemma," *American Political Science Review,* Vol. 91, no. 1 (March 1997), pp. 1-14.

6. "No other country has a system where the lists of voters are prepared afresh, on a systematic basis, and so close to the time of voting, as does Canada" (Boyer, *Election Law in Canada,* p. 425).

7. Boyer, *Election Law in Canada,* p. 426. He does not explicitly indicate any source for the 98 percent figure; it may originate in a study of 12 by-elections in 1978 that Courtney and Smith ("Registering Voters," p. 364) cite in their own work, though they note that the figure (98.1 percent) refers to the percentage of the names on the voters' list who were eligible (and thus is more a measure of accuracy than of coverage).

8. Norman Ward, *The Canadian House of Commons: Representation* (Toronto: University of Toronto Press, 1950), p. 204 (cited on p. 416 in Boyer, *Election Law in Canada*).

9. Terrence H. Qualter, *The Election Process in Canada* (Toronto: McGraw-Hill, 1970), p. 22.

10. See, in particular, Kenneth R. Carty, "Citizens, Electors, Voters and Parties in Canada or the Case of the Missing Voters List," in Courtney, "Registering Voters" (pp. 41-48).

11. *White Paper on Election Law Reform* (Ottawa: Queen's Privy Council for Canada, 1986). For a mention of earlier official pronouncements, see Black, "The National Register of Electors," pp. 8-9.

12. *White Paper on Election Law Reform*, p. 39.

13. *An Act to amend the Canada Elections Act, the Parliament of Canada Act and the Referendum Act.*

14. More exactly, the last enumeration was conducted between April 10 and 16 in all parts of Canada except Alberta and PEI, where agreements had been reached to use the lists produced from their most recent provincial elections (March 1997 and November 1996, respectively).

15. Bill C-63 also altered the hours of voting in federal elections across the country, in order to ensure that the election results would be made public at approximately the same time.

16. *Report of the Chief Electoral Officer of Canada on the 37th General Election* (Ottawa: Chief Electoral Officer of Canada, 2001), p. 58.

17. On terminology, Courtney rightly points out that the term "permanent voters list" is inaccurate, since there are always changes to be incorporated into the register (whatever its form), which is why he prefers "continuously maintained roll." See John C. Courtney, "Reforming Representational Building Blocks: Canada at the Beginning of the Twenty-First Century," in William Cross (ed.), *Political Parties, Representation, and Electoral Democracy in Canada* (Don Mills, ON: Oxford University Press, 2002), pp. 115-31, esp. p. 119. The current paper uses the former term because its usage is more widespread.

18. Courtney, "Reforming Representational Building Blocks."

19. Those provinces were Alberta, New Brunswick, Newfoundland and Labrador, Ontario, and Quebec. No doubt, provincial developments (not explained here) were in some cases linked to the initiative taken at the federal level; this is a topic that merits investigation in its own right.

20. Black, "The National Register of Electors."

21. Black, "The National Register of Electors."

22. In a sense, the 1980 election constituted an earlier precedent, since its proximity to the 1979 election led to a decision by Elections Canada not to carry out another enumeration. Still, the context was entirely different, with no thought at all being given to the idea of a permanent list. In fact, Courtney and Smith argue that the enumeration process at the time, which included a heavy reliance on revision, "proved that it is capable of responding fairly to instances of unanticipated crises" ("Registering Voters," p. 355).

23. *Royal Commission on Electoral Reform and Party Financing* [hereafter, RCERPF], *Reforming Electoral Democracy: Final Report* (Ottawa: Royal Commission on Electoral Reform and Party Financing, 1991).

24. Courtney, "Reforming Representational Building Blocks."

25. Courtney, "Reforming Representational Building Blocks," p. 125.

26. Courtney, "Reforming Representational Building Blocks."

27. See, for instance, Courtney and Smith, "Registering Voters," p. 358.

28. *1989 Report of the Chief Electoral Officer of Canada* (Ottawa: Chief Electoral Officer of Canada, 1989).

29. *1989 Report of the Auditor General of Canada*, esp. pp. 8-10, 20, at http://www.oag-bvg.gc.ca/domino/reports.nsf/html/8910ce.html

30. RCERPF, *Reforming Electoral Democracy*, Vol. 2, ch. 4.

31. "Closed list" approaches, such as the one employed in Britain, have a closing date that typically makes it difficult for individuals to be registered until a new list is prepared. See, for example, Qualter, *The Election Process in Canada*, pp. 18-22.

32. At the same time, of course, receiving these lists earlier would be of lesser value if they contained many omissions and inaccuracies.

33. Elections Canada, "Discussion Paper on a Continuous Register of Electors" (Ottawa: Elections Canada, April 1994), p. ii.

34. *Report of the Chief Electoral Officer of Canada on the 35th General Election* (Ottawa: Chief Electoral Officer of Canada, 1994), p. 25.

35. *The 1992 Federal Referendum: A Challenge Met: Report of the Chief Electoral Officer of Canada* (Ottawa: Chief Electoral Officer of Canada, 1994), p. 19.

36. *Report of the Chief Electoral Officer of Canada on the 35th General Election*, ch. 13.

37. The interview took place on August 22, 2000, at Elections Canada's headquarters, and lasted about two hours.

38. *Standing Committee on Procedure and House Affairs*, April 30, 1996. He responded by noting that Elections Canada has "been champing at the bit for this opportunity." See p. 1, at http:/www.parl.gc.ca/committees35...nce/10_96-04-30/haff10_blk101html,

39. House of Commons, *Debates*, October 22, 1996, p. 2, at http://www.parl.gc.ca/english/hansard//088_96-10-22/088GO1E.html

40. See, for example, *Report of the Chief Electoral Officer of Canada on the 36th General Election* (Ottawa: Chief Electoral Officer of Canada, 1997), p. 73.

41. It might be argued that this new orientation represents a natural and inevitable development in an agency preoccupied with operational imperatives, and that the increasing emphasis on technology would have occurred even without the influence of the auditor general's report. One also wonders if the attractiveness of a permanent list for Elections Canada, and for Kingsley personally, reflected a penchant for innovation within the new environment of commitment to technology — almost as an end in itself. Graham White offered this interpretation in his critique of the register at an IRPP-sponsored conference, "Transparency, Disclosure and Democracy: Assessing the Chief Electoral Officer's Recommendations," Ottawa, February 27, 2002.

42. Elections Canada, "Discussion Paper," p. 1; the committee was formally known as the Steering Committee — Continuous Register of Voters.

43. Elections Canada, "Discussion Paper," p. 1, original emphasis.

44. The executive summary, for instance, lists the "compelling reasons" for considering the establishment of a register. They are (in the order listed): growing problems with the way enumeration works, the possibility of savings from shared lists across jurisdictions, the advantage of reduced election periods, the acceptance by Canadians of technology to provide services, the use of registers in other countries and the register as a fundamen-

tal building block leading to electronic voting. Elections Canada, "Discussion Paper" (p. i).

45. The report that the project team ultimately produced — *The Register of Electors Project: A Report on Research and Feasibility* — indicated the establishment date as in late 1994 (Ottawa: Register of Electors Project Team, submitted to Jean-Pierre Kingsley, Elections Canada, March 1996, p. 10). However, January 1995 is the date referenced in the *Report of the Chief Electoral Officer of Canada on the 36th General Election*, p. 11.

46. *The Register of Electors Project*, p. 10.

47. The savings estimate that Elections Canada would eventually use in public, as it made the "business case" for changing registration regimes, was $30 million. To be clear, this is the amount that would be saved for each general election or referendum held subsequent to the recouping of costs associated with building and maintaining the register. Of this amount, $8 million is connected to the shortened election campaign. A critical analysis of the financial dimension of the changeover, a subject that clearly merits attention, is beyond the scope of this study.

48. The following portrayal is essentially concerned with elite-level politics and accords virtually no role to mass opinion. Thus, it is in fundamental agreement with Courtney's characterization of "indifference on the part of the public" ("Reforming Representational Building Blocks," p. 125). That said, during the legislative process Elections Canada did state, on at least two occasions, that its surveys indicated public support for a register, first in front of the Standing Committee on Procedure and House Affairs, April 30, 1996 (see p. 3 at http:/www.parl.gc.ca/ committees35...nce/10_96-04-30/haff10_ blk101html) and then during third reading of the bill, November 26, 1996 (see p. 8 at http://www. parl.gc.ca/english/hansard/107_96-04-26/107eGO1E.html). The *Report of the Chief Electoral Officer of Canada on the 36th General Election* also makes reference to supportive public opinion surveys (p. 12). Even if the survey results were not central to the pitch for the register, it is still unclear to what extent they could be construed as indicating strong public support. This is the case with regard to the summaries of two national surveys that Elections Canada made available to the author. The first, carried out by Angus Reid in July 1996, was limited to opinions about the sources that might be used to update a permanent list, and thus contained no evaluative questions about alternative registration systems or the principles they should embody. Moreover, proregister sentiment was no doubt accentuated, given the wording used in the survey's preface: "In order to eliminate duplication and reduce costs, consideration is being given to a process to replace federal enumeration." The second survey, carried out the following month by Environics, did not probe underlying principles, but did include general preference questions. One of the first questions was (unprefaced): "Elections Canada, which is the nonpartisan agency responsible for organizing and conducting federal elections, has proposed that Canada develop a register of electors, sometimes called a *permanent voters' list*, that would be updated regularly and would replace door-to-door enumeration at each election. Generally speaking, do you strongly approve, somewhat approve, somewhat disapprove or strongly disapprove of this idea?"

Approval was overwhelming, with 76 percent signalling support, 38 percent strongly so. Furthermore, support went up to 83 percent when respondents were told (near the end of the interview) that the list would save $30 million for each election, and more should the list be shared. These numbers are likely inflated, in no small measure because Elections Canada was identified as the sponsor. A slanting effect seems particularly likely given that Canadians would have had little information about permanent lists and, in the absence of public debate, would have reflected little on registration systems. Indeed, it is telling that only 3 percent of respondents had no opinion on this question, an unrealistically small percentage for such a low-information policy area. (In contrast, two questions on voter registration in a 2000 survey sponsored by the Institute for Research on Public Policy explicitly allowed for "don't know" responses, and found "no opinion" levels to be roughly 24 and 30 percent; these results are briefly discussed in the conclusion to the current paper).

49. *The Register of Electors Project,* p. 11.

50. For instance, at one point Gray praised the legislation during third reading by noting, "The register project also supports the goal of improved federal-provincial co-operation and the reduction of overlap and duplication" (House of Commons, *Debates,* November 26, 1996. See p. 8 at http://www.parl.gc.ca/english/hansard// 107_96-04-26/107eGO1E.html).

51. In fact, in 1998 the Elections Canada project team that developed the register won the Award for Leadership in Service Innovation, presented by the Association of Professional Executives of the Public Service of Canada and sponsored by Deloitte Consulting. A publication by the latter, *Elections Canada: National Register of Electors,* states that the register "eliminates the need for time consuming and expensive door-to-door enumeration" (Ottawa: Deloitte Consulting, no date), p. 1.

52. See also Courtney, "Reforming Representational Building Blocks," p. 125.

53. There is some Canadian literature demonstrating that incumbents do have an electoral advantage. See, for example, M. Krashinsky and W. Milne, "The Effect of Incumbency in the 1984 and 1985 Ontario Elections," *Canadian Journal of Political Science,* Vol. 19, no. 2 (June 1986), pp. 337-43, and by the same authors, "Some Evidence on the Effects of Incumbency in the 1988 Canadian Federal Election," in Leslie Seidle (ed.), *Issues in Party and Election Finance in Canada* (Toronto: Dundurn Press, 1991). See also David Docherty, *Mr. Smith Goes to Ottawa: Life in the House of Commons* (Vancouver: UBC Press, 1997).

54. Several years later, following the 2000 election, one member of the Standing Committee, Carolyn Parrish, was quite candid in drawing the link: "You see, a short electoral period is really great for the incumbents because it puts everybody else at a disadvantage. We've been advertising for three and a half years, so we're in good shape." *Standing Committee on Procedure and House Affairs,* March 1, 2001, p. 13, at http://www.parl.gc.ca/InfoComDoc/37/1/HAFF/Meetings/Evidence/haffev06-e.htm

55. The Reform Party's Stephen Harper complained about the rush to put the new system in place: "We are very concerned about this. I cannot understate this. We are already playing a guessing game here in the opposition about the timing of the next election, and we don't want to play a guessing game about the length as well." *Standing Committee on Procedure and House Affairs,* October 30, 1996, p. 8, at http://www.parl.gc.ca/committees35...nce/27_96-10-30/haff27_blk101.html

56. Opposition (Conservative) senators were more explicit in vocalizing their views about an advantage. Senator Murray said, "The government is in a hurry. I do not reproach it for that. I suppose that I, too, would be in a hurry if I enjoyed the lead in the public opinion polls which the government enjoys today" (Senate, *Debates,* December 3, 1996, p. 20, at http://www.parl.gc.ca/english/senate/deb-e/56db-e.html). His colleague, David Tkachuk, even wondered about the naïveté of the Opposition in the House for not immediately recognizing the partisan nature of the matter: "Why is there such a rush? It is only for the purposes of having a 36-day campaign in the election. I guarantee you, honourable senators, that if the Liberals were at 30 percent in the polls, we would not be rushing this through. As a matter of fact, the bill would not be here. It took a few days for the opposition in the other place to figure this out. I cannot believe that it took them so long, but we have been fighting the Liberals for a long time. We know them" (Senate, *Debates*, December 5, 1996, p. 12, at http://www.parl.gc.ca/english/senate/deb-e/58db-e.html).

57. The Reform Party was also against the staggered-hours provision that had been added to the bill late in the process.

58. In fact, some of the lengthiest discussions in the committee and in the House centred on privacy issues, particularly whether to include information on gender and date of birth, and on application of the 36-day campaign to by-elections — opposition parties feared that a snap call followed by a short election period would give them inadequate time to mount an effective campaign. (In the compromise solution, gender and date of birth are included in the register but not in the information made available to candidates or parties; in the case of by-elections, a minimum of 11 days is required between notification of a vacancy and issuing of the writs.) The implementation of staggered hours was also a topic of debate.

59. Liberal Party of Canada, *Creating Opportunity: The Liberal Plan for Canada* (Ottawa: Liberal Party of Canada, 1993).

60. Courtney and Smith, "Registering Voters."

61. *Proceedings of the Standing Senate Committee on Legal and Constitutional Affairs*, December 10, 1996, p. 2, at http://www.parl.gc.ca/english/senate/com-e/lega-e/42ev-e.htm

62. See *The Register of Electors Project*, pp. 11-12.

63. Liberal MP Marlene Caterall, a member of the Standing Committee on Procedure and House Affairs, can be singled out for her exceptional and consistent voicing of concerns about the impact of the register on participation and inequality. At one point she said that Elections Canada's approach "sounds a little bit like a version of negative option billing — the voter to take a positive measure to ensure he or she gets on the voters' list. This makes them different from somebody else who is put on the list as a result of the enumeration." She also worried that those who are illiterate, blind or speak another language would not be picked up in the updating process, which she suggested amounted to a "middle-class approach to publicity"(Standing Committee on Procedure and House Affairs, October 30, 1996, pp. 13, 15, at http://www.parl.gc.ca/committees35...nce/27_96-10-30/ haff27_blk101.html). Caterall's continuing preoccupation with inclusion and fairness is evident in her exchanges with Kingsley during a Committee session held on November, 21, 2002. See pp. 55-56, at http://www.parl.gc.ca/Info

ComDoc/37/2/HAFF/Meetings/Evidence/HAF-FEV07-E.HTM

64. *Report of the Chief Electoral Officer of Canada on the 37th General Election*, p. 59.

65. See Jerome H. Black, "Reforming the Context of Voting Process in Canada: Lessons from Other Democracies," in Herman Bakvis (ed.), *Voter Turnout in Canada* (Toronto: Dundurn Press, 1991), pp. 61-176. See also Richard Johnston, "Canadian Elections at the Millennium," *Choices*, Vol. 6, no. 6 (September 2000), p. 13.

66. See, for example, Centre for Research and Information on Canada [CRIC], "Voter Participation in Canada: Is Canadian Democracy in Crisis?" *CRIC Papers*, October 2001.

67. Jean-Pierre Kingsley, quoted in "Liberals Ignore Winds of Change...While It's Familiar Shores for Chrétien," *Toronto Star*, December 30, 2000.

68. See, for example, André Blais, Elisabeth Gidengil, Richard Nadeau, and Neil Nevitte, *Anatomy of a Liberal Victory: Making Sense of the Vote in the 2000 Canadian Election* (Peterborough, ON: Broadview Press, 2002), esp. ch. 3; and Jon H. Pammett, "The People's Verdict," in Jon H. Pammett and Christopher Dornan (eds.), *The Canadian General Election of 2000* (Toronto: Dundurn Press, 2001), pp. 293-317.

69. Blais et al., *Anatomy of a Liberal Victory*, ch. 3; Brenda O'Neill, "Generational Patterns in the Political Opinions and Behaviour of Canadians: Separating the Wheat from the Chaff," *Policy Matters*, Vol. 2, no. 5 (October 2001).

70. See the comments by Louis Massicotte, as quoted in CRIC, "Voter Participation in Canada," p. 13.

71. For instance, André Blais found that turnout dropped by 3 percent, on average, in the 1990s among the 91 countries he examined. See *To Vote or Not to Vote: The Merits and Limits of Rational Choice Theory* (Pittsburgh: University of Pittsburgh Press, 2001), pp. 33-36. See also Mark Gray and Miki Caul, "Declining Voter Turnout in Advanced Industrial Democracies, 1950 to 1997," *Comparative Political Studies*, Vol. 33, no. 9 (November 2000), pp. 1091-122. While there is a consensus that turnout has been declining, there is some debate as to its extensiveness, its timing across democracies and the uniqueness of the Canadian case. See, for example, Johnston, "Canadian Elections at the Millennium," pp. 14-15; and the references in CRIC, "Voter Participation in Canada," p. 6.

72. Were it not for the exceptional political developments in Quebec in 1993, particularly the rise of the Bloc Québécois as it mobilized the federal participation of Quebec nationalists, useful comparisons of turnout levels might have been made between the enumeration approach employed in the province and the (reused) list approach employed elsewhere.

73. Blais et al., *Anatomy of a Liberal Victory*, p. 57. For some earlier evidence of the effects of contacting on turnout (and vote direction), see Jerome H. Black "Revisiting the Effects of Canvassing on Voting Behaviour," *Canadian Journal of Political Science*, Vol. 17 (1984), pp. 351-74.

74. Candidates would, of course, still get the revised and official voters lists, but their usefulness would be limited by the fact that they are received late in the campaign, the former 10 days before election day and the latter 3 days in advance.

75. And, of course, there are other explanatory variables that would need to be taken into account.

76. *Report of the Chief Electoral Officer of Canada on the 37th General Election*, p. 90.

77. André Blais, Antoine Bilodeau, and Christopher Kam, "The Flow of the Vote between the 1993 and 1997 Elections" (unpublished manuscript, no date). The slightly higher figure in this study may be due to the authors' taking emigration into account in their re-adjustments.

78. *Report of the Chief Electoral Officer of Canada on the 37th General Election*, p. 90.

79. *Report of the Chief Electoral Officer of Canada on the 37th General Election*, p. 90.

80. For the 1988 election, the coverage figure of 95.99 percent cited by Courtney and Smith in "Registering Voters" is used (see note 4 in the current document). Estimates of the age-eligible population are based on various Statistics Canada sources and the IDEA Web site, at http://www.idea.int/voter_turnout/ northamerica/canada.html. Citizenship estimates were provided by Elections Canada, which had originally obtained them from Statistics Canada.

81. Citizenship estimates for election years, in particular, must be extrapolated from census data.

82. Elections Canada has published its own coverage estimates for these five elections — 95.5, 95.2, 95.9, 95.1 and 95.2 percent, respectively, indicating little temporal variation and no particular pattern. These figures are higher than those generated in this paper. According to one

agency official, this is because of the use of unadjusted population counts, which are several percentage points below the corrected figures that Statistics Canada emphasizes. Still, assuming that the undercounting is consistent, it is unclear why the estimates provided by Elections Canada differ from the pattern shown in figure 1.

83. *Report of the Chief Electoral Officer of Canada on the 36th General Election.*

84. *Report of the Chief Electoral Officer on the 35th General Election*, p. 96 (emphasis added).

85. Perhaps Elections Canada was able to take advantage of the focus on Quebec and concentrate its efforts and resources there.

86. *Report of the Chief Electoral Officer of Canada on the 37th General Election*, p. 62.

87. *Report of the Chief Electoral Officer of Canada on the 37th General Election*, p. 62.

88. *Standing Committee on Procedure and House Affairs*, March 1, 2001, p. 21.

89. The report's "main objectives were to evaluate the levels of satisfaction among electors and stakeholders and to identify areas that could be improved" (Elections Canada Research Studies, "2000 General Election Post-event Overview" [no date], p. 1, at http://www.elections.ca/loi/rec/overview_e.pdf).

90. Representatives included national directors, agents and members of Elections Canada's Advisory Committee of Political Parties.

91. *Standing Committee on Procedure and House Affairs*, March 1, 2001, p. 13, at http://www.parl.gc.ca/InfoComDoc/37/1/HAFF/Meetings/Evidence/haffev06-e.htm

92. *Standing Committee on Procedure and House Affairs*, March 1, 2001, p. 10.

93. *Standing Committee on Procedure and House Affairs*, March 1, 2001, p. 16.

94. *Standing Committee on Procedure and House Affairs*, March 1, 2001, pp. 20-21.

95. *Standing Committee on Procedure and House Affairs*, March 1, 2001, p. 13. Incidentally, Parrish's negative allusion to the federal register in the Ontario context stems from the province's decision to use it to generate the preliminary list of voters for the June 1999 election (and as the first step in establishing its own permanent list). Critics complained that the information obtained from the register was out of date and that the revision process was too limited and poorly organized. It was argued that all of this, in conjunction with a shortened election campaign (from 37 to 28 days), depressed turnout, especially among the less established and the poor. In turn, this had partisan implications, giving the incumbent Conservatives the advantage. For comments and references on the Ontario case, see Black, "The National Register of Electors," pp. 16, 20-21 and note 45.

96. *Standing Committee on Procedure and House Affairs*, March 1, 2001, p. 13.

97. *Standing Committee on Procedure and House Affairs*, March 1, 2001, p. 3.

98. See, for instance, Andrew Duffy, "Youth Tuning Out: Election Boss," *The Gazette* (Montreal), October 30, 2000.

99. The situation for new citizens appears to be better, though not perfect: Elections Canada reports that between 85 to 90 percent of new Canadian citizens agree to be added to the register (*Standing Committee on Procedure and House Affairs*, May 7, 2002, p. 30, at http://www.parl.gc.ca/InfoComDoc/37/1/HAFF/Meetings/Evidence/haffev63_e.htm).

100. Elections Canada kindly provided the author with this data set. According to its information, "Ipsos-Reid conducted a random telephone survey of Canadians that took place between November 28 and December 11, 2000. A total of 2,500 Canadians were surveyed." While the survey oversampled individuals between the ages of 18 and 34, the weighted version is used here. It is "representative of Canada's age and gender composition in accordance with 1996 Census data."

101. Not shown are 14 "don't know" cases, representing .5 percent of all respondents.

102. For those who were already registered, some corrections could have been made by telephone (e.g., address changes within the constituency), while others, particularly those involving a move to a new constituency, would have entailed a personal visit to the headquarters of the returning officer for completion of forms. Those who were not registered would have needed to apply in person to the returning officer (or, if they registered on election day, to other officials).

103. Blais et al., in their survey of the 2000 election, *Anatomy of a Liberal Victory*, report a similar pattern with respect to age and not receiving

a voter information card (see p. 60). In yet another survey, Pammett reports that young people, as well as lower income and lower educated citizens, "were more likely to report problems with being registered on the voters list" ("The People's Verdict," p. 312).

104. At the same time, students were among those most likely to take the initiative to resolve their registration situation — 9.6 percent, compared to 3 percent for the sample as a whole — reinforcing the inference that the category comprised exceptionally motivated young people.

105. These figures exclude those who took the initiative and those who replied "don't know."

106. Any empirical relationship between registration circumstances and turnout could, in principle, be interpreted as supporting the notion of either registration or turnout as the causal variable; in the latter instance, this would presumably entail reasoning along the lines that nonvoting intentions lead to indifference about registration matters. A partial case for interpreting registration as the antecedent variable, however, can be made by appealing, once again, to the substantial literature emphasizing the impact that institutional arrangements have on political participation. Perhaps also helpful in this regard is the use here of experience with the voter information card as the indicator of initial registration status. Since the card was sent out not too long after the election campaign got underway, responses concerning its receipt can be said to reference prior circumstances (though, in the context of a post-election survey, it is possible that some respondents, for whatever reason, incorrectly recalled those circumstances.) A potentially more credible challenge to the inference that registration is the causal variable involves considering "turnout intentions" not as an alternative causal variable but rather as part of a concern about spuriousness, that is, the possibility that the association between registration and turnout is only apparent, artificially linked by an underlying general lack of political engagement. This more encompassing sentiment would be reflected in disinterest in both registration matters and voting. This does not seem to be the case, however. As will be seen, the registration-turnout empirical association does not disappear when election interest and political knowledge are controlled for.

107. The logistic-based results are not shown but are available from the author upon request. An exception, where the OLS and logistic results are not similar, is pointed out below in note 112.

108. An examination of the betas, standardized regression coefficients, which are more suitable for across-variable assessments, reveals a coefficient of -.26 for not receiving a card and -.21 for the lowest age category.

109. Ideally, party identification should have been included in the analysis, but it is not available in the survey. On the positive side, Blais et al. demonstrate that political interest and information about politics are more important as correlates (see *Anatomy of a Liberal Victory*). Even so, the measures on hand might seem to provide only an approximation of the kind routinely employed. Instead of a question on political interest, there is one on election interest — that is, how closely individuals followed the 2000 election: "very closely, somewhat closely, not very closely or not at all closely." The two knowledge items are subjectively based and not objectively determined, which would have been preferable. Specifically, respondents were asked whether they regarded themselves as "very knowledgeable, somewhat knowledgeable, not very knowledgeable or not at all knowledgeable" about the parties and their platforms and about the voting process ("knowing where and when to vote and knowing what other options were in place if you could not get out to vote on election day"). Still, the way these variables behaved (their impact on turnout and their correlations with other variables) suggests their relevance for present purposes and that they have not produced misleading results. Finally, both the item on citizen duty ("It is important that people vote in elections") and the item on efficacy ("My vote really doesn't matter") are based on a 0-10 scale, agree-disagree format (appropriately recoded).

110. As note 106 suggests, this characterization can be related to a concern about the registration-turnout relationship being spurious; the results in column three provide the basis for dismissing such a worry. At the same time, it might be argued that registration experiences themselves have a bearing on political attitudes, including the possibility that individuals will become more interested as a result of political contact during the campaign.

111. The impact of the new registration system on participation inequality is not necessarily limited to differences in age, income and the like. A geographical dimension may also be relevant. The degree of coverage and accuracy achieved by the register might be expected to vary from one constituency to another, in part as a function of population mobility; presumably, this would be most evident in differences between urban (especially city centre) and rural ridings. Interprovincial disparities may also be evident, due in part to differences in the sharing and updating arrangements established with the provinces and territories. These aspects (not explored here) require a careful analysis that should also include a comparative assessment of the performance of enumeration vis-à-vis geographical disparities in coverage. Elections Canada does maintain the raw data necessary for setting up the dependent variables for such an analysis in the case of the register (i.e., coverage and accuracy estimates broken down by jurisdiction and constituency).

112. A multivariate version of this analysis (which included all of the variables indicated in the third regression model shown in table 4) provides some additional support for the presence of interaction effects. Focusing on the most consequential registration situation, not receiving a voter information card, interaction terms were created by multiplying the dummy variable for this registration experience by each of those representing the two lowest categories for the age, income and education series of variables and then examining the impact of these "product terms" alongside the original (or "main effect") variables. Three significant interaction effects, all in the expected direction, were observed. One was for the lowest age group, with a coefficient of -.08 ($p = .096$) alongside main effects for age, -.07 ($p = .012$) and not receiving a card, -.09 ($p = .012$), meaning that not receiving a card accentuated nonvoting by eight points for those between the ages of 18 and 24. The two others were for the income variables with a coefficient of -.13 ($p = .012$) for those nonrecipients with an income of less than \$20,000 and of -.08 ($p = .087$) for those in the second lowest income bracket (\$20,000-\$39,999); interestingly, the coefficients for the income variables as main effects were no longer statistically significant. Note that it is only in connection with this testing of interaction effects that the logistic analysis (see note 107) diverged from the OLS results: none of the coefficients for these six interaction terms achieved statistical significance, suggesting, as one reviewer put it, differences linked to their functional forms.

113. The survey sampled 1,278 adult Canadians during the period February 16 to April 2, 2000; the main results, though not the ones referenced here, are presented in Paul Howe and David Northrup, "Strengthening Canadian Democracy: The Views of Canadians," *Policy Matters*, Vol. 1, no. 5 (July 2000).

114. *Standing Committee on Procedure and House Affairs*, Evidence, May 7, 2002, p. 13, at http://www.parl.gc.ca/InfoComDoc/37/1/HAFF/ Meetings/Evidence/haffev63-e.htm#Int-227341

115. *Modernizing the Electoral Process: Recommendations from the Chief Electoral Officer* *of Canada Following the 37th General Election* (Ottawa: Elections Canada, 2001).

116. This was also the view of several speakers, most notably Graham White and John Courtney, at the IRPP-sponsored conference, "Transparency, Disclosure and Democracy: Assessing the Chief Electoral Officer's Recommendations," Ottawa, February 27, 2002.

117. Courtney and Smith, "Registering Voters," p. 433. Vote-encouraging activities may be especially important to ensure that enhanced coverage does not simply lead to the listing of *unlikely* voters who are relatively uninterested and uninformed. Indeed, without measures to promote participation itself, increased registration coverage may well lead to a lower official turnout rate.

118. E-mail and telephone communications (December, 2003 and January, 2004).

10

Canada's Democratic Malaise: Are the Media to Blame?

Richard Nadeau and Thierry Giasson

It would be impossible today to hold a discussion on democracy without according a central position to the media. The media have profoundly transformed electoral campaigns[1] and modified conditions of political governance to the point that the authors of one study[2] provocatively entitled their work *Do the Media Govern?* and that Timothy Cook was able to write that "American news media...are now part of the government."[3] In this context it is not hard to see the political dynamic in democracy as being more and more explicitly conceived of as a triangle consisting of interaction between the elected, the electorate and the media.[4]

This growing appreciation of the role of the media by political observers coincides with the appearance of two noticeable trends in most established democracies. The first is the decline in confidence on the part of citizens toward politicians and political institutions.[5] The second is the changing media coverage of politics, which is becoming increasingly negative and oriented toward partisan conflicts between political actors.[6] To many specialists it appears difficult to deny the existence of a link between these two developments. "Many scholars," writes Sören Holmberg, "...point to the media as one of the culprits behind the declining levels of political trust. And it is difficult to disagree."[7]

The preceding comments show the seriousness of the grievances against the media. They are reproached for both undermining the legitimacy of elected officials and exercising undue influence on their decisions. Patterson believes that "the press has gone way beyond the point of responsible criticism, and the effect is to rob political leaders of the public confidence that is required to govern."[8] Timothy Cook concludes that the undue influence of the media results in the diversion of the political agenda: "[T]he greatest pitfalls of governing with the news is that it provides an incentive for political actors to anticipate the needs of the news in deciding what to do, needs that often detract from extrinsic standards of governance."[9]

The charges levelled against the media are thus weighty. These accusations, disturbing in themselves, take on a particular significance given the expectations citizens and specialists have of the role of the media in a democracy. Hackett and Zhao aptly recall in this regard that the Royal Commission on Newspapers in Canada concluded, at the beginning of the 1980s, that "Canadians may not put newspapers on a pedestal but the great majority believe that newspapers, and the mass media in general, have responsibilities to the public different from those of other businesses,"[10] an observation that led them to conclude that "Canadians widely believe that news media should seek more than their own profitability" and that "as institutions central to public life, they are widely expected to function in the public interest."[11] The contribution to the public interest expected of the media is succinctly described by Entman: "The press," he writes, "is supposed to enhance democracy both by stimulating the citizenry's political interest and by providing the specific information they need to hold government accountable."[12]

In this article we will review the case against the media, concentrating on the most serious accusations brought against them, those of undermining the legitimacy of democratic institutions and provoking the rise in cynicism and apathy among citizens. We will examine the evidence produced to support this charge. We will note a certain rift between the weakness of the evidence and the seriousness of the accusations against the media. We will also note the growing gap, as have several observers, between a particular ideal of media coverage of politics and actual journalistic practices. This portrait, neither completely dark nor completely rosy, will inspire the recommendations that we will present to improve the contribution of the media to the quality of democratic life in Canada.

Who is Accused?

The best way to initiate the trial of the media is to concentrate on the identity of the accused. The term "video malaise," which has been widespread for a long time, indicates that the finger was first pointed at television. Lang and Lang, in their pioneering text, and Robinson,[13] who originated the expression, have been largely responsible for spreading the idea that the political journalism practised on television is principally responsible for citizens' lack of confidence in political actors and institutions.[14]

The "video malaise" hypothesis rests on three principal arguments. The first emphasizes the dominance of television news as a source of political information.[15] The second deals with the vulnerability of the accidental news consumer, who is the least sophisticated viewer. "Those who fall into the news," proposes Robinson, that is, those who absorb the news inadvertently because their television set is on, "are particularly likely to suffer from video malaise because they do not have the background of a good newspaper and political discussion with friends to help them understand and interpret the news."[16] Finally, according to the third argument, the conditions under which television journalism is practised are said to be at the root of the treatment of political news — short, superficial, episodic, instantaneous, oriented toward people and their motives rather than on issues — that is particularly responsible for undermining the confidence of citizens in the political process.[17]

The "video malaise" hypothesis makes television the principal source of the media problem in democracies. This view has been challenged since the early 1990s by Christina Holtz-Bacha, who emphasizes that the important distinction, from the point of view of media impact, is perhaps not television versus other media, but the content of the programs broadcast, regardless of the vehicle employed.[18]

This distinction between the medium and its content is important. It has informed writings on the issue for a decade, as attested by the presence, in numerous recent studies, of indicators that allow the types of content broadcast to be distinguished.[19] Noting the changes in the approach to the issue, Kenneth Newton proposes the term "media malaise" rather than "video malaise":

> Although most malaise theory concentrates on television (hence video-malaise), the problem does not lie only with television but with all forms of modern mass media, both print and electronic. Hence the term "media malaise" is preferred...The term is used broadly to cover those types of democratic pathology which are supposed to be caused, at least in part, by the modern mass media — political apathy, alienation, distrust, cynicism, confusion, disillusionment and even fear.[20]

Newton's words point to a notable shift away from the vehicle (television) toward the content (political journalism) as the source of media malaise. Thus it is journalistic treatment of politics in general, both in the written press and in the electronic media, that is in the dock. It is thus appropriate to open the trial of the media by focusing first on general criticisms levelled at the journalistic profession, before establishing whether these accusations are more serious or better founded in the case of television journalism in particular.

When Did the Incriminating Practices Begin?

The judgment passed by several authors on the media in general and political journalism in particular is severe, and some journalists themselves have added their voices to this indictment.[21] The portion of responsibility for the decline in confidence in government institutions attributed to journalists is large and, to make matters worse, the journalistic practices that are the root of this phenomenon have become accentuated over the past few decades.[22]

The idea of a change in journalistic practices since the 1960s in particular is important because it provides a benchmark against which to assess the current situation. There are some quite different perspectives on the past, as exemplified by two renowned critics of current journalistic practices, Larry Sabato and Thomas Patterson. Patterson contrasts the current style of political journalism, based on interpretation, with that which preceded it, based on the facts. The tone he adopts makes his own preferences clear:

> [I]nterpretative journalism has replaced or is supplanting an older descriptive style where the journalist's main job was the straightforward reporting of the "facts"...Today, facts and interpretation are freely intermixed in news reporting. Interpretation provides the theme, and the facts illuminate it. The theme is primary; the facts are illustrative. As a result, events are encompassed and joined together within a common theme. Reporters question politicians' motives and give them less of a chance to speak for themselves.[23]

Larry Sabato also thinks that journalism has changed over the past few decades, and that this evolution is not a positive one from the point of view of the quality of the democratic debate. What makes his viewpoint different from Patterson's, however, is his characterization of journalism in the United States before it took its current form. Thus, Sabato distinguishes three periods rather than two. During the first, which he dates from the beginning of the 1940s to the middle of the 1960s:

> [J]ournalists engaged in...lapdog journalism — reporting that served and reinforced the political establishment. Mainstream journalists rarely challenged prevailing orthodoxy, accepted at face value much of what those in power told them, and protected politicians by revealing little about their nonofficial lives, even when private vices affected public performance.[24]

This type of journalism, described as "complacent," and which hardly represented a golden age of American journalism, was followed by the practice of "watchdog journalism" for about a decade. During this period, "reporters scrutinized the behavior of political elites by undertaking independent investigations of their statements."[25] This interlude led up to the current form of journalism, "junkyard-dog journalism," a confrontational style that Sabato characterizes as being "often hard, aggressive and intrusive" and whose result is that "the news media, both print and broadcast, have sometimes resembled piranhas or sharks in feeding frenzy."[26]

This contrast between Patterson's and Sabato's opinions of what journalism was before it took on its present style is interesting from several perspectives. First, it shows that the definition of the ideal form of political journalism in a democracy is not unanimous. In particular, it recalls Sabato's comment that journalism that presented an essentially favourable attitude toward political actors and institutions is scarcely more desirable than the "junkyard dog" journalism prevailing today. Aside from their differences, these authors do agree in their condemnation of the current forms of political journalism, and in this they are not by any means alone.

Canada is not excluded from this assessment. For more than a decade, political pundits and communications analysts have noted radical changes in the practice of journalism north of the 49th parallel. The geographical proximity of the United States has allowed considerable penetration of Canadian airwaves by American news programs. Some see this situation as being responsible for the Americanization of Canadian journalistic practices and the content of political news coverage.[27] The negative tone, the emphasis on scandals and conflicts, the greater visibility given to journalists and their growing tendency toward commentary are just a few identifiable symptoms of the significant changes in Canadian media coverage of political affairs that have occurred over the past 20 years.[28] This switch in orientation seems to be gaining an increasing number of critics, as we will see in the following section.

What are the Charges?

The list of grievances levelled at political journalism is long. We will review these grievances and then examine the evidence presented to support the most serious accusation against the media, which is that they produce cynicism among citizens and apathy on the part of the electorate.

Harbingers of bad news[29]

The first and perhaps the most important grievance is the negative bias of media's political coverage. Patterson argues that journalism today has pushed the maxim that "bad news makes for good news" to its limit. Referring to the

American case, he claims "since the 60s, bad news has increased by a factor of three and is now the dominant factor of news coverage of national politics."[30]

Moreover, the extent and variety of the forms of negative journalism is revealed in writings on this topic. The increasing prominence given to political scandals,[31] the viciousness toward political personalities[32] and the excessive emphasis placed on bad economic news compared with good economic news are just a few manifestations of a phenomenon that appears to be quite generalized.[33] This is borne out by Westerstahl and Johansson with respect to Sweden, Hibbing and Theiss-Morse in the case of the House of Representatives in the United States[34] as well as numerous studies showing a progressive slide in the coverage of election campaigns in Canada, which were quite neutral or positive during the 1960s but have become increasingly negative over time.[35]

According to André Pratte, this tendency toward "requisite skepticism" in the fourth power is commendable, but it produces harmful effects when it lapses into "obligatory cynicism" or exaggerated criticism. "[W]e are the watch dogs of democracy," writes Pratte.[36] "It is the essence of this function that we be critical...The media have always emphasized the bad news, dramas, scandals, failures. This is not only inevitable, it is also necessary. Other people — advertising practitioners, public relations officers — are paid to broadcast the good news. Nevertheless, there is good reason to question the amplifying effect of the current media pugnacity." [Translation]

These comments of André Pratte's echo Robert Entman's analysis in *Democracy without Citizens*. In this work, Entman describes the retreat from investigative journalism in favour of confrontational journalism, citing the appearance of a dynamic he calls "aggressiveness without accountability." This dynamic, which is the result, according to this author, of journalists confusing vigilance (costly in time and effort) and aggressiveness (which would be a lesser form of investigative journalism), has the effect of increasing electors' cynicism, without making governments more accountable. This derivative of investigative journalism signals, according to Entman, "the faltering of accountability journalism, the seeming inability [of the media] to provide news that holds government to timely and consistent account, despite the trend toward increasingly skeptical if not cynical reporting."[37]

Stardom

The second accusation levelled at political journalists is that they create a barrier between elected and electors by assuming an unwarranted place in the news and in feature articles. The journalist's speech has taken precedence over that of the political actor, which is now reduced to short clips. Studies of the decrease in the time allocated to the politician's presence in favour of that of the journalist, particularly in television programs,[38] support this criticism of journalistic style, a criticism that can be likened to the accusation that journalists are deviating from their mandate in democracies. Sabato's criticism is the most damning in this regard: "especially in the post-Watergate era," he writes "the press is perceived as being far more interested in finding sleaze and achieving fame and fortune than as serving as an honest broker of information between citizens and government."[39] Taras echoes these sentiments in issuing a call to arms against the trend to celebrity among Canadian journalists:

> Journalists must step out of the stories they are covering. They should not be the stars of the show — the central focus of the events that they are reporting on. Political and community leaders who are being covered in TV news stories should be given enough "clip" time to express full sentences and communicate ideas. The reporter's voice should not be the only one heard in news stories.[40]

Denis Monière also refers to this situation in his comparative study of the production of televised news by public French language networks in France, Belgium, Switzerland and Canada. Monière observes that, following the example of American reporters, Canadian journalists allocate less speaking time to political actors than do their European colleagues. According to Monière, this observation could indicate that Canadian news practitioners have a more conflictual relationship with the political world.[41] The manner in which the words of political spokespersons were framed in stories broadcast on the four public networks studied by Monière essentially confirms this fact. In Europe, political personalities express themselves most frequently on the television news through face-to-face interviews. According to Monière, this mode of presentation "reinforces the seriousness and official nature of the broadcast" and leaves an impression of "deference toward the political class" on the part of journalists. [Translation] In Canada, the framing of political actors in news stories consists of quotations from press conferences or improvised press briefings ("scrums"). This conclusion "confirms once again that Canadian journalists favour a confrontational relationship with politicians."[42] [Translation]

Deviation from the agenda

The third grievance against journalists flows naturally from the second. Deviating from their mandate involves deviating from the political agenda. The argument takes two forms. The first, which is the most widespread, is that the media focus the attention of electors on superficial and secondary issues.[43] The importance accorded to candidates' gaffes, polls and party strategies during campaigns[44] and the increasingly frequent intrusions on politicians'[45] private lives would be manifestations of this phenomenon.[46] The second form of the argument has been developed for the most part by Cook and emphasizes the effects of the interaction between the elected and the media.[47] According to this view, government priorities are dictated too much by the media reaction as anticipated by politicians and not enough by the needs and concerns of the electorate.

Pedagogical shortcomings

An equally serious accusation deals with the pedagogical shortcomings of the media, that is, their inability to transmit complete, objective and relevant news, on most issues, to electors. This argument has been presented under a large number of guises, emphasizing various sources of possible bias in the diffusion of factual information. Rothman and Lichter, for example, state that journalists' ideological preferences have greatly influenced their coverage of the nuclear energy issue and that consequently "media coverage of the issue is largely responsible for public misperceptions of the views of scientists."[48]

Patterson maintains that "negative news misleads the people about social trends," which could explain the fact that "by two-to-one margins, Americans wrongly believed that crime, inflation, unemployment and the federal debt each increased."[49]

Structural explanations are generally provided to explain the pedagogical shortcomings of the media, which appear all the more surprising in that they continue to be apparent when sources of information increase, a paradox that Entman explains with the formula "abundance without growth"[50] to indicate the contrast between the increase in vehicles of information over the past few decades and stagnation in citizens' factual knowledge about politics.[51]

The first of these explanations emphasizes the fundamental objectives of the media and journalists, profit and visibility, respectively. According to this argument, neither the media, as businesses, nor journalists, as professionals, are interested, from a strictly rational point of view, in systematically offering their readers content that emphasizes information over entertainment or provides the necessary background for understanding the information presented.[52]

The second explanation emphasizes the impact of professional and organizational routines on the selection and treatment of news. Attraction to change is one of the most deeply rooted reflexes, according to Stimson: "Journalists pursue 'news' as a criterion of relevance. Change is news. Stability isn't."[53] In a study of political communication in France, Maarek presents another aspect of this kind of distortion:

> Frequently, journalists only portray politicians marginally, or indirectly with epithets relating to the orientation that the latter want to give their speeches. All the same, journalists have a tendency to devote

considerable coverage to politicians who "change" their point of view, when it is precisely these changes that adversely affect positive penetration of the political speech by giving an impression of quite detrimental instability.[54] [Translation]

This emphasis on change has an impact on the quality of news provided to citizens. Nadeau et al., who examined the determinants of media coverage of economic news, observe that: "Not only do media reports emphasize change, they also stress the importance and significance of observed change. Rather than reporting change as a temporary deviation from the norm, changes are reported as an indication of the development or the aggravation of a trend."[55]

Competition within the media industry and the speed with which news is disseminated could be leading the media to favour news that is easily accessible and can be quickly confirmed by their sources.[56] This news-selection method and a style of reporting that focuses on sensationalism contribute to creating a gap between the news disseminated and political reality. Ansolabehere, Behr and Iyengar remark on this contrast when they note that: "Simplicity, clarity, color and clear story lines are the hallmarks of news reports. These same qualities, of course, are generally absent from the fuzzy and ambiguous world of politics and public affairs."[57]

A final explanation, that of Gunther and Mughan, links the pedagogical deficiencies of the media to the weakness of the tradition of journalism as a public service in certain countries (notably the United States) and its progressive loss of ground in others (Great Britain and Canada, for example). According to the authors, this development has resulted in the appearance of "pathologies" in the media treatment of political activity that are deleterious to the quality of democratic debate. Thus Gunther and Mughan conclude that the decreasing quality of democratic life in the countries examined "derived from a reduced volume of policy-relevant information flowing to voters; from a shift from substantive issues to a focus on personalities and foibles of politicians, to the 'game' of politics and the excitement of the electoral 'horse race' and, more generally, the ephemera of politics; and from gratuitous editorializing by reporters."[58]

The temptation to editorialize

One fundamental accusation aimed at the contemporary form of political journalism, an accusation that to a certain extent cuts across most of the others, is that it relies on a restricted interpretative framework of political dynamics in a democracy. The effect of such "framing," according to Cappella and Jamieson, is to reduce the public policy process (or, to cite Page's expression, "deliberation"[59]) "to the sum of the leaders' self-interests and a chronicle of who won and who lost."[60]

The analytical framework favoured by contemporary political journalism, oriented toward strategic interpretation and conflict rather than consensus and factual information, has been given various labels: "strategy-driven," "conflict-based" and "strategic framing," all of which are geared to emphasize the deformed and diminished image of politics and politicians presented to electors. According to some[61] this journalistic style strangles public policy deliberation, others[62] believe it places too much emphasis on the struggle for power as opposed to the conditions under which it is exercised, and still others see it as discrediting the electoral process itself by reducing the broad debates of society to simple partisan issues, as Mendelsohn's particularly convincing work on the media coverage of the free-trade issue during the 1988 federal election shows.[63]

Pack journalism

An aggravating characteristic of political journalism is its homogeneity. "Pack journalism," as it is called, has numerous disadvantages. Conformity, aversion to risk and the pack mentality that characterize journalistic practices result in broad uniformity in the choice, treatment and interpretation of new policies.[64] This uniformity, which deprives citizens of the diversity of perspectives that normally produce competition and emulation,[65] reinforces the impact of the negative tendencies of contemporary political journalism (negative tone, stress on the actors' motives, etc.) by confronting citizens repeatedly and univocally with the same, devalued concept of politics.[66]

A harsh indictment

The foregoing shows that the list of grievances against the media's political coverage is long and full. Contemporary political journalists are blamed for exaggerating the bleaker side of the facts, usurping the role of elected politicians by giving themselves unwarranted visibility, diverting electors' attention toward secondary issues, failing in their educational role by disseminating incomplete and reconstituted information about the issues, giving themselves the authority to speculate about actors' motives and, to this end, presenting an interpretive framework that produces a belittling image of politics and politicians, and indulging in bandwagon behaviour that accentuates the limitations of their practices.

Beyond specific grievances, the two most serious accusations against the media are that they exercise undue influence in the process of determining the political agenda and they undermine citizens' confidence in political actors and institutions. Several authors specifically mention this second accusation. Patterson, for example, states that: "The media's bad news tendency has heightened Americans' disillusionment with the political leaders and institutions."[67] Sabato claims that "The electorate's media-assisted cynicism has been confirmed in a host of studies and surveys."[68] Cappella and Jamieson believe that the interpretation of politics favoured by the media is at the root of a spiral of cynicism that affects political actors as much as the media themselves, while Rothman, speculating on the long-term consequences of contemporary political journalism, concludes that: "Public cynicism...[is] growing in the United States and, in so far as journalists played a role in this growth they...contribute to the erosion of the very cultural elements which created a free society."[69]

Now that we have carefully outlined the charges, it is time to analyze the evidence supporting the most serious accusation, that of producing and perpetuating a level of cynicism toward political actors, institutions and processes that is deleterious to the quality and functioning of democratic life.[70] Before addressing the evidence as such, we should examine the conditions under which journalism is practised in order to determine whether they could be considered attenuating circumstances regarding the grievances levelled against political journalism.

Attenuating Circumstances: The Conditions under Which Political Journalism is Practised

There are numerous constraints that make a certain ideal-type of political journalism difficult to attain in a democracy. The leeway of political journalists who cover politics is limited by more or less formal constraints that can be attributed to television as a genre, professional routines and the commercial objectives of media companies. As Pratte says in his study *Le syndrome de Pinocchio*: "Journalists have neither the time, nor the means, nor the will to verify."[71] [Translation]

This suggests that the limitations of political journalism are due, in part at least, to the conditions under which it is practised. According to various authors, there are four constraints that contribute to restricting journalists' ability to produce news that is as rich and diversified as their detractors would like. Caught between a rock and a hard place, the product journalists present is the result of compromises among multiple demands, compromises that are inevitable to some and unacceptable for others.

Constraints of the genre
The first constraint with which the journalist has to deal is that of the demands of journalistic writing. The news is a literary genre that has its own canons to which the journalist is expected to conform. The comments of Reuben Frank, producer of the CBC Evening News, describe these expectations well:

Every news story should, without any sacrifice of probity or responsibility, display the attributes of fiction, of drama. It should have structure and conflict, problem and denouement, rising action and falling
action, a beginning, a middle and an end.[72]

Technical constraints

According to several commentators, the constraints associated with the production of televised news restrict even further the journalist's leeway in dealing with
the news.[73] Thus the specific imperatives of television production are added to
the constraints of journalistic writing in general. These constraints push the
journalist toward rapid production of brief, rather superficial news often
inclined toward an emphasis on personal experiences, image and emotions.

The analysis of Agnieszka Dobrzynska, who has examined the journalistic
practices of Canadian television reporters covering the 1997 federal election
campaign, confirms the existence of the same practical constraints in Canada.[74]
Journalists themselves point out the limited time available in news bulletins for
political or electoral information as an important determinant of the content
and form of their stories. Political and electoral content has to compete with
other categories of information (sports, culture, science) that must also be presented during the 22 minutes of airtime for a televised newscast.

Organizational constraints

The constraints that are specific to the dominant genre of political information,
television news, considerably limit the journalist's autonomy in the practice of
the profession. To these already weighty constraints are added the organizational pressures journalists must face. Bennett, in a short but illuminating article, effectively demonstrates the pressure of the organizational routines that go
along with "the beat," the demands of indexing and the tyranny exercised by
sources over journalistic practices.[75]

According to these routines, a journalist is typically assigned to a beat or a
story that he or she regularly has to follow based on information collected from
sources whose number is limited and whose make-up is almost unvarying.
Under this regime, journalists are caught in a stranglehold by the sources on
which they depend and the organization to which they are answerable.

This dependence on sources is in fact a recurring theme of the sociology of
journalists.[76] It is even greater if the journalist works in an organization where
the resources devoted to newsgathering are limited and the editorial policy
imprecise. Blais and Crête have shown that local journalists are often only the
conveyer belts of information from their sources (e.g., elected or municipal
officials).[77] Cormier notes that during the 1984 election there was a closer

convergence between media coverage and party messages (from the Conservative Party especially) on TVA than there was on SRC and CBC, and drew from this observation the general hypothesis that "the more structured the editorial policy, the less the journalistic treatment will conform with the communication objectives of the source."[78] [Translation]

These results are echoed in classic works of Sigal and Gans.[79] Sigal showed that, basically, the sources of American journalists barely extend beyond the triangle formed by the White House, the Pentagon and Congress. Gans used the image of a dance between two partners to illustrate the relationship between journalists and their sources, a dance that is largely, if not entirely, led by the sources, which were more active, dynamic, resourceful and motivated in their quest for publicity than were journalists in their quest for information.[80] Gandy uses the expression "news subsidies" [Translation] to describe this system, whereby journalists with very limited resources take advantage of information provided for free by their sources.[81] Zaller suggests that "the well-established reliance of reporters on their sources" can be attributed to journalists' lack of expertise and resources.[82]

The profitability constraint

Some claim that the heart of the unequal power relations between journalists and their sources is the limited resources the media allocates for handling information. Thus the pursuit of profitability would explain the media's desire to produce news at the lowest possible cost. This situation undoubtedly has an effect on news quality. Carper maintains that in general "the goals of marketing are in conflict with the role that the press should play in a democracy."[83] Reeves concludes that the imbalance between the resources provided to journalists to do their work and the means their sources have at their disposal (political parties, pressure groups, etc.) to influence the content of the news explains why "major news organizations routinely accept the assumptions and assertions of policy-makers."[84]

Journalists who cover political news must therefore do their jobs in a context of scarcity of resources, which prevents them from pushing their analytical or research efforts to the limit, unless they are given a specific dossier. Everything has to be done quickly and at the lowest possible cost to the company. Confronted with the numerous daily production deadlines that followed the advent of continuous information networks, journalists no longer have the time to do research or unearth alternative sources that might put into perspective or challenge the official speech they have to report.[85] According to Pratte, who cites the investigative journalist André Noël, the media have the means to allocate more resources to research and in-depth investigations but prefer to invest them in producing the "news of the day" [Translation] or in "news reports that are increasingly instantaneous, superficial and piecemeal" [Translation].[86] Media companies consider this kind of news report more profitable because it can be produced and aired more rapidly.

Still on the subject of the profitability constraints imposed on journalists, in his analysis of changes in the Canadian media landscape Taras points to the important fact that the American trend to produce information-entertainment seems to be well entrenched in Canada. Citizens whose knowledge of politics is said to be minimal prefer to be entertained than informed. The reaction of media companies, which are always looking out for the demands and tastes but not the needs of their consumers, has been to offer more entertaining but less educational content. As Taras suggests, "politics no longer sells" and has "taken a back seat to celebrity news, entertainment news, business news, sports news, and lifestyle news." He elaborates:

> The large conglomerates that own the TV networks but also major chunks of the world entertainment industry have a stake in promoting their own products — movies, books, celebrities, sports team, etc. — as news stories, and in appealing to audiences with news stories that are "lite and less filling" in order to boost ratings.[87]

News priorities are dictated by the commercial interests of media companies. In the name of synergy and profitability, the content of stories must both contribute to the effort to market "products" offered by various components of the large press conglomerates and be constructed to retain the attention of an apathetic television viewer audience that values being entertained above all.

Between a rock and a hard place

The conclusions presented here all seem to point to something of a paradox. How can one reconcile the image of the journalist who is at the mercy of his or her sources and the increasingly negative treatment of politics in the media? John Zaller has resolved this apparent paradox brilliantly in his important work.[88]

Zaller's thesis rests on the rationality of the actors. The media want to maximize their profitability, politicians their visibility and journalists their value-added, that is, their contribution as professionals to the depth and the quality of the news disseminated. These objectives are contradictory. The media, according to Zaller, are not very interested in presenting high-quality news that does not respond to the tastes of a public that, succumbing to the law of the least effort, will be content with a light diet of news described as entertainment.[89] Meanwhile parties do not seek to inform electors but rather to influence them, and to this end they use a whole range of more or less sophisticated means[90] in order to get their messages disseminated through the news media.

Zaller sees journalists as being caught in the crossfire: "Journalists are thus fighting a two-front war to control their professional turf. On one side, they must fend off market competition that forces them to dilute the news values that are their professional bread-and-butter. And on the other side, they must struggle with politicians to maintain control of their work market."[91] Their reaction to this double pressure explains the superficial character and negative tone of political news, argues Zaller. With few resources and under severe organizational constraints, journalists react by producing news reports that are rather superficial, homogeneous, predictable, focus on the political game and essentially conform to the dominant discourse of political elites. Subject to a sustained attempt by the parties to control the political agenda, these journalists, prompted by the desire not be manipulated, adopt an increasingly confrontational style.[92] This situation has led Bennett to suggest that journalists, seeking to escape the rather untenable constraints to which they are subjected, practise both "pack" and "attack" journalism.[93]

Dissatisfied journalists

Two conclusions emerge from this rapid overview of the conditions of the practice of political journalism. The first is that journalists are more and more dissatisfied, confronted with the problem of reconciling their professional ambition to produce high-quality news reports with the constraints to which they are subject.[94] This observation echoes an extensive survey of 1,400 journalists by Weaver and Wilhoit, in which the authors conclude that: "One of the most significant predictors of job satisfaction is the extent to which journalists see the organization as informing the audience."[95]

The second observation is that the organizational pressures on journalists have more influence on the journalistic product than pressures from their sources, as Zaller eloquently points out:

> A central tension of media politics is between journalists, who wish to produce a sophisticated news product, and ordinary citizens, who want something less sophisticated. The best evidence of the kind of product journalists would like to produce comes from markets in which they face relatively less competitive pressure to cater the mass tastes. In these markets — modern American newspapers, TV network news in the 1960s, and British television — we find a relatively high-quality news product and a determination to keep it so. But from markets in which competition is greater, especially TV news, we find a lower quality news product that is, one must assume, closer to what mass tastes in news actually are.[96]

Has the equilibrium been destroyed?

Over the past few years the growth of the phenomenon of press concentration has fuelled debate over the objectivity and variety of media coverage of politics.[97] Canada has not escaped this phenomenon, as demonstrated recently by concerns about editorial policies imposed by Can West Global on all its newspapers and those concerning amalgamation of Quebec companies Gesca and Québécor. The debate over the diversity of journalistic coverage of politics is obviously very old. It has been driven in Canada, as elsewhere, by two broad currents, a more conservative view that reproaches the media for being biased towards ideas and parties on the left of the political spectrum[98] and another, opposing trend that blames the media for being a cog in the establishment.[99]

A more recent direction in the debate over the objectivity of the media emphasizes the notion of equilibrium. This equilibrium between journalists' more liberal orientation[100] and media owners' more conservative one[101] is said to have contributed in the past to maintaining a certain amount of variety in the exchange of ideas, which feeds political debate. The weakening of the public service tradition in the media, combined with market deregulation and the resulting concentration of the news media has destroyed this equilibrium and caused the quality and diversity of journalistic treatment of politics to deteriorate.[102] The intensity of this debate recently reflects concerns about the contribution of the media to the quality of democratic life, to which we will return in our conclusion.

Are the Media Guilty?

Having outlined the accusations and the attenuating circumstances, it is now time to examine the evidence presented by contemporary political journalism's detractors to determine whether it is truly incriminating. But first, we will make three observations. The first is that the media generally, and political journalism specifically, will be deemed innocent as long as their guilt is not proven beyond a reasonable doubt. The burden of proof is thus on the side of the media's detractors (or accusers). This idea is clearly expressed by Pippa Norris: "It is incumbent on proponents of the media-malaise thesis," she writes, "…to demonstrate media influence at the societal level, if they can."[103]

The second observation has to do with the identity of the accused. Who is responsible for the increasing cynicism, television alone, or all the media? Does responsibility fall on a particular type of program? In other words, is this cynicism occasioned by exposure to political reporting in general, televised political news in particular, or entertainment programs? There again, is it the combination of a medium and a genre (televised news) that produces elector disenchantment?

The third observation deals with the logic of the evidence. Robinson's pioneering work[104] that introduced the "media-malaise" hypothesis and the work of his successors[105] rests on the type of proof that Patterson summarizes thus: "Unlike the situation of the '60s, increased news exposure is now positively correlated with a heightened mistrust of government."[106] The reasoning behind this evidence is clear. Because contemporary political journalism began adopting the character for which it is blamed in the late 1960s and the early 1970s, it is from that point in time that we should begin to observe a definite link between exposure to media coverage of politics and an increase in cynicism in the established democracies. Is this in fact the case?

Is the Evidence Convincing?

The evidence supporting the charges against the media has two characteristics that lessen its impact. The first is that it is circumstantial, based more on the coincidence between the decreasing confidence in political institutions and changes in journalistic practices than on the demonstration of a direct link between media exposure and the manifestation of a higher level of cynicism.[107] The second is that the evidence is rather old, and for a decade it has been severely shaken by a strong revisionist trend principally led by Pippa Norris.[108]

The media's detractors have pointed the finger at one vehicle, television, and one genre, political journalism. Moreover, as early as the beginning of the 1990s, Christina Holtz-Bacha showed that reading newspapers and exposure to television news was connected not positively but quite negatively to a composite indicator of political alienation. Noting that the reverse was true for entertainment media, she thus concluded that: "No connection was found between political malaise and the contents of political programming, which leads to the conclusion that the videomalaise thesis is unwarranted. Instead, political alienation and low participation are related to the use made of entertainment content in both television and press."[109]

The studies published in the following decade have, overall, confirmed Holtz-Bacha's conclusions. Bowen, Stamm and Clark concluded from their study based on a sample of voters in Seattle that: "Robinson's video-malaise theory is subject to a number of contingencies that limit its generality, including the probability that newspaper reliance may actually contribute to reduce political malaise,"[110] while Holmberg concluded from his reading of works on the Swedish case that "commercialized media is to blame."[111]

These kinds of conclusions overlap with Newton's, based on data from the 1996 British Social Attitudes Survey.[112] In this study, Newton examines the link between different types of media content and various indicators measuring information about voters: their interest in politics, their degree of cynicism, their confidence in political actors and institutions and their satisfaction with the functioning of democracy. His analyses show that reading newspapers (other than the tabloids) and watching television news have a positive effect on most of these indicators, while exposure to more entertainment-oriented programming (general television and tabloid) lowers them, albeit less markedly. These results lead Newton to conclude that the media-malaise hypothesis "finds little to no support" and that "it seems to be the content of the media, rather than its form which is important."[113]

Other studies contribute to exonerating the media. In Canada, Nadeau et al., for example, show that confidence in various political institutions (federal and provincial governments, courts, police, army, etc.) is not systematically linked to six different measures of media exposure.[114] This is similar to what Moy, Pfau and Kahlor conclude from their study based on 1996 American National Election Study data: that confidence in the presidency, Congress, the courts and the police is not linked to various measures of media exposure (including the nontraditional media and open-line broadcasts).[115]

The best documented rebuttal of the video-malaise hypothesis comes from Pippa Norris, who shows in a series of studies based on American and European data that reading newspapers and watching the television news are positively linked to indicators measuring political interest, information and participation.[116] What is more, Norris has also shown that this positive link between media exposure and political support has, contrary to what Patterson claims, remained essentially the same since the beginning of the 1970s. To Norris this seems to demonstrate that political journalism has not changed as much as has been claimed, because exposure to media coverage of politics seems to have the same positive effect on confidence in political actors and institutions now that it did in the past.

What would be the decision of a jury that had to convict or acquit the media of feeding cynicism in most of the established democracies? There would hardly be any doubt about the verdict. Based on the evidence presented and its inherent logic, the jury would acquit the media, undoubtedly after expressing its surprise at the harshness of the accusations, the baselessness of the evidence and its skepticism at the significance of the results regarding entertainment programming and media. (Why would political cynicism be associated with these kinds of coverage and not the television news, which should represent the most accomplished form of journalism today?)

Is this is the end of the story? No, because several questions remain unanswered. The first has to do with the evidence itself. Does it really let us get to the bottom of the question? If not, what evidence would allow us to dispose of the issue in a more satisfactory manner? Moreover, isn't this type of evidence too limited? Is the fact that there is no statistical association between media exposure and political cynicism enough to acquit political journalism? In other words, can one deduce from the statistical evidence presented by Pippa Norris that citizens in general are satisfied with the media and view their contribution to democratic life positively? Nothing could be less certain.

What if the Problem Lies Elsewhere?

The first factor that should be entered onto the record in the event of the trial being reopened is the ambiguity of the evidence of a positive link between media exposure and political support. The caution on the part of even those most skeptical of the media malaise hypothesis is noteworthy. Newton, for example, concludes in his article that "we should be cautious about making cause and effect statements. This article has talked in terms of associations...because it is exceedingly difficult to untangle cause and effect relationships in mass media research."[117] Norris expresses the same view when she concludes prudently: "Why should we find a positive link between civic engagement and attention to the news media?" she asks. "There are...possible answers, which cannot be resolved here."[118]

The major difficulty in interpreting the statistical link between media exposure and political commitment is the problem of selection, that is, how inclined are those voters who are most interested and most confident in political, media or other institutions to be more exposed to political news.[119] This factor increases both the difficulty of observing a positive association between media exposure and cynicism (the media-malaise hypothesis) and the ambiguity of works that arrive at the opposite result. Undoubtedly, this is why Newton hesitates to conclude that watching television stimulates political commitment,[120] and Pippa Norris merely presents her hypothesis of a virtuous circle between media exposure and civic commitment as being plausible but not proven.[121]

This caution, this reluctance to draw definitive conclusions of an association between indicators of media exposure and political commitment, also recalls Zukin's conclusion in his exhaustive study of the issue some twenty years ago. "The question of whether the mass media contributed to the growth of political malaise," he wrote, "...probably will never be satisfactorily answered."[122]

One day a more sophisticated methodology will allow us to resolve the issue clearly.[123] For now, "media malaise" supporters appear to have been defeated on their own ground, proving incapable of demonstrating a positive link between media exposure and cynicism. In addition, the fact that their opponents have achieved a modest victory and hesitate to conclude that being a media consumer increases support for political actors and institutions is a good indication that this debate, for the time being at least, does not lend itself well to definitive conclusions. Some might even be tempted to conclude that "media malaise" is still a good cause that has not been well defended, while others, in view of the harshness of the attacks on the media and the eloquence of some of its detractors, would perhaps be inclined to think exactly the opposite.

The uncertainty of conclusions on the "media-malaise" issue is an argument in favour of broadening a debate that has until now opposed those who think that the media exert a negative influence on political support and those who reject this hypothesis. Some recent observers have proposed that the issue be recast from the wider perspective of the decline in confidence not only in government institutions but also in almost all institutions, including the media.[124]

Confidence in the media and government institutions appears both to be weak and to have dropped.[125] Gallup polls show, for example, that only 21 percent of Canadians believe that values like honesty and integrity are high among journalists (14 percent have the same opinion of members of Parliament).[126] In addition, a study by Nadeau et al. shows that only 36 percent of Canadians have confidence in the media, an even lower proportion than that recorded for the federal and provincial governments (44 and 41 percent, respectively), and barely higher than the confidence expressed in unions, which brings up the rear at 29 percent.[127]

Among those who have pondered the common woes of the media and governments are Bennett et al.[128] Noting the existence of a very strong positive association between confidence in media and government institutions and the disappearance of all links between media exposure and government support when the variable measuring confidence in the media is included in the analysis, these authors conclude, "the traditional video-malaise notion needs to be revised. Jaundiced views of government and the media co-vary, raising the possibility that the public views both government and the media in the same vein."[129]

The work of Bennett's group reframes the media-malaise debate pertinently by clearly asking whether the simultaneous decline in confidence in the media and political institutions is a result of a decrease in support for institutions in general or whether it can be attributed to a dynamic that is specific to the relationship between journalists and politicians, a sort of vicious circle whereby the actors mutually reinforce the disrepute to which they have been subject. These questions remain unanswered: "Perceptions of the media and the government may rise and fall together. This may reflect a broader trend: that support for institutions in general has changed...but it might also represent the mutual destruction of government officials and the media."[130] To the ambiguity of the link between media exposure and confidence in political institutions, we therefore add that of the association between confidence in media and political institutions, as such.

One way to dispel this ambiguity is to examine media confidence in more detail. We have already noted that this confidence is rather weak and on the decline. The question is, why? In other words, are there data that would allow us to confirm, following Cappella and Jamieson, that "the public now tends to see the media as part of the problem, not part of the solution."[131]

There are many parts to the phenomenon of media confidence. Two of them appear to be decisive: equity and relevance. Studies of the perception of equity in television coverage of politics (the partisan press is a separate case) suggest that while the majority of voters in established democracies do not think television news is systematically biased against certain parties or political currents, a substantial minority think that it is.[132]

To this first source of discontent for some, we would add another, more important one, the lack of relevance. The lack of relevance of political news appears to be a fundamental aspect of media malaise. This malaise is manifested in two major complaints by voters. They believe that the media wield much too much influence, in other words, that they take up (and give themselves) too much airtime in news presentations. The data of Nadeau et al. are particularly explicit on this topic.[133] They show, first of all, the gap between perceived and desired media influence: one out of every two Canadians thinks that the media have too much influence in society, but only one out of twenty-five are satisfied with things as they are. They then show, and this is important, that this gap between the media's perceived and desired influence is positively linked to elector cynicism.

Electors do not reproach the media only for adopting too large a role. They reproach them for speaking to them about issues that do not interest them. On this point the collective that produced Crosstalk are eloquent. They write: "Journalists...might want to rethink the horse-race and strategy emphasis, not because of the scolding of political scientists, or even because of public criticism of the media's preoccupation with scandal and trivia. Our focus group reveals that horse-race journalism is neither useful nor interesting for the public."[134]

This is similar to the conclusion of Cappella and Jamieson, who explicitly mention this gap between the media's supply and the citizens' demand:

> The data from our studies indicate that people have strong opinions about media practices, believing that they choose stories that are more strategic than substantive and, once chosen, tend to slant the stories toward more strategic and sensational frames. The same people who hold these beliefs implicitly do not themselves select stories on the basis of more strategic headlines. To the contrary, their choices seem dictated more by topic than frame...Preferred news events included those that involved the news media least — debates, lengthy interviews, and unedited speeches.[135]

The weakness of the evidence of the harshest media detractors suggests that contemporary political journalism does not deserve the opprobrium to which it is subjected in some circles. However, the gap between what the media offer and citizens' expectations obviously creates a malaise. These expectations of the media are, however, qualified. Citizens' desire to see the media wield less influence goes in hand with a wish to see them play an even more active role as government watchdogs and protectors of citizens' rights against abuses of power.[136]

There is a new type of political reporting that is devoting itself to exactly this task: public journalism, or civic journalism. Defenders of civic journalism are pushing reflection on the links between political journalism and the quality of democratic life even further.[137] This journalistic practice places citizens' needs at the centre of the political coverage strategy generally and the electoral framework in particular.

From this angle, electoral news must principally focus on citizens' questions about issues they consider to be priorities and on party positions concerning these precise issues. The reporting in civic journalism must cover campaigns by uncovering ordinary citizens' experiences, the content of programs, local realities and election issues. Politicians get to speak in order to respond specifically to these needs. The preferred interlocutor for journalism is no longer the political actor but the citizen.[138] In contrast with the traditional model, media campaign coverage is no longer at the service of political organizations, but geared to listening to electors. In this context, news that deals with candidates' tours and the electoral strategies of political organizations becomes secondary.

The objective of this somewhat idealistic approach to political reporting, which originates in the United States and has been practised there since the beginning of the 1990s, is to stimulate political participation and deliberation by citizens as they are confronted with the broad issues that affect their communities.[139] The proponents of civic journalism are attempting to present a new conception of the media's audience. They reject the commercial vision that presumes their audience consists of consumers, victims or passive spectators.[140] Instead they consider media coverage of politics to be addressing communities of involved citizens who must be consulted, sensitized, informed and stimulated.

In this journalistic context, which seems to be a reaction to the media's loss of legitimacy in the public eye[141] and to critics who take aim at the harmful effects of traditional campaign journalism oriented toward partisan strategies and competition between candidates,[142] the media present themselves as social actors, vehicles of change in the markets they serve. They describe their explicit mission as being one of forging solidarity, outreach and pedagogy.[143] No longer are they just spectators and reporters of political or electoral events. In collaboration with citizens, practitioners of public journalism set priorities and design their coverage in order to offer their audience complete solutions to issues that concern them. The media thus serve as places for social actors to meet, deliberate and debate.[144]

Since 1990, more than 300 American media organizations have launched civic journalism initiatives of one type or another. Some of these experiments have produced worthwhile results for the media, politicians and electors. In 1996, the Poynter Institute for Media Studies conducted a study during the American presidential election in 20 communities where the local media (newspapers, radio and television) adopted various civic journalism models in their coverage of the final seven weeks of the campaign. In the 10 markets where electoral coverage was principally of the civic type, citizens' knowledge of general politics, candidates' positions and electoral issues had increased more than in the other 10 regions where the civic journalism approach was much less pronounced in the media coverage.[145]

Civic journalism thus attempts to respond to citizens' demands and needs with respect to political news. But there is a paradox. On the one hand, citizens claim to be dissatisfied with what the media offers. They would like to be able to get more analysis, debates and in-depth interviews in which journalists are more discrete. On the other hand, this call for a return to rigour and substance in the practice of political journalism seems puzzling when compared with citizens' real news consumption habits. The viewership for programs that offer news that is fuller and less commented upon by journalists is low. This is a considerable stumbling block with which defenders of civic journalism must contend.

Zussman, who paints a picture of Canadians' declining confidence in their public institutions and politicians, and Pratte and Zaller say that this contradiction can be explained by intellectual laziness, a rational ignorance displayed by the public toward information news programs.[146] Political news consumption habits seem to be controlled by the law of the least effort. This rational behaviour spurs citizens to consume (when they take the trouble to do so) political news that is briefer and more entertaining rather than serious and in-depth. Zussman argues that "what sells newspapers and attracts viewers are stories that portray conflict and controversy, and journalists are often rewarded based on these criteria. This approach is driven, in large measure, by what Walter Lippman called the public preference for the curiously trivial against the dull important."[147]

This situation is evident in the public disaffection experienced by the large Western public television networks (CBC-SRC, France2, PBS, among others) that are attempting to preserve a public service tradition by producing political programs with more rigorous and in-depth content. These broadcasters are losing large portions of their viewership to private networks that offer brief reports centred on conflict, leaders' images or political anecdotes whose objective is to keep viewers' attention by entertaining them.[148]

This gradual leakage in their audiences is a concern for public television services, which have to derive larger and larger proportions of their revenue from advertising sales.[149] In Canada the estimates vary, but available data indicate that between 40 and 50 percent of the operating budgets of the two Canadian public television networks comes from this source of financing.[150] This situation is prompting public networks to review their missions with a view to offering more commercial programs and stories[151] in order to increase their audience ratings, audience ratings that are driven by the tastes of a public that is apathetic and indifferent to politics and prefers to be entertained when they are watching the news.[152] The competition between public and private broadcasters is increasing to meet citizens' demands. This situation is leading to increasing uniformity in the content of reporting and a levelling in the quality of political news.[153] This levelling can only accentuate the increasing cynicism toward political actors. The mismatch between citizens' stated expectations vis-à-vis the news and their real news consumption habits is striking.

It is therefore appropriate, in the light of this observation, to conclude our article by briefly examining solutions that would allow the media to respond to citizens' wishes with respect to news and avoid the perverse effects of acceleration in the commercialization of televised political journalism.

What Should Be Done?

Some preliminary remarks are necessary before making recommendations on journalistic practices. First, we should note that even the most hardened critics of contemporary political journalism recognize the essential role the media plays in democracies, and they do not question the need for journalists to adopt a critical approach toward political power. On the contrary, this behaviour is valued and its opposite excess, complacency, is sometimes denounced just as vigorously.[154]

We should also point out that contemporary political journalism does not lack champions. Some think, for example, that the criticisms levelled at journalists are largely exaggerated, if not baseless.[155] Others maintain that the conditions under which journalism is practised are to blame, and that it is contradictory to want news that is both instantaneous and in-depth. Others, like Zaller, think it is to be expected that journalists and the media look after their own interests first and foremost, and that the market for news includes sufficient control and self-regulation mechanisms to adequately respond to citizens' needs.[156]

This is the perspective of Page, who believes that the media, even when functioning imperfectly, play their role adequately in the process of deliberation leading to the adoption of public policy.[157] Finally, others think that the media malaise debate is a false one, whether because the causes of the decline in government support lie elsewhere,[158] because the media malaise hypothesis has not been proven,[159] or because, contrary to the claims of champions of this school of thought, the dynamic between media exposure and political attitudes is not a vicious circle that leads to cynicism, but a virtuous circle that leads to commitment.[160]

It is with these qualifications and nuances in mind that we will now examine some remedies to the ills of political journalism. In so doing, we will also keep in mind that journalistic practices have structural roots (technological and economic) and they do not derive exclusively, or even principally, from the active encouragement of practitioners of the trade. The leeway journalists possess is rather circumscribed, as they frequently have few resources and are forced to deal with a restrictive editorial orientation and pronounced dependence on their sources. That said, they do have some freedom to manoeuvre, and in this respect we share Entman's view that some of the current problems in the media coverage of politics stem from the resistance of journalists themselves to questioning some of their practices, a situation that he calls "pressure without reform."[161] Our perspective, in the final analysis, borrows less from those who accuse the media of giving rise to political cynicism than from the current of works that observes a growing gap between the media coverage ideal as represented by so-called public service television and the contemporary forms of journalistic treatment of politics, a gap Robert Entman describes eloquently in his blunt, but not unfounded statement that "democracy has gained little from the rise of media power."[162]

In a certain sense, these remedies are self-evident. If the media wish to contribute more positively to democratic life, they will have to continue to be just as vigilant while becoming less omnipresent. The widespread perceptions of excessive media influence, Hallin's work on the "shrinking soundbite," the analyses of Entman, Jamieson, Pratte, Taras, Bennett, Patterson, Sabato, Cook and several others on the excessive power of the journalistic profession, and the complete absence of media accountability presents a whole array of data and perspectives that militate strongly in favour of recasting political reporting in favour of forms that would give a greater prominence to the facts, issues and politicians' speeches than to the journalistic interpretation of the same data. We believe with Patterson that "[t]he public interest would be better served if journalists recognized the limitations of their craft."[163] The objective of this strategic withdrawal by the media is better communication between elected and elector. In this we subscribe to Cook's argument that "in crafting public policy and practice, we should find ways for political actors to have more opportunities to reach each other and the public directly, without having to be channeled by the news."[164]

By re-establishing better contact between elected and elector, the media will fulfill their mission and serve democracy better. They would play a less conspicuous but more useful role by allowing citizens to listen to their elected politicians in a more direct and sustained manner, offering them more detailed information on the issues and dispensing with the continual references to the actors' motives and strategies, the usual interpretive framework for political events.

The predominance of this interpretive framework can be attributed to the homogeneity of journalistic practices. A product as uniform as political news interpreted through the prism of partisan motivation clearly does not offer the diversity and wealth of analytical angles that citizens want and that are desirable in a democracy. On the contrary, it contributes to a devaluation of the political process and the impoverishment of the information disseminated. Better access to the resources necessary to disseminate ideas would allow the conditions of press freedom to be met and possibly the monopoly of this reductionist framework for interpreting political events to be broken.

This objective could be partly achieved if civic journalism practices become more widespread within the media. The emphasis in this journalistic approach on voters' preoccupations and a thorough, detailed contextualization of social issues might help break the stranglehold of the dominant interpretation of politics, essentially based on a reading of the strategic and partisan motivations of political actors. Colette Brin's work (2000), which shows that journalists at the Radio-Canada and RDI were partly inspired by this professional approach in their coverage of recent election campaigns,[165] leads us to believe that positive changes might already be taking place in this area.

Nevertheless, the penetration of civic journalism remains limited. Traditional campaign coverage that focuses on surveys and party leaders' tours still predominates. This could be the result of reticence on the part of some journalists to call their professional routines into question[166] and, perhaps even more fundamentally, resistance on the part of media companies to investing the resources necessary to champion this type of journalistic project.[167] It should, however, be noted that the unquestioning adoption of the concepts of civic journalism could lead to other excesses. It would be easy for journalists who put effort into the mission of defending citizens' interests to fall into the stardom trap and give in to the temptation to editorialize. The objective of diversifying media coverage of politics, taking inspiration from the civic journalism stream, must not be achieved at the expense of re-establishing better contact between elected and elector.

The diversity of media coverage of politics that might emerge out of more widespread adoption of civic journalism practices would, in our opinion, better serve the interests of Canadians in general and possibly those of the youngest citizens, who are turning away from politics at a far greater rate than are their elders.[168] This diversification is an essential component of press freedom which, as Cook rightly reminds us, consists not only of guaranteeing the freedom of expression of those who have resources, but also of allowing the opinions of the less well-off to be disseminated.[169]

From this point of view the recent concentration of media companies is disturbing, particularly because the hopes that were placed in the spread of new vehicles of information (such as the Internet) to enrich public debate have not really materialized.[170] Solutions to the problem of excessive press concentration are always tricky and often difficult to put into practice.[171] That being said, the current state of tension between the imperative of press freedom and the reality of press concentration leads us to think that the interests of Canadian democracy would be well served by a wide debate over the issue of press concentration in Canada.

The ultimate objective of reflecting on the conditions under which political journalism is practised is to end up with a general balance sheet of the quality of media coverage of politics. Having done this, we conclude that the media must demonstrate more seriousness, rigour and originality if they wish to serve citizens better. This conclusion, which is neither a condemnation of the media in principle nor a suggestion that their practices be completely disrupted, highlights the importance of recent work by Gunther and Mughan.[172] These authors examined journalistic practices in 10 countries and concluded that citizens' needs and the requirements of democracy were better served in countries where the concept of journalism as a public service has strong roots. Their observations seem to show that the active involvement of the public sector, far from being an impediment to the free circulation of diversified and high quality news, greatly encourages the production and dissemination of news in established democracies.

We share this viewpoint, but unfortunately also agree with the analysis of these authors that "even countries with strong public-service broadcasting traditions are showing signs of following the trajectory of American television's 'infotainment' style of political coverage."[173] The analyses of Taras and of Pratte, and the conclusions of the report of the Mandate Review Committee CBC, NFB, Telefilm, chaired by Pierre Juneau in 1996, confirm that this situation also prevails in Canada.

The SRC, the French-language Canadian public broadcaster, has been confronted with two business conditions that have stimulated its shift toward a more commercial orientation. The environment in the communications industry has changed profoundly over the past 10 years.[174] Cable TV services have accelerated their penetration of the Canadian market, television networks and specialized services have multiplied and there have been major regroupings of private cable TV companies. This situation has caused considerable fragmentation of audiences in Canada, increased competition in the audience ratings battle and diluted news content in a flood of entertainment programs.

The decrease in federal government funding to the CBC over the past 15 years has contributed to the precarious situation of public television. The Crown corporation's parliamentary credits have been reduced by 36 percent since the mid-1980s. Canada holds the unenviable record of being the country that saw the largest decrease in funding to public broadcasting of all OECD member states between 1995 and 1997 (-16 percent).[175] With a global operating budget of one billion dollars, which is very modest compared with other large Western public broadcasting corporations,[176] the CBC has had to make up its shortfall by increasing advertising revenues. This objective has been achieved, according to the Juneau report, at the price of a commercial shift that has notably affected the nature of its programming.[177]

This commercial reorientation by the CBC is preventing it from completely fulfilling its mandate.[178] In its production of entertainment and information broadcasting, Canadian public television is distinguishing itself less and less from the other networks. Its broad mandate, as stated in the 1991 *Broadcasting Act*, is to present unique Canadian programming and produce broadcasts that inform, enlighten and entertain the Canadian people.[179] At this point in time, the achievement of these objectives is increasingly compromised. Hopefully this situation will change and Canada will, in the management of media space, revive the strong public service tradition that has for so long been one of its distinctive features.

Only public television that is free from political pressure and undue business constraints can truly hope to fulfill an informational and pedagogical mandate. Recent surveys show a majority of Canadian citizens recognize that the CBC, in spite of its commercial reorientation, still performs this task better than its private sector competitors. The news and public affairs broadcasts produced by the CBC are perceived as being more credible, fairer and as dealing with more diverse issues than those aired by its private or American competitors.[180] The conditions to allow this tradition of excellence to persist and become stronger have to be established as soon as possible.

High-quality public television is not only important for its regular audience, but for all viewers. Several studies have shown that the CBC is a reference for the private television networks in their treatment of political information.[181] The CBC's influence beyond its audience means that it has the characteristics of a public good and gives particular relevance to David Taras's pointed remark that "It may be a strange paradox of the Canadian condition that the people want to know that the public broadcaster is there, and they support its values even if they don't regularly watch or listen to the CBC themselves."[182]

Echoing the recommendations of the Juneau report, which proposes that the CBC be distinctive, have no advertising and be rooted in the regions, we favour a sizeable reinvestment of public funds in Canadian public television, and we would like to see a more effective method of financing (based on government credits or tax revenues) that is adequate, stable and free from political pressure. Various formulae are possible, taking the examples of public television broadcasters in other countries. One thing is for sure: the status quo is unacceptable, and the CBC's current method of financing is probably one of the most inadequate conceivable for high-quality public television in an advanced industrial democracy.

There is obviously a price to be paid for implementing the suggestions we have proposed. We believe, however, that adequate public television funding is a very profitable civic investment and Canadian society would be well advised to provide the CBC the necessary means to completely fulfill its mandate. If this were done, it would be possible to ensure the survival of a public news service that is free of all commercial and political imperatives and can truly offer profound and rigorous coverage of politics. In comparison with the uniform policies of its private competitors, the uniqueness of the CBC would emerge in no uncertain terms. Its broadcasts would thus respond more to citizens' news needs and expectations. This supported return to the public service news tradition would well serve the requirements of democracy in Canada.

Notes

1. Frederick J. Fletcher and Robert Everett, *Mass Media and Elections in Canada* (Toronto: Dundurn Press, 1991); R. Jeremy Wilson, "Horserace Journalism and Canadian Election Campaigns," in R. K. Carty (ed.), *Canadian Political Party Systems: A Reader* (Peterborough: Broadview Press, 1992), p. 500; David M. Farrell, "Campaign Strategies and Tactics," in Lawrence Leduc, Richard G. Niemi, and Pippa Norris (eds.), *Comparing Democracies: Elections and Voting in Global Perspective* (Thousand Oaks, CA: Sage, 1996), p. 170.

2. Shanto Iyengar and Richard Reeves, *Do the Media Govern?* (Thousand Oaks, CA: Sage, 1997).

3. Timothy E. Cook, *Governing with the News* (Chicago: University of Chicago Press, 1998), p. 164.

4. Stephen Ansolabehere, Roy Behr, and Shanto Iyengar, *The Media Game: American Politics in the Television Age* (New York: Macmillan Publishing, 1993); John Zaller, *A Theory of Media Politics: How the Interests of Politicians, Journalists, and Citizens Shape the News* (1999). Available from http://www.sscnet.ucla.edu/polisci/faculty/zaller/media%20politics%20book%20.pdf.

5. Neil Nevitte, *The Decline of Deference: Canadian Value Change in Cross-National Perspective* (Peterborough, ON: Broadview Press, 1996); David Zussman, "Do Citizens Trust Their Governments?" *Canadian Public Administration*, Vol. 40, no. 2 (summer 1997); Pippa Norris (ed.), *Critical Citizens: Global Support for Democratic Governance* (Oxford: Oxford University Press, 1999); Susan Pharr and Robert Putnam (eds.) *Disaffected Democracies: What's Troubling the Trilateral Countries?* (Princeton: Princeton University Press, 2000).

6. Thomas E. Patterson, *Out of Order* (New York: Knopf, 1993); Matthew Mendelsohn, "Television's Frames in the 1988 Canadian Election," *Canadian Journal of Communication*, Vol. 18, no. 2 (spring 1993); David Tarras, *Power and Betrayal in the Canadian Media* (Peterborough: Broadview Press, 1999); Richard Gunther and Anthony Mughan (eds.), *Democracy and the Media: A Comparative Perspective* (Cambridge: Cambridge University Press, 2000).

7. Soren Holmberg, "Down and Down We Go: Political Trust in Sweden," in Pippa Norris (ed.), *Critical Citizens* (Oxford: Oxford University Press, 1999), p. 119.

8. Patterson, Thomas E. "Bad News, Period." *PS: Political Science & Politics*, Vol. 29, no. 1 (March 1996, p. 19.

9. Cook, *Governing with the News*, p. 189.

10. Canada, *Royal Commission on Newspapers: Report* (Ottawa: Minister of Supply and Services, 1981), p. 36.

11. Robert A. Hackett and Yuezhi Zhao, *Sustaining Democracy: Journalism and the Politics of Objectivity* (Toronto: Garamond Press, 1998), p. 1.

12. Robert M. Entman, *Democracy without Citizens: Media and the Decay of American Politics* (New York: Oxford University Press, 1989), p. 3.

13. Kurt Lang and Gladys Engel Lang, "The Mass Media and Voting," in Eugene Burdick and Arthur J. Brodbeck (eds.), *American Voting Behavior* (New York: Free Press, 1959); Michael J. Robinson, "Public Affairs Television and the Growth of Political Malaise: The Case of 'the Selling of the Pentagon,'" *American Political Science Review*, Vol. 70, no. 2 (June 1976).

14. Authors whose perspectives differed from those of Robinson and his successors also pointed the finger at television. The advent of television ushered in, according to Martin Wattenberg (*The Rise of Candidate-Centered Politics* [Cambridge: Harvard University Press, 1991]); and David R. Spencer and Catherine M. Bolan ("Aperçu historique de la radiodiffusion électorale au Canada," in Frederick J. Fletcher [ed.], *La radiodiffusion en période électorale au Canada* [Montreal: Wilson-Lafleur, 1991]), a decline in parties, by allowing political leaders to communicate directly with electors (but see Larry M. Bartels, "Partisanship and Voting Behavior, 1952-1996," *American Journal of Political Science*, Vol. 44, no. 1 [January 2000], who challenges this position). In a perspective that is closer to the one that interests us in this article, Robert D. Putnam ("Bowling Alone: America's Declining Social Capital," *Journal of Democracy*, Vol. 6, no. 1 [January 1995a]; and "Tuning In, Tuning Out: The Strange Disappearance of Social Capital in America," *PS: Political Science & Politics*, Vol. 28, no. 4 [December 1995b]) claims that the penetration of television contributed decisively to eroding interpersonal links and confidence, erosion that brought with it a decrease in confidence in government institutions. (For a criticism of Putnam's thesis, see Michael Schudson, *The Power of News* [Cambridge: Harvard University

Press, 1995]; and Pippa Norris, "Does Television Erode Social Capital? A Reply to Putnam," *PS: Political Science & Politics*, Vol. 29, no. 3 [September 1996]).

15. Fletcher and Everett, *Mass Media and Elections in Canada*, p. 223; Ansolabehere et al., *The Media Game: American Politics in the Television Age*, p. 45; Denis Monière, *Démocratie médiatique et représentation politique* (Montreal: Les Presses de l'Université de Montréal, 1999), p. 9.

16. Kenneth Newton, "Mass Media Effects: Mobilization or Media Malaise?" *British Journal of Political Science*, Vol. 29, no. 4 (September 1999), p. 579.

17. Shanto Iyengar, *Is Anyone Responsible? How Television News Frames Political Issues* (Chicago: The University of Chicago Press, 1991); Roderick P. Hart, *Seducing America: How Television Charms the Modern Voter* (Thousand Oaks, CA: Sage, 1999); Taras, *Power and Betrayal in the Canadian Media*, p. 34.

18. Christina Holtz-Bacha, "'Videomalaise' Revisited: Media Exposure and Political Alienation in West Germany," *European Journal of Communication*, Vol. 5, no. 1 (March 1990).

19. Patricia Moy and Michael Pfau, *With Malice Toward All? The Media and Public Confidence in Democratic Institutions* (Westport, CT: Praeger, 2000); Vincent Price and John Zaller, "Measuring Media Exposure and Gauging Its Effects in General Population Surveys." Paper presented at the annual meeting of the American Political Science Association, San Francisco, California, 1996.

20. Newton, "Mass Media Effects," p. 579.

21. James Fallows, *Breaking The News: How the Media Undermine American Democracy* (New York: Pantheon Books, 1996); Taras, *Power and Betrayal in the Canadian Media*; André Pratte, *Les oiseaux de malheur: Essai sur les médias d'aujourd'hui* (Montreal: VLB Editors, 2000); Agnieszka Dobrzynska, "Analyse comparative du rôle des normes et pratiques journalistiques à la télévision dans la couverture de la campagne électorale fédérale canadienne de 1997," *Communications*, Vol. 21, no. 2 (winter-spring 2002).

22. Patterson, *Out of Order,* and "The News Media: An Effective Political Actor?" *Political Communication*, Vol. 14, no. 4 (October 1997); Larry J. Sabato, *Feeding Frenzy: How Attack Journalism Has Transformed American Politics* (New York: Free Press, 1993); Taras, *Power and Betrayal in the Canadian Media*.

23. Patterson "The News Media," p. 451.

24. Larry J. Sabato, "Open Season: How the News Media Cover Presidential Campaigns in the Age of Attack Journalism," in Mathew McCubbins (ed.), *Under the Watchful Eye: Managing Presidential Campaign in the Television Era* (Washington, DC: CQ Press, 1992), p. 128.

25. Van der Eijk's study of the impact of the transformation of the Dutch journalistic landscape on relations between the media and the party system shows an evolution similar to journalistic practices in that country: "The shift from the *zeil* identification to professional independence had serious consequences for political parties and other groups that had grown accustomed to easy access to, and uncritical coverage from, related, and hence friendly, media organizations. In the late 60s and early 70s, the major parties representing the various *zeilen* in Dutch society were suddenly confronted with what they often took to be journalistic hostility" (Cees Van der Eijk, "The Netherlands: Media and Politics between Segmented Pluralism and Market Forces," in Richard Gunther and Anthony Mughan [eds.], *Democracy and the Media. A Comparative Perspective* [Cambridge: Cambridge University Press, 2000]), p. 320.

26. Larry J. Sabato, "Open Season," p. 128.

27. Fletcher and Everett, *Mass Media and Elections in Canada*; Wilson, "Horserace Journalism and Canadian Election Campaigns"; Monière, *Démocratie médiatique et représentation politique*.

28. Quebec has not escaped this trend, according to renowned journalist and researcher Armande Saint-Jean ("The Evolution of Journalism Ethics in Quebec," in Valerie Alia, Brian Brennan and Barry Hoffmaster [eds.], *Deadlines and Diversity: Journalistic Ethics in a Changing World* [Halifax: Fernwood Publishing, 1996]). According to her analysis, Quebec journalism "apart from a few cultural particularities...follows the same patterns and trends as in the rest of Canada and, for that matter, North America" (p. 21.)

29. In the French version of the current article, the title, "Les oiseaux de malheur," is borrowed from the title of a book by André Pratte, editorial page editor of the Montreal newspaper *La Presse* (*Les oiseaux de malheur: Essai sur le mensonge en politique* [Montréal: Boréal, 1997]).

30. Patterson, "Bad News, Period," p. 17.

31. Patterson, "Bad News, Period"; Zussman, "Do Citizens Trust Their Governments?"

32. See, among others, Sabato, "Open Season," pp. 138-40; David McKee, "Fact Is Free but Comment Is Sacred," in Ivor Crewe and Brian Gosschalk (eds.), *Political Communications: The General Election Campaign of 1992* (Cambridge: Cambridge University Press, 1992); Matthew Mendelsohn and Richard Nadeau, "The Rise and Fall of Candidates in Canadian Election Campaigns," *Harvard International Journal of Press and Politics*, Vol. 4, no. 1 (winter 1999); Pratte, *Les oiseaux de malheur*, pp. 90-91. The descriptions of journalistic behaviour toward politicians — "feeding frenzy" by Sabato ("Open Season") and "character assassination" by McKee ("Fact Is Free but Comment Is Sacred") — are indicative of the vicious attitude attributed to the media.

33. David D. Harrington, "Economic News on Television: The Determinants of Coverage," *Public Opinion Quarterly*, Vol. 53, no. 1 (spring 1989); Richard Nadeau, Richard G. Niemi, David P. Fan, and Timothy Amato, "Elite Economic Forecast, Economic News, Mass Economic Judgments, and Presidential Approval," *Journal of Politics*, Vol. 61, no. 1 (February 1999).

34. Hibbing and Theiss-Morse add an interesting perspective to the rise in negative coverage of political institutions by linking it, in part, to a decline in the partisan press. "We have little quarrel," they write, "with the contention that media coverage of Congress has become more hostile over the course of the last few decades. To be sure, negative coverage of Congress is hardly new, although in the days of the partisan press it may have been easier to put the criticism in perspective. Today...Congress is short on defenders in the media." See John R. Hibbing and Elisabeth Theiss-Morse, "The Media's Role in Public Negativity Toward Congress: Distinguishing Emotional Reactions and Cognitive Evaluations," *American Journal of Political Science*, Vol. 42, no. 2 (April 1998), p. 482.

35. Jorgen Westerstahl and Folke Johansson, "News Ideologies as Molders of Domestic News," *European Journal of Communication*, Vol. 1, no. 1 (March 1986); John R. Hibbing and Elisabeth Theiss-Morse, *Congress as Public Enemy: Public Attitudes Toward American Political Institutions* (Cambridge: Cambridge University Press, 1995); Harold D. Clarke, Jane Jenson, Lawrence Leduc, and Jon H. Pammett, *Absent Mandate: The Politics of Discontent in Canada* (Toronto: Gage, 1984); T. H. Qualter and K.A. MacKirdy, "The Press of Ontario and the Election," in John Meisel (ed.), *Papers on the 1962 Election* (Toronto: University of Toronto, 1964); W. C. Soderlund, W. I. Romanow, E. D.

Briggs, and R. H. Wagenberg, *Media and Elections in Canada* (Toronto: Holt, Rinehart and Winston, 1984); Allan Frizzell and Jon H. Pammett, *The Canadian General Election of 1993* (Toronto: Dundurn Press, 1994); Mendelsohn and Nadeau, "The Rise and Fall of Candidates in Canadian Election Campaigns."

36. Pratte, *Les oiseaux de malheur*, p. 76.

37. Entman, *Democracy without Citizens*, p. 8.

38. Daniel Hallin ("Sound Bite News: Television Coverage of Elections, 1968-1988," *Journal of Communication*, Vol. 42, no. 1 [March 1992]) used the expression "shrinking soundbite" to describe the decrease in the duration of extracts of presidential canditates' speeches from 42 seconds in 1968 to less than 10 seconds during the 1990s. Studies by the Center for Media and Public Affairs (1994) have shown that at the beginning of the 1990s journalists' speaking time in a story on a presidential candidate was five times greater than that of the candidate.

39. Sabato, *Feeding Frenzy*, p. 2; see also Patterson (1997).

40. Taras, *Power and Betrayal in the Canadian Media*, pp. 223-24.

41. Monière, *Démocratie médiatique et représentation politique*, p. 109.

42. Monière, *Démocratie médiatique et représentation politique*, p. 109, shows that face-to-face interviews account for 19 percent, 45 percent, 71.9 percent and 79.5 percent of the types of interventions of political speakers on Radio-Canada, France2, RTBF (Belgium) and TSR (Switzerland), respectively. Inversely, extracts from press conferences account for 32.8 percent of interventions by political actors in the reports of Radio-Canada, but for 10 percent, 9 percent and 7.3 percent of the interventions presented in news programs on France2, RTBF and TSR.

43. Marion R. Just, Ann N. Crigler, Dean A. Alger, Timothy E. Cook, Montague Kern, and Darrell M. West, *Crosstalk: Citizens, Candidates and the Media in a Presidential Campaign* (Chicago: University of Chicago Press, 1996); Patterson, *Out of Order*, p. 36.

44. In Canada, Richard Nadeau, Neil Nevitte, Elisabeth Gidengil, and André Blais ("Election Campaigns as Information Campaigns," submitted to the *American Political Science Review*, 2001) present data for the 2000 electoral campaign showing that nearly three-quarters of stories broadcast dealt with various aspects of the electoral race rather than with the issues. Similar proportions emerged in the 1997 Canadian election and in other electoral studies in the United States and Great Britain (see Darrel West, *Air Wars: Television Advertising in Election Campaigns 1952-1996* [Washington, DC: Congressional Quarterly, 1997]; and Pippa Norris, John Curtice, David Sanders, Margaret Scammell, and Holli A. Semetko, *On Message: Communicating the Campaign* [London: Sage, 1999]). This preoccupation with polls and the "race to victory" ("horse-race journalism") was clearly expressed by Wagenberg and his collaborators (R. H. Wagenberg, W. C. Soderlund, W. I. Romanow and E. D. Brigg, "Campaigns, Images and the Polls: Mass Media Coverage of the 1984 Canadian Election," *Canadian Journal of Political Science*, Vol. 21, no. 1 [March 1988]), who conclude from this development that it "lend[s] credence to the fears of those who feel that essential democratic goals of the electoral process are being undermined" (p. 119).

45. Patterson, "The News Media"; Just et al., *Crosstalk*, 1996; Sabato, "Open Season," and Sabato, *Feeding Frenzy*.

46. Two Canadian studies appear to corroborate this argument. Nadeau et al. have shown that barely one in five Canadians believed at the time of the 1997 election, as the facts stated, that unemployment had decreased over the course of Jean Chétien's mandate and that an overwhelming majority of them thought, erroneously, that the lot of the First Nations was as enviable, if not better, than that of other Canadians or that crime had been on the rise over the course of the past few years (Nadeau et al., "It's Unemployment Stupid! Why Perceptions about the Job Situation Hurt the Liberals in the 1997 Election," *Canadian Public Policy*, Vol. 26, no.1 [March 2000a]; and Nadeau et al., "General Political Information, Issue-Specific Knowledge and Policy Preference," unpublished research manuscript, Canadian Election Study, 2000b).

47. Cook, *Governing with the News.*

48. Rothman and Lichter. "Elite Ideology and Risk Perception in Nuclear Energy," p. 383.

49. Patterson, "The News Media: An Effective Political Actor?", p. 452; see also Taras, *Power and Betrayal in the Canadian Media*, p. 41; and Richard Nadeau, André Blais, Elisabeth Gidengil, and Neil Nevitte, *Les médias et le soutien aux institutions politiques au Canada*, unpublished research manuscript, 2000c.

50. Entman, *Democracy without Citizens*, p. 8.

51. Michael X. Delli Carpini and Scott Keeter, *What Americans Know about Politics and Why It Matters* (New Haven: Yale University Press, 1996).

52. Kathleen Hall Jamieson (*Dirty Politics: Deception, Distraction, and Democracy* [New York: Oxford University Press, 1992], p. 11); John H. McManus (*Market-Driven Journalism* [Newbury Park: Sage, 1994]); Taras (*Power and Betrayal in the Canadian Media*); and James H. Kuklinski, Paul J. Quirk, and Jennifer Jerit ("Misinformation and the Currency of Democratic Citizenship," *Journal of Politics*, Vol. 62, no. 3 [August 2000], p. 794) also emphasize the fact that politicians are not necessarily interested in disseminating complete and high-quality information on the issues either. Consequently, neither of these actors offers citizens "a coherent and balanced package of information."

53. James A. Stimson, *Public Opinion in America* (Boulder: Westview, 1991).

54. Philippe, Maarek, *Communication et Marketing de l'homme politique* (Paris: Litec, 1992), p. 142.

55. Nadeau et al., "Elite Economic Forecast, Economic News, Mass Economic Judgments, and Presidential Approval," pp. 118-19; see also Fred W. Van Raaij, "Economic News, Expectations, and Macro-Economic Behavior," *Journal of Economic Psychology*, Vol. 10, no. 4 (December 1989), p. 484; and Paul B. Andreassen, "On the Social Psychology of the Stock Market: Aggregate Attributional Effects and the Regressiveness of Prediction," *Journal of Personality and Social Psychology*, Vol. 53, no. 3 (March 1987).

56. John Zaller, *The Nature and Origins of Mass Opinion* (New York: Cambridge University Press, 1992), ch. 11; Dobrzynska, "Analyse comparative du rôle des normes et pratiques journalistiques à la télévision dans la couverture de la campagne électorale fédérale canadienne de 1997."

57. Ansolabehere, Behr, and Iyengar, *The Media Game. American Politics in the Television Age*, p. 65.

58. Gunther and Mughan (eds.), *Democracy and the Media*, pp. 25-26.

59. It is interesting to note that Page's model (1996) of the discussion surrounding the creation and implementation of public policy rests explicitly on the politicians-media-electors triangle.

60. Joseph N. Cappella and Kathleen Hall Jamieson, *Spiral of Cynicism: The Press and the Public Good* (New York: Oxford University Press, 1997), p. 4.

61. Cappella and Hall Jamieson, *Spiral of Cynicism.*

62. Patterson, "The News Media."

63. Mendelsohn, "Television's Frames in the 1988 Canadian Election," 1993; and "The Media and Interpersonal Communications: The Priming of Issues, Leaders, and Party Identification," *Journal of Politics*, Vol. 58, no. 1 (February 1996).

64. Ansolabehere, Behr, and Iyengar, *The Media Game*, pp. 54-55; Sabato, "Open Season," pp. 131-32.

65. Sabato, "Open Season," p. 132.

66. Zussman, "Do Citizens Trust Their Governments?"

67. Patterson, "Bad News, Period," p. 19.

68. Sabato, "Open Season," p. 144.

69. Cappella and Hall Jamieson, *Spiral of Cynicism*; Stanley Rothman, "The Mass Media and Democratic Well Being in the United States," *International Journal on World Peace*, Vol. 13, no. 3 (summer 1996), p. 62.

70. An important nuance is the conceptual meaning of the notion of confidence. Several authors have stressed the fact that a prerequisite for an adequately functioning democracy is the critical vigilance of citizens toward government institutions, which entails a lot more skepticism than confidence (see Mark E. Warren [ed.], *Democracy and Trust* [New York: Cambridge University Press, 1999]). The accusation against the media is thus less that they maintain skepticism than that they feed cynicism, which is its exacerbated form (Patterson, "The News Media"; Cappella and Jamieson, *Spiral of Cynicism*).

71. André Pratte, *Le syndrome de Pinocchio: Essai sur le mensonge en politique* (Montreal: Boréal, 1997), p. 24.

72. Cited by E. J. Epstein, *News from Nowhere* (New York: Random House, 1973), pp. 4-5, and reproduced and translated by Michel Cormier, "Politique et télévision: Le cas du Parti conservateur lors de l'élection fédérale de 1984," in Jean Charron, Jacques Lemieux, and Florian Sauvageau

(eds.), *Les journalistes, les médias et leurs sources* (Boucherville: Gaëtan Morin, 1991), p. 50.

73. Gunther and Mughan (eds.), *Democracy and the Media*, pp. 20-21.

74. Dobrzynska, "Analyse comparative du rôle des normes et pratiques journalistiques à la télévision dans la couverture de la campagne électorale fédérale canadienne de 1997," pp. 86-88).

75. W. Lance Bennett, "Cracking the News Code: Some Rules That Journalists Live By," in Shanto Iyengar and Richard Reeves (eds.), *Do the Media Govern?* (Thousand Oaks: Sage, 1997); see also Jean Charron, *La production de l'actualité: Une analyse stratégique des relations entre la presse parlementaire et les autorités politiques* (Montreal: Boréal, 1994); Anne-Marie Gingras, *Médias et Démocratie: Le grand malentendu* (Ste-Foy: Presses de l'Université du Québec, 1999); and Dobrzynska, "Analyse comparative du rôle des normes et pratiques journalistiques à la télévision dans la couverture de la campagne électorale fédérale canadienne de 1997."

76. L.V. Sigal, *Reporters and Officials: The Organization and Politics of News Making* (Lexington: D.C. Healt, 1973); Jean Charron, *La production de l'actualité: Une analyse stratégique des relations entre la presse parlementaire et les autorités politiques* (Montreal: Boréal, 1994); Gingras, *Médias et Démocratie: Le grand malentendu*; Zaller, *A Theory of Media Politics*.

77. André Blais and Jean Crête. "La presse et la politique municipale dans deux villes du Québec," *Politique*, no. 2 (1982). p. 65.

78. Cormier, "Politique et télévision," p. 63.

79. Sigal, *Reporters and Officials*; Herbert J. Gans, *Deciding What's News: A Study of CBS Evening News, NBC Nightly News, Newsweek and Time* (New York: Pantheon Books, 1979); see also G. Tuchman, *Making News: A Study in the Construction of Reality* (New York: Free Press, 1978).

80. Gans, *Deciding What's News*, p. 116.

81. O. H. Gandy, *Beyond Agenda-Setting: Information Subsidies and Public Policy* (Norwood: Abex Publishing, 1982).

82. Zaller, *The Nature and Origins of Mass Opinion*, p. 315.

83. Alison Carper, "Marketing News," in Pippa Norris (ed.), *Politics and the Press: The News*

Media and their Influences (Boulder: Lynne Rienner Publishers, 1997), p. 46.

84. Richard Reeves, "Reporters and Public Officials: Who Uses Whom? Overview," in Shanto Iyengar and Richard Reeves (eds.), *Do the Media Govern?* (Thousand Oaks, CA: Sage, 1997), p. 101; see also John H. McManus, *Market-Driven Journalism* (Newbury Park: Sage, 1994); and William A. Dorman, "Press Theory and Journalistic Practice: The Case of the Gulf War," in Iyengar and Reeves (eds.), *Do the Media Govern?* for similar interpretations.

85. Dobrzynska, "Analyse comparative du rôle des normes et pratiques journalistiques à la télévision dans la couverture de la campagne électorale fédérale canadienne de 1997," p. 93.

86. Pratte, *Les oiseaux de malheur*, p. 49.

87. Taras, *Power and Betrayal in the Canadian Media*, p. 33.

88. Zaller, *A Theory of Media Politics*.

89. Zaller, *A Theory of Media Politics*, pp. 19-20.

90. Zaller (*A Theory of Media Politics*) explicitly showed the increase in the quality and quantity of means used by parties to win the battle for the agenda. According to several commentators, this trend is due to the decline of the partisan press. This phenomenon, the transformation of the links between the media and parties, illustrated in the case of the United States by Hibbing and Theiss-Morse in *Congress as Public Enemy: Public Attitudes Toward American Political Institutions*, and "The Media's Role in Public Negativity Toward Congress: Distinguishing Emotional Reactions and Cognitive Evaluations"; and in Zaller (1999), is also present in other democracies, as demonstrated by Taras for Canada (David Taras, *The Newsmakers: The Media's Influence on Canadian Politics* [Scarborough: Nelson Canada, 1990], p. 65), and Van der Eijk, "The Netherlands: Media and Politics between Segmented Pluralism and Market Forces."

91. Zaller, *A Theory of Media Politics*, p. 54.

92. Monière, *Démocratie médiatique et représentation politique*; Van der Eijk, "The Netherlands."

93. Bennett, "Cracking the News Code."

94. Taras, *Power and Betrayal in the Canadian Media*, p. 34; Pratte, *Les oiseaux de malheur*; Zaller, *A Theory of Media Politics*.

95. David H. Weaver and G. Cleveland Wilhoit, *The American Journalist in the 90s: US News People at the End of an Era* (Mahwah, NJ: Lawrence Erlbaum Associates, 1996), p. 24.

96. Zaller, *A Theory of Media Politics*, p. 51.

97. Hacket and Zhao, *Sustaining Democracy*; Gunther and Mughan (eds.), *Democracy and the Media*.

98. Barry Cooper, *Sins of Omission: Shaping the News at CBC TV* (Toronto: University of Toronto Press, 1994).

99. James Winter, *Democracy's Oxygen: How Corporations Control the News* (Montreal: Black Rose Books, 1996).

100. Rothman and Lichter. "Elite Ideology and Risk Perception in Nuclear Energy."

101. Ben H. Bagdikian, *The Media Monopoly*, 4th ed. (Boston: Beacon Press, 1994).

102. Hackett and Zhao, *Sustaining Democracy*; Gunther and Mughan (eds.), *Democracy and the Media*.

103. Pippa Norris, *A Virtuous Circle: Political Communication in Post-industrial Democracies* (New York: Cambridge University Press, 2000b), pp. 252-53.

104. Michael J. Robinson, "Public Affairs Television and the Growth of Political Malaise: The Case of 'the Selling of the Pentagon,'" *American Political Science Review*, Vol. 70, no. 2 (June 1976).

105. Austin Ranney, *Channels of Power: The Impact of Television on American Politics* (New York: Basic Books, 1983), pp. 75-79; Cappella and Jamieson, *Spiral of Cynicism*.

106. Patterson, "Bad News, Period," p. 19.

107. The most convincing demonstration of this viewpoint is *Why People Don't Trust Government*, edited by Joseph S. Nye, Philip D. Zelikow, and David C. King (Cambridge: Harvard University Press, 1997), which examines several possible explanations for the erosion of confidence in the American government and concludes that the media malaise hypothesis is one of the most plausible. This conclusion has, however, been challenged by Norris, in *A Virtuous Circle*, ch. 13.

108. Norris, *A Virtuous Circle*; Pippa Norris, John Curtice, David Sanders, Margaret Scammell, and Holli A. Semetko, *On Message: Communicating the Campaign* (London: Sage, 1999).

109. Holtz-Bacha, "'Videomalaise' Revisited," p. 73.

110. Lawrence Bowen, Keith Stamm, and Fiona Clark, "Television Reliance and Political Malaise: A Contingency Analysis," *Journal of Broadcasting and Electronic Media*, Vol. 44, no. 1 (winter 2000), p. 94.

111. Holmberg, "Down and Down We Go," p. 121.

112. Newton, "Mass Media Effects."

113. Newton, "Mass Media Effects," p. 577.

114. Nadeau, Blais, Gidengil, and Nevitte, *Les médias et le soutien aux institutions politiques au Canada*.

115. Patricia Moy, Michael Pfau, and LeeAnn Kahlor, "Media Use and Public Confidence in Democratic Institutions," *Journal of Broadcasting and Electronic Media*, Vol. 43, no. 2 (spring 1999).

116. Pippa Norris (ed.), *Critical Citizens: Global Support for Democratic Governance* (Oxford: Oxford University Press, 1999); Norris, *Virtuous Circle*.

117. Newton, "Mass Media Effects," p. 598.

118. Pippa Norris, *A Virtuous Circle? The Impact of Party Organizations and the News Media on Civic Engagement in Post-Modern Campaigns*, paper presented at the Joint Workshops of the European Consortium for Political Research in Copenhagen, 2000a (available from http://www.essex.ac.uk/ecpr/jointsessions/Copenhagen/papers/ws3/norris.pdf, p. 9).

119. Moy, Pfau, and Kahlor. "Media Use and Public Confidence in Democratic Institutions"; Nadeau, Blais, Gidengil, and Nevitte, *Les médias et le soutien aux institutions politiques au Canada*.

120. Newton, "Mass Media Effects," p. 598.

121. Pippa Norris's reticence to use an assertive, causal language proliferates in her work *A Virtuous Circle* (2000b) (for example, she says "It is not possible for us...to resolve the direction of causality...." [p. 18], and "The interpretation remains theoretical for we lack direct proof" [p. 309]). Moreover, one subsection of her work bears the revealing title "The Classic Chicken-and-Egg Issue of Causality." We should also point

out that if Norris rejects the "media malaise" hypothesis, she does not conclude that the negative coverage of issues is not without consequences. On the contrary, she demonstrates a link between the generally negative coverage of the issue of the Euro and mounting Euro skepticism.

122. Cliff Zukin, "Mass Communication and Public Opinion," in Dan Nimmo and Keith R. Sanders (eds.), *Handbook of Political Communication* (Beverly Hills: Sage, 1981), p. 382.

123. For example, several authors, including the current ones, favour the diachronic method (panel, rolling cross-section) to examine the issue of the media. On the other hand, one could question whether election campaigns, short as they are, are the best context in which to examine the long-term effect of the media on confidence in government institutions (see Norris et al., *On Message*). The "cultivation analysis" approach (Nancy Signorielli and Michael Morgan [eds.], *Cultivation Analysis: New Directions in Media Effects Research* [Newbury Park: Sage, 1990]), which states that the effect of the media is cumulative and long term, could undoubtedly inspire political observers in their research on the links between progressive change in the media environment (media and practices) and the secular decline in support for political actors and institutions.

The experimental method is rarely used (the exception is Cappella and Jamieson [1997]). The principle in this method is to present to randomly selected groups news sequences constructed according to descriptive and interpretive styles (Patterson, "The News Media") or according to a strategic or issue-oriented interpretive framework (Cappella and Jamieson, *Spiral of Cynicism*). Works based on this method are, all in all, not very conclusive for now. The minimal benefit of this type of experiment is that it collects participants' opinions of the type of news presented.

Finally, in addition to a number of methodological problems raised here, we add that of measures of media exposure. The work of Larry M. Bartels ("Message Received: The Political Impact of Media Exposure," *American Political Science Review*, Vol. 87, no. 2 [June 1993]), for example, raises important questions about the quality of media exposure indicators used in studies of the impact of the press and television.

124. Nevitte, *The Decline of Deference*; Nye, Zelikow, and King (eds.), *Why People Don't Trust Government*, p. 1.

125. Edmund B. Lambeth, "Public Journalism as a Democratic Practice," in Edmund B. Lambeth, Philip E. Meyer, and Esther Thorson (eds.),

Assessing Public Journalism (Columbia: University of Missouri Press, 1998), p. 34.

126. The percentages for the other professions included in the survey are as follows:

	%
Pharmacists	68
Doctors	62
Engineers	50
Police	53
University	45
Clergy members	44
Accountants	37
Pollsters	28
Entrepreneurs	21
Lawyers	19
Real estate agents	15
Advertising	14
Unionists	15
Parliamentarians	14

Source: *The Gallup Poll*, Vol. 59, no. 25 (April 14, 1999).

127. See Nadeau, Blais, Gidengil, and Nevitte, *Les médias et le soutien aux institutions politiques au Canada*. In comparison, no less than 84 percent of respondents expressed confidence in the police, 70 percent in public schools, 60 percent in the courts, 57 percent in the armed forces and 53 percent in churches.

128. Stephen Earl Bennett, Staci L. Rhine, Richard S. Flickinger, and Linda L.M. Bennett, "'Video Malaise' Revisited: Public Trust in the Media and Government," *Harvard International Journal of Press and Politics*, Vol. 4, no. 1 (winter 1999); see also Timothy E. Cook, Paul Gronke and John Rattliff, *Deconsidering the Media: The American Public's Changing Attitudes Towards the News*, paper presented at the annual meeting of the American Political Science Association, Washington, DC, August 2000; Moy and Pfau, *With Malice Toward All?*

129. Bennett, Rhine, Flickinger, and Bennett, "'Video Malaise' Revisited," p. 8.

130. Bennett, Rhine, Flickinger, and Bennett, "'Video Malaise' Revisited," p. 17.

131. Cappella and Jamieson, *Spiral of Cynicism*, p. 227.

132. See, among others, John Curtice, *Do The Media Matter?*, paper presented at the annual meeting of the Midwest Political Science Association, Chicago, April 1998, p. 9. This dissatisfied minority appears to be similar to the cur-

rent of works that examines the "hostile media environment" (see Robert Vallone, Lee Ross, and Mark L. Leeper, "The Hostile Media Phenomenon: Biased Perception and Perceptions of Media Bias in Coverage of the Beirut Massacre," *Journal of Personality and Social Psychology*, Vol. 49 [1985]; Richard M. Perloff, "Ego-involvement and Third Person Effect of Televised News Coverage," *Communications Research*, Vol. 16 [1989]; Albert C. Gunther, "Biased Press or Biased Public: Attitude Toward Media Coverage of Social Group," *Public Opinion Quarterly*, Vol. 56, no. 2 [summer 1992]) and claims that a good number of electors believe the media are hostile to their preferred political party.

133. Nadeau, Blais, Gidengil, and Nevitte, *Les médias et le soutien aux institutions politiques au Canada*; see also Cook, Gronke, and Rattliff, *Deconsidering the Media*, pertaining to this question.

134. Just, Crigler, Alger, Cook, Kern, and West, *Crosstalk*, p. 240.

135. Cappella and Jamieson, *Spiral of Cynicism*, p. 227.

136. Cook, Gronke, and Rattliff, *Deconsidering the Media*, p. 17.

137. See, among others, Jay Rosen, *What are Journalists For?* (New Haven: Yale University Press, 1999); Edmund B. Lambeth, "Public Journalism as a Democratic Practice"; Edmund B. Lambeth, Philip E. Meyer and Esther Thorsonin (eds.), *Assessing Public Journalism* (Columbia: University of Missouri Press, 1998); and Jay Rosen and Davis Merritt, *Public Journalism: Theory and Practice* (Dayton: Kettering Foundation, 1994).

138. Colette Brin, *Information électorale et innovation médiatique: agenda des citoyens ou événement hippique?*, paper presented at the Colloque des jeunes politologues, Quebec, 2000, p. 7.

139. Lambeth, "Public Journalism as a Democratic Practice," p. 17.

140. Rosen, *What are Journalists For?*

141. Lambeth, "Public Journalism as a Democratic Practice," p. 34.

142. Brin, *Information électorale et innovation médiatique: agenda des citoyens ou événement hippique?*, pp. 7-8.

143. Lambeth, "Public Journalism as a Democratic Practice," p. 18.

144. Lambeth, "Public Journalism as a Democratic Practice," pp. 27-29.

145. Philipp Meyer and Deborah Potter, *Effects of Citizen-Based Journalism in the 1996 Election* (St. Petersburg: Poynter Institute for Media Studies, 1996).

146. Zussman, "Do Citizens Trust Their Governments?"; Pratte, *Les oiseaux de malheur*, p. 232; Zaller, *A Theory of Media Politics*, pp. 14-20.

147. Zussman, "Do Citizens Trust Their Governments?" p. 250.

148. Denis Monière and Julie Fortier, *Radioscopie de l'information télévisée au Canada* (Montreal: Les Presses de l'Université de Montréal, 2000), pp. 16-17; Dobrzynska, "Analyse comparative du rôle des normes et pratiques journalistiques à la télévision dans la couverture de la campagne électorale fédérale canadienne de 1997," p. 87; Taras (1999, p. 128).

149. Matthew Fraser, "The CBC's Choice: Constellations or Core Competencies," *Policy Options*, Vol. 20, no. 7 (September 2000), p. 47.

150. Pierre Juneau, Catherine Murray, and Peter Herrndorf, *Making Our Voices Heard: Canadian Broadcasting and Film for the 21st Century*, report of the Mandate Review Committee (Ottawa: Minister of Supply and Services, 1996), p. 37; Taras, *Power and Betrayal in the Canadian Media*, p. 129; Fraser, "The CBC's Choice: Constellations or Core Competencies," p. 45.

151. Juneau, Murray, and Herrndorf, *Making Our Voices Heard*.

152. Taras, *Power and Betrayal in the Canadian Media*, p. 128.

153. Juneau, Murray, and Herrndorf, *Making Our Voices Heard*, pp. 72-75; Dobrzynska, "Analyse comparative du rôle des normes et pratiques journalistiques à la télévision dans la couverture de la campagne électorale fédérale canadienne de 1997," p. 87.

154. Sabato, "Open Season"; Pratte, *Les oiseaux de malheur*.

155. Schudson, *The Power of News*, pp. 16-33.

156. Zaller, *A Theory of Media Politics*.

157. Benjamin I. Page, *Who Deliberates? Mass Media in Modern Democracy* (Chicago: University of Chicago Press, 1996).

158. Bennett, Rhine, Flickinger, and Bennett, "'Video Malaise' Revisited"; Norris, *A Virtuous Circle*.

159. Newton, "Mass Media Effects."

160. Norris, *A Virtuous Circle*.

161. Entman, *Democracy without Citizens*, p. 8.

162. Entman, *Democracy without Citizens*, p. 129.

163. Patterson, "The News Media," p. 453.

164. Cook, *Governing with the News*, p. 190.

165. In her analysis of electoral information broadcast by Radio-Canada and RDI during the 1997 federal election and the 1998 Quebec provincial election, Brin (Information électorale et innovation médiatique, 2000), noted that the civic journalism movement made a conspicuous entry into the Crown corporation's coverage. In 1997, management openly incorporated this approach into its coverage strategy. Although traditional electoral journalism, which emphasizes candidates tours, campaign events and partisan strategies had been applied in 52 percent of the stories broadcast by Radio-Canada and RDI, 26 percent of the news segments had been developed according to a civic journalism angle. This proportion climbed to 32 percent in the 1998 Quebec election, when the management did not openly ask that civic journalism be practised (p. 15). Despite all this, horse-race journalism was still dominant in the two campaigns, especially on Radio One and news bulletins with large listenerships.

166. Brin, *Information électorale et innovation médiatique*, p. 21.

167. Lambeth, "Public Journalism as a Democratic Practice," p. 18.

168. André Blais, Elisabeth Gidengil, Richard Nadeau, and Neil Nevitte, *Anatomy of a Liberal Victory* (Toronto: Broadview Press, 2002).

169. Cook, *Governing with the News*, 1998.

170. Michael Margolis and David Resnick, *Politics as Usual: The Cyberspace "Revolution"* (Thousand Oaks: Sage, 2000).

171. Entman, *Democracy without Citizens*, p. 136.

172. Gunther and Mughan (eds.), *Democracy and the Media.*

173. Gunther and Mughan (eds.), *Democracy and the Media*, p. 431.

174. Juneau, Murray, and Herrndorf, *Making Our Voices Heard*, p. 72.

175. *OECD Communications Outlook 1999* (Paris: OECD Publications Service, 1999), p. 124.

176. *OECD Communications Outlook 1999* (Paris: OECD Publications Service, 1999), p. 124; Taras, *Power and Betrayal in the Canadian Media*, p. 179; Fraser, "The CBC's Choice."

177. Juneau, Murray, and Herrndorf, *Making Our Voices Heard*, pp. 72-73.

178. Juneau, Murray, and Herrndorf, *Making Our Voices Heard*, p. 95.

179. Taras, *Power and Betrayal in the Canadian Media*, p. 127.

180. Juneau, Murray, and Herrndorf, *Making Our Voices Heard*, p. 75; Taras, *Power and Betrayal in the Canadian Media*, p. 182.

181. See, among others, Mendelsohn, "Television's Frames in the 1988 Canadian Election"; and David Taras, "The Mass Media and Political Crisis: Reporting Canada's Constitutional Struggles," *Canadian Journal of Communication*, Vol. 18, no. 2 (spring 1993).

182. Taras, *Power and Betrayal in the Canadian Media.* p. 182.

11

Electoral Democracy in the Provinces

Donald E. Blake

Canada, like other Western democracies, is showing signs of declining public confidence in the institutions and processes of government. Distrust of politicians and cynicism about the processes of representative government are increasing. Turnout in elections is falling. More and more citizens are turning away from traditional political parties and toward protest parties, pressure groups, the courts and civil disobedience to achieve their goals or frustrate those of their opponents.[1] Political conflict exhibits a "decline of deference" as:

> new life was pumped into old issues and a staggering array of new issues were pushed onto the agenda as citizens mobilized and divided over such issues as the environment, women's rights, gay rights, the family, consumer rights, peace, multiculturalism, and race.[2]

A significant source of frustration is undoubtedly the electoral process. Our first-past-the-post system of electing members of national and provincial legislatures is biased towards the largest party and smaller parties with narrow regional appeal.[3] Governments elected by a majority of citizens are rare. Occasionally, because of inequalities in the size of electoral districts, the party forming the government will have fewer votes (but more seats) than one of its opponents. Changes in election-finance laws, ostensibly designed to level the playing field and prevent elections from being "bought," have led to charges that established parties are simply trying to protect their own position and thwart challenges by new parties or pressure groups.[4] The women's movement and other marginalized groups are impatient with a system that continues to deny them what they view as their fair share of representation.

Obviously fairness of elections is not the only important concern in a democracy. Legislative democracy is clearly an issue, given party discipline and government-party dominance of elected assemblies. Much government activity involves interaction with lobbyists and pressure groups, bypassing legislatures altogether. Some critics have argued that since the entrenchment of the Charter of Rights and Freedoms, the courts, catering to special interests, have usurped the role of elected representatives on a whole range of issues.[5]

Still, elections remain the principal mechanism for calling our representatives to account. Richard Katz calls them "the defining institutions of modern democracy."[6] Elections help to determine how power is exercised, by whom and for what policy objectives.[7] It is also difficult to see how we could do without them. One can envision a future in which technology permits direct and instantaneous voting by citizens on all sorts of issues, bypassing the need for electing representatives in elections. But, for now, and probably for a long time to come, we appear to be stuck with periodic elections, organized by officially recognized parties, competing for single seats in a system of territorial representation.

At the national level many steps have been taken to make elections more democratic. They have not included a shift to any form of proportional representation, which, some argue, is the only reform of any significance.[8] However, moves to eliminate gerrymandering and reduce differences among the populations of electoral districts have clearly made elections fairer. Most restrictions on the right to vote or be a candidate have been eliminated. Setting aside, for the moment, criticisms that election finance laws favour established parties, they have made political parties more accountable for the money they raise and spend, and have put them on a more secure financial footing. In recognition of the importance of the regulatory regime surrounding elections, the Royal Commission on Electoral Reform and Party Financing was established in 1989 to undertake an extensive review. Their "mandate concerned the most basic of democratic rights — the right to vote, be a candidate and to participate in free and open elections."[9]

However, Canadian citizens live in two political worlds. They are simultaneously members of the national polity and of the provincial polity in which they reside. Although part of the same federation, within the limits set out by constitutional provisions, such as the parliamentary system and the Charter of Rights and Freedoms, provinces are free to vary their constitutions, including their electoral systems, arrangements for redrawing constituency boundaries and the rules governing election campaigns. To the extent that public confidence depends on the vitality of democratic freedoms, the state of electoral democracy in the provinces must be considered at least as important as that at the national level.

For much of the twentieth century, the provinces figured prominently in litigation alleging provincial infringement of democratic rights such as freedom of speech, freedom of the press, freedom of assembly and freedom of association. The province of Quebec was particularly notorious in this regard. During the 1950s alone, seven civil liberties cases involving Quebec were considered by the Supreme Court of Canada. In a stinging indictment of Quebecers and their governments before 1960, Pierre Trudeau went so far as to question whether they considered democracy a legitimate form of government.[10]

Although the four Western provinces and Ontario extended the right to vote to women before they became eligible in federal elections, other provinces lagged behind, and women were not enfranchised provincially in Quebec until 1940. British Columbia prohibited most Asian Canadians from voting until 1947. As discussed in more detail below, since entrenchment of the Charter three provinces have had their electoral boundaries challenged in court. On the other hand, the first independent boundary commission was established by Manitoba in 1957. The pioneer in election expenses legislation was Quebec in 1963.

Studies of the provinces point to differences in history, wealth, demography and political culture,[11] all factors that have been associated in the comparative politics literature with the development of democracy.[12] Does the quality of electoral democracy vary across provinces as well?

Table 1 offers us some idea of what to expect in this regard. The table summarizes four major attempts to classify provinces in ways relevant to the quality of democracy: political development,[13] political culture,[14] economic preconditions for democracy[15] and institutional development.[16] All four studies imply that electoral democracy is less developed in all or part of Atlantic Canada. However, there is no consensus on which provinces are most developed. Three of the four studies put BC and Ontario in the top group based on an assessment of public opinion, political cleavage patterns, wealth or institutional development. Four provinces (Saskatchewan, Manitoba, Quebec and Prince Edward Island) appear in the top grouping in only one each of the four classifications. The absence of Saskatchewan on the institutional development measure is somewhat surprising given its record as a legislative innovator.[17]

In short, while there is reasonable consensus in the comparative politics literature, based on studies of mass political attitudes, about the level of political development in Atlantic Canada (low) and in British Columbia and Ontario (high), the placement of the other provinces is more debatable. Perhaps Dyck's institutional-development ranking is the most persuasive. While based mainly

Table 1
Provincial Groupings on Indicators of Development

Political development[1]	Political culture[2]	Economic preconditions[3]	Institutional development[4]
Modern	*Citizen societies*	*Affluent*	*Developed*
Saskatchewan	British Columbia	British Columbia	Ontario
British Columbia	Ontario	Alberta	Quebec
Prince Edward Island	Manitoba	Ontario	
Transitional	*Intermediate*	*Moderate*	*Intermediate*
Alberta	Saskatchewan	Saskatchewan	British Columbia
Newfoundland	Ontario	Manitoba	Alberta
Manitoba	Quebec	Quebec	Saskatchewan
Quebec	Nova Scotia		Manitoba
Ontario			
Traditional	*Disaffected*	*Hard-pressed*	*Traditional*
New Brunswick	New Brunswick	New Brunswick	New Brunswick
Nova Scotia	Prince Edward Island	Nova Scotia	Nova Scotia
	Newfoundland	Prince Edward Island	Prince Edward Island
		Newfoundland	Newfoundland

[1] Jane Jenson, "Party Systems," in David J. Bellamy, John H. Pammett, and Donald C. Rowat (eds.), *The Provincial Political Systems* (Toronto: Methuen, 176), p. 121.
[2] Richard Simeon and David J. Elkins, "Provincial Political Cultures in Canada," in David J. Elkins and Richard Simeon (eds.), *Small Worlds: Provinces and Parties in Canadian Political Life* (Toronto: Methuen, 1980), p. 68.
[3] Allan Kornberg, William Mishler, and Harold D. Clarke, *Representative Democracy in the Canadian Provinces* (Scarborough, ON: Prentice-Hall, 1982), p. 261.
[4] Rand Dyck, *Provincial Politics in Canada*, 2nd ed. (Scarborough, ON: Prentice-Hall, 1991), pp. 632-33.

on qualitative assessments, it is the most recent and incorporates differences on a wide range of indicators, including history, political culture, political institutions, the party system, the electoral system, leadership and policy.

The remainder of this study explores interprovincial differences on four important dimensions of electoral democracy: the fairness of the electoral map, laws governing who can vote and be a candidate, rules governing party and election expenses and election outcomes. Provinces are ranked on each dimension and compared to each other and to the federal level. The study concludes with an overall assessment of the state of electoral democracy in the provinces and the extent to which regional divisions, especially between Atlantic Canada and the rest of the country, persist.

Equality of Representation

Despite the importance of the equality principle in democratic theory, until entrenchment of the Charter of Rights and Freedoms in 1982, equality of the vote was not a major focus of representation concerns. For most of Canada's history, regular readjustment of constituency boundaries (after every decennial census) occurred only at the federal level, dictated by constitutional requirements for balanced representation across the provinces and mandated guarantees to small provinces and provinces with declining populations,[18] rather than concern for strict equality of the vote.[19] Gerrymandering, or the drawing of constituency boundaries to maximize partisan benefit, has been more of an issue, accounting, in part, for the decision in most jurisdictions to establish independent boundary commissions.

A member of the judiciary or a nonpartisan official such as the chief electoral officer chairs the typical independent commission. Other commission members will have no partisan affiliation although, in some cases, the government party and the opposition may recommend an equal number of commission members. Since 1982, virtually all commissions have been directed to respect the principle of voter equality, but are permitted to deviate from that principle to respect community of interest, municipal boundaries, minority representation and related considerations and to ensure that ridings do not become too large in geographical area. The commission generally will hold public hearings to receive suggestions on boundary adjustments and present its recommendations in a report to the legislature. In some cases, the commission may prepare a preliminary report that is the basis for further public hearings before a final report is completed. In all but two jurisdictions (Canada and Quebec), the legislature has the final say on boundaries and may make adjustments before finalizing changes.

Assuming that legislatures do not tamper too much with commission recommendations, these procedures should prevent gerrymandering. However, considerable latitude remains with respect to malapportionment, or the problem of unequal electoral district populations. As noted above, the most important court cases involving equality of the vote have been generated at the provincial level. The *Saskatchewan Reference* case[20] and the BC Civil Liberties Association challenge to electoral boundaries in that province,[21] have effectively established the limits to departures from the principle of one person, one vote. While the Supreme Court of Canada has argued that the Charter guarantee of the right to vote is a right to "effective representation" rather than strict equality, it has implicitly accepted a maximum 25 percent deviation as a reasonable standard.[22]

Nearly twenty years have elapsed since the appearance of the first systematic interprovincial comparison of redistribution procedures by R.K. Carty.[23] Since then the rules governing the timing of redistributions and the make-up of electoral boundary commissions have changed in several respects. As we shall see, the quality of democracy on this dimension has improved considerably.

Redistributions analyzed by Carty in Prince Edward Island, Nova Scotia, New Brunswick and Ontario were generated ad hoc, rather than dictated by a timetable given by statute. Ontario has since committed itself to a fixed schedule for redistribution by tying itself to *Canada's Electoral Boundary Readjustment Act*. The most recent redistribution in New Brunswick was still established at the discretion of the governing party, but it was the first independent boundary commissions used in that province.

In all provinces, except Quebec, the legislature continues to have the final say in implementing boundary revision recommendations. In most cases, changes made by the legislature are minor. However, they can be quite significant. The most recent (1994) boundary commission in Prince Edward Island recommended a new electoral map based on 30 electoral districts. However, the legislature subsequently reduced this to 27 electoral districts producing a significant increase in departures from the one-person, one-vote standard. Four of the districts had deviations exceeding 25 percent compared to none in the boundary commission plan.

Table 2 summarizes procedures for all ten provinces and for federal redistributions for the most recent boundary revisions. For jurisdictions with fixed timetables, redistributions normally occur every eight to 10 years either because the number of years is specified by statute or because eight years would typically cover two election cycles. For those without a fixed schedule, the interval is typically longer. The 1993 redistribution in New Brunswick was the first in nearly 20 years.

But again, PEI stands out. Its most recent boundary commission was established after the Supreme Court of Prince Edward Island ruled that the province's elections act violated the Charter of Rights and Freedoms.[24] It was required to fix an electoral map established in 1962. That map, together with provisions of the elections act, had established electoral districts where the minimum deviation from equality exceeded 30 percent, and the maximum reached 115 percent.

PEI is the only jurisdiction whose current boundaries were established by a commission containing members of the legislature.[25] In fact all of the commissioners were MLAs, albeit from both sides of the House of Assembly. Quebec is the only province with a permanent electoral boundary commission, consisting of the chief electoral officer, and two eligible electors elected for five-year terms supported by a two-thirds vote of the National Assembly. However, British Columbia and Manitoba also include their chief electoral officer as a member of boundary commissions. These two provinces also include members of the judiciary in redistribution exercises, as do Alberta,[26] New Brunswick, Newfoundland, Ontario, Saskatchewan and Canada. The Quebec and Nova Scotia commissions were the only nonpartisan ones without any members from the bench.

Table 2

Redistribution Rules[1]

	Year	Timetable	Composition	Deviation
Newfoundland	1993	Every 10 years	Judicial[2]	10% except for 25% in 1 district and 4 required districts in Labrador
Prince Edward Island	1994	Every third election	Bipartisan	25%
Nova Scotia	2002	Every 10 years	Independent	25%
New Brunswick	1993	Ad hoc	Independent with judicial involvement	25% except for 1 district
Quebec	2002	Every second election	Independent with CEO	25% except for 1 district
Ontario	1996	Every 10 years	Independent with judicial involvement	25% except in "extraordinary circumstances"
Manitoba	1998	Every 10 years	Independent with CEO and judicial involvement	10% south 25% north
Saskatchewan	2002	Every 8 years	Independent with judicial involvement	5% except 2 districts
Alberta	2002	Every second election	Judicial involvement with bipartisan appointment	25% 50% for up to 4 districts
British Columbia	Same	Every second election	Independent with CEO and judicial involvement	25% except in "very special circumstances"
Canada	Same	Every 10 years	Independent with judicial involvement	25% except in "extraordinary circumstances"

Source: Provincial election and representation acts supplemented by Elections Canada, *2002 Compendium of Election Administration in Canada.*
[1] For further details, see appendix, table 1.
[2] The 1995 commission consisted of a single judge. However, evidence obtained by the 1994 commission consisting of a judge and four commissioners, the commission established by statute, was made available to him.

Of course, one question to ask about any redistribution exercise is: how fair is the result? That has been perhaps the most important question since the entrenchment of the Charter of Rights and Freedoms in 1982. On the basis of a review of jurisprudence since then, Kent Roach has already concluded that "'One person, one vote' will not be the constitutional standard for distribution and districting in Canada."[27]

Roach bases his assertion on the comparatively large departures from the one person, one vote standard sanctioned by the courts — 25 percent and more. Australia, a country with similar geography and demography sets a maximum deviation limit of 10 percent.[28] In the United States, deviations are typically much less than 5 percent.[29]

The 25-percent limit was first endorsed in litigation respecting provincial electoral boundaries. In deciding the *Dixon* case (1989), Justice Beverly McLachlin, then of the BC Court of Appeal, ruled that the province's electoral map was unconstitutional on the grounds that so many electoral districts violated an equality of the vote standard. Rather than nullify the results of the most recent election based on those districts, she determined that a 25-percent deviation limit, then in effect at the national level and proposed by the Royal Commission on Electoral Boundaries (the Fisher Commission) that was examining BC's provincial boundaries,[30] would satisfy the constitutional requirement.

However, *Saskatchewan Reference* (1991) is the only case involving deviation limits to be decided by the Supreme Court of Canada, making it the definitive case on redistribution. In reviewing boundary proposals for Saskatchewan, the Supreme Court let stand legislative limits of plus or minus 25-percent deviation for the southern part of the province but as high as plus or minus 50 percent for the north. In doing so, a majority of the court (that now included Justice McLachlin, the judge in *Dixon*), argued that section 3 of the Charter, guaranteeing the right to vote, does not require absolute equality of voting power but rather the right to "effective representation." The court noted that geographical factors such as population density, difficulty of communication or community interests could mean that effective representation would entail deviations from voter parity. The decision implicitly endorsed the 25 percent deviation as acceptable in most cases but set no limit on the number of districts that could exceed this standard given the right circumstances.

As table 2[31] shows, following *Saskatchewan Reference*, the most recent boundary commissions in all jurisdictions except Prince Edward Island were given specific limits for deviations from voter parity. The commission in PEI decided, after reviewing the relevant jurisprudence, to work within a 15-percent deviation limit.

Commissions in five provinces in addition to Saskatchewan (Alberta, New Brunswick, Newfoundland, Ontario and Quebec) were given legislative authority to exceed the 25-percent limit in specific ways. Alberta allows for up to four districts with deviations as high as 50 percent. Its boundary commission produced two such constituencies. New Brunswick legislation specified that Fundy Isles be a separate electoral district. Accordingly the 1993 New Brunswick commission "recommended" a district whose population was 64 percent below the one-person, one-vote standard. Newfoundland legislation required that four districts containing certain specified communities be established in Labrador. Two of them had deviations that exceeded minus 25 percent. Quebec requires a separate electoral district for Îles-de-la-Madeleine. After the redistribution of 2001 that district had an electorate 76 percent below voter parity.

British Columbia specifies a 25-percent limit but allows greater deviations where "very special circumstances exist." A similar provision, "extraordinary circumstances," governs redistributions in Ontario, where the ridings produced by the federal Boundary Commission are also used in provincial elections. This escape clause was used most enthusiastically by the British Columbia Electoral Boundaries Commission. Six out of the 79 districts it recommended in 1999 have populations more than 25 percent below parity, although the smallest is "only" 34.3 percent below. No other jurisdiction in Canada, federal or provincial, has as many districts departing by more than 25 percent from parity. Only two federal districts (one in Newfoundland and one in Quebec) exceed a 25-percent limit calculated using a within-province electoral quotient. None of the Ontario districts exceeds the limit.

Federal redistributions are governed by rules that require boundary commissions to aim for a maximum deviation of 25 percent using a quotient obtained by dividing the provincial population by the number of seats to which the province is entitled. If electoral district populations are compared across provinces, however, the federal jurisdiction does not look so egalitarian. If one divides the combined population of the provinces by the total number of seats they have been allocated to obtain a "national quotient," the most recent redistribution produced 27 districts with deviations greater than 25 percent ranging from minus 71.6 percent (Labrador) to plus 25.4 percent (Scarborough Centre). However, federal redistributions are governed by an initial allocation of seats between provinces that is governed by the Constitution. As noted by Roach,[32] the rules that no province can have fewer MPs than senators and that no province can lose seats as the result of redistribution have constitutional status, making them immune to Charter challenge. Moreover, it would require unanimous consent of the provincial legislatures and federal parliament to change them.

What is the overall impact on voter equality of these variations in boundary revision procedures? Table 3 provides information on several different ways of measuring equality of the vote. The first column shows that provincial boundary commissions have produced maps with considerable range of deviations from their provincial electoral quotients. The average district in Nova Scotia, deviates by 14.2 percent. The average district in Saskatchewan, which has the strictest limits on deviations, outside the north, differs by only 1.8 percent from perfect equality even with northern districts included in the calculation.

The theoretical minimum percentage of the population required to elect a majority of the legislature is still relatively small in some provinces. It ranges from 44.2 percent in Quebec to 51.0 percent in Saskatchewan. Both Quebec and British Columbia (at 45.8 percent) have recently elected governments with fewer total votes than their nearest rivals. However, by a small margin, the federal map is worst of all.

Another measure of equality, the ratio of the largest district to the smallest district in each province, the "voting power ratio" in the table, also varies substantially across jurisdictions, with highs of 5.3 and 4.4 in Quebec and Newfoundland, respectively, and a low of 1.3 in both PEI and Manitoba. However, by this measure, inequality has also declined in every province as a result of their most recent boundary revisions. The most dramatic decline occurred in British Columbia, from 14.9 to 1.8.

The Gini index is one of the most commonly used measures of equality because its calculation is based on all district populations, not just a few extreme cases. It also has intuitively appealing mathematical limits. A province in which electoral districts had equal populations would score zero, indicating perfect equality. As populations diverge, the index approaches one, indicating complete inequality. All provinces have scores toward the low (equal) end, but there is still substantial interprovincial variation. Nova Scotia and Saskatchewan bracket the distribution with scores of 0.096 (comparatively unequal) and 0.013 (comparatively equal), respectively.

Still, voter equality in all provinces except Quebec is substantially greater than it was before the Supreme Court's ruling in *Saskatchewan Reference*. This conclusion is evident in comparing the Gini coefficient of inequality after the most recent redistribution in each province to the coefficient in the early 1980s. The largest changes are found in Alberta, British Columbia, New Brunswick and Prince Edward Island, where the coefficient dropped from approximately 0.20 or more to less than 0.10. The coefficients for Quebec for the two periods are quite similar, but the current map is slightly more inegalitarian than the one it replaced. The Gini coefficient for federal districts based on a national population quota also declined, from 0.121 to 0.086 across the 10 provinces.

Moreover, with the exception of Newfoundland, compared to the early 1980s the gap between Gini indexes for provincial and federal districts within the same province is also somewhat less. In the 1980s, federal districts in Newfoundland were substantially more egalitarian than provincial ones. The situation has now reversed. Populations of provincial electoral districts are now more equal than those in federal districts. This suggests, that on the whole, provincial commissions are being as strict as (or even stricter than) their federal counterparts.

Table 3
Equality of the Vote[1]

	Average absolute deviation[2]	Minimum for majority[3]	Previous voting power ratio	Current voting power ratio[4]	Previous provincial Gini index	Current provincial Gini index[5]	Previous federal Gini index	Current federal Gini index[6]	Rank on fairness of provincial electoral map[7]
Newfoundland	6.8	49.0	8.7	4.4	0.131	0.051	0.074	0.163	6
Prince Edward Island	8.4	49.2	5.6	1.3	0.295	0.054	0.010	0.024	5
Nova Scotia	14.2	45.4	2.7	2.4	0.155	0.096	0.085	0.045	1
New Brunswick	10.6	45.7	4.1	3.4	0.195	0.040	0.114	0.037	8
Quebec	12.7	44.2	5.1	5.3	0.075	0.088	0.097	0.019	2
Ontario	6.3	48.7	5.1	1.5	0.150	0.046	0.114	0.046	7
Manitoba	3.2	49.3	2.8	1.3	0.093	0.023	0.111	0.016	9
Saskatchewan	1.8	51.0	2.3	1.6	0.077	0.013	0.100	0.025	10
Alberta	9.1	46.2	5.2	2.1	0.219	0.062	0.077	0.042	4
British Columbia	10.3	45.8	14.9	1.8	0.201	0.071	0.105	0.054	3
Canada[8]	12.2	44.0	5.2	4.4			0.121	0.086	

[1] Figures for previous voting power ratio and previous federal and provincial Gini indexes are from R.K Carty, "The Electoral Boundary Revolution in Canada," *American Review of Canadian Studies*, Vol. 15 (1985): p.284. His figures are based on the most recent election through June 1984. The comparison may be affected by the fact that Carty's figures are based on election results not redistribution reports. All other calculations were made by the author using data from the most recent redistribution in each jurisdiction.

[2] Average deviation (positive or negative) of electoral district populations from the provincial quotient.

[3] Percentage of the population contained within the smallest 50-percent-plus-1 electoral districts.

[4] Ratio of largest to smallest electoral district.

[5] Gini index of inequality ranges from 0 (complete inequality) to 1 (complete equality).

[6] The federal Gini index measures inequality across federal electoral districts within the province. The figure in the Canada row measures inequality across all federal electoral districts in the country excluding Yukon and Northwest Territories.

[7] Ranking from 1 (least equal) to 10 (most equal) based on current provincial Gini index

[8] The figures in this row compare all federal electoral districts, excluding the territories. Current figures use data from the 2002 preliminary recommendations of the federal boundary commissions.

The final column in table 3 ranks the provinces from 1 (most inegalitarian) to 10 (most egalitarian) using the current provincial Gini index. There is no obvious cultural, economic or institutionalization pattern to differences among provinces. Two Western provinces, Manitoba and Saskatchewan have the most egalitarian electoral maps, while Alberta, despite comparable topography, is in the most inegalitarian half of provinces. British Columbia, Ontario and Quebec are the largest provinces with significant populations in remote or sparsely populated areas, but Ontario is relatively egalitarian compared to the other two. The Atlantic province of Nova Scotia is the most inegalitarian in the country, but New Brunswick is among the most egalitarian. Prince Edward Island, the last jurisdiction to involve incumbent politicians in redistribution, is more egalitarian than Quebec, the province with the most bureaucratized boundary-revision procedure.

In the early 1980s the principal differences were between those provinces whose redistributions had been triggered by statutory provisions (Newfoundland, Quebec, Manitoba, Saskatchewan and Alberta) and those without such legislative provisions. All five had substantially more egalitarian electoral maps than PEI, New Brunswick, Nova Scotia, Ontario and BC. With the exception of Alberta, they also had become more egalitarian over time.[33] Statutory provisions now appear less crucial. In the 1990s, redistributions in two of those provinces (PEI and New Brunswick) continued to be governed by ad hoc procedures, but their maps are not noticeably more inegalitarian than those in provinces with statutory timetables.

The Right to Vote and Be a Candidate

Voting restrictions

Section 3 of the Charter states that "every citizen of Canada has the right to vote in an election of members of the House of Commons or of a legislative assembly and to be qualified for membership therein." However, like all Charter provisions this one is subject to section 1, which allows "reasonable limits prescribed by law as can be demonstrably justified in a free and democratic society." While the right to vote is arguably the most important democratic right, as Richard Katz points out "no country allows all adults to vote."[34]

Katz identifies three categories of qualifications for voting, community membership, competence and autonomy.[35] The first category covers citizenship and residence requirements. The second typically includes age and mental health, although in the past "competence" requirements have been used to exclude racial groups and women. The autonomy requirement is mainly of historical interest and includes financial independence (used to justify restriction of the right to vote to property owners) and other markers of nondependency.

In Canada it might be expanded to include restrictions on the right to vote of election officials and judges on the grounds that those with legal responsibility for ensuring fairness should themselves have no part in elections. Most jurisdictions in Canada exclude at least two other groups, those incarcerated for criminal offenses and those convicted of corrupt or illegal electoral practices. In a sense, these groups have been excluded from the political community, at least temporarily.

All jurisdictions have established 18 as the minimum age for voting and, except for Nova Scotia and Saskatchewan, restrict the franchise to Canadian citizens. Nova Scotia enfranchises British subjects and Saskatchewan allows British subjects to vote if they were eligible on June 23, 1971. Table 4 summarizes the other qualifications (and disqualifications) for voting in provincial and national elections.

All but Newfoundland, Ontario and Canada establish a six-month residency requirement. In fact, Newfoundland stipulates that to be eligible a citizen must be resident in Newfoundland only on the day before polling day. All jurisdictions require that citizens be registered in order to vote, but all, except for Ontario[36] and Quebec, make it relatively simple to register on the day of the election itself. All jurisdictions permit some form of absentee voting, but in Ontario this must be done by proxy (i.e., by a delegate) — making it impossible for an absentee voter to ensure that her or his true preference has been registered.

Given Charter provisions, we would expect to find few exclusions from the franchise. New Brunswick is the most restrictive, disenfranchising key election officials, all inmates, no matter how insignificant their offenses might be, and those legally deprived of liberty or the right to manage their own property by reason of mental or physical infirmity. At the other end of the scale, Newfoundland has no exclusions, and Prince Edward Island has fewer restrictions than any other jurisdiction except Quebec.[37] Alberta, British Columbia, New Brunswick, Quebec, Saskatchewan and Canada treat election offenses as grounds for denial of the franchise, for up to eight years in the case of Alberta.

Again, there is no obvious pattern to differences among provinces in qualifications for voting. In numerical terms, the most restrictive jurisdiction insofar as voting is concerned is probably New Brunswick, which disenfranchises chief electoral officers and returning officers, all inmates, those convicted of corrupt electoral practices, as well as those legally restricted by reason of mental or physical disability.

The least restrictive is Newfoundland, which enfranchises all citizens and has no real residency requirement.[38] Ontario is next. That province disqualifies no one who meets basic citizenship and residency requirements. Ontario is followed closely by Quebec and Prince Edward Island. Quebec disqualifies only for election offenses, although these include failure to comply with financial

Table 4

Qualifications for Voting[1]

Jurisdiction	Minimum residency	Chief electoral officer	Returning officer	Disqualified from voting			Absentee provisions	Provincial rank on voter qualifications[2]
				Inmates	Conviction for election offenses	Other		
Newfoundland	No minimum							9.5
Prince Edward Island	6 months, district resident	Yes	Yes, except to break a tie				Mail ballot, unrestricted	8
Nova Scotia	6 months, district resident	Yes	Yes	Yes			Some restrictions	3
New Brunswick	6 months, district resident	Yes	Yes, except to break a tie	Yes	5 year disqualification	Legally restricted, mentally ill or physically infirm	Mail ballot, some restrictions	1
Quebec	6 months				5 year disqualification		Mail ballot, some restrictions	7
Ontario	No minimum, district resident						Proxy voting, unrestricted	9.5
Manitoba	6 months	Yes		Yes, if sentence 5 years or more [in Act but ruled of no force and effect by Manitoba Court of Queen's Bench 1999]			Mail ballot, unrestricted	6

Table 4 (continued)
Qualifications for Voting[1]

| Jurisdiction | Minimum residency | Disqualified from voting | | | | | Absentee provisions | Provincial rank on voter qualifications[2] |
		Chief electoral officer	Returning officer	Inmates	Conviction for election offenses	Other		
Saskatchewan	6 months, district resident	Yes	Yes, except to break a tie	Yes	5 year disqualification	Assistant chief electoral officer	Mail ballot, some restrictions	3
Alberta	6 months, district resident		Yes, except to break a tie	Yes[3]	8 year disqualification		Mail ballot, unrestricted	3
British Columbia	6 months, registered in district	Yes		Yes, If sentence 2 years or more	Up to 7 year disqualification	Deputy chief electoral officer	Mail ballot, unrestricted	5
Canada	No minimum, district resident	Yes		Yes, if sentence 2 years or more	5 to 7 year disqualification	Assistant chief electoral officer	Mail ballot, minimal restrictions	

Source: Provincial election and representation acts supplemented by Elections Canada, *2002 Compendium of Election Administration in Canada.*

[1] For further details see appendix, table 2.

[2] Provinces are ranked from 1 (most restrictive) to 10 (least restrictive).

[3] Except for inmates sentenced for 10 days or less or for nonpayment of fines.

reporting requirements by candidates or official agents. Prince Edward Island does not penalize election offenders, but it does disenfranchise its chief electoral officer and returning officers, a total of 28 people.

Of the remaining five provinces (Alberta, British Columbia, Manitoba, Nova Scotia and Saskatchewan), Manitoba appears to be the least restrictive. Its disqualifications are similar to those in British Columbia, but Manitoba is more forgiving of convicted felons, allowing those serving sentences of less than five years to vote compared to less than two years in BC, Alberta, Nova Scotia and Saskatchewan are more restrictive – no inmates are allowed to vote in provincial elections, but otherwise they are basically tied.

These considerations were used to quantify inter-provincial differences in the last column of table 4, again using a scale of 1 (least inclusive) to 10 (most inclusive).[39] Newfoundland and Ontario, polar opposites on most indicators of development, tie for most inclusive. The other three Atlantic provinces are found at both ends of the spectrum — Nova Scotia and New Brunswick at the low end and PEI on the more inclusive side. If ranked together with the provinces, Canada would appear toward the less inclusive end. It has low residency requirements, but, as of the 2002 election, more exclusions from voting than five out of 10 provinces.

Candidacy restrictions

As noted above, the Charter guarantees to Canadian citizens the right to "to be qualified for membership" in the House of Commons or a legislative assembly. However, Canada and the provinces, like most countries, regulate candidacy as well. According to Katz,

> [r]egulation of candidacy is forced by the conflict of democratic ideals and reality. The ideal is free and unfettered competition among all comers... [but] without some way of identifying candidates, the vote might be meaninglessly fragmented. Unfettered competition, far from being fair, may perpetuate (and magnify) the advantages (like private wealth) that some candidates enjoy, to say nothing of the possibilities of deceit and intimidation.[40]

There are at least two ways to determine eligibility to run for office. All provincial elections acts outline the necessary qualifications and procedures. However, some provinces also specify separately, in legislative assembly acts or the equivalent, who may sit in the legislature. In some cases these restrictions are more extensive. Typically these exclude individuals, such as civil servants or government contractors, who present potential conflict-of-interest problems. Direct

Table 5

Qualifications for Candidacy[1]

| | Nomination | Deposit | Return of deposit | Disqualified from candidacy or legislature | | | | Provincial rank on candidate qualifications[2] |
				Government employees	Election officials	Conviction for election offenses	Other	
Newfoundland	10 signatures, party endorsement	$100	15% of vote	Except if employed when house is not sitting or member of armed forces			Government contractors	4
Prince Edward Island	10 signatures	$200	Half the vote of the winner					8
Nova Scotia	5 signatures, signature of party leader	$100	15% of vote	Public employees in managerial or confidential positions		5 year disqualification	Members of or candidates for Parliament	1.5
New Brunswick	25 signatures, signature of party leader	$100	Half the votes of the winner				Mayors, councillors, judges, MPs or senators	4
Quebec	100 signatures, signature of party leader	none	N/A		CEO, returning officer	Yes, duration of disqualification not specified in Act	MPs, judges, official agents of party or candidates, persons who have not filed	8

Table 5 (continued)

Qualifications for Candidacy[1]

| | Nomination | Deposit | Return of deposit | Disqualified from candidacy or legislature | | | | | Provincial rank on candidate qualifications[2] |
				Government employees	Election officials	Conviction for election offenses	Other	
Quebec (cont.)							election expenses from previous elections, and members of electoral boundary commission if less than 3 months prior	
Ontario	25 signatures	$200	10% of vote	Federal or provincial, except members of armed forces and certain public officials	Returning officer, election clerk, enumerator, revision assistant	8 year disqualification	Government contractors	1.5
Manitoba	100 signatures, party endorsement	None	N/A		Election officer, revising officer, or enumerator	Convicted of provincial or federal offense		4

Table 5 (continued)

Qualifications for Candidacy[1]

	Nomination	Deposit	Return of deposit	Disqualified from candidacy or legislature				Provincial rank on candidate qualifications[2]
				Government employees	Election officials	Conviction for election offenses	Other	
Saskatchewan	4 signatures, party endorsement	$100	At least half the votes of winner	Government employees ineligible	Chief electoral officer; and CEO assistant	Up to 5 years disqualification	Federal or provincial judges, inmates	8
Alberta	25 signatures, party endorsement	$200	Half the votes of winner			5 to 8 years disqualification	MPs or senators	8
British Columbia	25 signatures, party endorsement	$100	15% of vote		Chief electoral officer, deputy chief electoral officer	7 years disqualification	MPs, federal judges, inmates with sentences more than 2 years	8
Canada	100 signatures (50 in large, sparsely populated districts), signature of party leader	$1,000	50% of deposit for 15% of vote, 50% for election expense statement	Yes (except for members of armed forces or reserves on active duty because of war)	Yes	5 to 7 years	Federal judges (except citizenship judges), members of provincial or territorial legislatures, inmates, public officials, person who has not filed election return from previous election.	

Source: Provincial election and representation acts supplemented by Elections Canada, *2002 Compendium of Election Administration in Canada*.

[1] For more detailed information, see appendix, table 3.

[2] Provinces ranked from 1 (most restrictive) to 10 (least restrictive).

restrictions on candidacy specified in elections acts as well as indirect ones contained in legislative assembly acts and civil service acts are both considered in this section.

In the provinces, qualifications for candidacy generally parallel those for voting. In fact, several elections acts simply state that eligibility to vote is the basic requirement for being nominated aside from fulfillment of procedural requirements.[41] Interprovincial differences in eligibility are summarized in table 5.

All jurisdictions require the signatures of eligible voters to secure a nomination although the range in the number required is considerable, from five in Nova Scotia to 100 in Quebec and for national elections. Deposit requirements are relatively low, nothing (in Manitoba and Quebec) and $100 or $200 almost everywhere else except for Canada, which demands $1,000. In keeping with the increased regulation of election expenses and public funding of political parties, discussed in the next section, all but Ontario require some official endorsement by a registered political party. Even in Ontario, party approval of nominations is implied by the requirement that candidates register with the chief electoral officer under the *Election Finances Act*. Since deposit requirements are relatively low or nonexistent, except for national nominations, the fact that substantial support is required (at least 10 percent of the vote) before the deposit is returnable cannot be considered much of a barrier to candidacy. Even for national nominations, where the deposit is higher, half the deposit is returned upon receipt of the required election expense statement, making the effective deposit only $500.

All jurisdictions except New Brunswick and Prince Edward Island specifically forbid those convicted of corrupt or illegal electoral practices from standing for office or sitting in the legislature. However, the restriction is implied in New Brunswick because eligibility to vote is a requirement for candidacy and those convicted of election offenses are not eligible to vote. By extension, certain election officials who are disenfranchised in most jurisdictions would also not be allowed to stand as candidates even if not explicitly disqualified in candidacy requirements. Ontario, one of the few jurisdictions that allows all election officials to vote, still prohibits some from standing as candidates.

Nova Scotia and Ontario prohibit some provincial and all federal employees from sitting in the legislature. Canada, Newfoundland and Manitoba restrict only their own employees, although they provide for leave of absence for those wishing to contest elections. Relatively few provinces specifically exclude MPs but, since the *Parliament of Canada Act* prohibits members of any provincial or territorial assembly from sitting in Parliament, the restriction is redundant. Moreover, since all provinces require members of their assemblies to be residents of their province, no one would be eligible to sit in more than one provincial assembly.

Exclusion of government employees from legislatures and Parliament is often justified on conflict-of-interest grounds. Similar reasoning applies to government contractors or suppliers, but only Newfoundland and Canada explicitly exclude them in their elections act or acts covering legislative membership. Another category of government employee, judges, is specifically excluded in British Columbia, New Brunswick, Quebec, Saskatchewan and Canada.

A ranking exercise comparable to that used for voter qualifications is more difficult in the case of candidates. Differences in formal nomination requirements, number of signatures and amount of deposit, are trivial. On the other hand, restrictions on candidacy by government employees, potentially the numerically largest group, are hard to assess because of the number of statutes that would have to be consulted in order to ensure completeness and difficulties in determining the number of government employees prohibited from sitting in provincial legislatures where the exclusion is specified as well as the ease with which they may obtain leave.

That said, the provinces appear to fall roughly into three groups if we use exclusions listed only in elections acts and legislative assembly acts. The least restrictive provinces are Alberta, British Columbia, Prince Edward Island, Quebec and Saskatchewan. On the more restrictive side we find Manitoba, New Brunswick and Newfoundland. The most restrictive, then, are Nova Scotia and Ontario. Provincial rankings on a scale of low (most restrictive) to high (least restrictive) are given in the last column of table 5.[42] Three of the four Western provinces rank on the high (less restrictive) end on this measure, but so do two of the four Atlantic provinces. The two most "institutionally developed" according to Dyck's scheme — Ontario and Quebec — rank at opposite ends. If we were to include in the rankings the rules governing candidacy at the national level, Canada would appear in the most restrictive group with higher deposit requirements and extensive disqualifications, including government employees, all election officials and most federal judges.

Party and Election Finance

Regulation of party and election finance in Canada really got started in 1963 with passage by the Quebec National Assembly of legislation governing candidate and party election spending. This was followed by the national *Election Expenses Act* (1974) *and Ontario's Election Finances Act* (1975). By 1990, all provinces except Alberta, British Columbia and Newfoundland had passed legislation establishing spending limits.[43] All provinces now have regulations covering one or more of the following areas: the amount and sources of party funds, spending and third-party advertising. However, Alberta still has no spending limits.

The arguments for regulation essentially rely on notions of equity and fairness. While competition is integral to electoral democracy, some measures may be necessary to protect voters from undue pressure and fraud. More recently, arguments have expanded to include a justification for public subsidies to parties and candidates. As summarized by Katz[44] these include the need to ensure that reasonable resources are available to all serious candidates, desirability of wide dissemination of information and competing ideas, relief from dependence on major contributors, and the desirability of freeing politicians from dependence on members of their own parties. In Canada and most provinces, a quid pro quo has resulted. Parties have agreed to submit to regulation in return for campaign subsidies or other benefits.

These regulations are not immune to criticism. By accident or design, they may restrict competition from new parties or nonparty groups.[45] Rules that allow only individuals to contribute to candidates or parties may disadvantage parties such as the New Democratic Party that depend heavily on contributions from trade unions or parties that rely on corporate donations. Spending restrictions can benefit incumbents over challengers who may have to spend more to compensate for an incumbent's advantage of name recognition and record of constituency service.[46] Incumbency effects in Canada are weaker than in the United States,[47] making restrictions on candidate spending less of an issue. However, restrictions on spending by parties or formulae that base campaign subsidies on electoral strength may give an advantage to larger, established parties over weaker or insurgent parties. Finally, restrictions on spending and advertising by nonparty groups raise serious free speech issues. As discussed below, such restrictions have been declared unconstitutional by the courts in challenges to federal spending laws and to legislation in British Columbia.

Table 6 summarizes the essential features of provincial regulation as well as legislation at the national level for comparative purposes. British Columbia, Manitoba, Newfoundland, Nova Scotia, Prince Edward Island and Saskatchewan (as well as Canada) have fewest restrictions. They have no limits on contributions but do require disclosure of donations over $50 in Nova Scotia and $250 elsewhere.[48] Detailed reporting requirements (not covered in the table) vary. Some provinces require formal disclosure by candidates and parties to a public official such as the chief electoral officer. Others require the information to be included in annual reports by parties.

Of the provinces limiting donations, Alberta and New Brunswick are the most permissive, followed by Ontario. Quebec is strictest with maximum donations of $3,000 to parties and candidates. All provinces limiting donations require disclosure as well.

Table 6

Party and Election Finance

	Amount	Source	Disclosure	Spending limits[1]	Reimbursement	Third party advertising	Provincial rank on contribution rules[2]
Newfoundland	No limit	Natural persons, only, citizens only, no anonymous contributions over $100	$100	Per voter limit	Candidate receiving 15% of vote	No restriction	3
Prince Edward Island	No limit	Individuals, corporations and trade unions, no anonymous contributions	Over $250	Candidates: $1.75 per elector	Candidate receiving 15% of vote, annual subsidy to parties	Name of sponsor	3
Nova Scotia	No limit	No anonymous contributions	Over $50	Per voter limit	Candidate receiving 15% of vote	Name of sponsor	3
New Brunswick	$6,000 to each party or association	Individuals, corporations and trade unions, no anonymous contributions	Over $100	$1 per voter	Candidate receiving 15% of vote, annual subsidy to parties	Name of sponsor	7
Quebec	$3,000 total to parties and candidates	Voters only, no anonymous contributions	Over $200	Candidates: $1 per voter; parties: $0.60 per voter	Candidate receiving 15% of vote; parties receiving 1% of vote reimbursed 50% of expenses	Name of sponsor	9.5

Table 6 (continued)
Party and Election Finance

	Amount	Source	Disclosure	Spending limits[1]	Reimbursement	Third party advertising	Provincial rank on contribution rules[2]
Ontario	$7,500 to each party, $1,000 to each constituency association not to exceed $5,000 aggregate, no anonymous contributions[3]	Individuals, corporations or unions	Over $100	Per voter limit	Candidate or party receiving 15% of vote	Blackout period to 22nd day before polling day	7
Manitoba	$3,000	No anonymous contributions over $10, only individuals	Over $250	Limits based on population and population density	Party or candidate receiving 10% of vote	Prohibited	9.5
Saskatchewan	No limit	No contributions from noncitizens outside Canada, no anonymous contributions over $250	Over $250	Limits based on population and population density	Party or candidate receiving 15% of vote	Advertising approved by candidate or party treated as election expense	3
Alberta	$15,000 to each party, $750 to association additional to parties and candidates ($1,500 during campaign)[4]	Individuals, corporations, unions, employee organizations	Over $375	No limits	None	Name and address of sponsor	7

Table 6 (continued)
Party and Election Finance

	Amount	Source	Disclosure	Spending limits[1]	Reimbursement	Third party advertising	Provincial rank on contribution rules[2]
British Columbia	No limit	No anonymous contributions over $50 and no more than $10,000 aggregate	Over $250	$1.25 per elector	None	Name of sponsor and financial agent	3
Canada	No limit	Canadian citizens or residents; anonymous contributions over $200 become property of Receiver General, no corporate or union contributions	Over $200	Per elector limit	Reimbursement for candidate receiving 15% of valid vote; for parties obtaining 2% of national vote or 5% of votes in districts if contested	$150,000 limit with a limit of $3,000 each to oppose or promote a candidate	

Source: Provincial election and representation acts supplemented by Elections Canada, *2002 Compendium of Election Administration in Canada.*

[1] Per voter spending limits on parties based on the number of registered voters in districts in which the party fields candidates.

[2] Provinces ranked from 1 (least restrictive) to 10 (most restrictive).

[3] Annual contributions to constituency associations must not exceed $3,000. Total contributions to candidates during campaigns are limited to $3,000.

[4] Annual total contribution to constituency associations must not exceed $3,750. There is a total party limit ($30,000) and candidate limit ($7,500) during campaigns.

As far as the source of donations is concerned, Quebec and Manitoba are clearly the strictest, permitting donations from voters only. The provinces that have no limits on contributions have few, if any, serious limits on sources, restricting them to citizens in one province (Saskatchewan) and banning anonymous contributions over $10 in another (Manitoba). The remaining provinces that restrict the size of donations also claim to restrict sources. However, it is difficult to determine who would not be eligible to donate in Alberta (individuals, corporations, unions and employee organizations can donate) or in Ontario and New Brunswick, where the lists are identical to Alberta's except for "employee organizations."

Campaign spending has attracted stricter regulation. Only one jurisdiction, Alberta, has no prescribed limit. While the amounts vary slightly, every other province uses a formula based on the number of voters to cap spending by parties and/or candidates.

All but two jurisdictions (Alberta and British Columbia) reimburse candidates and/or parties for some part of their election expenses. However, reimbursements are made available only once a minimum vote threshold has been achieved, ranging from 10 percent in Manitoba to 20 percent in Quebec. New Brunswick, Prince Edward Island and Quebec also provide annual allowances to registered parties based on their performance in previous elections.

The most controversial regulation, and the only one challenged in court to date, is restriction on so-called "third-party advertising," typically defined as advertising aimed at endorsing or opposing particular candidates that is not purchased by a candidate or registered party. Three jurisdictions (Nova Scotia, Quebec and Saskatchewan) effectively ban third-party advertising. British Columbia establishes a limit of $5000, but that was ruled unconstitutional by the BC Supreme Court in February 2000, a decision that has not yet been appealed. In the remaining provinces restrictions are nonexistent or minimal, requiring only the disclosure of the identity of the advertiser.

Ranking provinces in terms of party and election finance is somewhat more difficult than for the other dimensions of electoral democracy. On one hand, regulations exist to make elections fairer. On the other hand, litigants have successfully argued in court that restrictions on third party advertising violate freedom-of-speech guarantees in the Charter. Regulations at the federal level have been successfully challenged in the Alberta Court of Queen's Bench (June 1993), as have provincial regulations in BC. Federal legislation passed in spring 2000 to re-establish a national limit, albeit significantly more generous than the previous one — $150,000 per group of which no more than $3000 can be spent in a single riding — has already been struck down by the Alberta Court of Queen's Bench. However, that decision is being appealed by the federal government.

If we accept the arguments justifying restrictions on contributions on democratic fairness grounds, provinces fall into three groups — those with no contribution limits (PEI, Newfoundland, Nova Scotia, Saskatchewan and British Columbia), those limiting contributions and having disclosure requirements (New Brunswick, Ontario and Alberta), and two provinces (Quebec and Manitoba) that limit contributions, require disclosure and allow only voters to contribute to candidates or parties. The last column of table 6 ranks the provinces on this dimension. If ranked with the provinces, given changes that came into effect in January 2004, the national level would rank at the top.

The ranking would change if restrictions on third-party advertising are included, because four provinces at the lower end of the ranking (British Columbia, Nova Scotia, Saskatchewan and British Columbia), as well as Canada, either prohibit such advertising or attempt to limit it.

Ranking jurisdictions on spending limits or reimbursement schemes would also alter the order of provinces except for Quebec. For example, Alberta's rank would drop because, while it regulates contributions, it has no spending limits and no reimbursement scheme. On the other hand, Prince Edward Island's (and Canada's) rank would rise because it limits spending and subsidizes candidates and parties even though it has no contribution limits. This issue is revisited in the conclusion.

Election Outcomes

Election outcome is the final dimension on which electoral democracy in the provinces is assessed. There is a different quality to this dimension because it includes components that are related weakly or not at all to the legal framework governing elections (redistribution rules, voting and candidacy requirements, and party and election finance). The biggest debate about electoral systems, whether single-member-plurality systems are more or less democratic than proportional systems, is irrelevant to intra-Canada comparisons at present since all jurisdictions now have identical systems. The last remaining interprovincial variation disappeared with double-member ridings in Prince Edward Island before the 1996 election.

Nevertheless, there is general agreement that election outcomes exhibiting genuine competition are probably healthier for democracy than one-sided contests. Moreover, one-sided outcomes could be a sign that redistribution rules are less fair, overrepresenting rural areas, for example, or that elections have been manipulated by fraudulent means or influenced by disparities in financial resources possessed by the competitors. Indeed, these are reasons for introducing many of the rules and regulations discussed in previous sections.

Table 7

Election Outcomes

	Year	Turnout	Turnover last election (2000)[1]	Average turnover, last 5 elections	Effective number of legislative parties[2]	Female legislators	Proportionality[3]	Rank on proportionality[4]
Newfoundland	2003	72.0	41.7	18.4	1.8	20.8	87.9	7
PEI	2003	83.3	11.1	27.8	1.3	22.2	68.8	1
Nova Scotia	2003	65.6	9.6	29.6	2.7	9.6	88.2	8
New Brunswick	2003	73.6	29.1	33.2	2.1	13.0	90.8	10
Quebec	2003	70.4	24.5	18.1	2.0	30.4	82.4	5
Ontario	2003	57.0	35.9	35.0	1.8	21.3	76.6	4
Manitoba	2003	54.2	8.8	13.2	2.0	22.8	88.0	8
Saskatchewan	2003	70.5	5.2	25.8	2.0	19.0	84.0	6
Alberta	2001	52.8	13.3	15.7	1.2	19.3	74.1	3
British Columbia	2001	71.0	52.8	35.5	2.2	24.1	70.6	2

Source: Calculations by the author from official election results.

[1] Turnover is calculated by calculating the absolute difference between a party's percentage seat share in the most recent election and the preceding one, summing across parties and dividing by two to eliminate double counting. Average turnover is the average of similar calculations for the most recent election and the four preceding elections, effectively going back to the late 1970s and early 1980s.

[2] The effective number of parties is calculated by squaring each party's vote share, summing across parties, and taking the reciprocal of that sum. Essentially, it deflates the absolute number of parties in a legislature by taking each party's strength into account.

[3] Proportionality is calculated by calculating the absolute difference between percentage vote share and percentage seat share for each party, summing the differences, and dividing by two. That sum is then subtracted from 100. If all parties won the same percentage of votes as seats, the index value would be 100, signifying perfect proportionality.

[4] Provinces are ranked from 1 (least proportionate outcome) to 10 (most proportionate outcome).

Table 7 offers five measures of election outcomes. Three of these could, in principle, be directly affected by election rules — turnover, the effective number of parties and proportionality.[49] Turnout could be indirectly related if rules are perceived as so unfair that some eligible voters decide not to participate in the electoral game. There might even be an indirect link to the success rate of female candidates to the extent that candidate-subsidy programs make a difference or turnover creates openings in the legislature. In fact, however, none of these dimensions is correlated with the provincial Gini index, perhaps the best measure of electoral fairness. Statistical comparisons with the other dimensions (especially party and election finance) make little sense given the small number of cases and crudity of rankings. However, comparison among measures of election outcomes themselves offers another picture of life in provincial democracies.

Turnout rates differ substantially, ranging from below 60 percent in Alberta, Manitoba, and Ontario to over 80 percent in Prince Edward Island. The Islanders have consistently had higher turnout rates, but most provinces are experiencing lower rates, although only three (Ontario, Saskatchewan and Alberta) have lower rates than in national elections.

At the national level, Canada has had some of the highest turnover rates among democratic countries.[50] Alberta and Manitoba excepted, this also appears to be true at the provincial level over the five most recent elections in each province. Even provinces with relatively low turnover rates in the last election (Nova Scotia, Manitoba and Saskatchewan) have average turnover rates of roughly 25 percent or higher.

Higher turnover rates are not unequivocal signs of healthier democracy. Very high rates may produce a legislature populated excessively by amateurs. On the other hand, as documented in the United States, very low turnover limits opportunities for women and other marginalized groups.[51] However, as Lisa Young notes, "systemic barriers exist: they are only masked by low turnover rates."[52] Her own study shows that even in Canada, a country with very high turnover, under a best-case scenario it would take five general elections for the percentage of women in the House of Commons to reach 50 percent from the 13.2-percent level in 1988.[53] Still, turnover is obviously a necessary if not a sufficient condition for improving the representation of women.

However, turnover does not appear to be related to another measure of competitiveness — the effective number of parties (a calculation based on the number of parties in a legislature deflated by taking into account their relative strengths). Alberta has low turnover and a relatively uncompetitive system (effective number of parties equals 1.2). Manitoba has an even lower turnover rate, but close to perfect two-party competition in the legislature (effective number of parties equals 2.0). In fact the correlation between average turnover and the effective number of parties is weak (0.35) and not statistically significant. The chance of women being elected to the legislature is also presumed to be greater with higher turnover. However, that is not the case in the provinces. The correlation is not statistically significant and has the wrong sign (-0.34).

All but two provinces, New Brunswick and Nova Scotia, have percentages of legislators who are female comparable to or rather higher than that at the national level.[54] Again, there is no obvious pattern to interprovincial differences. Alberta, the province with the lowest average turnover rate, one party dominance, and low proportionality has one of the higher percentages of female legislators. The lowest percentage is found in Nova Scotia, a province with a much more competitive party system, higher turnover rate, and substantially higher percentage of New Democrats in the legislature, 15 of 52 compared to 2 of 83 in Alberta.

The proportionality index is perhaps the best intuitive measure of the fairness of election outcomes. This is certainly the position taken by advocates of proportional representation. It measures the relationship between vote shares and seat shares across parties in a given election; the higher the index number, the closer the relationship. A score of 100 represents a situation where the seat share of each party is equal to its vote share. While all provinces use the first-past-the-post method of election, proportionality differs substantially across the provinces, ranging from a low of 68.8 percent in Prince Edward Island to a high of 90.8 percent in New Brunswick.

The provinces with the most equal electoral maps as measured by the gini index, Manitoba and Saskatchewan, also have relative high proportionality scores. Conversely, Alberta, a province with a relatively unequal map and one-party dominance nearly equivalent to Prince Edward Island's, has low proportionality as well. However, Prince Edward Island has a much fairer election map. In other words, whatever is responsible for disproportionate outcomes, it is not the electoral map alone. In fact, the correlation between Gini scores and proportionality (0.18) is not statistically significant.

Provincial ranks on proportionality are given in the last column of table 7. The ranking provides no support for the view that the fairness of election outcomes varies by region. New Brunswick and Nova Scotia both have scores at the high end (ranks of 10 and eight, respectively), but Prince Edward Island ranks lowest. While proportionality is high in two of four Western provinces, Alberta and British Columbia rank very low. The last federal election generated a proportionality score of 81.8, higher than only Prince Edward Island, Alberta and British Columbia. Of course, alternative measures of election outcomes might yield different jurisdictional rankings. These alternatives are discussed in the next section.

Table 8

Provincial Rankings on Electoral Democracy[1]

	Electoral map	Voter qualifications	Candidate qualifications	Contribution limits	Spending limits	Proportionality	Female legislators
Newfoundland	6	9.5	4	3	5	7	5
Prince Edward Island	5	8	8	3	9.5	1	7
Nova Scotia	1	3	1.5	3	5	8	1
New Brunswick	8	1	4	7	5	10	2
Quebec	2	7	8	9.5	9.5	5	10
Ontario	7	9.5	1.5	7	5	4	6
Manitoba	9	6	4	9.5	5	8	8
Saskatchewan	10	3	8	3	5	6	3
Alberta	4	3	8	7	1	3	4
British Columbia	3	5	8	3	5	2	9

Source: Rankings based on author's judgement. Provincial election and representation acts supplemented by Elections Canada, *2002 Compendium of Election Administration in Canada*.

[1] Table entries are rankings from 1 (least democratic) to 10 (most democratic) on the measures described in the text.

Conclusion

Interprovincial differences on each of the dimensions examined in this study were summarized at the end of each section. As noted there, provincial rankings differ to some extent depending on what dimension is considered. Manitoba and Saskatchewan have the fairest electoral maps, election outcomes on the egalitarian side but diverge on voter qualifications: Saskatchewan is somewhat more restrictive than Manitoba on this count. The final section of this paper compares provinces more systematically across dimensions.

Table 8 contains provincial rankings for one or more indicators on each dimension. The rankings on voter and candidate qualifications, contribution limits and proportionality of election outcomes in table 8 are identical to those that appear in relevant sections above. In addition, the table contains rankings on one other measure of party and election finance (spending limits) and one additional measure of election outcomes (the percentage of female legislators). For quantitative measures such as the Gini index, female legislators and the proportionality index, ranking the provinces is straightforward. The province with the smallest Gini score (the least unequal) is given a score of 10, and the province with the highest score (the most unequal) is given a score of one. Ranks on the two measures of election outcome give higher scores to provinces with higher percentages of female legislators and higher proportionality scores.

Ranking the provinces on the other dimensions is more problematic. The interprovincial differences summarized above on qualifications for voting and candidacy and election finance are qualitative, and depend on how much emphasis is given to particular components — contribution limits versus disclosure requirements, for example, in the case of party and election finance. One could argue for including turnout in table 8 as another indicator of outcome. However, there is no consensus in the literature about what low (or high) turnout means. Low turnout may be an indication of alienation. On the other hand, it might be an indicator of widespread satisfaction with the status quo. High turnout may mean more ballots cast by voters with little information and poor understanding of election issues, possibly shaping the outcome in undesirable ways.[55]

None of these dimensions is linked to all of the cultural, economic and institutional differences discussed at the beginning of this paper. Rankings on female legislators resemble Simeon and Elkins's classification of the provinces on the basis of political culture. The "citizen societies" of Ontario, Manitoba and British Columbia are at the top, and two of the four "disaffected societies" (New Brunswick and Nova Scotia) are at or near the bottom. However, Quebec and Ontario, the most institutionally developed provinces in Dyck's scheme, rank relatively close to each other at the high end on only one dimension, qualifications for voting.

One might have expected differences on the basis of the ideological position of the governing party. However, none are apparent here and have been discounted in previous studies of redistribution rules[56] and party and election finance.[57]

Nova Scotia has relatively low scores on every indicator except spending limits and proportionality. Identification of the most democratic province is more difficult and depends on the importance attached to different measures. Quebec has the highest score (or is tied) on four of the seven indicators. However, three of the five indicators are measures based on party and election finance regulations. If one values voter equality more highly, Quebec does not look as democratic. Eight of 10 provinces have fairer electoral maps.

The placement of each province varies significantly depending upon the relative importance given to each dimension. Most provinces have high scores on more than one dimension and low scores on others. The objective of ensuring "effective representation" of Nova Scotia's minority Acadian population, enunciated in the *Report of the 1992 Electoral Boundaries Commission,* is largely responsible for the province's relatively inegalitarian electoral map.

While substantial interprovincial differences still exist, on the whole, the quality of democracy in the provinces has clearly improved. Huge improvements have been made to the electoral map. All but one province used nonpartisan redistricting procedures to create the electoral map that governed their most recent election. The one exception, Prince Edward Island, has since committed itself to a statutory timetable and an independent boundary commission. Almost all provinces have significant regulation governing contributions to and spending by political parties.

What about the provinces compared to the nation as a whole? Using a national quotient, that is, one person, one vote regardless of province, Canada's federal electoral map is more unequal than that for all but one province, Nova Scotia. It places more restrictions on the right to vote than Newfoundland, Ontario and Quebec. Seven out of 10 provinces have higher turnout rates. The proportion of legislators who are women is higher in six out of 10. In short, federal elections are not more democratic than provincial ones, and the national level is no longer unequivocally the leader in setting standards of fairness.

Boundary Revision Procedures

Jurisdiction/Year	Legal framework	Composition	Deviation
Newfoundland 1993	Every 10 years	5 members — one judge[1] appointed by chief justice and 4 members appointed by the Speaker of the House of Assembly	10% except for 25% in 1 district
Prince Edward Island 1994	Every third election[2]	Commission of 8 MLAs appointed by order-in-council[3]	25%[4]
Nova Scotia 2002	Every 10 years	Determined by Select Committee of House of Assembly; in 2002 consisted of 1 chair and 8 members	25%[5]
New Brunswick 1993	Ad hoc	2 judges (co-chairs) and 4 members[6]	25% except for 1 district
Quebec 2002	Every second election	Chief electoral officer and 2 electors approved by two-thirds of the National Assembly on a motion of the premier	25% except for 1 district
Ontario 1996	Every 10 years	As for Canada (see below)	25% except in "extraordinary circumstances"
Manitoba 1998	Every 10 years	Chief justice of Manitoba, president of the University of Manitoba, chief electoral officer	10% south, 25% north
Saskatchewan 2002	Every 8 years	Judge nominated by chief justice of Saskatchewan and 2 additional members appointed after consultation with leaders of the Opposition parties	5% except for 2 districts
Alberta 2002	Every second election	Nonpartisan chair, 2 electors recommended by government party, two electors recommended by Opposition	25% 50% for up to 4 districts
British Columbia 1999	Every second election	Chief electoral officer, judge or retired judge, person nominated by speaker after consultation between premier and Opposition leader	25% except in "very special circumstances"

Appendix Table 1 (continued)
Boundary Revision Procedures

Jurisdiction/Year	Legal Framework	Composition	Deviation
Canada **1996**	Every 10 years	Separate commissions for each province consisting of a judge appointed by the chief justice of the province and two provincial residents appointed by the Speaker of the House of Commons	25% except in "extraordinary circumstances"

[1] Evidence obtained by the 1994 Electoral Boundaries Commission, consisting of a judge and four commissioners — the statutory requirement — was made available to the 1995 commissioner, who was told that it "may be used." There were no additional public hearings associated with the 1995 report.

[2] Amendments to the *Electoral Boundaries Act* in 1994 stipulate that, in the future, a boundaries commission must be established within 90 days following every third general election

[3] Amendments in 1994 stipulate that future boundaries commissions will consist of a judge of the provincial Supreme Court, assisted by two commissioners who are not members of the legislature or government employees, one nominated by the premier and one by the opposition.

[4] The commission recommended 30 districts. This was reduced to 27 by amendment in the legislature following receipt of the commission's report.

[5] After consultation with the Mi'kmaq, the commission recommended that an Aboriginal seat not be established.

[6] The commission reported in 1992 and recommended 54 districts based on a 20 percent deviation. It was then given a revised mandate to establish 55 districts with Fundy Isles as one district and a maximum deviation of 25 percent for the remaining districts.

Appendix Table 2

Voter Qualifications

Jurisdiction	Qualified electors	Disqualified	Absentee Provisions
Newfoundland	18 years, Canadian citizen, resident in Newfoundland on day before polling day	None specified in *Elections Act*	Mail-in ballot for those who are qualified to vote and with reason to believe they will have difficulty voting, or are detained in penitentiary or jail or detained at Waterford hospital on the day prior to polling
Prince Edward Island	18 years, Canadian citizen, resident 6 months preceding date of writ and in polling division on date of writ	Chief electoral officer, returning officer except in case of a tie	Mail-in ballot for any reason
Nova Scotia	18 years, Canadian citizen or British subject, resident of province for 6 months, resident in electoral district	Chief electoral officer, returning officer, inmates serving sentences of 2 years or more	Mail-in ballot if cannot vote at special, advance or on ordinary polling day
New Brunswick	18 years, Canadian citizen, resident of province for 6 months, ordinarily resident in district[1]	Chief electoral officer, returning officer except in case of a tie, any inmate convicted of any offence, anyone legally institutionalized mentally or physically infirm, individuals convicted of corrupt or illegal electoral practices disqualified for 5 years	Mail-in ballot for absence from province, illness or infirmity
Quebec	18 years, Canadian citizen, resident of Quebec for 6 months (12 months if elector is outside Quebec)		Mail-in ballot for absence up to 2 years (2 year limit does not apply to government employees or employees of international organizations)
Ontario	18 years, Canadian citizen, resident in electoral district[2]	None specified in *Elections Act*	Proxy voting given absence for any reason
Manitoba	18 years, Canadian citizen, resident of province for 6 months[3]	Chief electoral officer, inmates still in Act but ruled of no force and effect by Manitoba Court of Queen's Bench, 1999	Mail-in ballot if voter expects to be absent and intends to return within 6 months
Saskatchewan	18 years, Canadian citizen or British subject if qualified,[4] resident of Saskatchewan for 6 months, resident of electoral district	Chief electoral officer, assistant chief electoral officer, returning officer except in case of a tie, those convicted within previous 5 years for	Mail-in ballot for members of the Canadian forces or spouse or dependent of member, operator or employee of long-distane transportation business,

Appendix Table 2 (continued)
Voter Qualifications

Jurisdiction	Qualified electors	Disqualified	Absentee Provisions
Saskatchewan (cont.)		corrupt electoral practices, all inmates	those incapable of going to polling place because of business commitments, health, students at educational institutions outside Saskatchewan, individuals participating in a job training or retraining program, those with concerns for safety, individual who has prior commitment and any other circumstances prescribed by the Chief electoral officer
Alberta	18 years, Canadian citizen, resident of province for 6 months, resident of electoral district[5]	Returning officers (except to break a tie), inmates of correctional institutions except those sentenced for 10 days or less or for nonpayment of fines, candidates convicted of corrupt practices prohibited from voting for 8 years	Mail-in ballot for physical incapacity, absence from electoral division, qualified inmates, candidate and official agents or scrutineers, residents of remote areas
British Columbia	18 years, Canadian citizen, resident of province for 6 months, registered in electoral district	Chief electoral officer, deputy chief electoral officer, inmates serving a sentence of 2 years or more, individuals convicted of corrupt practices prohibited from voting up to 7 years	Mail-in ballot for absence from province, disability or injury, weather or other environmental conditions, remote location, any other reason beyond individual's control
Canada	18 years, Canadian citizen, ordinarily resident in polling division	Chief electoral officer, assistant chief electoral officer, inmate serving sentence of 2 years or more, individuals convicted of corrupt or illegal electoral practices disqualified for 5 to 7 years	Mail-in ballot for any reason; Act includes "any other elector in Canada who wishes to vote in accordance with special voting rules"

[1] Under section 45(6) of the *New Brunswick Elections Act*, MLAs running for re-election can be on the list of electors in the district where they are normally resident, the district in or near the provincial capital in which they resided while an MLA or the district in which they are candidates. However, only one vote is permitted.
[2] Under section 15(1.1) of the *Ontario Elections Act*, those who cease to reside in the electoral district within two years of polling day are eligible to vote if they resided in Ontario at least 12 consecutive months before ceasing to be a resident, they intend to resume Ontario residency and their last Ontario residence was in the electoral district. The two-year limitation does not apply to those absent on government service or to those attending an out-of-province educational institution.
[3] Under section 35(1) of the *Manitoba Elections Act*, absence from the province for a definite purpose for a definite period of less than six months does not result in loss of residency.
[4] British subjects can vote if they qualified as voters on June 23, 1971 and ordinarily resided in Saskatchewan for six months preceding that day.
[5] Under section 40.1 of the *Alberta Elections Act* there is an exemption from the residency requirement for MPs, senators, provincial government employees, and their dependents.

Appendix Table 3

Candidate Qualifications

Jurisdiction	Qualifications	Disqualified	Nomination	Deposit	Return of deposit
Newfoundland[1]	Canadian citizen, 18 years, resident immediately preceding nomination day	Paid employees of government or public bodies (except those employed when the House of Assembly is not sitting, or members of the armed forces, legal advisors), government contractors	10 or more signatures, affidavit of candidate as to his/her qualifications including party affiliation, where affiliated, appointment of chief financial officer, appointment of auditor, endorsement in writing of political party where applicable or for use of "nonaffiliated" or no designation	$100	15% of popular vote or elected
Prince Edward Island[2]	Canadian citizen, 18 years	None specified in *Elections Act, Public Services Act* or *Legislative Assembly Act*	10 signatures, endorsement by party	$200	At least half the votes received by the winning candidate
New Brunswick[3]	Canadian citizen, 18 years, resident 6 months	Mayor or municipal councillors, federal or provincial judges, those ineligible to vote, senators or MPs	25 signatures, signature of party leader designation of official agent	$100	50% of the vote obtained by the winner
Nova Scotia[4]	Canadian citizen, 19 years	Member of, or candidate for federal parliament, provincial employees in managerial or confidential positions	Signature of 5 electors, letter signed by party leader or declaration of independent status	$100	Elected and/or obtained 15% of vote

Appendix Table 3 (continued)
Candidate Qualifications

Jurisdiction	Qualifications	Disqualified	Nomination	Deposit	Return of deposit
Quebec[5]	Canadian citizen, 18 years, resident 6 months	Judges, chief electoral officer, member of the electoral boundary commission, returning officers, official agent of a candidate or political party, MPs, persons convicted of indictable offence punishable for 2 or more years, a candidate in a previous election whose official agent has not produced a return of election expenses, an independent candidate who has not paid elections debts by December 31 in the year following the election, a person convicted of a corrupt electoral or referendum practice	100 signatures, signature of official agent, letter from party leader	None	Not applicable
Ontario[6]	Canadian citizen, 18 years, resident 6 months	Returning officer, election clerk, enumerator, revision assistant, anyone holding office, commission or employment in the			

Appendix Table 3 (continued)
Candidate Qualifications

Jurisdiction	Qualifications	Disqualified	Nomination	Deposit	Return of deposit
Ontario (cont.)		Government of Canada or Ontario at time of nomination except members of the armed forces, coroner, notary public, public school supervisory officer and members of boards and commissions[7]	Signatures of 25 electors, agreement to register with chief electoral officer under *Election Finances Act*	Act	10% of vote
Manitoba[8]	Canadian citizen, 18 years, 6 months residence	Election officer, revising officer or enumerator, those ineligible to sit in House of Commons or any provincial assembly, election offence, those receiving payment for office, commission or employment for Manitoba government (does not apply to employees of Crown corporations, JPs, members of statutory boards and commissions), leave-of-absence provisions for civil servants under *Civil Service Act* (leave-of-absence without pay for not longer than 90 days — every such application will be granted)	100 signatures, appointment of official agent, official endorsement by registered political party	None	Not applicable

Appendix Table 3 (continued)
Candidate Qualifications

Jurisdiction	Qualifications	Disqualified	Nomination	Deposit	Return of deposit
Saskatchewan[9]	Canadian citizen, 18 years, resident of province 6 months	Chief electoral officer, assistant chief electoral officer, election officers, federal or provincial court judge, 5-year disqualification for those convicted of corrupt electoral practices, inmates	4 signatures, appointment of business manager including written notice, written confirmation that is officially endorsed, is "independent" or does not want word "independent" to follow name on ballot	$100	At least half the votes obtained by the winning candidate
Alberta[10]	Canadian citizen, 18 years, resident 6 months	MP or senator, 5-8 year disqualification of candidate or chief financial officer reported under 36(1) of *Electoral Finances and Contributions Disclosure Act*, 8 year disqualification for expulsion from Assembly under *Conflicts of Interest Act*, 8-year disqualification for conviction for corrupt electoral practice	25 signatures, appointment of official agent, written confirmation that individual is the officially endorsed candidate of a registered political party or is an independent candidate	$200	At least half the number of votes obtained by the winning candidate
British Columbia[11]	Canadian citizen, 18 years, resident 6 months	Chief electoral officer, deputy chief electoral officer, inmates serving sentences of 2 years or more, MPs or federal judges, 7-year disqualification for illegal electoral practices	25 signatures, disclosure under *Financial Disclosure Act*, written endorsement by by 2 principal officers of registered political party[12]	$100	15% of vote

Appendix Table 3 (continued)
Candidate Qualifications

Jurisdiction	Qualifications	Disqualified	Nomination	Deposit	Return of deposit
Canada[13]	Canadian citizen, 18 years	Federally appointed judges (except citizenship judges), government employees (except members of armed forces or reserves on active service because of war), registrar of deeds in any province, government contractors, inmates, electoral officers, members of provincial or territorial assemblies, sheriffs, clerks of the peace or county or judicial district, Crown attorneys, those failing to file financial report as required by *Canada Elections Act*, 5-7 years disqualification for corrupt electoral practices	100 signatures (50 signatures in designated sparsely populated districts), appointment of auditor, signature of registered party leader or designate	$1,000	50% deposit for 15% of the vote, 50% for audited statement of election expenses with time limit

[1] Acts consulted: *Election Act, Act Respecting Legislative Disabilities and the Vacation of Seats in the House of Assembly, Conflict of Interest Act*.

[2] Acts consulted: *Election Act, Conflict of Interest Act, Public Services Act, House of Assembly Act*.

[3] Acts consulted: *Election Act, Legislative Assembly Act*.

[4] Acts consulted: *Election Act, House of Assembly Act*.

[5] Acts consulted: *Election Act*.

[6] Acts consulted: *Election Act, Legislative Assembly Act*.

[7] Exemption does not apply to this clause does not apply to members of the Ontario Labour Relations board, the Liquor Licence Board of Ontario, the Ontario Municipal Board, the Workplace Safety and Insurance Board, the Ontario Securities Commission, the Ontario Farm Products Marketing Commission, the Civil Service Commission, or the Board of Parole.

[8] Acts consulted: *Election Act, Legislative Assembly Act*.

[9] Acts consulted: *Election Act, Legislative Assembly and Executive Council Act*.

[10] Acts consulted: *Election Act, Conflicts of Interest Act, Electoral Finances and Disclosure Act, Senatorial Selection Act, Legislative Assembly Act*.

[11] Acts consulted: *Election Act, Constitution Act*.

[12] The Act allows for the endorsement to be withdrawn up until the end of the nomination period (15 days after the election is called).

[13] Acts consulted: *Canada Elections Act, Parliament of Canada Act*.

Notes

I acknowledge a debt for suggestions to André Blais, Paul Howe, Richard Johnston and anonymous reviewers for IRPP. Given the scope of the project and a tight timetable it would have been impossible to complete without the assistance of Carey Hill. This is a revised version of an article published by the IRPP in 2001.

1. See André Blais, Paul Howe, and Richard Johnston, "Strengthening Canadian Democracy: A New IRPP Research Project," *Policy Options*, Vol. 20, no. 9 (November 1999), pp. 7-9.

2. Neil Nevitte, *The Decline of Deference* (Peterborough, ON: Broadview, 1996), p. 5.

3. Richard Johnston and Janet Ballantyne, "Geography and the Electoral System," *Canadian Journal of Political Science*, Vol. 10, no. 4 (December 1977), pp. 857-66.

4. See Filip Palda, *Election Finance Regulation in Canada: A Critical Review* (Vancouver: The Fraser Institute, 1991).

5. F.L. Morton and Rainer Knopff, *The Charter Revolution and the Court Party* (Peterborough, ON: Broadview Press, 2000).

6. Richard S. Katz, *Democracy and Elections* (New York: Oxford University Press, 1997), p. 3. Katz looks at over 800 elections in 70 countries.

7. Lawrence LeDuc, "Elections and Democratic Governance," in Lawrence LeDuc, Richard G. Niemi and Pippa Norris (eds.), *Comparing Democracies: Election and Voting in Global Perspective* (Thousand Oaks, CA: Sage Publications, 1996), p. 344.

8. See for example, Henry Milner, "The Case for Proportional Representation in Canada," in Henry Milner (ed.), *Making Every Vote Count: Reassessing Canada's Electoral System* (Peterborough, ON: Broadview, 1999).

9. Royal Commission on Electoral Reform and Party Financing, *Final Report: Reforming Electoral Democracy*, Vol. 1 (Canada: Department of Supply and Services, 1991), p. 1.

10. Pierre Elliott Trudeau, "Some Obstacles to Democracy in Quebec," in Trudeau (ed.), *Federalism and the French Canadian* (Toronto: Macmillan, 1968), pp. 103-23.

11. A good summary is provided by Rand Dyck, *Provincial Politics in Canada*, 2nd ed. (Scarborough, ON: Prentice-Hall, 1991).

12. See for example, Seymour Martin Lipset, "Some Social Requisites of Democracy," *American Political Science Review*, Vol. 53, no. 2 (March 1959), pp. 69-105 and Deane Neubauer, "Some Conditions of Democracy," *American Political Science Review*, Vol. 61, no. 4 (December 1967), pp. 1002-9.

13. Jane Jenson, "Party Systems," in David J. Bellamy, Jon H. Pammett, and Donald C. Rowat (eds.), *The Provincial Political Systems* (Toronto: Methuen, 1976), p. 121.

14. Richard Simeon and David J. Elkins, "Provincial Political Cultures in Canada," in David J. Elkins and Richard Simeon (eds.), *Small Worlds: Provinces and Parties in Canadian Political Life* (Toronto: Methuen, 1980), p. 68.

15. Allan Kornberg, William Mishler, and Harold D. Clarke, *Representative Democracy in the Canadian Provinces* (Scarborough, ON: Prentice-Hall, 1982), p. 261.

16. Dyck, *Provincial Politics in Canada*, pp. 632-33.

17. Dale H. Poel, "The Diffusion of Legislation among the Provinces: A Statistical Analysis," *Canadian Political Science Review*, Vol. 9, no. 4 (March 1976), pp. 605-26. Saskatchewan first introduced 10 of the 25 innovations examined by Poel, more than any other province. While Poel's study covers legislative diffusion only until 1974, it does show that the implementation of independent electoral boundary commissions, pioneered by Manitoba in 1957, followed an adoption pattern that was different from that of any other legislation.

18. Constitutional rules guarantee that a province cannot have fewer members of the House of Commons than Senators from that province and that no province can lose seats as a result of periodic redistributions.

19. R.K. Carty, "The Electoral Boundary Revolution in Canada," *Canadian Review of American Studies*, Vol. 15, no. 3 (fall 1985), p. 274.

20. *Reference re Provincial Electoral Boundaries* [1991], 5 W.W.R. 1 (S.C.C.), 81, D.L.R. (4th) 16.

21. *Dixon vs. Attorney General of British Columbia* [1989], 4. W.W.R. 393, 413.

22. Royal Commission on Electoral Reform and Party Financing, *Final Report, Volume 1: Reforming Electoral Democracy* (Ottawa, 1991), p. 148. Also see the discussion in Keith Archer, "Conflict and Confusion in Drawing Constituency Boundaries:

The Case of Alberta," *Canadian Public Policy*, Vol. 19, no. 2 (June 1993), pp. 179-82.

23. Carty, "The Electoral Boundary Revolution in Canada," For a longer time series on electoral inequality in provincial legislatures, see Harvey E. Pasis, "Electoral Distribution in the Canadian Provincial Legislatures," in J. Paul Johnston and Harvey E. Pasis (eds.), *Representation and Electoral Systems: Canadian Perspectives* (Scarborough, ON: Prentice-Hall, 1990), pp. 251-54.

24. *Mackinnon v. Prince Edward Island* [1993], 101 D.L.R. (4th) 362 (P.E.I.S.C.).

25. Changes to the PEI *Electoral Boundaries Act* provide that the next redistribution will be by an independent commission consisting of a judge and two individuals who are not members of the legislature or Parliament and not provincial government employees. One will be nominated by the premier and the other by the Leader of the Opposition after consultation with other opposition party leaders. The province has also committed itself by statute to redistribution after every three elections.

26. The participation of the judiciary in Alberta is optional. The Alberta *Electoral Boundaries Commission Act* provides for a chair who must be the ethics commissioner, the auditor general, a university president, a judge or retired judge or someone whose "stature and qualifications" are similar. The chair of the 1996 commission was, in fact, a judge.

27. Kent Roach, "One Person, One Vote? Canadian Constitutional Standards for Electoral Distribution and Districting," in David Small (ed.), *Drawing the Map: Equality and Efficacy of the Vote in Canadian Electoral Boundary Reform* (Toronto: Dundurn Press, 1991), p. 65.

28. "Equality and Efficacy of the Vote," in Royal Commission on Electoral Reform and Party Financing, *Final Report: Reforming Electoral Democracy*, Vol. 1 (Canada: Department of Supply and Services, 1991), p. 140.

29. "Equality and Efficacity of the Vote," appendix C, p. 200.

30. British Columbia, Royal Commission on Electoral Boundaries for British Columbia, *Report* (Victoria: Queen's Printer, 1988).

31. A more detailed comparison is contained in the appendix.

32. Roach, "One Person, One Vote?"

33. R. K. Carty, "The Electoral Boundary Revolution," pp. 284-85. Carty attributes Alberta's exceptionalism to its use of different apportionment criteria for rural and urban districts.

34. Katz, *Democracy and Elections*, p. 216.

35. Katz, *Democracy and Elections*. For a more recent comparative examination of the right to vote in 63 democracies see André Blais, Louis Massicotte, and Antoine Yoshinaka, "Deciding Who Has the Right to Vote: A Comparative Analysis of Election Laws," *Electoral Studies*, Vol. 20, no. 1 (March 2001).

36. Urban residents in Ontario can obtain a certificate of entitlement to vote up to the day before polling day. Rural residents can be registered on polling day itself if vouched for by a registered voter.

37. The disqualifications in table 4 are based on a reading of the relevant elections act. Other statutes that specify disqualifications may have been missed.

38. Citizens must be "ordinarily resident" in the province prior to an election, but no minimum period of residence is stipulated.

39. Since Newfoundland and Ontario are tied for top spot in this ranking, they are each assigned the rank of 9.5, i.e., the average of 9 and 10. Manitoba, and British Columbia follow with scores of 8, 7, 6 and 5, respectively. Nova Scotia, Saskatchewan and Alberta are also tied so they are given the average of the next three ranks (4, 3 and 2). New Brunswick, the most restrictive province, ranks lowest. Similar calculations are used below to rank provinces on candidacy restrictions and election finance rules.

40. Katz, *Democracy and Elections*, p. 246.

41. Nova Scotia is the only jurisdiction to stipulate a minimum age for candidacy, 19, that is different from that for voting.

42. See endnote 39 for an explanation of the procedure used to assign ranks in the case of a tie among provinces.

43. See F. Leslie Seidle (ed.), *Provincial Party and Election Finance in Canada* (Toronto: Dundurn Press, 1991).

44. Katz, *Democracy and Elections*, pp. 263-64.

45. Some have argued that public funding of political parties leads to (or is produced by) a cartel joining dominant parties in the system, in effect constraining voter options. See Heather MacIvor, "Do Canadian Parties Form a Cartel?", *Canadian Journal of Political Science*, Vol. 29, no. 2 (June 1996), pp. 317-34. For a rebuttal of MacIvor's argument, see Lisa Young, "Party State and Political Competition in Canada: The Cartel Model Reconsidered," *Canadian Journal of Political Science*, Vol. 31, no. 2 (June 1998), pp. 339-58.

46. See Gary Jacobson, "Public Funds for Congressional Campaigns: Who Would Benefit?", in Herbert Alexander (ed.), *Political Finance* (London: Sage Publications, 1979), pp. 99-127.

47. John Ferejohn and Brian Gaines, "The Personal Vote in Canada," in Herman Bakvis (ed.), *Representation,, Integration and Political Parties in Canada* (Toronto: Dundurn Press, 1991), pp. 275-302.

48. However, Saskatchewan requires contributions to be made to a federal party and then channelled back to the provincial one. This effectively discriminates against the Saskatchewan Party, which has no federal equivalent. Legislation to eliminate that restriction has been passed but had not been proclaimed at the time of writing.

49. For a study of electoral volatility at the national level in Canada using the turnover index, see Donald E. Blake, "Party Competition and Electoral Volatility: Canada in Comparative Perspective," in Herman Bakvis (ed.), *Representation, Integration and Political Parties in Canada* (Toronto: Dundurn Press, 1991), pp. 253-73. For a national level study on Canada using the proportionality index, see R. Kent Weaver, "Improving Representation in the Canadian House of Commons," *Canadian Journal of Political Science*, Vol. 30, no. 3 (September 1997), pp. 473-513.

50. Peter Mair, *Party System Change: Approaches and Interpretations* (New York: Oxford University Press, 1997), pp. 218-19.

51. See Susan J. Carroll, *Women as Candidates in American Politics* (Bloomington: Indiana University Press, 1985); and Carol Nechemias, "Changes in the Election of Women to U.S. State Legislative Seats," *Legislative Studies Quarterly*, Vol. 12, no. 1 (February 1987), pp. 125-42.

52. Lisa Young, "Legislative Turnover and the Election of Women to the Canadian House of Commons," in Kathy Megyery (ed.), *Women in Canadian Politics: Toward Equity in Representation* (Toronto: Dundurn Press, 1991), p. 95.

53. Lisa Young, "Legislative Turnover and the Election of Women," pp. 91-95. Her "best case" assumes the percentage of women who are candidates increases by five percentage points in each election and that women are given a six point advantage in being nominated in winnable ridings.

54. Female representation in most provinces reached or exceeded the federal level in the early 1990s. See Donley T. Studlar and Richard E. Matland, "The Dynamics of Women's Representation in the Canadian Provinces," *Canadian Journal of Political Science*, Vol. 29, no. 2 (June 1996), p. 273.

55. See, for example, Richard Rose, "Evaluating Election Turnout," in *Voter Turnout from 1945 to 1997: A Global Report*, 2nd ed. (Stockholm: International IDEA, 1997), pp. 35-47.

56. See Carty, "The Electoral Boundary Revolution in Canada."

57. See F. Leslie Seidle, "Preface," in F. Leslie Seidle (ed.), *Party and Election Finance in Canada* (Toronto: Dundurn Press, 1991), pp. xix-xxii.

12

Introducing Direct Democracy in Canada

Matthew Mendelsohn and Andrew Parkin

The 2000 federal election campaign in Canada featured a shallow debate on the merits of direct democracy. The Canadian Alliance suggested, somewhat timidly, that citizens should be allowed to initiate binding referendums on issues of their choice. Other political parties and the media generally derided this idea. Indeed, many commentators refused to engage in a debate on the merits of the citizen-initiated referendum, choosing instead to characterize it as nothing more than a device for attacking immigration levels or women's access to abortion services. When satirist Rick Mercer of the television program *This Hour Has 22 Minutes* launched his own "citizen-initiated referendum" to change Alliance leader Stockwell Day's first name to Doris, the die was cast and the concept of direct democracy became an object of ridicule. As is often the case during election campaigns the issue did not get the kind of thoughtful consideration that it deserves. In this paper we would like to begin a more serious discussion of the question of whether, and how, direct democracy should be used in Canada.

Introduction

Referendums[1] are becoming more common in many liberal-democratic societies.[2] Over the past decade, Western Europeans have been called upon to vote with increasing regularity on a range of issues, including membership in the European Union and the ratification of its treaties, the devolution of powers to regional assemblies, changes to the electoral system, and the legalization of abortion and divorce. In Switzerland, Italy, and in the US — where citizens themselves are able to submit questions to the electorate and vote directly on laws — the number of questions that are being placed on the ballot has been increasing.[3] It is fair to say that where there is direct democracy it is being increasingly used, and where there is no direct democracy its introduction is being increasingly debated.[4]

Canadians are no strangers to the referendum. In addition to the 1898 vote on prohibition, there have been two national votes — on conscription in 1942 and on the Charlottetown Accord in 1992 — both of which were dramatic events in the political life of the country. Referendums at the provincial and territorial level have been more common: since 1990, there have been referendums in New Brunswick (on video lottery terminals), Quebec (in 1995, on sovereignty), in Newfoundland (in 1995 and 1997, on the constitutional protection of denominational schools), in Saskatchewan (in 1991, on public funding for abortion, balanced budget legislation, and mandatory referendums on constitutional amendments), in British Columbia (in 1991, on direct democracy), in the Northwest Territories (in 1992, on the division of the territory), and in Nunavut (in 1997, on the composition of the new legislature). In 2002, there was also a referendum-like consultation in BC on the process of negotiating treaties with First Nations. These examples represent only a small fraction of the referendums held throughout Canadian history.[5]

In recent years, a case has been made for expanding the scope of direct democracy. At times, citizen groups on the left have called for issues such as free trade to be put to a vote, and have advocated the use of the referendum as one means of reinvigorating public life and civil society.[6] More famously, the more frequent use of referendums has been a rallying cry for populists on the right. The Canadian Alliance, for example, pledged to "allow Canadians to bring forward citizen-initiated referendums to put their priorities on the national agenda through a Canada-wide vote"[7] and to "seek the consensus of all Canadians through judicious use of national referenda, both on issues having significant implications for Canadian society and on proposed changes to the country's Constitution."[8]

During the 2000 federal election campaign, the Alliance's proposals were singled out for criticism by their opponents. Some worried that if relatively small numbers of citizens were allowed to initiate referendums, Canadians would find themselves dragged into repetitive votes on matters that were either frivolous or deeply divisive. Others argued that the wider use of referendums would be incompatible with Canada's system of representative and responsible government[9] — a system in which the executive is responsible to the legislature and sovereignty is vested in the Crown rather than "the people" — and as such would constitute an unwelcome "Americanization" of Canadian politics.[10]

The discussion that took place during the campaign could hardly be characterized as an informed debate of the merits of introducing direct democracy in Canada. In part, this was due to the Alliance's own failure to articulate a credible and consistent position on how and when referendums might be used. In part this was because many of those who spoke out against the notion of citizen-initiated referendums were themselves not called upon to defend the status quo. It may have been easy to poke holes in the Alliance's policy; it would have been more difficult to defend the position that the Canadian parliamentary system currently provides for the adequate representation of citizens, affords elected representatives ample opportunities to debate the merits of government legislation, and affords the public the possibility of influencing government decisions.

What was also overlooked in the discussion was the fact that, generally speaking, Canadians appear to be cautiously supportive of the idea of allowing the public to play a more direct role in political decision-making. When asked directly in a survey conducted by the IRPP in March of 2000, "Overall do you think that referendums are good things, bad things, or don't you think they make much difference?," a majority (57 percent) said they were good things. Eight percent said they were bad things, and 28 percent felt they didn't make much difference. When asked in another survey a more general question about public involvement in decision-making — "If the general public was more involved in decision-making on our big national problems, do you think we would be more likely to solve our problems, less likely to solve our problems, or that it would make no difference?" — just over 50 percent of Canadians said more likely, compared with 16 percent who said we would be less likely to solve our problems (the remaining third of respondents said it would make no difference or had no opinion).[11]

However, the support for direct democracy does not appear to be very deep: only 37 percent of Canadians on the IRPP survey said that they could think of an issue on which they would like a referendum held. And when asked whether referendums should always, sometimes, rarely or never be held on a selection of possible issues, most supported the use of referendums only "sometimes."[12] On none of the suggested issues did a majority of Canadians feel that referendums should always be held (see figure 1).

Some provincial governments have already responded to what they perceive as a popular desire for reform. Both Alberta and British Columbia now require that an amendment to the Canadian constitution be approved by voters in a referendum before it can be passed by the provincial legislature. BC and Saskatchewan have gone further by adopting laws enabling citizens to initiate referendums (or in the case of Saskatchewan, nonbinding plebiscites) on any issue within the province's jurisdiction — although in neither province has a

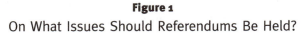

Figure 1

On What Issues Should Referendums Be Held?

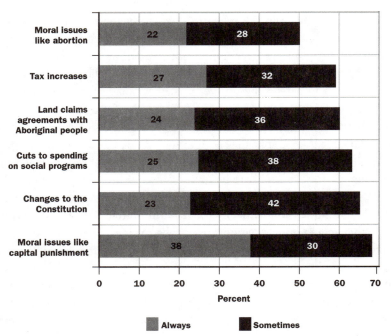

Question Structure: "Do you think Canada should always, sometimes, rarely or never have referendums on...?"
Source: IRPP, Strengthening Canadian Democracy Survey (March 2000).
N=1,278 (except "capital punishment" N=592; and "abortion" N=686).

vote of this kind actually been held. Manitoba and Ontario have adopted laws mandating referendums in order to gain approval for measures such as tax increases.[13] Other provinces, notably New Brunswick, currently are considering ways of enabling referendums.

As a result of these changes and proposals, direct democracy has been gradually working its way into the mainstream of Canadian politics. Our concern, however, is that this has occurred in an ad hoc manner without adequate attention being paid to the question of what type of direct democracy is most appropriate for Canada, and when and how it should be deployed. The failure of political elites to consider and assess different modalities of direct democracy is likely to favour the advent of inappropriate types. "Inappropriate types" are those forms that are least consistent with the best values and traditions of Canadian democracy, and that could end up undermining some of its primary achievements.

The criteria

In evaluating the referendum device, we will examine the claim put forward by the advocates of direct democracy. That is, do referendums provide greater scope for citizen participation in political decision-making and shift power from elites to the general public? Our own criteria, however, will not simply mirror the ones set out by the advocates of direct democracy. We will also examine the effect that referendums are likely to have on some of the most valuable features of Canadian liberal democracy. In our view, these include:

- the protection of minority interests, so that majority rule does not become majority tyranny
- the fairness of the political process, so that all citizens have a reasonable opportunity to raise their concerns and to influence the views of others
- informed decision-making, so that citizens have access to the information they need to be able to make choices that are in their best interest
- political accountability, so that voters can hold someone to account for the consequences of public policy decisions

The protection of minorities, fairness, the quality of decision-making and accountability are therefore crucial litmus tests against which referendum practice must be evaluated, along with the question of whether the use of referendums actually increases the power of the general public. Thus, in reviewing the experience of other countries, our goal will be to identify those particular forms of direct democracy that can best meet the goals of referendum proponents, while still preserving the best elements of the Canadian liberal-democratic tradition.

With these criteria in mind, we will highlight four important ways in which referendum processes may differ. First, referendums and their outcomes can be more or less majoritarian — that is, they differ in the degree to which they allow for "winner-take-all" scenarios. Conversely, they can incorporate integrative practices, designed to promote compromises between different interests and provide some protection for the interests of minority communities. Referendums are sometimes thought to be intrinsically majoritarian devices that undermine compromise and fail to integrate the viewpoints of competing groups. If this is indeed the case, it would be a highly damning criticism in a country as diverse as Canada.

Second, referendum processes can be more or less deliberative — that is, they differ in the extent to which they promote thoughtful public debate. Deliberative referendum campaigns allow citizens to develop their opinions through participation in collective public dialogue; at the other end of the spectrum are referendums that tabulate the standing opinions of citizens on the issue at hand.

Democracy is as much about public discourse as it is about voting, and only after a process of debate, in which the positions of all sides can be tested within the public sphere, will the wisest choices be made. What interests us is the extent to which such a process can be made part of a referendum campaign.

Third, referendums can be more or less controlled by political elites. The process can be regulated so as to give the lead role to established political parties and to restrict the ability of others to set the agenda or influence the outcome. Or a framework can be established that provides for a much larger role for interest groups, social movements, and individual citizens. Who can initiate referendums and under what rules will be an important determinant of their effectiveness in empowering citizens.

Finally, referendums can be used to accomplish more or less sincere objectives. Theoretically, the intent of a referendum is to solicit the public's views on a given issue. In practice, referendums are typically deployed strategically by elites who are interested not so much in knowing the public's mind as in achieving more self-interested objectives — such as bringing about a particular result or maintaining the unity of their party in the face of a divisive issue. The timing of a referendum, the wording of the question, and the rules of the campaign are generally set with such strategic objectives in mind. There is of course no way to prevent governments from using referendums to further their strategic ends and tactical goals will be part of any process. Yet some referendum regimes encourage the tactical use of referendums, while others promote referendums designed to solicit feedback from the population on the direction of policy. The crudely tactical use of referendums is, in fact, part of the reason why proponents of direct democracy are often disappointed with the actual practice of referendums.

These four criteria allow us to distinguish between different referendum practices on the basis of important principles of liberal democracy and Canadian democratic practice. First, there must be a reasonable expectation that the referendum regime will promote integration and avoid creating unnecessary divisions between the country's diverse communities — linguistic, regional and cultural. Second, Canadian democracy is about more than simply voting. It is also about talking. Ideally, voting is but the final stage of a larger process of discussion among citizens, a process through which citizens learn about one another, debate public issues, and ultimately develop public judgement that is reflective of collective needs and values. Third, referendum procedures must be evaluated on the basis of whether they ensure an appropriate mix of party, interest group, and citizen participation in the process. Too little participation by political parties can undermine the coherence of the process and the accountability of government, as we have seen in California, while too much control by established elites defeats the very purpose of introducing referendums. Finally, a tool like the referendum must be evaluated not simply on the basis of whether it allows citizens to vote more frequently on a wider range of issues, but on whether it is used sincerely — that is, with the genuine intention of extending citizens' control over government and their influence on policy issues of their own choosing.

Overview of our argument

The paper is structured as follows. We begin by reviewing a range of referendum models that are currently in use in various liberal-democratic societies. In the next section, we assess these models in light of a number of specific issues that are often raised in discussing referendums — issues such as the rules governing campaigns, the ability of voters to make good decisions, and the effect of referendums on key institutions and actors. On this basis, we turn in the final section to a discussion of the best forms of direct democracy for Canada.

In general, we conclude that many of the hopes of the proponents of direct democracy — notably that the process is one that allows "the people" to bypass elites in order to enact policies with widespread public support — are misplaced. Referendum contests are often disputes between competing narrow interests or competing groups of elites, with the battlefield merely having shifted from the floor of the legislature to the ballot box. The timing of a referendum, the wording of the question, the terms and tone of the campaign, and even the interpretation of the result all tend to be determined by elites.[14] Referendums often have little to do with grassroots democracy.

Referendums also do not usually provide the public with an opportunity to make policy, although they often provide a way to veto proposals made by political elites. The referendum on the Charlottetown Accord is a good example. While the referendum allowed the public to defeat the accord, it provided no mechanism though which the public could set the constitutional agenda or suggest alternatives. In and of itself, therefore, the use of referendums will not make a political system more democratic. Moreover, there is a risk that referendums can actually damage the integrity and effectiveness of the democratic system, depending on how they are integrated into existing structures. That said, their wider use, under the right conditions and governed by the right rules, can serve to improve the quality of Canadian democracy and make government decisions more responsive to public concerns. Moreover, we believe their expanded use to be inevitable and it is therefore essential to think through how they can be most effectively and democratically used. Our objective is to identify those circumstances and models of referendum practice that preserve the best elements of Canadian liberal democracy while at the same time revitalizing it. Accordingly, we put forward three key recommendations:

- Referendums should generally be used to ratify constitutional amendments, but such referendums should be used only following a people's convention on the issue.
- Governments should initiate referendums more frequently, but these are best used in cases when the government is genuinely uncertain about the direction to take, and perhaps even prepared to remain neutral during the campaign.
- The "indirect" form of the citizen-initiated referendum should be adopted. Unlike the direct initiative, which allows citizens to place questions directly on the ballot, a successful petition drive under the indirect initiative requires governments to introduce the measure into the legislature and hold hearings on the question, and permits amendments to the proposal before it goes to the electorate.

Direct Democracy around the World

Direct democracy exists in many forms. In this section, we review some of its most instructive variants, in order to sketch out an array of options from which Canadians might choose. We will describe how direct democracy is used in each case, as well as comment upon its majoritarian as opposed to integrative qualities, its deliberative nature, the degree to which it is controlled by political elites as opposed to political outsiders, and the sincerity of its use.

There are three general classes of referendums: those initiated by the government at its own discretion, those referendums which must be held by law, and those initiated by the population through the collection of signatures (see figure 2). Government-initiated referendums, used at the discretion of the government, have been held in most liberal democracies, although in many countries, including Canada, their use has been sporadic. Obligatory referendums are held where a government is required by law or custom to submit certain kinds of legislation to a popular vote. Australia and Ireland, among other countries, require that referendums be held in order to ratify constitutional amendments. Increasingly there are also calls to oblige governments to submit non-constitutional issues to a referendum, such as tax increases or the incurring of a budgetary deficit. The citizen-initiated referendum is prevalent in many US states, Switzerland, Italy and New Zealand, though there are important variations in the form it takes in each jurisdiction. We will highlight three distinct types: the direct, the indirect, and the abrogative initiatives. We will also review in more detail the Swiss case that combines various forms and merits separate attention.

Figure 2

Types of Referendum

1. Government-initiated referendums
2. Obligatory referendums
   Obligatory constitutional referendums
   Other obligatory referendums (nonconstitutional)
3. Citizen-initiated referendums ("the initiative")
   Direct initiative
   Indirect initiative
   Abrogative initiative

The citizen-initiated referendum ("the initiative")

The United States

There is no single American model of direct democracy.[15] There has never been a national referendum, constitutional amendments are not submitted to referendums, there is no provision for the initiative at the national level, and each state has its own unique arrangement (currently 24 states allow for some form of citizen-initiated referendum).[16] We will single out for attention two states with contrasting systems of direct democracy: California, where the use of the direct form of the initiative has attracted world-wide attention, and Massachusetts, which allows for an indirect form of the initiative. The one element that is common to all jurisdictions across the US is the application of a series of court decisions (with *Buckley v. Valeo* [1976] being the most sweeping) that have struck down attempts to limit campaign spending on the grounds that such limits constitute an unwarranted restriction of free speech. Unrestricted campaign spending makes the US experience very different from anything that would ever materialize in Canada. Unrestricted spending also makes it difficult for observers of American politics to distinguish the effects of the initiative from the effects of the initiative in a context where there are no limits on spending. The folly of the Californian direct democracy experience is *sui generis* and a product of a lack of campaign spending limits and elements of the political culture and is unlikely to be reproduced elsewhere. Because of this, it is important to be cautious in the conclusions we draw from the American experience and to look carefully at the initiative in countries other than the US.

The direct initiative (California)

Under the terms of the direct initiative — which is permitted in 18 states — voters who gather enough approving signatures from fellow voters within a given period of time are able to place a measure before the electorate in a referendum (the number of signatures and the time for collecting them vary from state to state). If the measure passes, it becomes law.

The California variant promotes a mix of sincere and strategic practices. On the one hand, it is genuinely open — any group can launch a petition drive on any issue of its choice and succeed in putting it to a vote. The process is legally structured so as to allow for any type of initiative and political outsiders of various stripes have successfully changed legislation. Different political eras have tended to produce different types of initiative outcomes. Progressive measures were common in the 1920s, while more recently, conservatives have prevailed on "law and order" and taxation issues, and progressives have come out on top on environmental and consumer rights issues. On the other hand, the process is not necessarily fair to all participants. One generally needs access to a large pool of financial resources in order to be competitive in an initiative campaign. Consequently, such campaigns are often launched for insincere reasons, such as sapping opponents' resources or forcing the legislature to act to avoid becoming embroiled in a messy initiative campaign.[17] In such instances, the initiative is no more than a strategic weapon deployed by those with deep pockets.

The California initiative regime is not designed to promote deliberation. There are no formal mechanisms to ensure that voters have adequate opportunities to learn about the proposed measures. The state does mail out a voters' pamphlet (which few voters read) that summarizes the measures and arguments for and against, but beyond this, voters are offered little help in their deliberations. There are, for example, no state-sponsored public debates. Likewise, there is no system requiring different intervenors to register with "yes" or "no" committees in order to make the process more transparent, and there is no easy way for the average voter to track the sources of campaign funding. As it is, the debate largely takes place on television, in the form of 30-second commercials. Moreover, many measures often appear simultaneously on a single ballot, limiting the amount of time that voters can devote to a consideration of each. Because of this, many voters do not bother to participate, and those that do tend to give perfunctory consideration to the issues.

The majoritarian flavor of the Californian initiative stems from the fact that there is no formal mechanism to guarantee minority interests a say in the outcome of the vote. There is, for instance, no requirement that a measure gain approval in a minimum number of regions or electoral districts. Nor is there a process that would allow groups other than those who sponsor an initiative to have a say in the question wording. While majority opinion is one important consideration in democratic decision-making, the absence of any protection for minority interests — as opposed to minority rights, which are enforced by the courts — is a concern because some minorities may consistently find themselves on the losing side of important initiative campaigns. Moreover, the low turnout in most initiative votes means that when the "majority" prevails, it is often quite a narrow coalition of groups that has come together to advance their own interests, not a true majority of the voting population.

Finally, the California initiative process is not controlled by the established political parties. Interest groups with either large memberships or significant financial resources can launch petition drives, as can less stable and more diverse coalitions of smaller or less well-off groups that come together to pool their resources. Increasingly, wealthy individuals or industry associations can single-handedly succeed in having questions placed on the ballot. In short, the principal players in Californian politics are not the elected state representatives but loosely knit coalitions of advocacy groups, professional and industry associations, wealthy private citizens and professional political consultants.[18] Party leaders do sometimes play a role in the initiative campaigns themselves — they are often key spokespersons for one side or another and often sponsor petition drives — but the impetus for political change now usually emerges from outside the parties. However, this does not mean that power has been transferred to what would be generally understood as "the public"; rather, it has been transferred to a different group of political insiders with financial resources.

One final issue deserves mention. Amending legislation that has been passed via the initiative process is impossible without another initiative. This is problematic because in practice most legislation at same point requires amendment, not to undermine its objectives but to better achieve them. One can never be certain of the precise effects of a law until it is implemented. Circumstances may change so as to require new legislation, but each law passed through the initiative remains on the books until it is rescinded through the initiative. And some laws are written so as to prohibit amendment unless the change is approved by a super-majority. These qualities serve to "constitutionalize" an increasing proportion of the state's legislation, as laws passed via the initiative are placed beyond the reach of the legislature acting on its own. As these laws are layered one on top of the other, a system is created that is increasingly incoherent, that fails to meet its intended objectives, and that cannot respond to new situations, or, ironically, new public demands. In short, it is a system at odds with good governance. The Californian case, though, is at one end of the spectrum of initiative politics and, as we will see below, there are a variety of regulations that can be incorporated into the referendum regime to prevent many of the worst excesses seen in California.

The indirect initiative (Massachusetts)
The indirect initiative is the form adopted in many of the northern US states, such as Maine, Michigan and Massachusetts. It differs from the direct initiative

in that the satisfaction of the petition signature requirement does not mean that the question is placed directly on the ballot for a vote. Rather, the question goes first to the state legislature where it is submitted to a public legislative hearing. Several outcomes are then possible: the legislature may place the question on the ballot, with or without amendments; it may submit its own proposal along with the original one (allowing voters to choose between them or vote for neither); or it may pre-empt a referendum by enacting legislation that responds to the general spirit of the original proposal.

The indirect initiative process is more deliberative than the direct in that it explicitly provides for public dialogue in the form of legislative committee hearings. The hearing process allows the public to offer more than a "yes" or "no" final verdict, and provides a process whereby the strengths and weaknesses of the proposal can be assessed and improvements considered. It is also more integrative than the direct initiative. Although the majority still rules once the measure is submitted to a referendum, at the earlier stage it is possible to amend it so as to incorporate the concerns of minority groups. The process is more controlled by political parties because they play a key role in the legislature in organizing the debate and shaping the choices that voters are called upon to make, though interest groups and other coalitions can still force issues onto the agenda. In this way, the indirect initiative allows outsiders to force issues onto the agenda and lets voters pronounce on issues, but the important features of accountable and representative government are preserved.

The indirect initiative thus has several advantages over the direct initiative: it allows the legislature to develop counter-proposals that integrate concerns from groups other than those sponsoring the initiative; the legislature is able to respond quickly to changed circumstance or unforeseen consequences by amending legislation passed through the initiative; and it encourages political parties to play a prominent role in the process. These factors help avoid "majority tyranny" and promote greater deliberation and a form of debate that is more organized and therefore more accessible to voters — producing more considered decisions on their part. The key disadvantage of the indirect initiative is that it does not guarantee that voters can force a vote on an issue of their choosing in exactly the way they want. If voters regularly see their proposals blocked or changed beyond recognition by the legislature, their confidence in the process may erode.

An alternative indirect initiative process takes place in New Zealand. There, citizens gather signatures for a referendum question, but no legal text accompanies the proposal. If the initiative is eventually passed in a referendum, the issue is then turned over to the legislature (and therefore the public service) to turn the general statement of intent into actual legislation. At that point, the ordinary legislative process begins, and the final legislation may end up incorporating the views of groups other than the original proponents.

The abrogative initiative: Italy

The abrogative initiative — referred to in Italy as the *referendum abrogativo* — provides voters with an opportunity to overturn legislation that has been passed by parliament. In order to initiate the process, 500,000 signatures must be collected within a period of 90 days. Then the Constitutional Court must decide whether the question is eligible to be put to a popular vote (some laws, such as international treaties or budget measures, cannot). In order for the initiative to pass and overturn the existing law, at least 50 percent of eligible voters must turn out to vote. Governments can pre-empt the initiative by adopting a revised law in place of the one in question, and even a referendum win can be tentative because governments have sometimes replaced the defeated law with a similar measure.[19]

As used in Italy, the abrogative initiative allows voters to make good on one of the traditional promises of the direct democracy: when political elites conspire to suppress widely held views of the general public, the public can rise up and say "no." This power can be most effectively exercised when parties and elites seek to protect their own interests at the expense of what voters see as the public interest. For example, the abrogative initiative was used to bring about change to the electoral system over the objections of the major parties in Parliament.

In practice, the abrogative initiative is not merely a public veto. Those considering initiating a popular vote often make known what amendments could be made to the existing law that would be sufficient to cause them to abandon the petition drive. This initiates a dialogue with government officials and provides those outside of government (including smaller political parties as well as citizens' groups) with a voice in shaping legislation. Its effect in practice is to distribute political power more widely throughout the political system.

In Italy, the abrogative initiative has been used by both the Radical Party on the left and a variety of Catholic groups on the right. Catholic groups mobilized large numbers of voters in their 1974 attempt to repeal the law legalizing divorce and in their 1981 attempt to repeal the law liberalizing access to abortion, but failed on both occasions. The Radical Party has sponsored a large number of abrogative initiatives; while many of these have been defeated, they nonetheless have prodded the political system to move more quickly in adopting a variety of progressive measures, most notably a law liberalizing access to abortion. Nevertheless, it is true that under the terms of the abrogative initiative, the power of the government remains formidable. Governments have been able to use their discretion to pass laws that respond to no more than the spirit rather than the details of a proposal, and governments have also been known to dissolve parliament in order to avoid a referendum altogether.

The abrogative initiative thus does not shift power decisively away from governments in favour of other parties and groups, but instead promotes dialogue among a variety of political actors aimed at developing compromise solutions. This makes this form of referendum much less majoritarian and more deliberative than the direct initiatives of some American states. The danger with both the indirect initiative and the abrogative initiative, however, is that in favouring compromises negotiated by the leaders of parties and citizen groups, the referendum process may lose a great deal of its appeal — the possibility of producing a decisive outcome that political elites are required to obey.

Switzerland

The overwhelming majority of all national referendums held over the past 50 years have taken place in Switzerland. There are five different forms of the referendum in Switzerland at the national level, with the three most commonly used being the obligatory constitutional referendum, the abrogative initiative and the citizen-initiated constitutional referendum. We will focus on the latter, although the abrogative initiative is also crucial to the workings of Swiss direct democracy. Referendums are a regular feature of Swiss politics, and they are tightly interwoven into the general process of government.

In Switzerland, the collection of 100,000 petition signatures is needed to launch a campaign to change a provision of the constitution. Because the constitution contains so many provisions, issues that might elsewhere be considered "ordinary legislation" end up being contested in the constitutional arena of initiative politics. Once the necessary signatures are collected, the measure is tabled for discussion in parliament. The government can then choose from a number of options: it can let the question be put to voters in a referendum, it can submit an alternative proposal to the voters alongside the one put forward by the petition's sponsors, or it can enact a legislative measure deemed satisfactory by the petition's sponsors. The success rate for initiatives is low, with only 10 percent that make it to a vote eventually winning approval in a referendum.[20] The approval rate for government counter-measures is higher. In approximately one-quarter of all cases, the original proposal is withdrawn by its sponsors after negotiations with the government produce an acceptable legislative response, leading many observers to describe this initiative process as "indirect."[21]

It has been argued that even though most initiatives are defeated, at the heart of most new legislation in Switzerland is an initiative drive. Some have referred to Switzerland as a case of "negotiated" direct democracy because the referendum is part of the ongoing bargaining that takes place within government.[22] Many initiatives are launched by small groups, but before coming to a vote, these minority views are transformed through consultation into proposals that are acceptable to the majority.

The Swiss initiative process can be characterized as both deliberative and integrative because it incorporates the practice of negotiation and compromise among political actors — actors that include representatives from both the canton and federal levels of government, political parties, interest groups, and citizen movements. In this sense, the initiative is part and parcel of the larger Swiss tradition of "amicable agreement"[23] in which political rivals cooperate with one another in order to get things done. Legislation in Switzerland is made the subject of an elaborate process of consultation before it is passed by parliament. This process — known as *Vernehmlassung* — serves to "referendum-proof" a considerable amount of legislation and make subsequent initiative challenges less necessary. Even when an initiative campaign is launched, it often serves as a means of extending the process of consultation rather than forcing a "yes or no" majority vote.

The non-majoritarian nature of the Swiss initiative also derives from the fact that measures must receive the support of a "double majority" in order to pass — a majority of all voters, as well as a majority of voters in a majority of the individual cantons. As a result, a regionally concentrated majority cannot pass measures without the support of voters in a significant number of other cantons. Furthermore, in order to get an abrogative initiative on the ballot in Switzerland, one requires either the collection within three months of 50,000 signatures from voters, or a vote of eight of the 26 canton legislatures. This second provision, that less than one-third of the canton legislatures can force a national vote on a piece of federal legislation, highlights the nonmajoritarian and federal nature of Swiss direct democracy. Its effect is to encourage extensive discussion and negotiation with the canton governments before the federal government proceeds to enact contentious legislation.

The initiative process in Switzerland is sincere in that its main purpose is generally to obtain the views of voters rather than to accomplish ulterior objectives. It is open for use by anyone and even small citizen groups have been successful in placing issues on the ballot and at using the threat of the initiative to spur the government into action. Political parties in Switzerland have more control over the process than do politicians in the direct initiative states of the US by virtue of the parliamentary hearings and subsequent negotiations with initiative sponsors. Swiss politicians play a central role in helping to "broker" the outcomes of initiative campaigns, thus exerting some control over the process, but control that is clearly shared with a wide range of political actors.

The obligatory constitutional referendum: Australia

We move now to consider referendums that are required under the terms of the constitution. This is a familiar issue for Canadians, and, because many of our institutions and traditions are strikingly similar to those of Australia, it is instructive to examine its process of constitutional amendment.

The case for using a referendum to ratify constitutional amendments is an easy one to make. The idea of popular sovereignty that underpins much of the discourse of democracy implies that citizens collectively remain the ultimate authority in a democratic society and by virtue of this must be consulted directly whenever the terms under which they have consented to be governed are changed. More pragmatically, it can be argued that because the constitution structures the political system and influences the outcomes of future decisions, any changes to it should be subject to a more rigorous process of ratification than is the case with ordinary legislation.

In Australia, a proposed amendment to the constitution must be passed by referendum. It must receive over half of the votes cast across the country, along with a majority of the votes cast in at least four of six states. By virtue of this double-majority requirement — which in practice means that the three small-est states can veto an amendment — referendums in Australia are nonmajoritarian in that "majority rule" is qualified by the federal principle.

At first blush, the referendum process in Australia appears to be fairly deliberative. Parties are involved in the campaigns, issues tend to be of high importance, votes are not held during regular elections, and, because only one or two amendments are usually considered at the same time, each one usually attracts considerable voter attention. However, because the process has tended to be highly controlled by established political parties — with the government proposing constitutional amendments and the government and opposition parties acting as the main antagonists in the ensuing campaign — it has been highly partisan and governed by strategic considerations. Governing parties initiate referendums for tactical purposes, and opposition parties oppose them for the same reason. In the end, many voters simply vote according to their partisan loyalties, undermining the deliberative nature of the process. Because of the strategic and insincere nature of many referendums — with the device used to pursue partisan objectives rather than build national consensus around key issues — the process has not proven to be very integrative.

In practice, referendums on constitutional amendments in Australia have proven very difficult to pass — in fact, the overwhelming majority (36 of 44) of proposed amendments have failed.[24] This has led some to conclude that referendums on constitutional amendment are problematic in and of themselves — that allowing the people a direct vote on constitutional changes adds an inordinate level of complexity to the process which only serves to ensure that the constitution will ossify in the face of successive referendum defeats. We doubt, however, that such conclusions are warranted. It is true that many voters are cautious by instinct and tend to vote to preserve the status quo unless a strong case can be made for change. However, many of the proposed amendments that have been defeated in Australia were proposed by a Labor government interested in transferring powers away from the states and into the hands of the Commonwealth government. This shift in the division of powers was opposed by the opposition parties and much of the public. One can argue, then, that in these cases the referendum served exactly the purpose for which it was intended: it allowed the citizenry to block a proposed change to the fundamental law of the land which was seen as advancing the partisan interest of the governing party.

In the 1999 referendum on the proposal for an Australian head of state, a people's convention was held prior to the referendum. The purpose of the convention was, in part, to generate more discussion and deliberation among the general public prior to the vote being held, but was also designed to limit the partisanship that had undermined previous campaigns. By moving the process of initiating the referendum and formulating the question out of the hands of parties, it thus constituted an "ambitious attempt at taking normal politics and partisanship out of referendums."[25]

The relevance of the Australian experience for Canada seems clear. Unless there is a popular consensus on the need for and nature of constitutional change, amendment will be difficult, regardless of whether a referendum or some other process is used. Canada has always had great difficulty achieving successful multilateral constitutional change to the satisfaction of all major partners in confederation. Multilateral constitutional amendment is inherently difficult because the consent of almost every provincial government must be secured in order to proceed. We will return to this theme later in our recommendations, but it should be underlined that the difficulty of securing constitutional amendments lies with the politics of constitutional change in complex societies, not the use of the referendum device itself. In Canada, constitutional change is going to be difficult regardless of the process used.

Government-initiated referendums

Government-initiated referendums are increasingly common and increasingly called for by the public. Since such referendums are not obligatory, governments can hold them or refrain from holding them as they see fit. The reasons why a government might opt to call a referendum are varied and include the desire to: add legitimacy to a policy through public ratification; free itself from having to take a stand on a controversial issue; strategically manage division within its own party; or respond to public demands for a referendum. The government may also feel that it has no choice but to call a referendum because precedents or conventions exist which make its use virtually mandatory. The bottom line, however, is that governments are unlikely to choose to call a referendum unless it is to their advantage. Even when the public calls for a popular vote on an issue, the government usually only accedes when it perceives that it is in its interest to do so. That government-initiated referendums are often used for strategic reasons undermines their effectiveness as a tool of public participation.

There is often no principled reason why governments choose to turn some issues to the people, and not others. The United Kingdom held no vote when it joined the European Economic Community in 1973, confirmed its membership by referendum in 1975, but (unlike France, Denmark and Ireland) did not hold a referendum in 1992 when it ratified the Maastricht Treaty. What differed in each case was not the nature of the decision but the strategic calculations of the country's political leaders — calculations regarding their standing with the electorate and the management of dissent within their own party.

Government discretion over whether to hold a referendum raises serious questions about the sincerity of the process. The more a referendum becomes a device deployed for partisan purposes, the more the process is likely to constrict opportunities for a genuinely open and inclusive public debate. Moreover, governments are likely to avoid calling a vote precisely when one might be most warranted — for instance, in the face of a particularly controversial policy decision that had not been widely discussed during the previous election campaign. Government-initiated referendums are often used to reinforce the position of the major political parties in the legislature. For example, Quebec legislation on referendums on sovereignty makes the premier and the leader of the opposition the leaders of the two opposing coalitions. These referendums are often highly deliberative, but debate tends to be controlled by established political parties and is not very open to political outsiders.

In sum, in the case of government-initiated referendums, the determining factor in the decision to put a question to the people is mainly political expediency. Because of this, the use of direct democracy can end up exacerbating, rather than alleviating, public disaffection with the political process. While there is often public support for the use of a government-sponsored referendum — for example, almost all Quebecers recognize that a referendum is the only legitimate way to begin a process leading toward secession — the public can also become disenchanted with the strategic use of the referendum device, deployed only when the government believes it has a good chance of winning.

On the other hand, there are instances when the government is not heavily attached to one outcome over the other and is sincerely prepared to let the public have a say. In Ireland, for example, the government turned to the electorate in 1984 to decide whether British citizens should have a right to vote in Irish elections and in 1972 to decide whether the voting age should be lowered from 21 to 18. Such genuine consultative actions, in which the government does not become the chief proponent of one side or the other, can, as we will discuss in the final section, contribute to the health of democracy. But too often the population is only brought in at the end of a process to endorse or reject a government proposal, with the government using all of the resources of the state to cajole the population into acquiescence. It is not altogether surprising that such referendums often leave a bitter aftertaste. However, a decision early in the policy process to allow the public a greater say on an issue the government does not feel strongly about, with the governing party remaining neutral, has in other countries produced more edifying democratic effects.

Concerns about Direct Democracy and How to Regulate Its Use

Each of the referendum models we outlined above functions quite differently depending on the rules governing its use. In this section, we examine how the regulatory regime under which a referendum is conducted helps to determine the effects of the process on the quality of liberal-democratic politics. In doing so, we will review some of the main objections to direct democracy: that direct democracy weakens political parties and accountability, places unrealistic demands on voters, jeopardizes the rights of minorities, and unduly favours well-financed interests.

Do referendums weaken political parties and undermine accountability?

It is often argued — by both advocates and critics of direct democracy — that one effect of the use of referendums is to weaken political parties. The argument in brief is that parties become less relevant once the power to initiate, draft and pass legislation is turned over to the electorate. Parties play a lesser role in determining the public policy agenda and in organizing and defining the terms of political debate. The stronger the regime of direct democracy, the more likely it is that those seeking to influence public policy will put their time and money into the referendum rather than the electoral process.

We take any potential threat to parties seriously; we consider parties essential to the smooth functioning of a democratic system. In a liberal democracy, voters must be able to hold someone to account for the consequences of public policy decisions. Voters also must perceive that they are presented with meaningful choices during elections. In our view, this means that political parties must continue to play the leading role in the political process. By developing policy platforms and selecting slates of candidates for political office, parties effectively present voters with alternatives from which to choose. While a system of direct democracy that permits other actors to break the oligopoly of the major political parties would be a positive development, one that did permanent damage to parties' long-term viability would not. But the evidence from other jurisdictions shows that while the referendum may force parties to change and may help new parties grow (both of which can help revitalize democracy and parties themselves), it does not lead to their demise.[26]

In the case of government-initiated referendums, parties clearly play a key role both in determining when a vote will be held and on what question, and in organizing the debate — either by leading the "yes" and "no" sides or by taking positions which serve to guide voters. In those cases where ad hoc organizations play an important role in the campaign, these organizations are often led and staffed by party activists. Even the citizens' initiative, which is cast as the biggest enemy of parties, can be used to their advantage by invigorating their role in policy innovation. More specifically, by sponsoring or supporting initiatives, parties can succeed in recruiting new supporters and in shifting political debate to a ground more favourable to their own electoral success. The Radical Party in Italy has been particularly successful at sponsoring referendums that furthered its own agenda, and party leaders in the US states often lead initiative campaigns designed to force issues onto the agenda that bring their own supporters out to the polls during the simultaneous elections.[27] Referendums and initiatives may curtail the ability of political parties to unilaterally set the legislative agenda, but they do not create a process that is beyond the reach of parties.

Referendums can strengthen parties in other ways as well. For instance, they can be used by political leaders to manage conflict within their own parties or governing coalitions. Instead of taking a stand on a key issue that divides party supporters, party leaders can adopt a more neutral stance and choose to have the issue decided directly by the voters. Such a strategy has been employed many times in Europe — the 1975 UK referendum on the European Community, for instance, allowed dissenters within the governing Labour party to campaign against the country's membership in the organization without placing the government's hold on office at risk. Similarly, referendums allow parties to remove a divisive issue from the realm of electoral politics. In Quebec, for example, the Parti s was able to win power in 1976 only after promising that it would not pursue its goal of sovereignty-association without first gaining support for the proposal in a referendum. This strategy effectively decoupled the issue of secession from other election issues and allowed the party to become a stronger electoral force. Referendums also provide opportunities for small parties: by taking a position in a referendum campaign, they can potentially attract more publicity and gain credibility. This is especially likely to occur if the major parties are aligned on one side of the referendum question. For example, the Charlottetown referendum provided the nascent Reform Party with an opportunity to gain national prominence.

Some worry that the referendum threatens governmental accountability, but again, this concern is overstated. In the case of government-initiated or obligatory constitutional referendums, governments clearly remain account-able to the electorate for the decision to use the referendum device itself (or to initiate the process of constitutional change). And all parties remain account-able to the electorate for their conduct in the referendum campaign. With the abrogative initiative, governmental accountability is in fact accentuated. Under normal rules of accountability, governing parties can only be held responsible for their governing record during periodic election campaigns — campaigns that inevitably focus on many issues. With the abrogative initiative, other actors can force governments to take more immediate responsibility for their policies and defend them before the electorate.

On the other hand, a plausible argument can be made that the direct initia-tive diminishes accountability. The Californian case raises the most concerns: there, the accumulation of laws passed through the initiative effectively curtails government choice. Governments are required by the virtue of initiative out-comes to allocate spending to a variety of specific purposes, and as a result they have very little discretion left in budgeting or establishing priorities. As Peter Schrag has persuasively argued, the limits placed on property taxes by Proposition 13 in California mean that "regardless of the demand for public services [and regardless of public opinion on the question]...budgets are [usu-ally] balanced with spending reductions, not revenue increases," with programs enjoying popular support being cut because of the restrictions that have been placed on the state's ability to raise revenue.[28] When the proliferation of initia-tive outcomes serves to paralyze the hand of government, the ability of voters to effectively hold public officials to account for public policy is undermined.

However, even in the case of the direct initiative, one can design processes to preserve some measure of accountability. Some states have "sunset" provisions that allow the legislature to amend laws passed by initiative after three to five years. Other states put restrictions on what issues can go to the ballot, with many excluding initiatives on spending measures. This guarantees that the legislature still has control over the budget process — a key element of an accountable gov-ernment. Thus, while the risks to accountability are much higher with the direct initiative than with other forms of referendum, even here rules can be put in place to prevent the worst excesses that characterize the California system.

Can voters make sensible decisions?

One major objection to the use of the referendum is that voters are not up to the task of making sensible decisions on policy issues. Some suggest that voters quite simply are not knowledgeable enough or are too busy to think about policy issues in detail. In our view, this is a legitimate concern and to raise the issue is not evi-dence of an anti-democratic bias. The demands of decision-making in a complex society may indeed be too high for those who do not have time to immerse themselves in policy on an ongoing basis. This criticism must be adequately addressed before one can responsibly endorse the wider use of referendums.

All of the available evidence suggests that voters make "reasonable" decisions during referendum campaigns, that is, decisions that — as far as possible given the range of options presented to them — are consistent with their underlying preferences, values, and interests. This does not mean that all voters know all the details about the issues in front of them. Instead, most voters rely on a variety of short-cuts when casting their vote, taking into account:

- the positions of party leaders and interest groups whom they trust
- the current economic situation, resisting change during poor economic times, particularly if it involves new spending
- the motivations of the individual or group who sponsored the measure;
- their general ideological or value orientation
- their own self-interest
- their degree of uncertainty about the issue at hand, tending to vote "no" when unsure[29]

Taken together, these short-cuts enable voters to take decisions that are generally sensible, in that they are consistent with their underlying preferences and values.

This of course does not mean that the decisions made directly by voters will be the "right" or "best" ones, judged by whatever academic standard one cares to employ. But neither will be those taken by governments. It is no more legitimate to condemn referendums because voters might make the "wrong" choice than it is to condemn elections because voters might elect the "wrong" party. What we can ask is whether or not voters are able to make decisions that accurately reflect their general values, or whether on the contrary referendums so befuddle them that they end up voting differently than they would have if given more time to study the question. The evidence suggests that such befuddling does not regularly occur.[30]

That said, it is possible to identify those institutional arrangements that establish the conditions that make it easier for voters to make good choices. Four factors contribute to voter competence: (1) having time to devote to thinking about the issue; (2) receiving information about the issue; (3) having opportunities to discuss the issue; and (4) receiving cues about where prominent groups, parties and individuals stand on the issue.

The amount of time that voters have to focus on an issue will be affected by the number of questions on the ballot, as well as by whether or not the referendum is being held at the same time as an election. If there are many questions, most will receive inadequate attention from voters; and if the vote is held at the same time as the election, voters' ability to focus either on the election or the referendum question will suffer. Rules restricting the number of questions that can be placed on the ballot are therefore appropriate to facilitate sensible decision-making by voters.

Second, voters require adequate information, and to this end one should seek to maximize the availability of differing points of view through the mass media. The concern, however, is that the side with greater financial resources could monopolize the airways. For this reason we favour regulations designed to ensure that different sides in a referendum campaign can gain a public hearing. This means the provision of free air time. And the regulatory body overseeing elections, in negotiation with the key figures in the campaign, should send out information packages to all households, which would include factual information, arguments advanced by all sides, the position of prominent individuals and groups, and the source of funding (if applicable) for the competing sides.

Third, in order to foster public discussion we endorse regulations that encourage the creation of public forums — accessible public spaces where voters can hear and respond to the arguments advanced by both sides in a referendum campaign, and where both sides are given an opportunity to debate with their opponents. This type of exchange adds to the deliberative character of the voter's decision-making process. Regulations could be put in place that ensure that at least one televised debate between campaign leaders be held during each referendum campaign and that there be television and Internet broadcasting of any parliamentary committee hearings that precede the referendum. We also advocate measures similar to the Danish law that provides public money to those organizing a public meeting on the issue at hand only if each side is equally represented at that meeting.

Fourth, it is important that voters receive adequate cues about the positions taken by prominent groups on referendum issues. As analysis of voting behaviour in the 1992 referendum on the Charlottetown constitutional accord has shown, the decisions of many voters were influenced not so much by their own assessment of the accord's merits, but by the positions taken on the accord by prominent figures.[31] Many of these cue-givers, however, may support or oppose a measure for reasons different from those in charge of the official "yes" or "no" campaigns. For this reason, it is important that third parties be permitted to spend money during campaigns to promote their distinct perspectives (although this spending should be subject to regulation). Otherwise, voters may miss receiving signals about where different interests stand. One study of the 1995 Quebec referendum found that cues from third parties — such as labour and business organizations, students, environmentalists and farmers' unions —

were conspicuously absent from press coverage.[32] Taken together, all of these measures will facilitate better decision-making in referendums by voters.

Does the referendum threaten minorities?

One of the main criticisms of direct democracy is that it is a tool that is used to undermine the status of minorities. The argument is that referendums allow the majority to bypass whatever checks and balances may constrain the legislature and to impose its will upon unpopular groups. The concern rests on the important principle that democracy is about far more than "majority rule" and liberal democratic societies now widely recognize that there must be limits on what the majority can do. Those who raise concerns about threats to minorities during referendums often point to a number of well-known examples from American states, where anti-gay rights ordinances and measures restricting minority language services have all passed by referendum. They have also pointed to the 2002 BC referendum on the process of negotiating treaties with the province's First Nations. In this case, British Columbians were asked to voice, by means of a postal ballot, their support of or opposition to eight principles that might guide the government in treaty negotiations. This alarmed many observers since the exercise seemed to imply that the extent to which the rights of First Nations peoples would be actualized in the form of treaties might somehow depend, not on constitutional principles, the directives of the courts, or the give-and-take of the negotiating teams, but rather on the goodwill of the non-Aboriginal majority.

In considering this aspect of direct democracy, it is important to distinguish among several separate concerns that are too often conflated. The first issue is whether referendums threaten minority rights; the second is whether they threaten the policy preferences of minority groups; and the third is whether they are likely to exacerbate divisions between distinct cultural groups in multicultural societies.

On the question of minority rights, referendums theoretically can harm rights in two ways: by allowing for the passage of measures that repeal or violate these rights, or by allowing for the defeat of measures that would see new rights entrenched. In practice, however, measures that violate constitutionally protected rights would be struck down by the courts, whether these measures were passed through a referendum or not. For this reason, referendums represent little threat to established rights. On the other hand, one could plausibly argue that a requirement that new rights be approved by referendum could make the entrenchment of expanded conceptions of rights more difficult.

Research from jurisdictions that allow for citizen-initiated referendums has produced somewhat contradictory findings. Barbara Gamble's study of the record in the US, for instance, leads her to argue that "the majority has indeed used [the citizen-initiated referendum] to deprive political minorities of their civil rights." She reviewed 78 citizen-initiated referendums on civil rights at the state and local levels and found that 78 percent of these "resulted in outcomes that constituted a defeat of minority interests."[33] But Shaun Bowler and Todd Donovan dispute the implication of her findings. They note that in practice many antiminority measures that receive media attention in the US fail to pass, or, if passed, are later struck down by the courts. Crucially, even when they do pass and withstand court challenges, it is not clear that the result differs from the policy that the legislature would have enacted in the absence of a popular vote. They argue that "it has not been empirically established that direct democracy necessarily produces outcomes that are decidedly more anti-minority than those produced by legislatures."[34]

Consider for example the expanded conceptions of rights for same-sex couples, rights that some have suggested might be difficult to win through a referendum. The fact is that the provision of state benefits for same-sex couples has been difficult to pass through the legislature as well. Even the NDP government of Bob Rae in Ontario was unable to pass such legislation, which was instead introduced only when the government of Mike Harris felt compelled to do so by the courts. Likewise, it is not at all clear whether parliamentarians or the public would be more likely to pass legislation in favour of same-sex marriage, and it is the courts that have driven this issue forward. Extending rights is difficult, whether by referendum or otherwise, and it is the courts that stand as the best protection for minorities.

It must also be remembered that referendums can be used to compel legislatures to extend protections or benefits to minority groups. In the United States, for example, many of the first states to extend the franchise to women did so through the means of the direct initiative. In the case of Denmark, the referendum has been frequently used to protect minority rights,[35] and in the case of Switzerland, one team of researchers has concluded that not only do voters tend to vote against antiminority propositions, but they tend to vote to broaden protections for civil rights.[36] The experiences of other countries caution against taking recent US experience as the most indicative.

The second issue of concern in regards to minorities is not that referendums will violate minority rights, but that they will target programs and services that benefit minority groups. It is claimed that while the legislative process can be structured to give minorities a voice in law-making (even if minority groups do not get everything they want), similar compromises and concessions may not characterize referendum voting. In considering this objection, one must first recall that it is a mistake to assume that the adoption of direct democracy introduces a threat to minorities where no such threat previously existed. The government of Ontario did not need a referendum to repeal affirmative action legislation in 1995, or to reduce assistance to the poor through a variety of measures; the same goes for the re-criminalization of aspects of homosexuality by the Thatcher government in the UK. We argue, therefore, that the question is not whether referendums can target minority groups — this is true of all decision-making devices — but whether there are ways to design the process in order to minimize the potential for majority tyranny and whether there are processes that can facilitate the integration of minority concerns into legislation.

Ideally, legislation in a representative democracy is the outcome of a process in which representatives weigh the concerns of their own supporters against a number of other concerns, including those brought forward by opponents, experts and public servants. While those with little economic clout can easily be shut out during this process, it is nonetheless true that minorities can sometimes secure some moderation or amendment to legislative proposals so as to accommodate their concerns. This is as it should be: it is inherently healthy in a democracy for majorities to negotiate with minorities in an attempt to find solutions acceptable to as broad a range of citizens as possible.

At first blush, the opposite appears to be the case with direct democracy: the process seems designed to allow the majority to make the law as it sees fit. Referendums also appear to force voters to offer a simple yes or no response, with no opportunity to make approval conditional on the incorporation of amendments designed to accommodate specific minority concerns. The status of minorities can therefore be threatened not because referendums explicitly target minorities, but because policy is now being made through a process in which there are fewer opportunities for minority concerns to be taken into account. The referendum process appears to be inherently more majoritarian and less deliberative than policy-making by representatives.

In our view, however, this is not an argument for forbidding referendums on contentious issues. Rather, it is an argument for designing the referendum process carefully, with a view to tempering its majoritarian dynamic. As we saw above, some referendum processes (notably the indirect initiative) require that the proposed measure be subject to public hearings prior to the vote, a step that allows minority groups a chance to engage the proposal's sponsors in debate. Furthermore, the legislature should be permitted to amend laws passed by popular vote, allowing laws that have unanticipated adverse effects to be changed without another referendum. These guidelines do not prevent majorities from passing laws that some will see as "targeting" minorities, but what they can do is minimize the possibility that majorities will act via the referendum impetuously, without giving others an adequate opportunity to raise concerns.

Third, in discussing the potential impact of direct democracy on minority groups, special consideration should be paid to the case of societies historically divided along religious, ethnic or linguistic lines into two or more constituent national or cultural communities. Typically such communities are unequal in size — in which case direct democracy poses a particular problem because the larger community could impose its will on the smaller one, overriding any tradition of cross-community accommodation that may have taken root among political leaders. This was one of the concerns voiced about the BC referendum on treaties. Even if it was conceded that the outcome could do nothing to weaken the status of constitutionally protected Aboriginal rights, some argued that the holding of the referendum would only serve to reinforce mistaken public views about the treaties, inflame opinions, and make the process of building cross-community understanding more difficult.

The question of how to avoid sowing the seeds of division compels us again to think about how the process should be designed. What safeguards can be put in place to minimize the risk that a referendum can be used by the majority community as a means of circumventing the need to take the interests of its minority counterpart into account? The most obvious is the stipulation that a "double" or "compound" majority be required in order for the referendum to pass. Double majorities are most appropriate in federal systems — as noted above, double majorities are required both in Australia and in Switzerland. In Canada, the compound majority threshold could be integrated into the process by requiring that voters in Quebec and some combination of other provinces must vote in favour of the question in order for it to pass. If this were done, the referendum could in fact provide greater protection to Canada's regions than does the standard legislative process, with governments often making decisions without significant support from all parts of the country. (With the possible exception of votes held at the local level, double-majority provisions may not be practical in the case of referendums affecting Aboriginal peoples in Canada, given that the Aboriginal population is small and geographically dispersed. Divisiveness in this case is best minimized by means of a number of other regulations discussed in this paper that are designed to make referendum processes more fair, deliberative and integrative.)

The insistence that referendums be structured in such a way as to limit their majoritarian character, however, might well clash with the very impetus behind the referendum itself. It needs to be acknowledged that some of the support for direct democracy in Canada stems from a dissatisfaction with the compromises reached among elites. Regulations requiring double majorities in effect reproduce these compromises as constraints on direct democracy. They also arguably undermine one of the main purposes of a referendum, which is to allow that majority to speak. Nevertheless, in designing the referendum process, a balance must be found between allowing the majority to make decisions and ensuring that the referendum is not used as a weapon by one community against the other. In our view, this balance could be achieved by ensuring that federal referendum legislation incorporate a compound majority provision, a provision that would encourage the building of pan-Canadian alliances on important questions and ensure that legislation can be passed directly by voters only when there is broad consensus.

While we have tried to outline how different rules can temper direct democracy's majoritarian character, it remains the case that referendums can be disruptive in certain contexts — namely when societies are deeply divided on an issue of fundamental importance. Does this mean, however, that referendums in such situations should always be avoided? This is far from clear. In some cases, the alternative to a referendum — the avoidance of the issue and the preservation of the status quo, or the striking of a bargain among elites without public endorsement — can be even more divisive. As André Blais has noted, tensions between Canada's two major linguistic communities have been kept manageable because of the use of referendums in Quebec (in 1980 and 1995), and the political situation might have been further improved had more referendums been held. For example, popular ratification (by double majority) of the 1982 constitutional package would have added legitimacy to the deal and, if it had passed in Quebec, might have prevented two decades of constitutional conflict.[37]

Another interesting case to consider is that of the 1942 Canadian referendum on conscription. The conventional chronicling of this episode blames the referendum itself for polarizing the country's two linguistic communities, focusing on how the vote enabled a national majority to excuse Prime Minister King from a promise he had made to the minority. Yet this interpretation does not consider that the government would likely have been compelled by the course of events to introduce conscription anyway, with or without a referendum. Moreover, Canadians were already deeply divided on the issue, and the referendum merely served to highlight — and not create — this division for the benefit of King, his ministers, and the country. By so doing, the referendum helped to reinforce King's predisposition towards a cautious approach to the imposition of conscription, and arguably contributed to his government's relatively effective management of the crisis.[38] Again, the lesson is that referendums are neither inherently divisive nor benign. Their effects are determined by the rules according to which they are conducted, the political circumstances in which they are held, and the motives and actions of the political actors that seek to make use of them.

Is the referendum process fair?

Even if one has a commitment in principle to direct democracy, one could still reject it as unworkable because it is not fair to all citizens. This concern stems most notably from the often unequal access to the funds necessary to wage a successful campaign. Some American scholars have expressed concern that "well-financed measures enjoy a significantly greater chance of winning than those that are poorly financed."[39] In Switzerland similar concerns have been occasionally raised, although the lack of spending restrictions has not led to a spiralling escalation of spending because it would be so out of place with the Swiss political culture. In the case of the UK, the parliamentary committee on standards in public life noted that "there is a serious risk of a gross imbalance in resources." As evidence, they point to the 1975 UK vote on membership in the European Community, when the "yes" side outspent the "no" side by a factor of 20 to one, and to the 1997 referendum on devolution in Wales. In the latter case, the committee observed that the campaign and spending were "very one-sided, with the last-minute No organisation seriously under-funded...and a fairer campaign might well have resulted in a different outcome."[40] These concerns about spending are real, but need qualification.

First, it is important that we not hold direct democracy to an unrealistic standard. The existing electoral and legislative process is not beyond reproach, and the unequal distribution of wealth in democratic societies creates advantages for those with resources regardless of whether decisions are made through representative or direct democracy.

One should also note that the record around the world is replete with cases of successful referendums championed by less-than-wealthy interests and failed campaigns launched by well-organized interests with ample resources. In the US in particular, broad-based coalitions — such as consumer groups or those concerned about a particular environmental question — have often been successful in using the initiative to further their agenda. In contrast, narrow industry groups that have turned to the initiative after failing to secure passage of measures through the legislative process have met with repeated defeat. Put simply, the group with the most money does not always win. (It should be underlined that in the US, high spending is often used successfully to defeat initiatives through the purchase of a great deal of advertising that serves to confuse voters and make them reluctant to risk change, but such spending is much less successful at securing the passage of initiatives.) In the case of government-initiated referendums on high-profile issues, financial resources are usually of distinctly secondary importance: individuals often have standing opinions on the question at hand, and the news media can be counted on to ensure that both sides receive extensive coverage. Furthermore, when coalitions of elites put forward referendum proposals, they are often defeated by underfunded grassroots coalitions.

Yet the case for imposing limits on campaign spending remains strong, not only because the amount of money spent has been identified as one important variable influencing outcomes, but for a variety of other reasons as well. First, many referendums, particularly government-initiated ones, concern issues of fundamental importance to the political community, such as the constitution, devolution, or international treaties, and any perception that the process is unfair has a direct effect on the esteem in which citizens hold the overall system of government. Second, unlike the ordinary legislative process, referendums hold out the promise that the public has a direct say in decision-making. Thus, to the extent that the perception takes root that only the wealthy have influence, an important part of the very purpose of the exercise is undermined. Third, and more generally, high-spending referendum campaigns have the potential to further erode public trust in the political process because of the way in which they play to the advantage of groups seeking to use the device for less than sincere purposes. For example, in some US states those with access to the necessary funds have been known to qualify questions for a vote knowing that they would most likely lose, doing so only in order to sap the financial resources of their poorer opponents. For example, in Colorado, an antitobacco initiative qualified for the ballot with the support of many in the medical profession. The tobacco industry responded by rapidly qualifying an initiative that would require insurance companies to pay for "alternative healers." Why? The tobacco industry reasoned that the medical profession would be forced to protect their own interests and divert their resources to fight against the alternative healers measure, thereby reducing the time and money available to support the antitobacco measure. Clearly, the regulation of spending is one of the most effective ways to limit the ability of interest groups to qualify measures in the absence of a genuine level of popular support for them.

We therefore support the imposition of controls on campaign spending (including spending on the signature gathering that might launch a citizen-initiated referendum), as was the case for the 1992 referendum on the Charlottetown Accord and the two Quebec referendums on sovereignty.[41] A discussion of which specific regulations are best is beyond the scope of this paper, but we contend that it is important that groups unaffiliated with the two sides be permitted to spend their own resources, subject to spending restrictions. We also think that some form of public funding for campaign committees should be considered, especially in cases where groups with little resources might otherwise be unable to defend their interests in a citizen-initiated referendum campaign launched by their more well-financed opponents. The UK parliamentary committee on standards in public life concluded that "if a referendum is to be fair...[it is] essential that both sides of the argument should be funded at least well enough to enable them to put their case before the voters."[42] Exactly how public funding would be allocated, and whether public funding to campaign organizations should be in the form of the provision of "core funding" to each side or should take another form, are technical questions that we will not consider in this paper. Finally, it is crucial to make it very clear who is funding referendum campaigns because this information provides an important cue to voters about what is at stake. Making the funding of campaigns transparent in this way often serves to undermine material advantages because voters can vote against big spending groups that they do not trust. Whatever the precise means adopted, these various practices related to campaign spending and the disclosure of the origin and size of campaign contributions would make the politics of referendums in Canada significantly different in character from that which is frequently witnessed in the United States. Finally, it almost goes without saying that the government should be prohibited from using the resources and agencies of the state to advocate on behalf of one side of the issue, although in the UK referendums of 1975 on the EEC, of 1997 on devolution, and of 1998 on the Good Friday peace accord, the government did just that.

The issue of fairness goes beyond campaign spending. Another important issue is the wording of the question. In the US, while the proponents of initiatives are permitted to phrase the question, the law requires that each question deal with a single issue. The final say on what constitutes a single issue is given to the courts.[43] Court intervention in referendums is far from unusual. In Italy, the courts must approve the question that goes before the public during abrogative initiatives. In 1998 in Portugal, the Supreme Court ruled that the government's proposed referendum question on the European Union was insufficiently clear to be asked.[44] Most US states do not allow the initiative's proponents to write the summary description or title of their propositions, both of which are left to public servants, preventing voters from being overtly misled by the title or the summary. Similar provisions should be replicated in Canada, should the initiative be adopted here.[45]

As mentioned above, there should also be rigid restrictions on the number of questions that can be placed before voters at any give time. This can be accomplished by setting the threshold for signature collection at a high enough level to deter all but the highest profile issues from qualifying for the ballot. The relative ease with which measures can be qualified in Switzerland has meant that a single election cycle can feature numerous ballot questions, many of which are highly technical. An electorate faced with a large number of questions is easily overwhelmed. Many voters feel that they are faced with too many decisions and do not have sufficient time to find out about the issues.[46] In such circumstances, many respond by voting "no" or by not voting at all. The bottom line is that the electorate's ability to exercise reasoned control of the law-making process is undermined when faced with too many issues.

There is also the question of whether the governing party should have a free hand in writing the question in the case of government-initiated referendums — an issue of particular interest to Canadians in light of concern over the government-designed questions used in previous Quebec referendums on sovereignty. Government-initiated referendums give the ruling party a great deal of power, including the final say in terms of when to call a vote, on what issue, and what question to submit to the public. The government's decisions naturally are taken to maximize its advantage in the ensuing campaign. This is inescapable and few governments would be willing to call a referendum unless they retained control over key elements of the process. However, subtle differences in the wording of a question can be important, and in a close campaign, the wording alone can make all the difference. The question then arises: without removing the government's prerogative to write the question, can anything be done to enhance the fairness and credibility of the process?

One option would be to require that the question be approved either by the official opposition or by a vote of two-thirds of the legislature, though in such cases the effect would be to allow the opposition to veto a referendum question which the government wanted to ask. Another option would be to allow the opposition to place an alternative question on the ballot in the event that they object strenuously to the one the government has chosen. Such processes are not unheard of: in Switzerland, the government often places a "counterproposal" on the ballot next to the citizen-initiated question, and in 1993 a referendum took place on the subject of the status of Puerto Rico in which the contending parties were each allowed to word their preferred option and have it placed on the ballot.[47] In Quebec, it is possible that the presence of two questions could lead to an interesting result: simultaneous majorities for sovereignty and federalism.[48] The right of both the government and the official opposition to place their preferred question on the ballot is one option worthy of serious consideration.

An alternative is to require televised public legislative hearings on the subject of the question itself before it is written by the government. In effect, this means that the question text would become a subject of public debate well before the campaign begins. In any future referendum on Quebec sovereignty, this would mean the government would announce its intention to hold a referendum on the subject and then seek public input and debate on what question wording would be most clear and fair. This contrasts with the existing practice, whereby the question is written secretly by the government with the goal of advancing its own strategic objectives. In the case of the federal legislation currently governing the conduct of referendums in Canada, it is notable that, while the law stipulates that the question must be debated by parliament, the time for debate is limited, and there is no provision for the question to be examined by a parliamentary committee either before or after its wording is finalized.[49] Hearings on the question itself would provide interested groups with an opportunity to voice their concerns regarding clarity and fairness. Issues relating to the meaning and implications of different types of questions can come to the fore in the course of public hearings. We argue that this public airing of views and concerns would make it more difficult for a government to ask an overtly ambiguous question.

Any of these measures would have resulted in a more meaningful consultation on the treaty process in BC than that which was in fact conducted in 2002. Public hearings on the questions prior to the vote, for instance, would have shone the spotlight on the misleading nature of some of the statements appearing on the final ballot, raising the public's awareness of the way in which the exercise was designed more to cater to the prejudices of the government's core supporters than to engage citizens in meaningful deliberation about an issue crucial to the public's future. Had a compromise ballot been produced in cooperation with the official opposition in the legislature or even with First Nations organizations, the process would have been more educational (for all sides) and more productive. As in our Quebec example, such a scenario may have produced contradictory results — majorities in favour of propositions that policy experts might deem irreconcilable — but this is surely a more constructive outcome than the engineering of a clear majority in favour of a series of one-sided and overly simple propositions.

Does direct democracy empower voters?

One of the fundamental theoretical justifications for the referendum is that it empowers citizens. But in practice this is only partly true. While both government-initiated referendums and obligatory referendums give voters the power to veto proposed changes, the ability to initiate change remains in the hands of the government. Furthermore, governments often choose to use these referendums in order to advance their own strategic objectives and not because they genuinely wish to give the public a more direct role in decision-making.

In the case of the abrogative and the indirect initiatives, however, citizens clearly have a greater role to play since it is they who initiate the process. At the same time, elected representatives remain front and centre: these referendums provide an effective means through which voters can engage with parliamentarians, rather than bypass them. In our view, these forms of the referendum offer a balance between the need to increase voters' influence on the political agenda and the need to sustain the important organizational, accountability and integrative functions performed by elected officials.

On the surface, the direct initiative seems to go further in satisfying the proponents of direct democracy by transferring power to citizens. Such an assessment is somewhat misleading. In the case of the US, at least, the degree to which the public is empowered is questionable. While the impetus for the spread of direct democracy has been the public's demand for a means to ensure that its views prevail over the more narrow interests of powerful groups and individuals, today the direct initiative can produce the opposite result: powerful but narrowly-based interests make use of the device to defeat propositions that arguably have a broad base of support. They do so by raising strong enough doubts in the minds of voters to incline a majority to shy away from change.

Thus, in many US states, the direct initiative has become a device that is more often than not deployed strategically by rival parties and interest groups to advance their own narrowly-based interest. The professionalization of every aspect of the process has served to ensure that the gap between the ideal of direct democracy and its practice in these US states has become almost unbridgeable. The implication is that an "open" process with little direct control by political parties does not guarantee that voters will be empowered; in fact, it is the presence of appropriate regulations and the maintenance of an important if circumscribed role for parties that increases public influence over policy.

Of course, the experience with the direct initiative in Switzerland is very different from that of the United States. One reason for this is that the initiative is integrated into the unique Swiss process of government — a process that we noted has been described as "negotiated direct democracy." This means that the initiative operates within a distinct political culture that is both more deliberative and less majoritarian than that of the US or Canada. For this reason, one should be wary of concluding that the Swiss experience with the direct initiative could be easily replicated elsewhere.

Recommendations

Does Canada need more direct democracy? Would the holding of more referendums on a wider range of topics make a constructive contribution to the political life of the country? We say that it would. Between elections, Canadians often feel shut out of the political decision-making process. The extent to which the executive, and particularly the prime minister and closest advisors, exercise tight control over the legislative agenda is exceptionally high in Canada.[50] In Canada, the power of the executive is not tempered by an elected or effective senate, as in Australia; by the formal separation of the legislature from the executive, as in the US; by a strong system of legislative committees, as in Germany; by widespread public consultations, as in Switzerland; or by a tradition of independence among individual legislators, as in the UK. Thus, while the governing party may be sensitive to public opinion, there remain fewer opportunities in Canada than elsewhere for those outside of the prime minister's inner circle — be they lesser ministers, backbenchers, opposition parties or citizens themselves — to influence public policy. There are few reliable mechanisms for transmitting public concerns to the government and having them reflected in decision-making, which is damaging to the quality of democratic life. We therefore endorse the referendum as one possible reform that can help redress this situation. However, this does not mean that any type of direct democracy is advisable. Some forms of direct democracy are compatible with Canadian political values, while some are not.

Government-initiated referendums

We recommend that governments use the referendum more frequently, particularly when they are in fact uncertain or divided on an issue, and so genuinely seeking the guidance of voters (as was the case, for example, in the May 2001 referendum in New Brunswick on the use of video lottery terminals). When the purpose of a referendum is to consult the population and not just to cajole them into giving their approval, it can be used both more creatively and to greater effect. If the government is prepared to remain neutral during the campaign, its own credibility is not linked to a given outcome and the stakes of the referendum for the parties are not necessarily high. Furthermore, the outcome of the vote is less likely to be tied to the popularity of the government launching the referendum and more likely to reflect citizens' views on the substance of the issue at hand. If the government were genuinely uncertain about its preferred path, it might be inclined to allow for more public input: the referendum, for example, could be preceded by a period of consultation in the form of parliamentary committees soliciting advice on the range of options to consider and, eventually, the precise wording of the question that should be asked. With the major political parties not compelled to adopt the rigid roles of leaders of "yes" and "no" options, legislators and parties could cooperate in the development of alternatives and by so doing show themselves to be relevant actors in the policy-making process. The referendum itself would not have to offer a single, final, yes-or-no choice: on rare occasions on particularly important issues, multiple ballots could be used over a period of time, with earlier ballots offering voters more than two options from which to choose. Governments often face important issues on which they have no clear opinion or are divided internally, and we suggest that one source of guidance in such circumstances is the public itself.

It is important that the public not come into the process only at the final stage, to say yes or no to a question that it did not write, on an issue that it may not have wished to discuss. On some issues, the referendum should be part of a larger process of public dialogue. A perfect example is the citizens assembly on electoral reform currently underway in British Columbia. It is the assembly, and not the government, that will write the option to be put to a referendum in that province in 2005, and it will do so only after engaging in an innovative process of consultation and deliberation. Clearly such a process could be used only occasionally, but when faced with important choices, governments, through the use of commissions, could choose to facilitate conversation rather than advocate on behalf of one position. By so doing, the referendum and consultation process could provide citizens with a more genuine say in government.

Obligatory constitutional referendums
The argument for using the referendum in the case of constitutional amendments is strong: the government has an obligation to seek the consent of the people when proposing to change the rules that govern the exercise of political power. However, in the wake of the Charlottetown Accord, it is clear that referendums on major constitutional changes in Canada are likely to prove very difficult. To merely formalize the convention that referendums be used for major amendments does nothing to facilitate and improve the process of constitutional change. The difficulty in Canada is that the amending formula for major change is exceptionally onerous. This is not something that will be easy to alter and so one must look to processes that can help facilitate consensus building.

Focusing on an all-or-nothing vote as the final stage in the process of constitutional amendment seems misplaced. Instead, greater attention should be paid to maximizing public input in the earlier stages of constitutional discussions, before the terms of amendment have been finalized. One form this might take is a "people's convention," along the lines of that used in Australia on the question of replacing the Queen as head of state or, again, a citizens assembly such as the one now active in BC. Such a consultative exercise should not be confused with the ones that preceded the Charlottetown Accord, including the Spicer Commission. There is a great deal of difference between processes that allow only for the public airing of grievances, and processes explicitly invested with the authority to debate issues, work through problems, and issue recommendations on the content of the proposal and the question to be submitted to a referendum. When a public body knows that it is actually integrated into the decision-making process, it is more likely to adopt a thoughtful and integrative approach. The Australian process itself was not without its problems, but it did serve to focus choices, interest the public, and contribute to more informed decision-making.

We recognize that changes to Canada's constitutional amending formula are unlikely. Bearing this in mind, we suggest that the process for initiating and debating constitutional amendments be formalized. We do not insist that the use of the referendum become legally obligatory, but do suggest that if a referendum is to be used, it be preceded by a people's convention. This convention would be charged with formulating the precise proposal and drafting the referendum question — hence issuing a recommendation to the population for popular approval. The convention should be made up of appointed delegates and delegates elected specifically to participate in the convention. These suggestions are designed to facilitate the integration of Canada's diverse communities, promote the brokerage of competing interests in a more public way, and as a result facilitate the passage of amendments.[51] The use of such conventions would decouple the issue at hand from the popularity of the governing party. When the governing party itself sponsors the referendum and establishes the terms of debate, it becomes difficult for unpopular governments to secure victory in a referendum, even when the proposal is one that the population might otherwise support.

Obligatory referendums on other policy matters

Some governments of late have proposed that certain policies — notably tax increases — should be prohibited unless first approved by referendum. This would not constitute what we term a sincere use of the referendum. Such proposals are far more concerned with the tactical use of referendums to entrench one ideological agenda rather than with any genuine commitment to the enhancement of popular control over government. The use of the referendum in this way would not allow the public to choose between competing policy options — such as tax increases versus cuts to spending on health care — but would simply make it more difficult for future governments to reverse the policies of their predecessors. In fact, requiring referendums on some measures of ordinary policy-making but not others steals control away from the public: the referendum requirement means that some options are more difficult for governments to pursue. The result is that governments will be more likely to choose the easier course of action, even if it is not the choice the public would prefer.

By proposing the expansion of direct democracy in such a crass way, one may end up deepening rather than redressing the public's distrust of government. The public opinion data collected by the IRPP and presented in figure 1 indicate that the population generally recognizes that it is the government's responsibility to make important budgeting decisions: while the majority say that referendums on tax increases and cuts to social spending should be held at least sometimes, fewer than 30 percent say they should always be held. Moreover, the number supporting referendums in each of the two cases is remarkably similar, suggesting that the population does not want to place some budgeting decisions in a special category while leaving others to the ordinary political process.

The citizen-initiated referendum

We endorse the use of referendums as a means of enhancing public participation in politics and of enabling citizens to exert a more direct influence over the direction of public policy. For this reason, we believe that in addition to government-initiated referendums, citizens themselves should have the opportunity to place issues on the political agenda and bring them to a vote. However, we do not support the adoption in Canada of the direct initiative. Our reasons:

- Of all the types of referendum, it is the most majoritarian: measures can be passed by a narrow majority of voters without requiring that they first be made the subject of a process of dialogue or bargaining among different groups that might lead to the development of compromises.
- For the same reasons, it is the least likely variant to promote the type of deliberation that is a necessary prerequisite of good decision-making. Direct initiative proposals are drafted in private by narrowly-based groups, and much of the debate about the measures takes the form of competing TV ads.
- It poses the greatest threat to the principle of governmental accountability, since parliament is likely to be constrained by measures passed without its input and that it might not be able to amend or repeal

For these reasons we argue that the direct initiative is not compatible with the better traditions of Canadian liberal democracy, especially those related to the search for accommodation among different groups. While it is true that Switzerland has successfully used the direct initiative consistent with these traditions, the Swiss case is *sui generis*: its direct initiative works only in the context of other elements within its political system.

As we have noted, the indirect initiative offers a viable alternative. What is crucial to the indirect initiative are those things which take place between the launching of the initiative and the referendum vote — namely, the submission of the proposal for consideration by parliamentary committee, the ensuing opportunities for the proposal to be amended, and the option for the government to enact a measure in response. (In the case of New Zealand, what is important are the activities that occur after a successful popular vote but before the adoption of legislation, activities which mirror the ordinary legislative process.[52]) In contrast to the direct initiative, then, the indirect initiative is embedded in a process that is both deliberative and integrative. It is conducive to the maintenance of accountability, in that governments and parties must take some responsibility for the proposals put to voters, or, in the case of New Zealand, the legislation eventually adopted.

There are a number of technical questions to consider. For example, how easy should it be to get a question on the ballot? This is affected by three factors: the number of petition signatures required for a measure to qualify, whether a minimum number of signatures needs to be collected within specific geographic areas, and the length of time permitted for the collection of signatures. We argue that these thresholds should be set high enough to ensure that only those few initiatives with a broad base of support can qualify.[53] Most importantly, the rules should require that initiatives have some support in all areas of the country. There is also the question of whether, once put to the vote, an initiative must win a double majority in order to pass. We argue that, as in other federations such as Australia and Switzerland, measures should be required to pass in a minimum number of provinces, including the province of Quebec. Taken together, these requirements will mean that only groups with a broad base of national support will be able to effectively launch petition drives. These broadly based national groups would include political parties. Because of parties' organizational resources, we believe that the initiative could turn out to be the parties' best friend, revitalizing their policy-making role and providing opposition parties with an opportunity to play a constructive role in government.

Imaginative uses of the referendum

Regardless of the type of referendum used or the issue at hand, the range of options available to government is far wider than usually thought. We typically think about referendums as a one-shot, all-or-nothing contest. But this is not the only possible arrangement. In fact, in other jurisdictions, referendums have been used far more imaginatively. Referendums can be used creatively in a variety of ways to help manage conflicts, alleviate tensions, settle issues, and enhance the legitimacy of political decisions.

In the first instance, the use of nonbinding advisory plebiscites should be considered. Canadians are perfectly capable of helping governments set priorities and choose among alternative courses of action. In our view, they are less willing than they once were to simply await the outcome of cabinet meetings to discover whether taxes will fall or the Canada Health and Social Transfer (CHST) will be increased. Plebiscites that asked Canadian voters to weigh the options of tax cuts, social spending and debt reduction are feasible and consistent with their political abilities. Using the referendum in this manner would allow for meaningful public input into policy-making while retaining for governments their leadership and decision-making responsibilities.

A second option is to have more than one referendum on the same issue. This does not mean bringing the same issue to the population over and over again in the hopes of achieving a desired result, as has occurred in Quebec with the issue of sovereignty and in Denmark with the issue of the European Union. Rather, it means involving voters in a genuine dialogue with their representatives. By means of a series of direct consultations, for instance, voters can become involved in the process of revising successive drafts of important pieces of legislation; at each stage, certain amendments could be approved and others discarded. At the end of the process, voters would be able to pronounce upon a text that they had had a direct hand in creating. This is not too different from the process that was used in Newfoundland to secure its entry into confederation — a process that included two sequential votes, with the first vote having multiple options on the ballot. The process that led to the creation of the new canton of Jura in Switzerland was even more complex, featuring a series of referendums, through which the canton of Bern approved the right in principle for Jura to secede and form its own canton, the people of Jura voted to secede, regions within Jura voted on whether to stay in Bern or join the new canton, and the people of Switzerland voted to accept the new canton, the constitution of which was written by a popularly elected constituent assembly.[54] What is instructive in this case is the way that the use of multiple referendums was combined with deliberative forums in an ongoing decision-making process, with the public consulted formally at various stages of the process to give their assent. Such an elaborate form of consultation could only be used sparingly — by no means do we believe that Canadians want to be bombarded with a never-ending series of cascading referendums. Nor do we believe that this would lead to good policy. But on key issues such as changing the electoral system or Senate reform, they could be highly appropriate.

Conclusion

Whatever the form of referendum used, the process should be governed by the different regulations that we have highlighted throughout this paper, including restrictions on campaign spending and disclosure of the sources of funding, the provision of free broadcast time and the distribution of information to voters by the nonpartisan agency governing the vote, the use of parliamentary committees to facilitate public debate about the choice of the question, strict limits on the number of questions that can be placed before voters at any one time, and the requirement that referendums pass by a double majority that accords regional vetoes. Taken together, these measures would serve to ensure that the referendum process is as deliberative as possible, that its majoritarian nature is tempered by adequate integrative measures, that it is as fair as possible, and that it does not displace parties or parliament from their central role in political decision-making. We argue that the types of referendum we have recommended, when combined with these rules, can lead to a form of direct democracy that is compatible with the essential values of Canadian democracy. Such a process would provide citizens with greater opportunities for participation in decision-making and with more direct influence over public policy, without undermining the practice of responsible and accountable government, allowing the process to be captured by narrow interest groups, or facilitating majority tyranny. Importantly, it would make legislation on important questions more sensitive to and representative of the views of the public, something we should value in a democracy.

Our argument has been that the enhancement of democracy requires much more than an increase in the number of opportunities for citizens to vote, though this is one part of the picture. It requires an increase in the opportunities for citizens to participate in political deliberation: to engage each other and their elected representatives in a meaningful conversation in which not only the political executive, but also parliamentarians, interest groups and the general public have a meaningful say in decision-making. The increased use of direct democracy, properly structured, can help in achieving this goal.

Notes

This paper stems in part from an international conference on referendums funded by the Donner Canada Foundation. The authors would like to acknowledge the Foundation's support. The authors also thank André Blais, Richard Johnston, Hugh Segal, Paul Howe and Simon Hug for their very helpful comments on a previous draft of this manuscript.

1. There are many different types of referendum. In this paper we will be drawing attention to these differences as the need dictates, though we will use the general term "referendum" to refer to all of them. This paper will not deal with the mechanism of recall, whereby an elected representative can be unseated by means of a citizen-initiated vote in her or his constituency. We exclude it from our discussion because its use raises issues that are significantly different from those raised by the referendum. We would like to stress that we believe the circus that was the 2003 California gubernatorial recall election has absolutely zero relevance for a serious discussion of whether to introduce the use of the referendum in Canada.

2. Laurence Morel, "The Rise of Government-Initiated Referendums in Consolidated Democracies," in Matthew Mendelsohn and Andrew Parkin (eds.), *Referendum Democracy: Citizens, Elites, and Deliberation in Referendum Campaigns* (London: Palgrave, 2001).

3. For instance, in the US there were a total of 323 state-wide initiatives between 1991 and 1998, compared with 276 in the 1980s, which itself was very high compared to previous decades. See Steven Craig, Amie Kreppel and James G. Kane, "Public Opinion and Support for Direct Democracy: A Grassroots Perspective," in Matthew Mendelsohn and Andrew Parkin (eds.), *Referendum Democracy: Citizens, Elites, and Deliberation in Referendum Campaigns* (London: Palgrave, 2001).

4. We do not examine the reasons for this increase, but we do take as a given that an important shift in political attitudes has taken place, the effect of which has been to make citizens more confident in their own ability to make key policy decisions and less confident in the ability of their elected representatives to do so on their behalf.

5. For a full history of the referendum in Canada, see Patrick Boyer, *Direct Democracy in Canada: The History and Future of Referendums* (Toronto: Dundurn Press, 1992), chaps. 2 and 3.

6. Judy Rebick, *Imagining Democracy* (Toronto: Stoddart, 2000), pp. 91-104.

7. Canadian Alliance, *A Time for Change: An Agenda of Respect for all Canadians* (1st ed., October 2000), p. 20.

8. The policy platform of the Reform Party, the Alliance's predecessor, was more detailed. The Reform Party called for binding national referendums on the issues of capital punishment and abortion, and also stated that the government "should not be permitted to run a deficit or to raise tax levels unless authorized by a national referendum." In the case of changes to the constitution, the party supported a new amending process that would "replace the ratification power of Parliament and the provincial legislatures with that of the people, as expressed in binding referenda." Finally, the party supported the idea that citizens should be able to "initiate binding referenda on new legislation and constitutional amendments." See Reform Party of Canada, "Principles and Policies," 31 August 1998, at *www.reform.ca/bluebook/* (this Web site is no longer available).

9. This objection would only be valid if efforts were made to make referendum results binding on governments and the Crown in such a way that the legislature itself was bypassed altogether, or the prerogatives of the governor general (however theoretical they may be) were abrogated. But this is not what is generally meant by a "binding" referendum in the Canadian context. It is true that Manitoba's *Initiative and Referendum Act*, passed in 1916, was overturned by the courts precisely because it was held to unduly constrain the powers of the lieutenant governor (the act stipulated that a measure passed by voters would become law, without requiring that it receive royal assent). But current proposals for direct democracy in Canada generally do not propose to do away with the need for royal assent, nor would it be necessary to do so (see Boyer, *Direct Democracy in Canada*, p. 89). Rather, a referendum can be understood as binding in the sense that the government of the day commits itself to following the results of the popular vote, and there is nothing in law or convention that prevents a government from doing so.

10. This criticism of the referendum device was made in an earlier context by Richard Cashin. See his comment in Citizens' Forum on Canada's Future, *Report to the People and Government of Canada* (Ottawa: Minister of Supply and Services, 1991), p. 141.

11. Centre for Research and Information on Canada (CRIC), "Portraits of Canada 2000," surveys conducted in October 2000 by Environics and CROP ($N = 2,019$). The survey is available on the Web sites of CRIC, at www.cric.ca, and of the Canadian Opinion Research Archive at Queen's University, at www.queensu.ca/cora

12. It was the issue of abortion that caused respondents the greatest reservations, again highlighting the wise strategic choices of parties during the election campaign to use this issue to criticize the Alliance's position.

13. See Tim Mowrey and Alain Pelletier, "Referendums in Canada: A Comparative Overview," *Electoral Insight*, Vol. 3, no. 1 (January 2001), p. 19. Available on the Web site of Elections Canada at *http://www.elections.ca*

14. Arthur Lupia and Richard Johnston, "Are Voters to Blame? Voter Competence and Elite Maneuvers," in Matthew Mendelsohn and Andrew Parkin (eds.), *Referendum Democracy: Citizens, Elites, and Deliberation in Referendum Campaigns* (London: Palgrave, 2001).

15. The classic text on the initiative in the United States is quite critical: David Magleby, *Direct Legislation: Voting on Ballot Propositions in the United States* (Baltimore: Johns Hopkins University Press, 1984). For a more favourable view of the initiative, see Thomas Cronin, *Direct Democracy: The Politics of Initiative, Referendum and Recall* (Cambridge: Harvard University Press, 1989).

16. Shaun Bowler, Todd Donovan and Caroline J. Tolbert (eds.), *Citizens as Legislators: Direct Democracy in the United States* (Columbus: Ohio State University Press, 1998).

17. Elisabeth Gerber, *The Populist Paradox: Interest Group Influence and the Promise of Direct Legislation* (Princeton: Princeton University Press, 1999).

18. Peter Schrag, *Paradise Lost: California's Experience, America's Future* (Berkeley: University of California Press, 1999).

19. Pier Vincenzo Uleri, "Italy: Referendums and Initiatives from the Origins to the Crisis of a Democratic Regime," in M. Gallagher and P.V. Uleri (eds.), *The Referendum Experience in Europe* (London: Macmillan Press, 1996). pp. 106-25.

20. Alexander H. Trechsel and Hanspeter Kriesi, "Switzerland: The Referendum and Initiative as a Centrepiece of the Political System," in Michael Gallagher and Pier Vincenzo Uleri (eds.), *The Referendum Experience in Europe* (London: Macmillan Press, 1996).

21. Wolf Linder, *Swiss Democracy: Possible Solutions to Conflict in Multicultural Societies* (New York: St. Martin's Press, 1994), p. 100.

22. Trechsel and Kriesi, "Switzerland," p. 192.

23. Jurg Steiner, *Amicable Agreement Versus Majority Rule: Conflict Resolution in Switzerland* (Chapel Hill, NC: University of North Carolina Press, 1974).

24. Brian Galligan, "Amending Constitutions Through the Referendum Device," in Matthew Mendelsohn and Andrew Parkin (eds.), *Referendum Democracy: Citzens, Elites, and Deliberation in Referendum Campaigns* (London: Palgrave, 2001).

25. Galligan, "Amending Constitutions."

26. See, for example, Ian Budge, "Political Parties in Direct Democracy," in Mendelsohn and Parkin (eds.), *Referendum Democracy.*

27. See Elizabeth Gerber and Simon Hug, "Legislative Response to Direct Legislation," in Mendelsohn and Parkin (eds.), *Referendum Democracy.*

28. Schrag, *Paradise Lost*, pp. 21, 65.

29. These conclusions benefit from the findings of Shaun Bowler and Todd Donovan, *Demanding Choices: Opinion and Voting in Direct Democracy* (Ann Arbor: University of Michigan Press, 1998); and of Arthur Lupia, "Shortcuts versus Encyclopedias: Information and Voting Behavior in California Insurance Reform Elections," *American Political Science Review*, Vol. 88, no. 1 (March 1994), pp. 63-76.

30. See, for example, Bowler and Donovan, *Demanding Choices.*

31. Richard Johnston, André Blais, Neil Nevitte, and Elisabeth Gidengil, *The Challenge of Direct Democracy* (Montreal and Kingston: McGill-Queen's University Press, 1996).

32. Richard Jenkins and Matthew Mendelsohn, "The News Media and Referendums," in Mendelsohn and Parkin (eds.), *Referendum Democracy.*

33. Barbara S. Gamble, "Putting Civil Rights to a Popular Vote," *American Journal of Political Science*, Vol. 41, no. 1 (January 1997), pp. 246, 254, 262.

34. Shaun Bowler and Todd Donovan, "Popular Control of Referendum Agendas: Implications for Democratic Outcomes and Minority Rights," in Mendelsohn and Parkin (eds.), *Referendum Democracy*.

35. Palle Svensson, "Denmark: The Referendum as Minority Protection," in Michael Gallagher and Pier Vincenzo Uleri, *The Referendum Experience in Europe* (London: Macmillan, 1996).

36. Bruno S. Frey and Lorenz Goette, "Does The Popular Vote Destroy Civil Rights?", *American Journal of Political Science*, Vol. 42, no. 4 (October 1998), p. 1343.

37. André Blais, comments delivered at the conference "Maturity or Malaise? The Growing Use of Referendums in Liberal-Democratic Societies," held at Queen's University, Kingston, May 1999.

38. See J.L. Granatstein and J.M. Hitsman, *Broken Promises: A History of Conscription in Canada* (Toronto: Oxford University Press, 1977).

39. Cronin, *Direct Democracy*, p. 215.

40. Committee on Standards in Public Life (United Kingdom), *Standards in Public Life: The Funding of Political Parties in the United Kingdom. Volume 1: Report and Appendices* (The Stationery Office, October 1998), paragraphs 12.45; 12.32. Available at: *http://www.official-documents. co.uk/document/cm40/4057/contents.htm/volume-1/ volume-1.pdf*.

41. For a review of the rules governing the conduct of these referendums, see Mowrey and Pelletier, "Referendums in Canada."

42. *Standards in Public Life*, paragraph 12.31.

43. The question of how one interprets what constitutes a "single issue" is often the subject of debate, and different state courts interpret the provision in different ways (see Daniel Hays Lowenstein, "California Initiatives and the Single-Subject Rule," *UCLA Law Review*, Vol. 30, no. 5 (June 1983), pp. 936-75).

44. The proposed question was: "Do you agree with the continuing participation of Portugal in the construction of a European Union within the framework of the treaty of Amsterdam?" Translation courtesy of Simon Hug.

45. Note that the existing legislation governing citizen-initiated referendums in Saskatchewan allows the government to submit the citizens' proposal to the courts in order for its wording to be clarified. See Mowrey and Pelletier, "Referendums in Canada," p. 19.

46. Steven Craig et al., "Public Opinion and Support for Direct Democracy."

47. We are grateful to Lawrence LeDuc for bringing this case to our attention.

48. Such a result would create confusion, but nonetheless it would be a truer reflection of the public's preferences than either a "yes" or a "no" answer to a single option. Arguably, the result would be constructive: since a good number of voters would have shown themselves to be supportive of both options, it would be harder for politicians to divide the Quebec electorate into two great hostile camps. In any event, any political crisis unleashed after such a scenario would be less severe than the one that would follow a narrow "yes" vote to sovereignty (presuming many sovereignist voters remained committed to their province remaining a part of Canada, as is currently the case).

49. See Boyer, *Direct Democracy in Canada*, appendix 2.

50. Donald J. Savoie, *Governing from the Centre: The Concentration of Power in Canadian Politics* (Toronto: University of Toronto Press, 1999).

51. Matthew Mendelsohn, "Public Brokerage: Constitutional Reform and the Accommodation of Mass Publics," *Canadian Journal of Political Science*, Vol. 33, no. 2 (June 2000), pp. 245-72.

52. We recommend that the referendum vote be held only after the measure has been considered by Parliament and legislation drafted — as is the case in Massachusetts, but not in New Zealand.

53. In the case of the existing legislation in the provinces of British Columbia and Saskatchewan, the thresholds are set too high (10 percent and 15 percent, respectively), making it very difficult for any measure to qualify. Without making it so onerous, we believe that the number of required signatures should be relatively high (about 8 percent of the electors in the previous election), the time period for collecting these signatures should be comparatively short (150 to 180 days), and there should be geographic requirements that guarantee that the measure has some support in all regions of the country (the signatures of perhaps three percent of electors in each province should be required).

54. For more details, see Linder, *Swiss Democracy*, pp. 65-68.

Notes on Contributors

David Beatty is a legal commentator on human rights and constitutional and labour law. He is the author of *The Ultimate Rule of Law* (Oxford University Press, 2004).

Jerome H. Black teaches political science at McGill University. Over the years, he has published in the areas of women and politics, the political participation and representation of ethno-racial minorities, Canadian immigration and refugee policy, strategic voting, voter turnout and voter registration.

André Blais is a professor in the political science department at Université de Montréal, a researcher at the Centre interuniversitaire de recherche en économie quantitative (CIREQ), a researcher at the Center for Interuniversity Research and Analysis on Organizations (CIRANO) and a fellow of the Royal Society of Canada. His research interests are elections and voting, public opinion and methodology.

Donald E. Blake is a professor emeritus of political science at the University of British Columbia, where he taught from 1970 to 2004. He has published widely in the areas of parties, elections and public opinion. He was a contributor to the Royal Commission on Electoral Reform and Party Financing in Canada (the Lortie Commission) and served as an advisor to electoral boundary commissions in British Columbia and Yukon.

John C. Courtney is a political scientist at the University of Saskatchewan. He is the author of several studies on representational systems, electoral boundary readjustments, party leadership and party conventions. Recent books include *Do Conventions Matter? Choosing National Party Leaders in Canada* (1995) and *Commissioned Ridings: Designing Canada's Electoral Districts* (2001). He also contributed to the Canadian Democratic Audit series, *Elections*. Professor Courtney received the University of Saskatchewan's Distinguished Researcher Award in 2001 and will be awarded the earned D.Litt. degree by the University of Saskatchewan in 2005.

Jean-Pierre Derriennic is a professor in the political science department at Université Laval.

Tom Flanagan is a professor of political science at the University of Calgary and a fellow of the Royal Society of Canada. He is also the chief political adviser to Stephen Harper, the leader of the Conservative Party of Canada, and managed Mr. Harper's two leadership campaigns as well as the 2004 national election campaign of the Conservative Party.

Thierry Giasson is a doctoral candidate and lecturer in the department of political science at the Université de Montréal. His research deals with political communication and marketing. Specifically, he is interested in the mediatization of political speeches, electoral communication, televised debates, and the design and impact of politicians' images.

Paul Harris retired as the chief executive of the New Zealand Electoral Commission in 2003. Since then he has been an electoral consultant in Indonesia, East Timor and Yemen, where he is currently the technical director in the IFES (International Foundation for Election Systems) office in Sana'a. From 1979 to 1994 he lectured at Victoria University of Wellington. He was the principal research officer for the Royal Commission on the Electoral System in 1985-86.

Paul Howe is an associate professor of political science at the University of New Brunswick in Fredericton and a research fellow at the Institute for Research on Public Policy (IRPP). Previously he was the research director of the governance program at the IRPP. His research interests include political participation, political culture and public opinion.

Richard Johnston is a professor and the head of political science at the University of British Columbia. He specializes in the study of elections, public opinion and representation, and is the author or co-author of five books on Canadian and US politics, as well as numerous journal articles and chapters.

Louis Massicotte teaches political science at the Université de Montréal. He is the main author of *Establishing the Rules of the Game: Election Laws in Democracies* (University of Toronto Press, 2003), a comparative study of election laws in some 60 democratic countries. He has been involved in the democratic development of 13 countries in Eastern Europe and in Africa. He is currently advising the minister responsible for the reform of democratic institutions in Quebec on electoral system reform.

Matthew Mendelsohn was appointed the deputy minister and head of Ontario's Democratic Renewal Secretariat in January 2004. He is on leave from Queen's University, where he is an associate professor in the department of political studies and director of the Canadian Opinion Research Archive at Queen's University.

Richard Nadeau is a professor of political science at the Université de Montréal. He has published more than 80 scientific papers on electoral behaviour, public opinion, political communication and the media. He was a member of the Canadian Election Study from 1997 to 2003. He has commented on political news in the media on numerous occasions. He was also a special adviser to the premier of Quebec and to the leader of the official opposition.

Andrew Parkin is the director of research and program development at the Canada Millennium Scholarship Foundation. A political scientist by training, he has written extensively about Canadian politics and society in both the academic and popular press. From 2000 to 2004, he served as assistant director for research and subsequently as co-director at the Centre of Research and Information on Canada (CRIC), where he oversaw an extensive series of studies on Canadian public opinion and political institutions.